THE LEVEL UP! EXCLUSIVE OFFER TO OUR READERS

Thank you very much for buying Level Up! The Guide to Great Video Game Design!
If you happen to meet me at a book signing or a video game conference or a taco shop
just present this page and I will draw you your very own customized level design—free of charge!

Signed, Scott Rogers

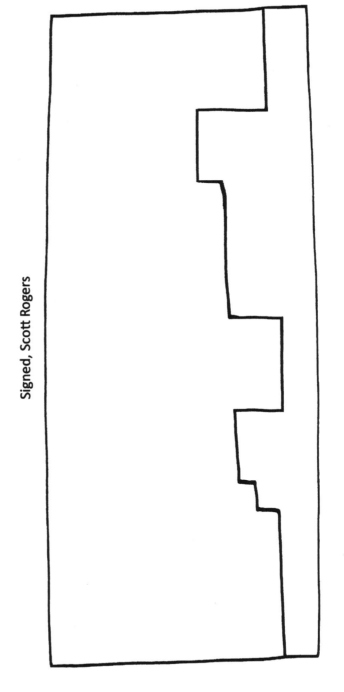

LEVEL UP!
THE GUIDE TO GREAT VIDEO GAME DESIGN

Scott Rogers

WILEY

A John Wiley & Sons, Ltd., Publication

ISBN 978-0-470-68867-0

A catalogue record for this book is available from the British Library.

Set in 10 on 12pt Swiss721BT-Light by Toppan Best-set Premedia Limited
Printed in the US by RR Donnelley

To Brenda Lee

who always thought this would make a great book.

I love you.

Publisher's Acknowledgments

Some of the people who helped bring this book to market include the following:

Editorial and Production
VP Consumer and Technology Publishing Director: Michelle Leete
Associate Director—Book Content Management: Martin Tribe
Associate Publisher: Chris Webb
Assistant Editor: Colleen Goldring
Publishing Assistant: Ellie Scott
Project Editor: Juliet Booker
Content Editor: Céline Durand-Watts
Development/Copy Editor: Gareth Haman
Technical Editor: Noah Stein

Marketing
Senior Marketing Manager: Louise Breinholt
Marketing Executive: Kate Batchelor

Composition Services
Compositor: Toppan Best-set Premedia Limited (HK)
Proof Readers: Sarah Lewis and Gill Whitley
Indexer: Robert Swanson

CONTENTS

FOREWORD

Scott set out to write a handbook; a general text that any designer can pull off their shelf or call up on their PC or e-reader when they want to get back to fundamentals. A sort of Scout Handbook or Farmer's Almanac for game creation. Scott has even included the kind of clear and simple illustrations you might find in these evergreen texts.

When any team in sports, any military unit, or any human endeavor wants success, they start in one place: with the basics. How many times have we heard after a big win, "It's all about fundamentals." One of those fundamentals I've found valuable in game design is the concept of "doing one thing, well." Well, Mr. Rogers has done just that with his handbook.

Whether you are starting out as a new designer or are a veteran who's stuck on a difficult problem, pull this handbook off the shelf, get back to the fundamentals, and I'll bet they trigger some inspiration that will take you beyond.

Danny Bilson
Executive Vice President of Core Games, THQ
February 2010

ABOUT THE AUTHOR

After discovering that game designers have more fun, Scott Rogers embarked on a 16-year-(and counting) career in video games. He has helped design many successful video games including: *Pac-Man World*, the *Maximo* series, *God of War*, *Drawn to Life* series and *Darksiders*. Scott is currently a creative manager for THQ and lives just outside nuclear strike range of Los Angeles with his lovely wife, two children and many, many action figures.

PRESS START!

IF YOU ARE ANYTHING LIKE ME...

… then you'll read the first page of a book before you buy it. I find that if I like the first page, then I'll probably like the whole thing. I have noticed that many books have an exciting excerpt on the first page in order to grab the reader's interest, such as:

The zombie's filthy claws clutched hungrily at Jack's shirt, even as his blade split the creature's head like a ripe melon. A firm kick to its headless torso sent it sprawling down the stairs into the greedy mob that surged forward like a wave. The corpse's undead brothers and sisters paused their onslaught until they realized the decapitated body was just dead meat. Their hesitation gave Jack a second to spare a glance over his shoulder and see that Evelyn had finally reached the helicopter. Jack braced himself for the oncoming mob. "Get that thing started! I can't hold them off forever!" he yelled, as he severed several greedily clutching hands from their wrists. "But, Jack!" Evelyn screamed back, frantically flipping switches. "I don't know HOW to fly a helicopter!"

Not that I would ever resort to such cheap tactics in *this* book. I have also noticed that some books try to gain respectability by publishing a positive quote from an industry professional or famous person on their first page:

I learned more from reading the first page of Level Up! The Book of Great Video Game Design *than I learned in working for 25 years in the video game industry!*
A very famous game designer[1]

---

[1] No doubt you are smart enough to have realized that this isn't a real quote, because there isn't a very famous game designer. Unless you count Shigeru Miyamoto, the creator of Mario. Drat! I should have translated the above quote into Japanese!

You obviously don't need someone else to tell you how to make up your mind. Just by picking up this book, I can tell you are a discriminating reader. I can also tell you are seeking the straight truth on the creation of video games. This book will teach you the who, what, where and, most importantly, how to design video games. If you have an interest in arcade games, boss fights, chili, deadly traps, ergonomics, fun, giant hydras, haunted mansions, islands and alleys, jumps, killer bunnies, leitmotifs, Mexican pizza, non-player characters, one-sheet designs, pitch sessions, quests, robotic chickens, smart bombs, the triangle of weirdness, un-fun, violence, whack-a-mole, XXX, Y-axis and zombies, then this is the book for you.

Before we start, keep in mind that there are many ways to approach game design. All of them are valid, as long as they can communicate the designer's ideas. The tricks and techniques found in *Level Up!* are MY WAYS of creating game design.

Another quick reminder, when I say "I designed a game" this is an oversimplification. Video games are created by many, many, many talented people (you'll be introduced to them shortly) and to give the impression that I did all the work myself is not only incorrect but egotistical[2]. There is no "I" in team[3].

The majority of the games I've helped design were single player action games, so many of the examples found in *Level Up!* will be skewed towards that perspective. It's just the way I think. But I have also found that most of the gameplay concepts are transferable to many different genres of games. It won't be too hard for you to translate my advice to your own game, no matter what the genre.

Another thing before we get started. If you are looking for a single chapter about gameplay, don't bother. Because EVERY chapter in this book is about gameplay. You should be thinking about gameplay all the time and how things affect the player, even when designing passive elements like cutscenes and pause screens.

Since you have made it this far, I may as well start by actually telling you the bad news first. Making video games is very hard work[4]. I have worked in video games for over 16 years and on games that have sold millions of copies.

---

[2] It's a small industry. No one can afford to piss anyone off! Be a nice, hardworking person and you'll go far.

[3] Ironically, there is a "me."

[4] I once had an employer who would walk the halls of our office muttering how "video games are a haaaard business." I used to laugh at him back then, but I don't any more. He was right.

But in that time, I have learned that making video games is also the best job in the world. It can be thrilling, frustrating, rewarding, nerve-wracking, hectic, boring, vomit-inducing, and just plain fun.

NO, YOU CAN'T HAVE MY JOB

Over the course of my career, I came up with some **Clever Ideas** and learned some **Universal Truths**. For your convenience, I have added these at the end of each "level."

I also learned a couple of **very important things**. You can tell they are **very important** because they are written in all bold letters. The first **very important thing** I learned was:

GAME DESIGNERS HAVE MORE FUN

I know this, because my first job in the video game industry was as an artist[5]. Back in those 16-bit days, video game artists drew images with pixels. There are several great 16-bit artists, like Paul Robertson and the teams that made the Metal Slug and classic Capcom fighting games; but for me, drawing pictures out of pixels is like drawing with bathroom tiles. Here is what a drawing I made out of pixels looks like:

Anyway, as I was "pushing pixels" I heard the sound of raucous laughter coming from the group of cubicles next to mine. I peered over the wall to see a bunch of video game designers yukking it up and have a good ol' time. For the record, I was not having a good ol' time pushing pixels. I realized, "Those game designers are having more fun than I am! Making

---

[5] Actually we were called "pixel pushers" and "sprite monkeys", neither of which, despite how cute those terms sound, were ever meant as a compliment.

video games should be fun! I want to have fun! I want to become a game designer too!" And so I did. I eventually worked my way up the ladder to become a game designer. After I became a real game designer, I learned the second **very important thing**:

NO ONE ON YOUR TEAM WANTS TO READ YOUR DESIGN

This is a horrible thing to discover, but it is something every game designer needs to hear. Here I was, a brand new game designer with brand new game designs ready to go, and no one wanted to read any of them! What was I to do? In order to solve this problem and get my colleagues to read my design documents, I started drawing them as cartoons. And guess what? It worked. They conveyed the ideas I wanted to get across to my team mates. And I've been designing games this way ever since, many of which have gone on to become top-selling titles. That is why you will find many cartoons, so you will continue reading and understand the ideas presented. If you do, then you can apply them to your own design and become a great designer, too.

WHO IS THIS BOOK FOR?

Why *you*, of course. Provided you are one of the following people.

A working video games professional. There are lots of books about video games design, but most of them are full of THEORY, which I have never found very helpful while making a game. Don't get me wrong, theory is great when you are at a game developers conference or one of those wine and cheese affairs we game designers always find ourselves at. But when I am working on a game, with my sleeves rolled up and blood splattered all over the walls[6], I need practical nuts n' bolts advice on how to solve any problems I may encounter. I mention this because I assume that some of you reading *Level Up!* will be experienced video game professionals. I hope you find the techniques and tips in this book useful in your day-to-day work. Not that this book doesn't have uses for beginners.

I'm talking about you, **future video game designers**. Remember, one page ago when I told you I was a pixel pusher? There was a point to that story, which is *I was just like you.* Maybe you're also an artist who is tired of hearing the game designers laughing it up over in the other office. Or a programmer who knows he can design a better enemy encounter than the knucklehead currently doing it on your game. Or maybe you are a tester who wants to move up in the world, but you don't know how to do it. When I wanted to become a video game designer, there weren't any books on the subject. We had to learn everything from other game designers. I was lucky to have a mentor and an opportunity to work as a game designer. If you don't have either of these things, don't fret. Read this book; I will be your mentor. All *you* need to do is follow my advice, be prepared, and take advantage of the opportunity when it finally arrives.

This book is also great for **students of video game design**. Back when I started making games, I didn't take any classes on video game design— because they didn't exist! I just made stuff up as I went along! And I made a lot of mistakes. This is why I wrote this book: so you can learn from all **my** mistakes before they become **your** mistakes too.

Finally, this book is for **anyone who loves video games**. I love video games. I love to play them. I love to make them and I love to read about making them. If you want to make video games, then you must love them too. Ironically, I know several people who work in video games that freely admit they do not like to play video games. That does not make any sense

---

[6] Figurative blood. To my knowledge, no one has died from making a video game.

to me. Why would you work in video games if you do not love video games? They are fools. They should just step aside and let someone who loves video games make video games. Someone like you.

Ready? Great! Let's find out how to make games!

ACKNOWLEDGMENTS: EVERYTHING I LEARNED ABOUT WRITING A BOOK

I hope you found *Level Up! The Guide to Great Video Game Design* to be educational and inspirational. What I've learned is that books don't write themselves and writers can't write without support and inspiration from lots of great people. I couldn't have written *Level Up! The Guide to Great Video Game Design* without the love, help, and support of the following family and friends:

Brenda Lee Rogers, Evelyn Rogers, Jack Rogers, Noah Stein, Hardy LeBel, Dr. Brett Rogers, Jackie Kashian, Danny Bilson, Laddie Ervin, Tim Campbell, THQ games legal department, Jeremiah Slackza (for requesting the Platform Primer), mentors William Anderson and David Siller, Mark Rogers, Eric Williams, George Collins, Scott Frazier (my first test audience), Andy Ashcraft, Paul Guirao, Tommy Tallarico, Joey Kuras, Ian Sedensky, Evan Icenbice, Brian Kaiser, Jason Weezner, David O'Connor, Jaclyn Rogers, Dr. Christopher Rogers, Patricia Rogers, Anthony Rogers, The GDC selection committee of 2008, Disneyland's original imagineers, the Los Angeles customizing gang, the editors at John Wiley & Sons, Ltd: Juliet Booker, Gareth Haman, Katherine Batchelor, Ellie Scott, and most importantly, Chris Webb for making that call. And special thanks to Cory Doctrow for the glowing GDC review that kicked all of this off. I owe you a drink, mate.

And a big thank you to YOU for buying this book. Now go and design some great games! I can't wait to play them!

LEVEL 1
WELCOME, NOOBS!

This chapter is written especially for people who are new to video games and how they are made. If you are not a n00b[1], then feel free to skip it. However you are going to be missing out on a lot of great stuff. Don't say I didn't warn you.

Within the academic gaming community, there are many different definitions for what qualifies as a game. Some scholars insist that "a game needs to be a closed formal system that subjectively represents a subset of reality[2]." Others say that games need to have "players in conflict with each other[3]." I think those definitions are trying too hard to sound smart.

Games, while complex, are often simpler than that. Bernard Suits[4] wrote that "playing a game is a voluntary effort to overcome unnecessary obstacles." This is a pretty amusing definition, but still a bit too scholarly for my taste. Let's keep things simple. Let's consider hand ball. You only need one player for hand ball—where's the other players to be in conflict with? Bouncing a ball against a wall without missing it is hardly a metaphor for reality; unless you lead a very boring life. Let's face it, sometimes a ball bouncing against a wall is just a ball bouncing against a wall.

---

[1] A n00b is short for "newbie", or someone who is new to a game. While the term predates the Internet, it became popular with MO communities. Not a particularly flattering term, as it implies inexperience and/or ignorance: only a real n00b would read a footnote defining what a n00b is!

[2] "What is a Game?", Chris Crawford in The Art of Computer Game Design, 1982.

[3] "What is a Game?", Kevin Langdon in The New Thesaurus, 1979.

[4] The Grasshopper: Games, Life and Utopia, Bernard Suits, 1978.

Playing hand ball may therefore seem like a time-waster, but a time-waster becomes a game when you add rules and an objective. A rule may be to throw the ball with your right hand and catch it with your left, or to not drop the ball. A victory condition could be that you have to catch the ball ten times in a row. A failure state would be if you violated any of the rules or victory conditions. Once those criteria have been met, you have created a game. Ironically, while simple, hand ball was enough of a game to inspire the creators of one of the earliest video games: *Tennis for Two*.

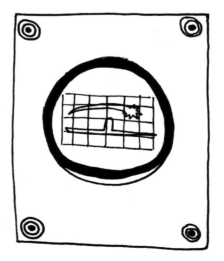

Tennis for Two

So, let's ask this basic question:

Q: What is a game?
A: A game is an activity that:
   - requires at least one player
   - has rules
   - has a victory condition.

That's pretty much it.

Now that you know what a game is, let's ask:

Q: What is a video game?
A: A video game is a game that is played on a video screen.

Sure, you can start complicating the definition and add requirements about devices, peripherals, control schemes, player metrics, boss fights, and zombies (and don't worry; we'll tackle these things soon enough). But by my reckoning, that is pretty much as simple as it gets.

Oh, there's one other thing to consider at this early stage. The game's **objective**. You should be able to sum a game's objectives up quickly and clearly. If you can't, you've got a problem.

Danny Bilson, THQ's EVP of Core Games, has a great rule of thumb about a game's objective. He says that you should be able to sum up the game's objectives as easily as those old Milton Bradley board games did on the front of their box. Check out these examples taken from real game boxes:

Battleship: sink all of your opponent's ships.

Operation: successful operations earn "Money." Failures set off alarms.

Mouse Trap: player turns the crank which rotates gears causing lever to move and push the stop sign against shoe. Shoe tips bucket holding metal ball. Ball rolls down rickety stairs and into rain pipe which leads it to hit helping hand rod. This causes bowling ball to fall from top of helping hand rod through thing-a-ma-jig and bathtub to land on diving board. Weight of bowling ball catapults diver through the air and right into wash tub causing cage to fall from top of post and trap unsuspecting mouse.

Ok, so maybe not with that last one. The lesson is, you need to keep your game objectives simple. Speaking of simple games, let's take a moment to travel back to the dawn of video games. They had to start somewhere, right?

A BRIEF HISTORY OF VIDEO GAMES

The 1950s. The dawn of television, 3-D movies, and rock 'n' roll. Video games were invented in the 1950s too, only they were played by a very few people on very large computers. The first video game programmers were students in the computer labs of large universities like MIT and employees of military facilities at Brookhaven National Laboratories. Early games like *OXO* (1952), *Spacewar!* (1962), and *Colossal Cave* (1976) had very simple or even no graphics at all. They were displayed on very small black and white oscilloscope screens.

After playing *Spacewar!* at the University of Utah's computer lab, future Atari founders Ted Dabney and Nolan Bushnell were inspired to create *Computer Space*, the first **arcade** video game, in 1971. While (despite the name) the first arcade games could be found in bars, arcades dedicated to video games began appearing by the late 1970s.

Asteroids
(Vector Graphics)

Galaxian
(Raster Graphics)

Early arcade games like *Asteroids*, *Battlezone*, and *Star Castle* were rendered in **vector graphics** (images constructed from lines). After color **raster graphics** (images constructed from a grid of dots called pixels) were introduced, cartoon-inspired video game characters appeared. Characters like Pac-Man (Namco, 1980) and Donkey Kong (Nintendo, 1982) became pop culture icons virtually overnight.

During the early 1980s, three styles of game machines dominated arcades: **uprights** (cabinets which the player stood in front of while they played), **cocktail tables** (arcade games set into the top of a small table, allowing the player to sit down while playing), and **cockpits** (elaborate game cabinets that allowed the player to lean or sit down to further enhance the gaming experience).

Arcade Cabinet   Cocktail Table   Arcade Cockpit

In the mid-1980s, arcades began springing up everywhere and video games took the world by storm. Game genres and themes became more varied, while gaming controls and cabinets became more elaborate with realistic controllers and beautiful graphics decorating uniquely designed cabinets. You could sit back-to-back in a two-player spaceship cockpit while playing *Tail Gunner* (Vectorbeam, 1979), battle Klingons from a replica of Captain Kirk's command chair in *Star Trek* (Sega, 1982) or drive in an actual Ferrari Testarossa that moved and shook in *Out Run* (Sega, 1986). By the late 1990s, many arcade games started to resemble mini theme-park rides complete with rideable race horses, gyroscopically-moving virtual simulators and fighting booths that allowed players to battle virtual foes using actual punches and kicks. The most elaborate of these arcades was Virtual World's BattleTech Centers; steampunk-themed arcades with linked "battle pods[5]"

---

[5] In the mid-1990s, I had the pleasure of going to a BattleTech Center on several occasions. The battle pods were a video gamer's dream come true. The player sat in a photo booth-sized cockpit. Dual control joysticks and foot pedals operated the mech's movement. Triggers and thumb switches fired the arsenal of weapons. Surrounding the pod's video monitor were banks of dipswitches—each one actually having a function within the game from activating tracking devices to venting overheating weapons. It took at least one gaming session (about a half hour) just to learn what all the switches did! It was as realistic a gaming experience as I've ever had.

that allowed 8 players to fight each other while stomping around in giant virtual "mechs."

These elaborate arcade games required lots of floor space and were very expensive to maintain. In the late 1990s, home systems began to rival and eventually surpassed the graphics seen in most arcade games. Arcades went out of business by the dozens. The video games became replaced with more lucrative redemption machines[6] and games of skill like skeeball. With the liquidation of arcades, many cabinets ended up in the hands of private collectors. The golden age of video game arcades was over.

Most recently, arcades have become social and virtual experiences. **LAN gaming centers** combine retail and social space to allow players to play computer and console games on a per-hour basis. Many have upgraded to feature large-scale gaming experiences held in movie theater-sized venues. Internet cafes are similar to LAN centers but with an emphasis on cultivating a café-style environment.

Social gaming has also expanded in another direction. Companies such as Disney and the Sally Corporation have started merging traditional amusement **dark rides**[7] with gameplay to create new arcade-style experiences. For example, *Toy Story Midway Mania* at Disney's California Adventure (2008) whisks a four-player cart past a succession of giant video screens where players compete in a variety of carnival-style shooting games. Players are sprayed with air and water to simulate different visual effects in the game. The circle of modern arcade gaming and home gaming has come full circle with the release of a Wii version of the *Toy Story Midway Mania* attraction.

Who knows? Perhaps these new attractions will become the backbone of a new hybrid arcade/amusement park filled with virtual games and interactive dark rides.

---

[6] Redemption machines are those claw catcher "games" you see in American toy stores and supermarkets. Personally, I would rather play the lottery than try my luck with one of these vending machines, which are rigged to (almost) guarantee you to lose. However, if you are ever in Japan, I recommend playing them as they are winnable and are usually stocked with some very cool toys and prizes.

[7] A "dark ride" is an amusement park attraction that has guests ride past scenes of (usually) audio-animatronic characters. Famous examples of dark rides include Disneyland's Pirates of the Caribbean and Haunted Mansion.

Atari 2600

Nintendo Entertainment
System (NES)

Playstation One (PSX)

A **console** is a gaming platform that can be used in the home. A microprocessor runs the electronic device, which sends a video display signal to the user's TV set or monitor[8]. Unlike the dedicated controllers of an arcade machine, a home console controller has enough buttons, triggers, and analog controls to allow for a variety of games to be played. And unlike the dedicated motherboards in early arcade games, which could only hold one game, console games use cartridge, CD, and DVD media to allow players to quickly change games. From the late 1970s onwards, there have been many home consoles. Some of the more popular and/or well known previous generation ones include the Atari 2600 and Jaguar, the Mattel Intellivision, the Colecovision, the Nintendo Entertainment System and Super Nintendo, the Sega Genesis and Dreamcast, and the 3DO interactive player. Current consoles such as the Playstation 3, Xbox 360, and Nintendo Wii continue to bring gaming into the homes of millions of gamers worldwide.

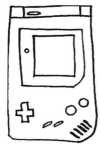
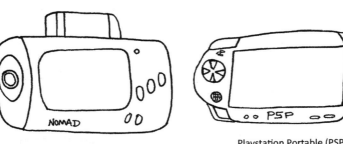

Nintendo Game Boy

Sega Nomad

Playstation Portable (PSP)

Like arcade games, **handheld games** have a visual display, a processor, and controller, but are small enough to fit in the hands of the player. The first handheld titles were dedicated to only one game per unit. *Auto Race* (Mattel Electronics, 1976) used a digital display while the Game & Watch series (Nintendo, 1980) featured a more appealing liquid crystal display.

[8] One console exception is the wonderful Vectrex portable game system (Smith Engineering, 1982). The Vectrex's processor, screen, controller and even one game were all in a self-contained, portable system.

Microvision (Milton Bradley, 1979) was one of the earliest handheld systems to have switchable cartridges. Handheld gaming took off when Tetris became a phenomenon on the Gameboy (Nintendo, 1989), the forerunner of the Nintendo DS[9]. Recent handheld systems have become quite powerful. The Sony PSP's processor can run the equivalent of a Playstation One game. That's quite a jump since the digital blips of Mattel Football!

Handheld gaming, particularly on mobile devices, is becoming more and more popular. Games for cellular phones are quick and less expensive to make. In a few short years, the number of mobile game developers has exploded. Are these mobile games and devices the future of gaming?

Commodore 64 (C64)   Macintosh Plus   Personal Computer (PC)

As **personal computers** (or **PCs**) became popular in the late 1970s, both video game programming and video game playing became more common. An entire generation of game developers started off in their bedrooms, programming games on their PCs. These early games were stored on tape drives and floppy discs. While early computer video games attempted to emulate games found at arcades, the addition of the keyboard allowed greater user input, giving rise to unique game genres including the text adventure game. Longer periods of time spent at the computer also meant longer gaming experiences and simulations; construction and management and strategy games started to become popular. As the computer hardware, memory, and storage evolved to CD and DVD media, computer games became more detailed, more involved, and more complex. The rise of the **first person shooter** (or **FPS**) can be attributed to the popularity of the mouse controller. By the mid-1990s the computer was the ultimate gaming platform. Several gaming genres, particularly strategy, FPSs, and **massively multiplayer online** games (or **MMOs**) remain very strong on the computer platform.

[9] Not ironically, the Nintendo DS bears several design semblances to the original Game & Watch series devices.

GAME GENRES

Over the years, gaming has splintered off into many different genres and subgenres. A game genre is used to describe the style of gameplay.

Action: games that require hand/eye coordination to play. The action genre has several subgenres:

- **Action-adventure**—this combination of genres features an emphasis on item collection and usage, puzzle solving, and long-term story-related goals. Examples: the *Prince of Persia* and *Tomb Raider* series.
- **Action-arcade**—any game presented in the style of early arcade games with an emphasis on "twitch" gameplay, scoring, and short play time. Examples: *Dig Dug*, *Diner Dash*.
- **Platformer**—a platform game often features a mascot character jumping (or swinging or bouncing) through challenging "platform" environments. Shooting and fighting may also be involved. At one time, the platformer was the most popular subgenre in gaming. Examples: Nintendo's Mario titles (*Super Mario World*, *Mario 64*, and *Super Mario Galaxy*).
- **Stealth**—an action game with an emphasis on avoiding enemies rather than directly fighting them. Examples: the *Metal Gear* series and *Thief: The Dark Project*.
- **Fighting**—a game where two or more opponents battle in arena settings. Fighting games are distinguished from action games for the depth of their player controls. Examples: the *Street Fighter* series and the *Mortal Kombat* series.
- **Beat 'em up/hack 'n' slash**—these games have players battle against wave after wave of enemies increasing in difficulty. Examples: *Double Dragon*, *Castle Crashers*.

Shooter: shooters focus primarily on firing projectiles at enemies. While fast-paced and "twitch" oriented, like action games, this genre has evolved to include several subgenres that are distinguished by their camera view:

- **First person shooter**—a shooter as seen from the player's perspective. The tighter camera view is more limiting but more personal than in a third person shooter. Examples: *Quake*, *Team Fortress 2*.
- **Shoot 'em up**—shoot 'em ups (or shmups for short) are arcade-style shooters where players shoot large quantities of enemies while avoiding hazards. The player's avatar in a shmup is usually a vehicle (such as a spaceship) rather than a character. They can be presented from several different camera angles. Examples: *Space Invaders*, the *Contra* series.

- **Third person shooter (TPS)**—a shooter where the camera is placed further behind the player, allowing for a partial or full view of the player's character and their surroundings. Despite the wider view, the emphasis on gameplay remains on shooting. Examples: the *Star Wars Battlefront* and *Grand Theft Auto* series.

Adventure: adventure games focus on puzzle solving, and item collection and inventory management. Early adventure games were solely text based. Examples: *Colossal Cave*, the *King's Quest*, and *Leisure Suit Larry* series.

- **Graphical adventure**—this subgenre has players use a mouse or cursor to click to uncover clues and navigate around. Examples: *Myst*, *Monkey Island*, and the *Sam and Max* series.
- **Role-playing game (RPG)**—this subgenre is based on pen and paper role-playing games like *Dungeons and Dragons*. Players choose a character class and increase their statistical abilities through combat, exploration, and treasure finding. Characters can either be specific characters or generic character classes. Examples: *Star Wars: Knights of the Old Republic* and the *Mass Effect* series.
- **Massively multiplayer online role-playing game (MMORPG)**— an RPG that can support hundreds of players together in one environment. MMORPGs are known for player vs player gameplay, repetitive gameplay or "grinding", and group battles or "raids." Examples: *World of Warcraft*, *DC Universe Online*.
- **Survival/horror**—players attempt to survive a horror scenario with limited resources, such as sparse ammunition. Examples: the *Resident Evil* series, the *Silent Hill* series.

Construction/management: this genre has players build and expand a location with limited resources. They can be based on stories or "toys." *SimCity* and *Zoo Tycoon* are examples of this genre.

Life simulation: similar to the management genre, but revolving around building and nurturing relationships with artificial life forms. *The Sims* and *Princess Maker* titles are both life simulators.

- **Pet simulation**—based on the Tamagotchi digital pet pocket games, though often now much expanded, pet simulators revolve around nurturing animals through feeding and relationships. *World of Zoo* is an example of this.

Music/rhythm: the player tries to match a rhythm or beat to score points. They can be as simple as the game *Simon* or as complex as *Rock Band*.

Party: party games are specifically designed for multiple players and are based on competitive play. More often than not, gameplay is presented in the minigame format. Examples: *Mario Party* and *Buzz!*

Puzzle: puzzle games are based on logic and pattern completion. They can be slow, methodical or use hand/eye coordination. Examples: *The Incredible Machine* or *Tetris*.

Sports: these are games based on athletic competitions, whether they are traditional or extreme. It is common to see annual versions of these titles. Examples: the *Madden* series, the *Tony Hawk* series.

- **Sports management**—rather than directly playing the sport, players manage players or teams. Examples: the *FIFA Manager* series, the *NFL Head Coach* series.

Strategy: from chess to *Sid Meir's Civilization*, thinking and planning are the hallmarks of strategy games. They take place in both historical and fictitious settings.

- **Real time strategy (RTS)**—similar to turn-based games, these faster-paced games focus on the "four X's": expansion, exploration, exploitation, and extermination. RTS has become the dominant strategy subgenre. Examples: *Command and Conquer* series, the *Dawn of War* series.

- **Turn-based**—the slower pace of these games allows players time to think, providing more opportunity for strategy to be employed. Examples: the *X-Com* series, the *Advance Wars* series.

- **Tower defense**—a relatively new subgenre on PC and handheld systems where players create automated projectile-shooting "towers" that keep enemies at bay. Examples: *Defense Grid: The Awakening*, *Lock's Quest*.

Vehicle simulation: players simulate piloting/driving a vehicle, from a sports car to a spaceship. Emphasis is placed on making the experience as "real" as possible. Examples: *Lunar Lander*, *Densha de Go! 64*.

- **Driving**—players race and upgrade vehicles, from motorcycles to hovercrafts. Driving games can be ultra-realistic experiences or more action oriented. Examples: the *Gran Turismo* series, the *NASCAR Racing* series, *Wave Race* and *SSX*.

- **Flying**—players pilot aircraft either for the pleasure of flying as in the *Microsoft Flight Simulator* series or into combat as seen in the *Ace Combat* and *Blazing Angels* series. You can even fly into outer space as in *Starfox* and the *X-Wing/TIE Fighter* series.

This list of genres and subgenres attempts to scratch the surface. Adult games, serious games, advert games, and vehicular combat are other classifications that fit within several of the genres above. As games combine several genres and subgenres, new ones are constantly being created. For example, the *Grand Theft Auto* series now combines action-adventure, third person shooter, driving, life simulation, and action-arcade genres into one game! *Tuper Tario Tros.*[10] seamly combines *Super Mario Bros.* and *Tetris*! What's next? What will be the most popular game genre in the future? Who knows? Perhaps you will create it!

WHO MAKES THIS STUFF?

Just as there are many types of games, there are many types of people who make them. In the early days of video game development, games were initially created by individuals; one example is the original *Prince of Persia*, which was made by one person[11] programming, designing and animating the entire game. He even composed the game's music! Teams eventually became bigger as commercial video game development became serious and games required two or three programmers to make.

Artists joined development teams as players began to demand better-looking games. Games were initially designed by whichever team member had the good idea. Finally, when game content became too involved to do alone, a dedicated design position was created. While team members on current teams can still wear many hats, specialization is becoming increasingly necessary as games become bigger, more complex, and take longer to make.

Video game teams that produce games are known as **developers** or **development teams.** They are similar to a production team that makes a movie or TV show—several creative people all working together to create entertainment. An average production team includes numerous members, as outlined in the following sections.

PROGRAMMER

Using programming languages such as C++ and Java, a **programmer** writes the code that allows a game's text and graphics to be displayed, develops the control systems that allow a player to interact with the game, creates the camera system that allows the player to view the game world, programs the physics system that affects the player and game world, writes the AI system that controls enemies and object scripting ... you get the idea.

---

[10] You can play Tuper Tario Tros. by Swing Swing Submarine at http://www.newgrounds.com/portal/view/522276.

[11] The one-man development team in question is Jordan Mechner.

One programmer may work exclusively on tools to help team members build the game more efficiently. Another programmer may write code to simulate real-world physics making water look realistic or develop inverse kinetics for characters. They may even work solely on sound tools to play music and effects.

Like many of the jobs in the game industry, programming jobs are becoming more specialized. Regardless of the position, a programmer needs to have an excellent understanding of mathematics, 2-D and 3-D graphics, physics, particle systems, user interface, artificial intelligence, input devices, and computer networking. These skills are always in high demand and some programmers make a good living as contractors, moving from project to project as "hired guns", writing code and providing temporary solutions to beleaguered teams.

ARTIST

In the early days of video games, programmers created all a game's art. Because that early art was so blocky and crude, we now call placeholder game art "programmer art[12]." Thank goodness real artists came along. One of the first artists working in video games was Shigeru Miyamoto, who created Mario and Donkey Kong. He was able to create memorable cartoon characters with an 8-bit CPU using only 2-bit pixels. That's a lot of personality per pixel! There were a few exceptions in the early days, such as *Dragon's Lair* (Cinematronics, 1983) and *Space Ace* (Cinematronics, 1984), beautifully animated games created by ex-Disney animators like Don Bluth, but those games were rare exceptions because they employed laser discs to play the video footage. Eventually, new, better hardware with more

[12] I apologize to any programmers reading this, but I didn't make this term up.

memory, color depth and the ability to display larger graphics meant artists could create more detailed images, backgrounds and characters like those seen in beautifully hand-drawn and animated games such as *Darkstalkers* (Capcom, 1994) and *Metal Slug* (SNK, 1996).

As high-end computer software became more affordable to developers, 3-D graphics, which had been limited to movies like *Tron* (Disney, 1982) and Pixar's animated shorts like *Luxo Jr.* (1986), began appearing in games. *Myst* (Broderbund, 1993) and *Donkey Kong Country* (Nintendo, 1994) used prerendered 3-D graphics. True 3-D graphics had been in arcade games as early as *Battlezone* (Atari, 1980), but when the Playstation arrived in 1994, game developers became inspired to use 3-D to create more realistic worlds and characters for home consoles.

Just like with programming, video game art has become a specialized job. A **concept artist** uses both traditional medium and computers to draw game characters, worlds, and enemies. **Storyboard artists** illustrate the game's cinematics and sometimes elements of gameplay design to be passed along to other artists and animators. **3-D Modelers** and **environmental artists** build characters and environments using programs such as Maya and 3D Studio Max. **Texture artists** literally paint surfaces onto 3-D models and locations. **Visual effects artists** create spectacular visual effects using a combination of 2-D and 3-D art. A **user interface (UI) artist** designs icons and elements that are used in the game's interface and HUD. **Animators** animate the player character and create cutscenes exactly like they do in big budget animated movies. **Technical artists** help every artist on the team by doing a variety of tasks, including rigging models to allow animators to move them and teaching fellow artists the latest tools and technology. The **art director** supervises the work of all the artists while maintaining the artistic vision for the entire project. Regardless of what kind of art position you are interested in, make sure you study the basics and keep drawing!

DESIGNER

Director, planner, producer[13], lead designer, or senior game designer—no matter what the job title is, the designer's role is the same: create the ideas and rules that comprise a game. A **game designer** needs to possess

---

[13] There's more to a producer's job than game design and in some cases, a producer doesn't even design the game. But what are you doing skipping ahead anyway?

many, many skills[14], least of which is to love to play games. As a game designer, you should be able to tell the difference between a good and bad game and, more importantly, communicate why. Remember, "because it sucks" is *never* an acceptable answer.

Just like with programmers and artists, design is becoming a specialized profession. **Level designers** create paper maps, build "grey box" worlds using 3-D programs, and populate the levels with everything from enemies to treasure. **System designers** develop how the game elements relate to one another, whether it is the game's economy or technology tree. **Scripters** use tools to write code that allow things to happen within the game, from springing a trap to choreographing a camera movement. **Combat designers** specialize in player vs enemy combat and "balancing" the player's experience. The **creative director** maintains the vision of the game while supervising the other designers; often offering suggestions for improving their work.

There is one other task that a designer is responsible for: that the game is "fun." However, I will leave this can of worms unopened until later in the book. I hope you can stand the suspense.

PRODUCER

Overseeing the entire game development team is a **producer**. Originally, producers were designers who also managed the work of their team members. A producer's role has expanded dramatically over the years.

The producer's responsibilities include hiring and building teams, writing contracts, contributing to the game's design, managing the team's work schedule, balancing the game's budget, resolving disputes between

---

[14] According to Jesse Schell in his book The Art of Game Design (Morgan Kaufmann, 2008), a "well-rounded" game designer understands animation, anthropology, architecture, brainstorming, business, cinematography, communication, creative writing, economics, engineering, history, management, mathematics, music, psychology, public speaking, sound design, technical writing, and visual arts. I think it's a pretty accurate list.

creative and programming leads, acting as the team representative to upper management and publishers, coordinating the creation of outside resources such as art, music and cutscenes, and arranging testing and localization. Producers are usually the first team member on and the last team member off of a game's production. More often than not, you will find producers acting as the public face of the game; talking to the press and public about the game they are managing[15].

Because there are many things for a producer to do, often you will find assistant and **associate producers** helping out with day-to-day tasks. Sometimes the task can be as "trivial" as ordering dinner for a team that is working late. Believe it or not, some of those "menial" chores are some of the most important that a producer can provide to a team.

Regardless of how helpful producers can be, some development studios consider producers to be an unnecessary part of development. Others feel that producers should not have any creative control, just manage the game's production and schedule. As with designers, the role and influence of a producer varies wildly across the industry.

TESTER

Do you like to play games? Do you like to play games over and over? Do you like to play the same level over and over and over and over and over and over and over and over again? Then testing is for you!

While **testers** work long hours, work in cramped environments, and have to play games to a degree that many would classify as mind-numbingly boring, being a tester requires more skills than you may think. A good tester has patience, persistence, and great communication skills to report back any

[15] Producers often end up as the "face of the game" because they are the one team member that can keep all of the moving parts straight!

problems (or "**bugs**") they find in the game. It's not a glamorous job, but without testers, we would be plagued with games that crash upon loading, have crappy cameras, broken combat systems, and unfair difficulty balances.

Quality assurance (or **QA**)[16] is crucial to the successful completion of a game. Publishers hold games to a rigorous standard of quality so the game that you buy is (mostly) bug free. That standard can only be met by thoroughly testing a game for weeks, if not months. Only once it has passed muster with the QA department is a game truly ready to be released to the public.

Testing is a great gateway job position for newcomers to the game industry, I have seen testers go on to become designers, artists, producers, and even heads of studios. You can find out a lot about games in a short time by working as a tester. Testers prevent games from sucking. Remember that the next time you think about making fun of a tester.

COMPOSER

In the earliest days of video games, music was nothing more than crude beeps and bloops to accompany the game's action. But how many of you can still hum the music to *The Legend of Zelda* or the *Super Mario Bros.* theme?

Music is extremely important to the gaming experience, and a **composer** creates that music. Most modern composers create their music on a keyboard or synthesizer, as they can be used to simulate any musical instrument. As sound technology has improved, many composers have created actual "live" and orchestral pieces; this requires a whole new set of skills, including conducting an orchestra. I won't even pretend to know how to do that—I have no idea what all that baton waving means!

Home versions of modern audio software are powerful enough to mix and master professional-sounding samples. If you want to become a composer, then write some music, record it, and get your samples into the hands of a game producer. As someone who has reviewed lots and lots of composers'

---

[16] Quality assurance is just a fancy way of saying "test department."

audio resumes, I can tell you it goes something like this: the designer has a specific idea for the style or feel of music in his mind. If your music sample matches what the designer wants, then they will contact you for the job. What matters most is that your music is unique and fits the needs of the game. Look at the success of a movie score composer like Danny Elfman. He composed very distinct music for *Beetlejuice* and *Pee Wee's Big Adventure*, and soon everyone wanted his style of music in their own movies.

Writing music for games is somewhat different than writing music for movies. Most game themes are either very short or have to repeat over and over again. Being able to compose powerful and exciting music with these limitations in mind will make your music more appealing than someone who just writes "songs[17]." Don't worry, I'll cover more about music in Level 15.

SOUND DESIGNER

Unlike a composer who creates the music for a game, the **sound designer** creates all the sound effects that are used in a game. Go ahead and fire up a game, turn off the sound and try playing it. Do you notice that the game just isn't the same without sound effects? Often, there is a lot of information that is delivered to the player via sound. These audio cues are the sound designer's responsibility to create.

Personally, I think sound design is a lot of fun. Games tend to come to life once sound is added to them. That is why it is important to even have placeholder sound effects. Mixing and blending sounds to create something no one has ever heard before is pretty cool. However, a good sound designer needs to understand the game he is working on and how to create sounds that help the player with the game. Some sound effects need to sound "positive" to encourage the player that they are doing something right or collecting something good. Other sounds warn players of danger or possible bad choices. A sound designer can make a sound effect sound happy, deadly, scary, or like a big pile of treasure. Or sometimes all the above!

If you want to be a sound designer, you also need to take direction from people who may or may not know what they want. For example, see if you can create a sound effect based on the following description: "I need this creature to sound like a phlegmy cougar from hell … but make it sound more shriek-ey than growl-y[18]." Did you do it? Congratulations! You are now ready to be a sound designer.

---

[17] Don't let that comment cause you despair, songwriters. There are still plenty of games that use traditional songs; in particular, sport and rhythm games.
[18] Sadly, yes: this was an actual direction to a sound designer. And yet, he still delivered a great sound effect.

WRITER

Unlike Hollywood, where **writers** come up with the initial ideas for a movie, video game writers are usually hired pretty late in the game's production process. If you want to be the "idea guy" then I suggest sticking to game design.

That's not to say that writers don't contribute to games. However, a writer is not usually a full-time team position. Most likely they are a freelancer who is brought into the game's production for one of the following reasons:

- To rewrite the design team's story into something that makes sense once everyone on the team realizes that it is drivel.
- To write dialogue for the game characters and cutscenes once everyone on the team realizes that writing good dialogue is actually hard to do.
- To make elements in the game clearer to understand, as in the case of instructional or directional prompts.
- To write the games manual and any fictional support material, such as character biographies, that will appear on the publisher's website.
- To add some "star power" to the back of the box. This comes and goes depending on how important the game industry is feeling about the worth of "name writers" at the time.

The upside of being a writer in the game industry is that there is usually plenty of work, as long as you don't mind doing different writing jobs and working for different companies. If you want to be a game writer, you obviously need to know how to write, use proper grammar, and know how to write in screenplay format. But the most important thing to know is how to write for video games. They are very different than writing a book or movie. Fortunately, this book has a whole chapter[19] on how to do this. Good thing you are reading it!

Well, now you know all the different employment possibilities in video games, right? Wrong! People don't generally know this, but there is a second career path in video games: publishing.

HAVE YOU THOUGHT ABOUT PUBLISHING?

Publishers provide the funding for game development teams, manage the game's production, handle any legal issues, manufacture the game, and

---

[19] Level 3, to be exact.

provide public relations and marketing for the game. They even handle distribution of the finished product. Here are some of the more common positions found in publishing:

PRODUCT MANAGER

Much like a game producer, a **product manager** works with the development team and manages them based on the agreed production schedule. They help determine production priorities for the game's production, act as an intermediary between the studio and the publisher's legal department, review and approve milestones, and make payments to the studio. They also work with the ESRB[20] to secure a rating for the game.

At some publishers, the product manager has extensive say in the game's content. At others, the product manager is there to make sure the game's development goes smoothly. All I know is, I'm glad I'm not the one making the schedule.

CREATIVE MANAGER

When people ask me what I do as a **creative manager** for THQ, I tell them "I have the job that people think of when they think of working in video games." To be honest, working as a creative manager isn't just "thinking up and playing games all day." But sometimes it is.

Creative managers are usually game designers or writers who are working in publishing. Like product managers, a creative manager's involvement on a game can vary from publisher to publisher. In my own experience I have worked with teams to create and develop games, written game pitches, and worked with licensors to create game concepts. One of my most common responsibilities is to play game builds[21] and make sure that they remain true to the core idea and are "fun."

The best benefit a creative manager can provide is what I call the "**thousand foot view**" (as in looking down on the game from a thousand feet in the air, not looking at thousands of feet!); an unbiased viewpoint on a game that can help root out weakness in the game's design and construction. When they aren't solid I need to provide the team clear

---

[20] ESRB stands for the Entertainment Software Ratings Board, an organization that determines a game's rating (in the US, at least).
[21] A "build" (or a "burn") is an in-progress version of the game that can be played either on a computer or a special console.

feedback on how gameplay can be improved or give advice on how the team can explore another creative direction.

Creative managers also work with marketing and public relation departments to provide press materials to make sure a game is shown in the very best light.

ART DIRECTOR

An **art director** is similar to a creative manager, but only deals with the game's art. Art directors can help a team create a visual style for their game and take their game in directions that weren't previously considered by the team. An art director can help the team globalize the visual language of their game to make it clear to the player. Art directors also work with the marketing teams to create packaging materials (such as the cover of a game's box) or wrangle assets that are needed to publicize the game.

TECHNICAL DIRECTOR

A **technical director** comes from a programming background. They review and recommend tools and software to teams to help them work more efficiently. They provide technical support and advice when there are deficiencies in a team's programming staff. They also help perform **due diligence** on a new team to help assess whether they can actually make the game they are being hired to make.

AND THE REST . . .

There are other publishing positions that aren't directly involved in making games, but are important to creating and selling a game nonetheless. **Business development** staff build relationships with studios, hold game pitch meetings and review prospective game demos. They make deals with external studios and find emerging studios to acquire. If you ever own a gaming studio, odds are you'll meet a lot of business developers. A **lawyer** negotiates all the contracts and makes sure the production team isn't creating content that will get the publisher into any legal trouble. A **brand manager** creates the marketing strategy to promote and advertise a game. They develop print material such as manuals and box covers. A **public relations manager** talks to gaming magazines and organizes press events to show the game off in the best possible light. A **quality assurance manager** runs the test department, organizing and relaying the bug sheets back to the developer.

In addition to production and publishing, there are many others who interact with development teams and publishers. A **talent recruiter** searches for new talent and helps get them employment with developers and publishers, **game reviewers** play the games before they come out and write reviews and interviews for magazines and online sites, and **licensors** work for major entertainment companies to make sure their brands are properly represented in games based on their properties.

As you can see, there are plenty of options if you want a career in games. But I say forget all those other jobs. You want to find out how to make great game designs, right? Trust me, game design is where the real fun is!

But to make great games, you need great ideas. Where do you get great ideas? Let's find out!

Level 1's Universal Truths and Clever Ideas:

- A game is an activity with rules and a victory condition.
- Your game objective should be simple, like that of a 1950s board game.
- Game genres come in all shapes and sizes. Don't be afraid to mix and match.
- Gaming technology is always improving. Adapt or get left behind.
- It takes all kinds of people to make video games.

LEVEL 2
IDEAS

Let's talk about *making* video games. To most people, making a video game is a mystery. The average party conversation goes like this:

So, you program video games? Is it hard to write all of that code?

No, I said I *design* games.

Oh, so you draw the characters? That must be fun.

No, I don't draw them. That's what an artist does.

I don't get it. If you don't code the games or draw the games what *do* you do?

Apparently nothing.

At this point in the conversation I then tell people that games are made by elves. All I have to do is leave a game design idea in the middle of the room overnight and in the morning the elves have made the game[1].

OK, this is not entirely true.

You have to leave a *good* idea out for the elves to make into a game. Which begs the question: "Where do **good ideas** come from?"

---

[1] They also make shoes, Christmas toys and cookies the same way.

IDEAS: WHERE TO GET THEM AND WHERE TO STICK THEM

↑
Every good idea borders on the stupid.
Michel Gondry[2]
↑

I like this quote because many game ideas often sound stupid. Try these on for size:

- A yellow creature eats dots while being chased by ghost monsters.
- A plumber jumps on the heads of mushrooms to find his girlfriend.
- A prince rebuilds stars by rolling balls of junk into bigger balls of junk.

All of those stupid-sounding ideas ended up being games that made lots and lots of money. I guess they aren't so stupid after all. To me, the lesson is, never dismiss a game idea, even if it does sound stupid.

So, where do I get my own stupid ideas to turn into video games? The traditional way to get an idea is to get inspired. The good news is that a good game idea can come from anywhere. Here is a list of things I do to get inspired. I suggest you try them yourself the next time you need to come up with an idea.

1. **Read something you normally wouldn't read.** I once attended a roundtable discussion with the famous game designer Will Wright. Mr. Wright said he got his inspiration for his games from Japanese gardening, architectural design, and biology. I replied that was great, as long as you were into Japanese gardening, architectural design, and biology; but what about "normal folks" who were into comic books, sci-fi movies, and video games? But to tell the truth, I realized that I knew what the answer to my question was even as I asked my question.

   One of the reasons why video games sometimes feel the same is that many game developers love the same stuff. There's nothing wrong with liking video games, comics, and movies; however when developers all get their inspiration from the same things, games start to feel the same. When popular movies come out, their themes start to show up in games. When popular games come out, you find their mechanics being

---

[2] While Michel Gondry doesn't make video games, he does make excellent movies like Eternal Sunshine of the Spotless Mind, The Science of Sleep, and Be Kind, Rewind. I suggest you add them all to your Netflix lists immediately.

used in other games. Games start to feel derivative. You also get that creepy synchronicity when developers put out similar games at the same time[3]. Take the time to expand your educational horizons, even just a little. You don't have to get a degree in the subject; just thumb through a magazine or two, spend an afternoon at the library or research something new on the Internet. In other words, stop reading so much crap and break the cycle, fanboy!

2. **Take a walk, drive or shower.** When the active part of your brain is being occupied by a familiar activity like walking or driving, then your subconscious is free to start wandering and making connections it would normally never make. These connections often lead to great ideas. Besides, many game designers could stand an occasional shower. Please make sure though that if you drive to get ideas, you invest in a hands-free recording device or stop your car first before you jot down your thoughts.

3. **Attend a lecture.** I love the Game Developer's Conference because I get inspired by the game design lectures and discussions. I often end up with a notebook full of ideas. Make sure you share some of your ideas with your fellow game designers, too. It's always good to "stretch your idea's legs" to find out where it bends and where it breaks. Just be prepared to be told your ideas are stupid[4].

4. **Play a game, preferably a bad one.** Playing a good[5] video game has its benefits, but I find it more educational to play a bad game. As you play a bad game, look at the things in the game that were done poorly. Then think about what **you** would do to improve them. Consider how many people "invented" the airplane before the Wright Brothers built and flew their plane. Sometimes it takes several iterations on an idea before it works successfully.

5. **Regardless of the above, follow your passion.** You never know when you'll get a chance to use something you love in a game design. Even if you do read comics and play video games, if you really love something, that love will shine through in your game. Satoshi Tajiri designed *Pokémon* as a game version of his love for collecting insects. Dave Jaffe turned his love for Ray Harryhausen movies into *God of War*. Shigeru Miyamoto often turns his real-world hobbies into game designs. If you follow your passions, designing your game won't even feel like work.

[3] This is the same phenomenon that gave us two volcano-themed movies in one year, Dante's Peak and Volcano, back in 1997.
[4] And then when someone tells you your idea is stupid, you can retort with Michel Gondry's quote!
[5] I realize that "good" is extremely subjective. Good could mean highly rated, best-selling, competently made or even just damn cool.

It's one thing to have a good idea; it's another thing to have a *marketable* one. During the course of my career, I have been told many times (usually by my colleagues in the marketing department) that my idea is a "designer's idea", which means that they think my idea one that I would love to play but it isn't marketable to the general gaming public. Personally, I am torn with this assessment. On the one hand, I can understand their desire to make a game that will sell. If your game sells, that means you can make more games.

But on the other hand, before I am ready to give in to "the suits" I am reminded of all of the innovative games that have been created over the years. I am sure that at one point the designers of these games were told by their marketing colleagues that their idea was too weird, too unmarketable, or too stupid. If that were the case, then games like *PaRappa the Rapper*, *The Sims* or *Braid* would have never been made.

However, let me tell you a little secret. Come a little closer … a little closer … too close!

↑   *If you think something is innovative, it just means you haven't been paying attention.*   ↑

                                                                       Scott Rogers

While I am sure there is probably still a completely original idea out there in the galaxy of ideas, the majority of gameplay design works by each game building upon its predecessor. I truly believe that this strategy is one of the keys to creating great game design. Even the most innovative games like the aforementioned *PaRappa*, *Sims*, and *Braid* had their predecessors in *Simon*, *Sim City*[6], and *Blinx: the Time Sweeper*.

Here's another secret. My idea isn't even original. Raph Koster charted the evolution of the shoot 'em up genre in his book *A Theory of Fun for Game Design* (Paraglyph, 2004). Taking Raph's chart as inspiration, I will show you the evolution of gameplay design within the platform game genre.

---

[6] Will Wright, the creator/designer of The Sims, is one of, if not the smartest guy in video games. His genius is that his entire video game career appears to be dedicated to the iteration of a single idea. His creations, Sim City, Sim Ant, Sim Earth, Sim City 2000, The Sims, and Spore, showcase the natural evolution of a single idea (the world building simulation) to literally galactic proportions. That he has been able to develop and polish this idea over the years is a luxury of which any game designer would be envious.

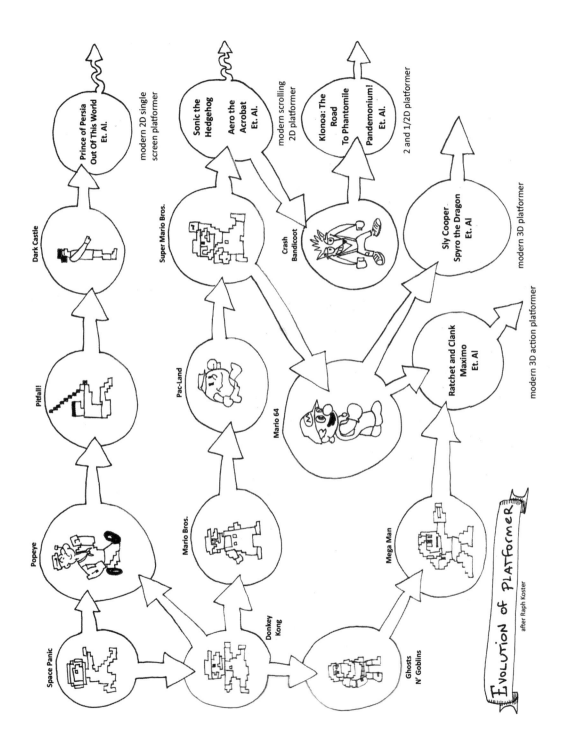

Evolution of Platformer

after Raph Koster

- *Space Panic*'s (Universal, 1980) walking character climbed ladders and dug holes to temporarily stun enemies.
- *Donkey Kong* (Nintendo, 1981) added jumping and a power-up that could defeat enemies.
- *Popeye* (Nintendo, 1982) introduced moving collectables and environmental mechanics that the player could interact with.
- *Pitfall!* (Activision, 1982) added alternate moves including vine-swinging and hopping on alligators' heads.
- *Mario Bros.* (Nintendo, 1983) added a second player and enemies that could be defeated by the player's skill rather than just a power-up.
- *Pac-Land* (Namco, 1984) featured a world map, a variety of themed levels and dynamic hazards.
- *Ghosts 'N' Goblins* (Capcom, 1985) featured multiple weapons including projectiles, health (in the form of armor that shattered off), and combatable "boss" monsters.
- *Super Mario Bros.* (Nintendo, 1985) launched a wave of imitators who were inspired by its tight controls, whimsical environments, and creative level design.
- *Dark Castle*'s (Silicon Beach Software, 1986) hero Duncan could "hide" from enemies. It was also the first game where players didn't immediately die from falling, but rather ended up in the dungeon.
- *Mega Man* (Capcom, 1987) introduced themed stages ending with similarly themed bosses who possessed powers that could be gained by the player once they were defeated.
- *Crash Bandicoot* (Universal, 1996) used 3-D models and environments to create the camera view called "2.5-D."
- *Mario 64* (Nintendo, 1996) brought all of the gameplay of the Mario platform games into true 3-D.

As you can see, each idea builds upon the next. Each game designer inspires the one that comes after them. Or as Pablo Picasso once said, "Bad artists copy. Good artists steal."

Now that you have a great game idea to start with, you have to ask yourself:

WHAT DO GAMERS WANT?

I believe that most gamers don't know what they want until it is shown to them. That is why it is important for game designers to have ideas born from passion. To have a vision of what their game is supposed to be.

Gamers can feel when developers are passionate about their games. They can smell it like a dog smells fear. Don't be afraid to hold onto your unique vision: just be aware that it may not turn out exactly how you envisioned.

But that didn't really answer the question did it? Okay, here's a simple answer:

GAMERS WANT GOOD GAMES[7]

Of course, there is no guarantee that your game will be good. While no one sets out to make bad games, bad games still get made. You can lay the blame of a bad game at the feet of a multitude of reasons, which we will be covering later on.

Tim Schaefer, the designer of *Psychonauts* and *Brütal Legend*, says that all good game characters are **wish fulfillment**. They give the player a chance to be something they aren't in the real world. I think the same is true about games *in general*. Games should *make players feel something that they aren't in the real world*: powerful, smart, sneaky, successful, rich, bad, or heroic.

As you are developing your idea, you need to know "What audience is my game for?" The rise of casual gaming has created an entirely new market; gamers that aren't interested in grinding away at a game for hours at a time. You need to decide who your game idea is for: the casual or the hardcore player. You can rule out certain design decisions early on by setting the audience in stone near the beginning of the idea development process.

Don't forget to ask this important question: "What is the age of my audience?" Having made dozens of "kid's" games, I have observed a useful fact about kids and games. Kids always want what is made for an audience older than their own age group. For example, an 8-year-old kid wants to play a game that is made for a 10-year-old kid. A 10-year-old kid wants to play a game that is made for a 13-year-old kid. A 13-year-old kid wants to play a game that is made for an 18 year old. Many kids aren't interested in playing games directly targeting their age range. If asked, they will tell you "that's a game for my little brother." Believe me, in kid language, there is no greater put down!

Developers, especially ones who have never made a game for kids before, tend to oversimplify and talk down to younger audiences. They say "we don't want this game to be too challenging because it is for kids." Don't make that mistake. Kids are far smarter and way better gamers than we give

---

[7] Yes, this is in ALL CAPS and bold because it is a VERY IMPORTANT THING.

them credit for. Often, they pick up on concepts faster than many adults. There are some limitations you have to consider when making games for kids though. First is that their little hands can't perform overly complex control schemes. The second is with an audience in first grade or younger (6 to 7 years old), they may not be able to read many complex words or long amounts of text. And watch the swearing.

WHY I HATE "FUN"

"Is it fun?" is the question I dread the most when coming up with new game ideas. Many gaming academics have attempted to define what fun is. Designer Marc LeBlanc breaks down fun into eight categories: Sensation, Fellowship, Fantasy, Discovery, Narrative, Expression, Challenge, and Submission[8]. While the classification of fun is an interesting exercise, I don't find it that helpful "in the field." There are always problems. For example, a game idea (or mechanic, or boss fight, or whatever) can sound fun "on paper" but may not be fun once you get it working in the game. Or it may work, but only be fun to you.

The problem with fun is, like humor, it is completely subjective. Even if I find something fun the first time I play it, it will almost certainly not be fun on the hundredth go. This ultimately happens to all game developers while working on a game. You will play the same level hundreds of times over the course of the production. Then you start to lose all objectivity. I distinctly remember several times when a producer would come in and ask:

---

[8] Taken from Mark's GDC lecture and corresponding website: http://www.8kindsoffun.com/.

When it comes to fun and games I have found there is only one truth:

YOU HAVE NO GUARANTEE THAT YOUR GAME IDEA IS GOING TO BE FUN

You can try to skew the odds in your favor by basing your game on existing, proven gameplay style, but more often than not, you end up with a "clone" game. Look at how many lousy first person shooters and survival horror games have been made.

Because developers always lose their objectivity during the course of production, I have created the "**Theory of Un-Fun**."

↑ *The Theory of Un-Fun states: start with a "fun" idea. As you develop the game, if you find something in the game that is not fun (or un-fun), then remove it. When you have removed all of the un-fun, then all that should be left is the fun.* ↑

Seems like common sense, right? And yet I have encountered many developers that have left bad gameplay mechanics and ugly art and broken cameras in their games because they got used to them or couldn't recognize them as problems. They just didn't possess the objectivity to see that something in their game was not fun. Of course, you need to start with a game idea that is fun to begin with. Otherwise, when you have removed all of the un-fun you'll be left with nothing!

The theory of un-fun must be applied several times during the game's development. Stop what you are doing and take a look at the game. Make a list to determine what is making the game "un-fun." It could be a crappy camera. Lousy controls. You could have bad animations. The game may be too hard. The game may be too easy. A producer I once worked with gave me a great piece of advice when it came to ideas. "Don't be too dear." And what he meant was don't be afraid to kill bad ideas. In other words, kill the un-fun. Don't worry, there are plenty more ideas where those came from.

BRAINSTORMING

When coming up with ideas, I like to brainstorm. To brainstorm properly, you need the following five things:

1. A working brain
2. Something to write with

3. Something to write on
4. A place to work
5. Collaborators, preferably ones who also have working brains.

Before you start brainstorming, you need to set some ground rules. First, there is no such thing as a stupid or bad idea. Say yes to everything at this stage. Make sure you collaborate with people from other disciplines than game design: programmers, artists, testers, writers. The more diverse your brainstorming group is the better[9]. People always surprise me with what they bring to the idea creation process.

Think about all the things you want your game to be. Then write them down. Your goal is to free associate an idea as far as it can go. Milk the idea completely. When you have reached the ridiculous, then squeeze it once more and let it go. Here are some of the notes from one of my brainstorming sessions:

---

[9] Keep in mind that everyone you invite to your brainstorming session should understand how to make a game though, otherwise you might waste a lot of time on unrealistic ideas.

KART RACING BRAINSTORM

SPEED RELATED:

GO SO FAST THAT YOU CAN SKIM WATER
LEAP LONG GAPS/ VIBRATE THROUGH
WALLS/ LEAVE TRAIL OF FIRE/ DODGE
BULLETS/ CREATE A SONIC BOOM/
GET BULLET-TIME (TIME SLOWS)/
AVOID DETECTION OF NON-HUMAN
DEVICE/ DRAG OTHER CHARACTERS
IN YOUR WAKE (SLIP STREAM)
DRIVE DONUTS TO CREATE TORNADO
ROCKET BOOST/ TEAM SPEED BOOST

DAMAGE RELATED:

FLAME BLAST (FROM EXHAUST OR
GOUT FROM FRONT)
BACKWARDS ATTACK = STICKY
BOMBS - BOUNCING BETTY BOMB
FORWARD ATTACK = BULLET /
HEAT-SEEK
WHANGING ON CAR - KNOCK PARTS
LOOSE/ HEALTH LEECH/
SHIELD LEECH/ WEAPON/POWER
UP STEAL
POWERFUL BOMB THAT YOU MUST
SHOOT BEFORE IT EXPLODES
ATOM BOMB FORCE FIELD
(CHARGES UP THEN HURTS
ALL NEARBY)

As you can see, the topics didn't really relate exactly to each other; sure, they are all things you may find a combat/driving game to have. The ideas don't have to be original at this stage either; you are merely cataloging ideas and concepts. As you design them further, then you can start thinking of things like originality or even fun.

When I am brainstorming, I like to write on a very big whiteboard. You may prefer to use lots of Post-It notes. Index cards work pretty well too. It doesn't matter. What matters is that these ideas get recorded. Even if they don't work out, you can always use them for some other game.

An excellent exercise you can use to brainstorm your game idea is to create the box and the manual. What would the cover image be? What would the bullet points on the back of the box read? How would you communicate the game in a black and white, 16-page manual? By placing these limitations on your idea, you can streamline your idea to the bare essentials. Here's an example of the back of game box that you can use as a template.

BREAKING WRITER'S BLOCK

What do you do when the ideas won't come? There's no need to be ashamed. Everyone gets creatively stopped up from time to time. Here are a few tricks to try when you are dealing with writer's block.

1. **Narrow your focus.** Maybe you are trying to think of too many things at once. Tackle your problems one by one by making an outline or breaking things down to a minute level if you have to. Give yourself a time line to complete each of these tasks, but don't take days. Try to get them done in hours.

2. **Take a walk or exercise.** Everyone knows the brain is fueled by blood. Don't let that blood coagulate in your butt; get outside and move around. When your blood starts circulating again, the new ideas will be coming back in no time.

3. **Deal with something else that may be distracting you.** Sometimes when I am stuck it is because I am worrying about something else. It may be an unfiled expense report or a floor that needs vacuuming. Take a break and deal with whatever is bothering you. When it is done, it won't be a concern anymore!

4. **Jump ahead to the good stuff.** Sometimes you have to come up with ideas for game features that may not excite you as much as other parts of the game. If these are bogging you down, then go ahead and jump to the good parts. Take some time to design a boss fight rather than worrying about the UI design. However, I recommend this ONLY as a last resort as it can be very dangerous! The truth is that games are built around schedules, deadlines, and budgets. If you don't get your work done on time and choose fun over the drudge work, the game, the whole team, and even the company can suffer. Don't procrastinate. Time management is very important, so be responsible.

5. **Change your environment.** I find that my office is full of distractions. E-mail beckons, video games call out to be played, and game design documents flutter their little pages at me, begging to be read. When this happens, I get out of my office and go to the nearest conference room to work. Or sometimes I go outside to sit in the sun and get some "vitamin Duh."

Once you have your list of ideas, it is time to get critical. Start narrowing down your list. Some items will immediately jump out as "keepers", while others are clear losers. Be merciless. It is better to have more good ideas than you can use than to have a game be full of lots of bad ideas.

Present these ideas to another party. Miyamoto has his "wife-o-meter" where he presents his ideas to his wife. If she hates them, they get thrown away. I used to have the executive assistants in my office take a look at game ideas. Someone who has no vested creative interest in your ideas will often give you the clearest and most honest insight.

Now that you have your ideas, let's put them to good use!

Level 2's Universal Truths and Clever Ideas:

- All gamers want are good games.

- You have no guarantee that your game is going to be fun.

- Start with a "fun" idea. As you develop the game, remove the "un-fun." All that should be left is the fun.

- Don't be so dear with your ideas. Throw out some good ideas along with the bad if they don't fit or have more than you need.

- Ideas are cheap, it's how you use them that matters.

- If you're stuck, take a break—but don't procrastinate.

LEVEL 3
WRITING THE STORY

Almost since the dawn of gaming, designers have debated which is more important: story or gameplay? Some designers believe games require a story to engage the player. Other designers think a story is what people use to describe play when it is finished. Pro-story designers reply that games are an artistic medium used to tell a story. Anti-story designers counter that a story is what you watch while the game loads. Designers at Game Developer Conferences all around the world face off against each other: one group yelling "*Bioshock*!" while the other side shouts "*Doom*!" back. Silly designers. They are both right and wrong. A game doesn't need to have a story, and yet it always has a story. Perplexing? While you are chewing that over, let's look at the classical definition of "story" as taught by everyone from Aristotle to very famous screenwriters. Here's the most basic structure of a story:

1. First, there is a **hero** who has a **desire**.

2. Our hero encounters an **event** that throws his life into disarray and interferes with obtaining the desire. This event causes a **problem** for the hero.

3. The hero tries to overcome the problem ...

4. … but his method fails.

5. There is a **reversal of fortune**, which causes more trouble for the hero.

6.   An **even greater problem** is created for the hero that puts the hero at greater risk.

7.   Finally, there is **one last problem** that threatens the hero with the **most risk of all**.

8. The hero must **resolve the final problem**...

9. ... in order to gain his **object of desire**. And everyone lives happily ever after. Well, until the sequel anyway.

Remember that no matter what your story is about, a story ALWAYS has a beginning, middle, and end. Hollywood has spent many years analyzing and deconstructing the story. Don't feel like you have to reinvent the wheel; learn what they have. Read screenwriting books, take classes, visit screenwriting websites. But you don't have to feel chained to a standard story structure like Joseph Campbell's "Hero's Journey" or Syd Field's "Three Act Structure." Try using another medium's structures to tell your story. How is a story told in a song? In a TV news report? In a Homeric poem? Or try looking to non-Western-world storytelling for inspiration.

Just remember that video games are an interactive medium, and as William Shakespeare reminds us, "The play's the thing." That was one guy who knew story, and he was pretty smart for someone who never played a video game. If gameplay is the meat of the game, then story should be the salt: just enough will add flavor but too much can ruin everything and kill you.

Some games don't even have stories. Games like *Tetris* or *Bejeweled* or even *Pac-Man* don't need them to be engaging for the player. However, they still generate a **narrative**, which literally means "an order of events." Since we humans perceive time as linear, we express our experiences linearly as well—even if they aren't presented in a traditional story structure. Let's look at it this way:

Every time a person plays a game they create a narrative. There are an infinite number of narratives that the player can create. As a designer, you need to look at all[1] of the narratives possible and find out how to make them ALL fun. The goal is to create multiple narratives that the player will enjoy playing.

In a narrative, the player is the "hero" of the game. The designer needs to look at the game from the player's perspective and be aware of the ordering of the events and experiences that will eventually help the play create the narrative. As each experience builds on the next, the goal is to create rising emotional states for the player. Then the designer can design systems to choreograph these interesting experiences which in turn create emotions. Savvy? How about an example instead?

Left 4 Dead uses an **artificial intelligence** called the "Director" to control the game's pacing. Depending on the player's "stress level", which is calculated using many variables including health, skill, and location, the Director then adjusts the number of zombies that attack, what items like ammo and health are generated, and even the music. In the end, the game itself generates a unique and dynamic play experience for the player. However, since most developers don't yet have technology like *Left 4 Dead*'s Director, it is up to the designer to create these situations as best they can within their own games.

When you are designing a game, it is extremely important to know the narrative that the player will experience. You'll find that the player's narrative can end up quite different to the game's story. **Remember to never mistake story for gameplay, and similarly never mistake gameplay for story.**

I am also a firm believer that almost ANYTHING can be made into gameplay. Don't feel like you are limited by subject matter. Look at games

---

[1] Or as many as you can guess will happen. It's like playing a massive session of "what if." However, as these possibilities can stretch on to infinity, it might not be worth the time investment to predict everything. That's why when something happens that the designer didn't expect and doesn't break the game, we're more than happy to call it a "feature" and move on!

like *Mr. Mosquito* (the player is a mosquito who drinks the blood of a family), *SimCity* (the player builds and manages a city), and *PaRappa the Rapper* (dog raps to win the love of his flower girlfriend).

Still don't believe me? Let's look at the classic and simple story *Little Red Riding Hood*. This children's story has all the elements you'll need to make a great video game:

1. Little Red Riding Hood walks through the forest to Grandma's house = classic player exploration. Give Red some goodies to collect to fill up her picnic basket (inventory system) and have her jump over a fallen log or two on her way.
2. Red meets the Big Bad Wolf = the player has her first enemy encounter. Of course, you can't kill off the wolf yet ... (unless the enemies are "wolf minions").
3. Carrying a full basic set of goodies (gating mechanism), Red reaches Grandma's house (next level), where she finds "Grandma" waiting in bed.
4. Red questions "Grandma's" true identity ("what big eyes you have"). This can take the form of a quiz, a puzzle, or even a rhythm game.
5. "Grandma" is revealed as the Big Bad Wolf and Red and the wolf battle to the death = boss fight[2]!

See? Even a "simple" classic story can still offer all the elements to make an exciting and varied video game[3]!

---

[2] We all know that Little Red Riding Hood ends with Red being eaten by the wolf and having the woodcutter save her, but where is the fun in that? Why watch a cutscene when you can have a boss fight? It's not my fault boss fights weren't invented when they wrote this story. Personally, I think my ending is better.

[3] OK, the story of Little Red Riding Hood might not make for a very LONG video game, but it can be made into a game nonetheless.

THE TRIANGLE OF WEIRDNESS

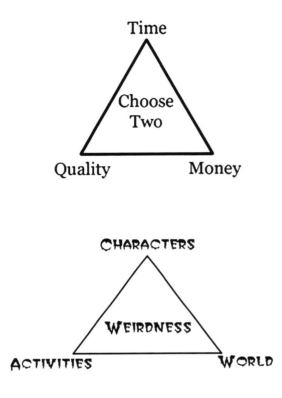

I am sure you have heard of the famous production triangle (see opposite).

One of the best things about video games is that, technical restraints of your chosen platform aside, you are limited only by your imagination.

Developers can craft virtual worlds that feature non-Newtonian physics, bizarre characters, and absurd quests. However, it is possible to go crazy with creativity, especially when writing the game story. This is why I created the "**Triangle of Weirdness**." Notice the difference in the choices on the triangle of weirdness: characters, activities, and world.

Unlike the production triangle where you can have any two points, you can only choose **one** corner on the triangle of weirdness. Choose any more than that and you risk alienating your audience.

Let's take a look at three examples of how to apply the Triangle of Weirdness to your story and world:

While the *Wizard of Oz* features weird characters such as a Tin Man, a Lion, and a Scarecrow, the land of Oz was a pretty typical fairy tale location when it was created in the 1900s. The characters of the *Wizard of Oz* have desires readers can relate to: courage, love, and wanting to return home.

While the main characters of *Star Wars* are familiar (the young hero, the princess in distress, the charming rogue), and their desires are familiar (join the war effort, defeat the villains, get the girl), it is the world of *Star Wars* that is weird with its Jawas, Wookies, Jedis, and a Cantina populated by the craziest-looking scum in the galaxy.

Monty Python and the Holy Grail features typical (if not archetypical) characters: King Arthur and his knights of the round table. These stalwart knights travel through medieval England on their quest for the Holy Grail. However, that quest is filled with weird activities like designing shrubs for the knights that say "Ni!" or being slaughtered by the killer rabbit of Caerbannog.

It is possible to go too far. Movies like *Dune* (1984) and *The City of Lost Children* (1995), or video games like *SkullMonkeys* or *Muscle Man March,* while incredibly unique and creative, just left many audiences feeling like they "didn't get it." And nobody likes to feel stupid.

What do these games and movies have in common? They all violate the Triangle of Weirdness. Do so at your own peril …

When developing a game story, you will find there are three different types of people in your audience.

1. Players that are into your story as it happens.
2. Players that want to get into your story in depth.
3. Players who don't care what the story is at all[4].

Making your story appealing to all three types of players can be a challenge. The best rule of thumb is to always make the story be in service of the gameplay and not the other way around. Here are some tips on involving story into the game.

- To satisfy players that are looking for a deeper experience, provide details but make sure they don't get in the way of the story. For example, *Bioshock* and *Batman: Arkham Asylum* both have non-mandatory collectable audiotapes that reveal deeper story details to the player without intruding in on the main story.
- Players that are just along for the ride will "A button" their way through audio cues and cutscenes that reveal story points. Make sure your game's story is also revealed through gameplay and level design to prevent it being skipped entirely by the player; otherwise, the player will get lost and confused[5]. You can also introduce story as gameplay by making them playable flashbacks or puzzles.
- Start your story as late into the action as possible. This can be in the middle of a boss fight, at the end of a level, or during a car chase. Keep in mind, this works best for games with traditional story. I'm not sure it's such a good idea to start a puzzle game of *Tetris* with dozens of tiles raining down on the player.
- Always keep your stories lively and moving. Professional screenwriters will introduce a change in the plot or action every 15 minutes. Even with non-story games, play sessions are becoming "bite-sized" so they're short enough for players to enjoy in short bursts.

---

[4] I can't take credit for this observation. This statement was made by Ken Levine, the director of Bioshock, during his excellent 2009 GDC speech.
[5] Yeah, I know. It's their own damn fault if they get confused for skipping the cutscenes in the first place, but remember the first rule of responsible game design: love thy player.

Speaking of surprises, there is a trend in game stories that I blame squarely on Hollywood: the twist/surprise ending. While it is fun to be taken by surprise, I believe there is merit to a predictable ending. Remember that wish fulfillment I said players want? People like it when the good guys win and the bad guy lose, and yet that's the oldest story in the book.

Take, for example, the James Bond movies of the 1980s. When I was growing up, I loved to go see those films. Even before I saw them, I knew that Bond was going to use a cool new gadget and drive an awesome car, defeat the villain's scheme, save the world, and end up with the hot girl. So, if I knew all of these things, why did I bother watching the movie? For me, the fun was the twists and turns the story took. I knew the WHO, the WHAT and the WHY, but I didn't know the HOW.

There is a delight in predicting how things will turn out. It makes the player feel smart, like they "called it" in an election or solved a mystery. Besides, life is unpredictable enough as it is, why not give your audience a little predictability? The point I am making is you don't have to be especially clever when writing your story, just entertaining.

Conversely, something that I don't find very clever is a video game story where the main character has amnesia. Amnesia ranks as the number one video game cliché of all time, but I understand why game writers do this. It's an attempt to approximate the lack of information about the characters and the world as a player begins the game. However, it ultimately becomes an excuse for the writer to be an "unreliable narrative" and intentionally omit information to the player in order to create a "shock ending." It just feels forced and frankly, isn't fair to the player.

Instead, here is a great theory about the value of surprise vs suspense from classic director Alfred Hitchcock. Imagine that there are two men sitting at a table talking about baseball. The conversation lasts for about five minutes, when suddenly, there is a huge explosion! This shocks the audience but that surprise only lasts about 15 seconds.

However, here is how you can get a greater impact from your audience. Start the scene by showing the bomb under the table. The bomb is set to explode in five minutes. The two men discuss baseball while the audience is squirming in their seats thinking "Don't just sit there talking about baseball! There's a bomb under the table! Get out of there!" By making the audience aware of the danger the characters are in, the audience gets emotionally involved. By the time your scene reaches its climax, you have created more excitement with your audience than just the surprise of the bomb exploding[6].

Another thing to consider when developing your story is "what is at stake?" Many video games are about saving the world from evil or destruction. But just like every movie doesn't have to be a slam-bang blockbuster, not every video game has to be about saving the world. Small themes can be just as important as big ones. In my opinion, using a theme for your story other than "violence solves all problems" is a worthwhile pursuit. It worked for games like *Frogger*, *Zoo Tycoon*, and *Braid*.

TIME TO WRAP IT UP

Ending games can be just as hard as starting them. In the good old days, there wasn't an end to a game, just a kill screen[7]. Or they just ran forever, frequently wrapping their scores around like your car's odometer. Then along came *Dragon's Lair*, and everyone wanted to know whether Dirk rescued the Princess or not. The video game story was born.

How long should a game be? In the old days, the average was 20 hours. In the really old days, it was 40. Nowadays, most games average 8–10 hours of playing time; however, depending on the game, this length might not always be appropriate. You'll have barely scratched the surface of *Fallout 3* after 8 hours. I recommend ending the game when you feel like you have left the player feeling satisfied. You can leave plot points dangling to encourage replayability or to open up storylines for sequels, but in the end play fair with the player. Let them feel like they accomplished everything they needed to do during the game.

---

[6] Hitchcock also recommends that you don't actually kill the characters in this scenario. In the case of video games, the game would be over!

[7] A kill screen originally wasn't the "game over" screen, but rather a screen that appeared due to a programming error or design oversight. The most famous kill screen from classic gaming is the 256th level of Pac-Man. At this point, due to a bug half the screen becomes garbled data, which keeps the player from collecting all of the dots and clearing the board to move on. Arcade owners had to unplug or "kill" the game to start it back up again.

Some games even offer extra experiences so the player can continue playing after the story has ended. Multiple endings, minigames, unlockable and downloadable content or "deleted levels" (akin to deleted scenes on a DVD) will let your player return to your world without having to hear the same story over again. If you create a world that the player wants to play in, they will want to come back to play.

Or you can just throw away all of the previous advice and write your story at the last minute. Some development teams concentrate solely on the gameplay and create the storyline last. They claim it works. Personally, I think it would make me nervous.

Oh, I almost forgot to talk about one of the most important things about your game's story: the title! There are several ways to approach naming your game. They include:

- The literal title
- The action/cool title
- The punny title
- The "purple cow" title[8].

A literal title makes it easy to figure out where the title came from. It can be the name of your main character, like *Sonic the Hedgehog* or *Voodoo Vince*. It can be the main location of your game, like *Castle Wolfenstein* or *Saint's Row*. Or you can name your game after a gameplay activity or component like *Command and Conquer* or *Boom Blocks*.

The action/cool title is a title that captures the spirit of the game without mentioning any of the game characters or locations. I think games like *Darksiders, Brütal Legend*, and *Gears of War* all have cool titles.

The punny title is a title that makes you appreciate the cleverness of the title. *Just Cause, Half Life*, and *System Shock* are all good examples of punny titles. As puns are word play, you have to be careful as your audience may not get the reference or think the pun is funny. Humor is so subjective.

A purple cow title is one that makes your customer stop in their tracks and stare. It compels the reader to wonder why the title was chosen. Once the player has played the game, they understand the significance. Purple cow titles include *LittleBigPlanet, Far Cry*, and *Resident Evil*. The advantage to a purple cow title is once you've associated the word with their titles, it's hard for other people to use those words without conjuring up the image of the

---

[8] The term "purple cow" comes from the poem by Gelett Burgess who wrote: "I never saw a purple cow, I never hope to see one. But I can tell you anyhow, I'd rather see than be one."

game. It's going to be a long time before anyone thinks of using the word *Halo* in their game title …

No matter what naming convention you use, I think that shorter titles are better than longer ones. First of all, they are easier to remember and say. I like to keep them to two or three syllables like *Star Wars*, *Don-kee Kong*, *Pac-Man* or *Hey-lo*. I think this started because of marquee sizes on arcade cabinets: they needed to attract the player's attention, create some mystery, and describe the gameplay. "Defender" is still one of the best game names ever: it perfectly sums up the game in one three-syllable word.

Secondly, shorter titles are easier to make into logos for your game's start screen and read on the cover of a game's box. Don't forget to consider marketing aspects when you are creating your game's title. If you have to use a longer title or a subtitle, then still try to keep it short. *Uncharted: Drake's Fortune* combines a couple of purple cows to make a pretty good title. Players will want to know who Drake is and what his fortune is. Uncharted gives you the image of exploring or sailing into unknown and dangerous territory. Conversely, *Batman: Arkham Asylum* lets you know who you are playing and where it takes place.

Try to name your game sooner than later. I have always preferred the titles developers created over those made up by someone else in the team. If you wait too long, a publisher's marketing department will have to come up with the game's name for you—and believe me, you don't want that.

When you have finally named your game, you may discover that your great title is already in use or trademarked by someone else. Make sure you do a check with your publisher's legal department to make sure you can use your title before you become too attached to it. Even a quick word search on the Internet will help get you started.

CREATING CHARACTERS

Fellow designer Andy Ashcraft believes that video game developers only care about telling the second act of their story. I tend to agree with him. However, games that do that are missing an important part of the storytelling process[9]. In games, the second act is the grind that moves the player towards the third act which is the completion of the story; usually the last level and a boss fight. They skip the all-important first act to "cut to the chase." In video games, this is either done with a cutscene

---

[9] Remember, all stories have what? A beginning, middle and end.

or, even worse, the game's manual—which no one ever reads[10]! This is a mistake. The first act is where the player is given an opportunity to find out about and care about the character. However, I believe you need that first act to get the player to bond with the character, even if you kill that character off repeatedly (common in video games) or radically change them into a killing machine. Case in point, you don't need to look any further than the movie *Robocop*.

In the film *Robocop*, the audience is introduced to police officer Alex Murphy. He's an honest cop and a decent guy fighting crime in futuristic Detroit. By page 25 of the script, you actually care about the guy and feel bad when he's gunned down by criminal scumbags. The second act kicks off when Murphy is rebuilt as the cyborg Robocop. Now this movie had several video game adaptations made, and in all of them, Murphy's death was only shown as a cutscene. The player would start the game as Robocop and the killing of bad guys would commence immediately[11].
But in our hypothetical Robocop game, why not start with Murphy as a cop? The first level of the game would have Murphy tracking down the bad guys and end with his death. The player would have time to bond with him, making his death and resurrection have much more of an impact.

---

[10] Maybe I am exaggerating a little, but c'mon. When was the last time you really read a game manual? Then again, when was a game manual worth reading?

[11] Just so you realize that I'm not a complete idiot, I do know why the developers of Robocop began the player as Robocop. (1) It's more appealing to play as a criminal-blasting cyborg than as a fragile human; (2) game carts in 1988 didn't have the memory to store two completely different player character models, and why would you go through all of the work to create them, especially if you were only going to be the human player character for one level; and (3) the game is called Robocop, not "Guy who gets shot and eventually becomes Robocop."

Death should mean something to the player, especially when it isn't the main character dying. When was the last time you cried when a game character died? (Other than when you accidently deleted your save file?) Writers forget that you have to care about a character first if it is going to mean anything when you kill him. And the solution isn't to make the character a relative or part of a meaningful relationship, especially if that character is killed off in the first cutscene. I remember playing a game that opened with the player's relative getting murdered after interacting with him for one level. I didn't feel the righteous anger that the player felt for the rest of the game because I knew the character for such a short time. Invest the time in these characters, even if the ultimate goal is to kill them off.

Even better, make the character important to the player somehow. They can provide information on how to play the game, be the economy system (like the proprietor of the game's store), or provide health power-ups to the player on a regular basis. When that character is taken out of the game, the player will feel the impact. Spoiler alert, but in my humble opinion, the only game character whose death felt impactful was Aeris in *Final Fantasy VII*. Aeris filled many roles for the player; she was a damsel in distress, one part of the hero's love triangle, a character who contributed solutions to the problems in the plot, and a "playable" part of the gaming party. When she died, her loss to the player was felt on many levels. Build up your game characters before you tear them down. Make their loss count.

Your party members don't have to be human: the deaths of Agro the horse in *Shadow of the Colossus* and Dogmeat the dog in *Fallout 3* have similar effects on players. All that matters is that your player has a bond with these characters to feel the loss when it happens.

All this talk about death has bummed me out. So, what about humor in games? Most writers agree that comedy is harder than drama. However, I believe that the secret to humor is character. My favorite first person shooter is *Team Fortress 2,* and I believe it is one of the funniest games I have ever played. The game doesn't feature humor like other games have; you won't find physical gags, "hilarious" jokes, or burping and farting. What makes the game so funny is how true the characters are to themselves. From the wry Australian sniper who has to defend his occupation to his parents, to the Russian heavy gunner who is overly fond of "sanviches." All of the game characters' appearances, animations, and vocal barks reinforce their personalities, raising them from stereotypes to truly original (and funny) characters.

If your game character is defined by a profession or activity, then make sure that the majority of the activities they do are related to that profession or activity. For example, if your player character is a demolitions expert, they aren't going to negotiate their way into a prison level to free their pal. They are going to BLOW IT UP! Heck, they may even blow up a door rather than turn the knob. When we were creating *Maximo*, we decided that he was an impatient guy, always in a hurry to rescue the princess or get into a fight. He didn't even stop to open a treasure chest; he just kicked it open, collected the treasure, and went on his way. If you start with your character's personality you will end up with some interesting animations and gameplay. Remember, characters have many motivations: success, revenge, love, acceptance, escape, hunger, responsibility, knowledge. Many characters have more than one; often conflicting motivations. Knowing their motivations will help you determine what your character will do and say. The result will be a much richer character.

Mortimer!
It's short for Mort...
Which is latin for death...

Speaking of character, just like giving your game the right title is important, it is equally important to name your character correctly. Would you name a strapping barbarian hero Mortimer? Only if your hero is a parody or it's a comedy game. Names carry great weight. It is important to give your character the right name. Baby books are a great place to start. I like names that have some significance to the character's personality or what their occupation is. *Star Wars* has some of the best names. What does the name Luke Skywalker tell you about the character? Luke feels like a simple, homespun name fitting for a farm boy who yearns to "walk among the stars[12]."

It's also fun to have characters' names juxtapose each other. Two of my favorite character names are from *When Harry Met Sally*. Billy Crystal's character is named Harry Burns—a curmudgeonly, burned out name if ever there was one. Meg Ryan's character is Sally Allbright. She's positive, romantic, and a little naïve. While these names are pretty blatantly obvious, they give you a quick snapshot of the character's personality.

[12] Did you know that Luke Skywalker's original name was Luke Starkiller? This name change provides a great lesson: never give your character a name that gives away the ending of your story!

Comedic characters need appropriate names too. Guybrush Threepwood, Spongebob Squarepants, and Larry Laffer aren't heroic sounding names, but they are totally appropriate for the humorous games they are in. The only rule of thumb is when you look at an image of the character; the name fits what you see.

A FEW POINTERS ON WRITING FOR KIDS OF ALL AGES

Just because you are writing game stories for kids, doesn't mean it has to suck. The most common mistake kid game writers make is trying to make the story too simple. I have often heard developers protest over using complex ideas and themes because "it's for kids!" But think about children's literature. Children's classics like *Where The Wild Things Are*, *Heidi* or *The Chronicles of Narnia* are full of complex themes, interactions, and emotions. If it's good enough for kid's books, it should be good enough for kid's games. Coming of age doesn't only mean that the main character can carry a sword!

Another great thing about kid's games (heck, this applies to all games) is that you can teach your players things without them even knowing it. I am not talking about "edutainment", but the type of entertainment you used to find in movies and comic books. As a kid, I remember a *Batman* comic book in which I learned about famous comedians of the 1920s, the opera *Pagliacci*, African masks, and how paraffin wax discolors with age. That's some pretty impressive knowledge to gain from a "kiddie story." Don't be afraid to educate as well as entertain. Who knows, your players may learn something while they are having fun … and you may learn something as you are writing your story.

WRITING FOR LICENSES

A **licensed game** is when you create a game based on a pre-existing intellectual property[13]. This can be a character or world first seen in a movie, comic, real life, television, or even another video game. *Star Wars, Batman, Harry Potter*, and *Spongebob Squarepants* are all licensed characters and worlds, known as properties. The property is licensed by a publisher or

---

[13] There are also plenty of IPs that exist in the public domain: Cinderella, The Wizard of Oz, Dracula, The Three Musketeers, The Bible, Dante's Inferno to name a few. Remember to base your own work on the original material and not on someone else's interpretation.

developer, which means that a fee is paid to use the property for a game (or several games). The group who owns the original property is called the **licensor**. Licensors are groups like Lucasfilm, DC Comics, J.K. Rowling or Nickelodeon (to use examples from above). However, just because the **licensee** has paid to make a game using the character, that doesn't mean they can make any game they want. A licensee has to work with the licensor to adhere to the brand. For example, a licensor may not want their character to kill enemies. Therefore, the developer has to design their game around these "brand limitations." Some properties are pretty lenient to what developers can do with their properties, while others are very strictly moderated.

Don't dismay about having to stay within the confines of a license. With a good licensing partner, you can design a game that allows room for creativity. For example, I was working on a licensed game that had seen over 10 games previously based on it. Not looking forward to making just "another installment" of the property, we talked with the licensor about making the game in a genre that wasn't just a standard platformer. After we made our pitch, the licensor confessed that they were tired of creating the same style of game over and over, but had never considered taking the gameplay in another direction. The licensor gave us a lot more freedom than we had previously thought we had and, in the end, we produced a solid game. Just because you are working on a licensed game, don't assume that you are locked in to the "same old, same old." It never hurts to ask.

Here are a few tips I've picked up from working on licensed games:

- Find out about the license inside and out. Read, watch, play everything you can on it. Go deep whenever possible. If you go in directions that aren't obvious or use characters that are more obscure, the fans of the brand will appreciate it. Every licensed game should be a celebration of the license and a big "thank you" to the fans.

- Uncover the "big issues" early. Talk to your licensor and find out what the big "no no" issues are. Doing this will save you a lot of headaches and prevent you from making resources that will have to be changed later in production. For example, one game used hamburgers as a power-up. When the character ate them, he became invulnerable. However, even though it was never mentioned in any of the license's episodes, one of the main characters (one that was a playable character in our game) was a vegetarian. We had to change the power-up because the show's creators didn't like that we had their character "eating meat."

- Get as much material as possible from the licensor. Television shows have "bibles"—detailed documents that outline the show characters and worlds. Established comic books have years of back issues that make great reference material. If your license is still in production (for example, if you are making a game for a movie with a simultaneous release) get hold of scripts, animatics, storyboards, and production photos as soon as possible.

- If you are working on a movie license, visit the set (if applicable) and take your own reference pictures. Anything that helps you replicate the world of the license as closely as possible.

- Respect the license, but find ways to make it your own. A two-hour movie may not have enough material to allow you to create an 8–10 hour game. Work with the licensor to expand the fiction to help you "fill in the gaps." Don't be afraid to bring your own interests to the party; those interests may fit in better to the brand's license than you may think.

There is much more I could tell you about writing stories, but I won't. This should get you started with *your* stories. Now, let's get back on track and talk about the foundations of gameplay: what I call the Three Cs!

Level 3's Universal Truths and Clever Ideas:

- Some games need a story. Some games don't. All games need gameplay.

- A story always has a beginning, middle and end.

- Never mistake story for gameplay.

- Almost ANYTHING can be made into gameplay.

- Create a world the player will want to play in, and they will come back to play.

- Make death matter.

- Keep names short and descriptive.

- Don't underestimate kids: they're smarter than you think.

- Stay true to a license, but don't be afraid to "make it your own."

LEVEL 4

YOU CAN DESIGN A GAME, BUT CAN YOU DO THE PAPERWORK?

A Japanese game director once visited the studio where I worked to impart his wisdom to our team about his philosophy of game design, which mainly had to do with how much money his latest game had made. As he was leaving, he asked our team a cryptic question: "I believe making games is like fishing" he said. "When I return, you will tell me why this is so." If he had been wearing a cape, I'm sure he would have swooshed it mysteriously as he left.

I spent a lot of time thinking about just exactly how making games was like fishing. In the end, I decided that making games is **nothing** like fishing. Fishing is quiet and slow and involves waiting for something to happen that may never happen[1]. I also decided that this game director was full of crap. So I developed my own analogy.

Making games is like making chili (bear with me—it'll make sense). Like making chili, you first need a recipe and that recipe is the game's documentation. Having the right recipe is important. You are not making soup or stew. You want to make sure your documentation not only covers what is in it, but how it can be made: just like a recipe. Be sure to follow the recipe, but be

[1] You may be able to tell from this statement that I do not enjoy fishing.

mindful that it will have to change, especially if something doesn't go right. And, just like making chili, remember that you can season to taste. Some parts of the game will be "meatier" than others and you will want to adjust your game to make those parts more pronounced.

Next step is to assemble the ingredients. Just as a chili needs ingredients, a game's design needs people and tools to make the game. You'll also need the right equipment to make your game, just like you'll need spoons and pots and pans and a stove to make your chili. However, you might not have exactly what you need at hand. Sometimes you will have the team and resources you want, sometimes you have to improvise with what is available. That's okay; I hear cowboys made some pretty good chili with nothing more than a campfire and a tin can.

Add these ingredients together. The beauty of chili is that it usually works no matter how you prepare the ingredients. You can carefully cut and chop everything or just throw it together in a big pot. Some game productions are very methodical and well organized. Others are a mad dash to get all of the elements into the game as soon as possible. Just make sure you follow the recipe so you don't forget anything. Prepare the ingredients in the right order. Always brown the meat **before** you add it to the pot. (I learned that one the hard way.)

In chili, everything is brought to a boil and then left to simmer. **Crunch time** reminds me of boiling: a frantic burst of energy and effort to get everything in and running. However, if you boil for too long, you can ruin the chili, burn the pot, and catch the stove on fire. Games and studios have been destroyed by too much crunch time, so be responsible. **Game polishing** and **bug squashing** reminds me of chili simmering. Chili isn't ready the moment you finish assembling it. You need to take the time to make it just right. Games, just like chili, need time to be iterated on, improved, and seasoned. **Bugs**, code, art and design problems with the game, need to be found and fixed. That takes time. Allow for that time, just like you need to allow for cooking time with chili. Sometimes it's good to let the team play with a part of the game to find out what works and what doesn't. I find that chili always tastes better the day after you have made it.

Your chili may need something added to it at the last minute to make it work. Unless you've royally screwed it up, chili can usually be salvaged. I've seen troubled games get turned around at the eleventh hour. However, I don't recommend making games this way. It can lead to stomach upset. Chili can also deceive. It may look horrible, but still taste delicious. Some games may not be perfect, or even pretty, but if they have good gameplay they can still entertain. Good games and good chili satisfy the soul as well as the stomach. (Or the head, if you think with your stomach.)

You see? Making games is **exactly** like making chili. Take that, Japanese game director[2]!

So you've learned how to make chili, but what about making games? To make a game, you need to start with a game design document. There are actually four documents that will guide you through preproduction:

1. The one-sheet
2. The ten-pager
3. The beat chart
4. The game design document.

Each of these documents has a specific use during the preproduction/ production of a game and eventually all evolve into the same document: the **game design document**, or **GDD** for short.

Ironically, a typical GDD is anything but short; many of them average over 300 pages. Now, this is not a hard and fast number. Some are much shorter, some are much longer. The GDD for *Grand Theft Auto* would be significantly longer than the GDD for *Tetris*.

Game designers have struggled with just how long a game design document should be. There is a movement within the game development community to keep the game design document as short as possible, for a variety of reasons. In the end, I believe a GDD should be just long enough to accurately describe what is going on in the game. However, don't let that intimidate you. The other documents—the one-sheet, the ten-pager, and the beat chart—are all steps to help you reach your goal of a completed GDD.

There is no official format for any of these documents. What I'm showing here is just one way to present the information. For example, video game consultant Mark Cerny presents his GDD material in a single page per topic, bullet point format. He claims this simple presentation is easier for his team mates to read and digest. Use what works best for you. Just remember, the goal of great game design documentation is **communication**: communication to the player, to your team members, and to your

[2] I don't blame him for his bad analogy. I am sure they don't have very good chili in Japan.

publishing partners. The clearer the communication, the easier it is going to be to get your coworkers excited about your ideas. Got it? Good. Let's start writing!

WRITING THE GDD, STEP 1: THE ONE-SHEET

The one-sheet is a simple overview of your game. It is going to be read by a variety of people including your team mates and publisher, so you need to keep it interesting, informative and most importantly, short. It should be no longer than … you guessed it … a single page. You will find two examples of one-sheets in Bonus Levels 1 and 2. You can create them anyway you'd like, just as long as you include the following information:

- Game title
- Intended game systems
- Target age of players
- Intended Entertainment Software Rating Board (ESRB) rating
- A summary of the game's story, focusing on gameplay
- Distinct modes of gameplay
- Unique selling points
- Competitive products.

Most of these terms are self-explanatory, but here are a few you may not know:

ESRB RATINGS[3]

The ESRB is a self-regulatory organization that enforces a rating system as well as advertising and online privacy principles for software in the United States and Canada. The ESRB's creation is similar to the comic book industry's Comics Code, which was created to enforce content and morality guidelines in conjunction with concerned parent groups. However, the ESRB's rating system more closely resembles that of the MPAA's movie rating system (G, PG, PG-13, R, X). Games are reviewed and assigned a letter rating according to content.

---

[3] The ESRB is the American rating system. There are several other international systems including the Pan-European Games Information (PEGI), the UK's British Board of Film Classification (BBFC), and Germany's Unterhaltungssoftware Selbstkontrolle (USK). Their age and content restrictions vary by country.

Currently, there are six ratings that can be assigned by the ESRB:

eC (Early Childhood): contains no material parents would find inappropriate.

E (Everyone): may contain fantasy, cartoon or mild violence, and infrequent use of mild language.

E10 (Everyone 10+): may contain more fantasy, cartoon or mild violence, and mild language and suggestive themes.

T (Teen): may contain violence, suggestive themes, crude humor, minimal blood, and infrequent use of strong language.

M (Mature 17+): may contain intense violence, blood and gore, sexual content, and strong language.

AO (Adults Only 18+): not suitable for people under 18—may contain prolonged scenes of intense violence, graphic sexual content, and nudity.

While the ESRB's guidelines are effective in informing parents what titles are appropriate for their children, there is stigma attached to some of the ratings within the development community and fanbase.

Many gamers consider eC to be for "baby games", as this rating most frequently appears on edutainment and licensed titles for young audiences. At the other end of the scale, no brick and mortar retailer in America will carry a game with the AO rating. It's the industry's equivalent to an X rating in film. Therefore most publishers and developers won't even consider making games for this rating and will take great pains to prevent their titles from having this rating[4].

Competitive products (or **"comps"**) are games that are similar to your game design idea that have already been released. Listing comps helps your reader understand what your game is going to be about. However, make sure that when you choose your comps you pick games that people are (a) very familiar with or (b) are successful. Publishers and marketers are very aware of how well or poorly a game sold. If you choose a comp of a game that did badly, a potential publisher may get scared off. Like I say, "always pick a winning horse."

Unique selling points (or **USPs**) are the "bullet points" found on the back of the box. As a rule of thumb, there should be around five USPs. (A number I developed when I realized you can only really fit five bullet

---

[4] This happened on The Punisher (THQ, 2005), where the player could curb-stomp and feed criminals into a woodchipper during interrogations. The scenes were so graphic that the developer changed the camera angles and displayed the action in black and white to bring the AO rating down to an M.

points on the back of a game box.) Remember "amazing graphics" and "awesome story" or "sequel to the award-winning game" don't count. All games should have or be these things (though only if it actually is a sequel in the case of the last one). Besides, gamers can smell that marketing BS a mile away. USPs should be the unique features that make your game stand out from the crowd. Here are some examples. Let the spin begin!

- Multiple gameplay modes, including 256-player cooperative gameplay.
- Over 1000 tunes from popular bands.
- Explore an open world and 200 levels that allows the player to go anywhere.
- Mow through your enemies using the blastinator, the skull-defiler, and the awesome fire-ant anguisher!
- Experience lifelike physics and groundbreaking special effects with the new Realitech engine!
- Download additional costumes and content over the Internet.

As you can see, USPs should get the reader excited about the features of a game without going into lengthy detail about them. Exposing more of that detail is what the ten-pager is all about.

WRITING THE GDD, STEP 2: THE TEN-PAGER

Now that you have completed you game outline, it is time to expand upon that information and flesh out the details.

The **ten-pager** is a "broad stroke" design document that lays out the spine of your game. The intent is for readers to quickly understand the basics of the final product without going into excruciating detail. Keeping your ten-pager interesting may be the most important part of your document. Remember, the people that are going to finance your game are going to be reading this. Be sure to provide plenty of visuals but keep them relevant. Don't go overboard with fancy fonts and ornate layouts. Readability is the key. Creating your ten-pager in PowerPoint or a similar program will assist you with formatting. This will allow you to present it electronically during a pitch meeting or print it out as a "leave behind" handout.

No matter which document you are creating, the goal is to make it interesting enough so your reader wants to continue reading it. Ask yourself as you write your ten-pager, "who is my audience?" There is a big difference between a ten-pager that is being circulated around your team vs one that is going to be presented to a marketing department. Here are some examples of how you should skew the information in your ten-pager for each audience type:

Production Team	Marketing/Executives
Provide clear diagrams of gameplay	Show exciting conceptual images
Use short, punchy sentences	Text in bullet points form
Use specific terminology to get your intention clearly across	Use vivid, descriptive examples
Compare gameplay to appropriate games, even vintage titles	Use successful, modern games as comparative titles

While the above table shows two different audiences for a ten-pager, that doesn't mean you have to write two different documents. Just remember that both audiences will be reading it[5].

Keep in mind that the 10 pages of a ten-pager are more what you'd call "guidelines" than actual rules. Feel free to go over or under[6] the 10-page count as long as you succinctly communicate the basics of your game design. By the way, you will find an example of a ten-pager in Bonus Level 3.

THE RULE OF THREES

Before we start writing our ten-pager, here is a **very important rule of thumb**, that I use when creating a ten-pager:

THREE IS A MAGIC NUMBER

History has observed that all good things come in threes. Don't believe me? Observe!

- The Holy Trinity of Christianity
- The *Star Wars* trilogy (the original good ones)
- *Goldilocks and the Three Bears*
- Three's a crowd

---

[5] Then again, sometimes you might want to make a version that caters to one audience over another ... it never hurts to be prepared.
[6] Preferably under.

- Asimov's three rules of robotics
- *Three Men and a Baby*
- Getting to third base.

This rule will be coming up further on in this book, but for now, my point is that people like things in threes; especially when you are providing examples. The logic behind the **rule of threes** is this:

- The first example gives the reader an idea of what you are talking about, but can still mislead them.
- The second example gives the reader something to compare or contrast the first example with.
- The third example gives another example that can complement or contrast the other two, keeping your examples from feeling binary or contrived.
- Anything past three just gets too long and boring: never be too long or boring.

Now that you know the rule of three, use this power for good! When you are listing out your examples in your ten-pager, group them in threes. History will thank you.

TEN-PAGER OUTLINE

PAGE 1: TITLE PAGE

- Game title
- Intended game systems
- Target age of players
- Intended ESRB rating
- Projected ship date.

Game Logos: When creating your game title for your ten-pager, I suggest creating a placeholder logo. Choosing the proper font for your title allows you to convey the genre of your game quickly without the need for pictures.

Fun time! See if you can guess the game genres suggested by the fonts below.

SUPER MAGIC WORLD

VERY FAST CARS

DUDE WITH SWORD

PAGE 2: GAME OUTLINE

- Game story summary
- Game flow

Game Story Summary: Using your one-sheet's story outline as a starting point, flesh out your game's story. Keep in mind, your story outline still shouldn't be more than a few paragraphs long; but that shouldn't stop you from telling the beginning, middle, and end. Your readers will want to know if your hero ever rescues the princess! (He does.)

Game Flow: Briefly describe the flow of the game's action in the context of the locations the player will find themselves in. For example: "*Tomb Raider: Legend* is a third person action-adventure that finds archeologist Lara Croft searching the jungles of Bolivia to the mountains of Tibet for the mysterious Ghalali key; an artifact which may be the key to finding Lara's own long lost mother."

This brief game flow outline tells the player who they are playing (Lara Croft), the camera angle (third person), and genre of gameplay (action-adventure) as well as painting a picture of game locations (Bolivia and Tibet) and the player's goals (seek the Ghalali key and solve the mystery of Lara's mother).

Go ahead and list the environments that the player will find themselves in. Make sure you point out any special gameplay that may occur in these locations.

Other questions that should be answered by the game flow include:

- What are the challenges the player encounters and the methods by which they can overcome them?
- How does the progression/reward system work? How does the player grow as the challenges increase?
- How does the gameplay tie into the story? Does the player encounter puzzles that grant access to new areas when solved? Do players have to fight bosses that bar their progression?

- What is the victory condition for the player? Save the universe? Kill all of the enemies? Collect 100 stars? All of the above?

If your game doesn't feature a character, then concentrate on the environments the levels of play represent. For example, while the puzzle game *Peggle* has no main character, each level represents the challenges of a "Peggle Master" who lives in a particular location.

If you are working on a sports game, are there any special events like bowl games or stadiums that the player will compete in? If you are making a driving game, concentrate on tracks or races. The key is always to take the reader through the gameplay experience while creating vivid images of the game's locales and activities.

PAGE 3: CHARACTER

Up to this point, you have gone into some detail about the character the player is controlling (or the vehicle they are driving) in regards to the story. Here is where you want to highlight a few specifics about your character. Age, sex, and other "dossier"-style background material can go here … as long as you feel it does your character justice. Don't go listing your character's blood type if it doesn't add anything to your game. But if it does, then mention it.

Concept art is a must when dealing with characters. What does your character look like?

What is the character's backstory? How did they end up in this predicament? What is their personality type? How do they respond to the challenges in the game? For example, when I worked on *God of War,* we were constantly referring to Kratos as "brutal" and everything he did in the game, from killing enemies to opening treasure chests, had to reflect that personality.

How does all of this information about the character relate back to gameplay? Does the character have any signature moves, abilities, weapons or attacks? For example, Mario has his jump and stomp attack while Simon Belmont from *Castlevania* has his whip. What other gameplay does the character do? Driving, flying or swimming? Make sure you allude to every major style of play in your game.

Show a basic map of the character controls. Find an image of the controller (it's easy to find these online) that will be used to play your game, whether it's a mouse and a keyboard or a Wii Remote, and show where the controls are going to go. For example, here is a control map for a PS3 action game:

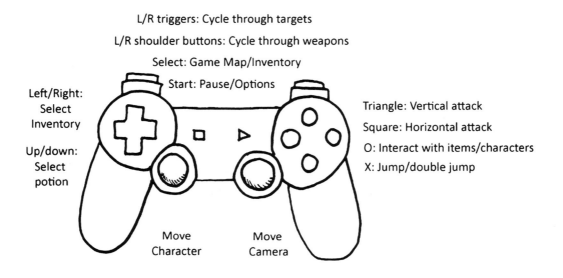

L/R triggers: Cycle through targets

L/R shoulder buttons: Cycle through weapons

Select: Game Map/Inventory

Start: Pause/Options

Left/Right:
Select
Inventory

Up/down:
Select
potion

Triangle: Vertical attack

Square: Horizontal attack

O: Interact with items/characters

X: Jump/double jump

Move
Character

Move
Camera

PAGE 4: GAMEPLAY

Remember that big list of gameplay genres from Level 3? Here is where you apply those game genres to your game. Start with the gameplay and detail out how the sequence of play is presented. Are there multiple story chapters? Or is your game divided up into levels or rounds? Are there any cool scenarios like driving while shooting or running away from a giant boulder? Call attention to them. Include your big set pieces, as they will get your reader interested in your game. Use your USPs from your concept overview here. Don't forget to outline any minigames, and include a short description and illustration. Diagrams are a great way to illustrate otherwise hard-to-imagine gameplay concepts.

Once you have written about your gameplay, go into detail about any platform-specific features. What game features capitalize on the platform's hardware? Does your game utilize a memory card or a hard drive or is it downloadable? Does it use a camera or a motion controller? Is your multiplayer mode played split screen? Cover these details because they will be important for readers to understand what technology requirements will be needed to produce your game.

PAGE 5: GAME WORLD

Present some images and descriptions of the game world. List out environments mentioned in the story. Provide short descriptions that outline what the player will find there. How do these locations tie into your story? What mood is being invoked in each world? What music will be used? How are all of the locations connected within the game world as well as for the player? Include a simple map or flow chart diagram to show how the player would navigate the world.

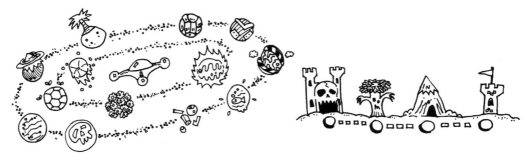

It doesn't matter if your map is a path or a galaxy, as long as it shows the player where to go.

PAGE 6: GAME EXPERIENCE

There is a fancy German word, **gestalt**, which translates as "the whole" of something. Gestalt can be found being used by stuffy film and art critics to describe the overall feeling of a work of art or the ambiance of a restaurant. But don't let the term's fancy-pantsy-ness fool you; the concept of gestalt is fantastic when applied to video games. To make a game feel like a complete experience, you need to account for the feel of the starting screens, your cinematics, your music, your sound design, the camera ... in other words, the whole, or the gestalt of your game.

So now that you know what gestalt means, what is the overall gestalt of your game? Humorous? Horrific? Thrilling? Hardcore? Foreboding? Sexy? How is this feeling going to be presented to the player from the very beginning of your product? Look to DVD movie menus and packaging (especially deluxe editions) as inspiration, as they usually do a great job of capturing the feel of the movie with just a little music, some fonts, and a few visuals.

Are there any special modes or interfaces for your gameplay? These can be special modes such as the "attack copter" gameplay in *Call of Duty 4: Modern Warfare* or Rubi's "Rage Mode" in *Wet*.

Here are a few other important questions about the game's experience you should answer for the reader of your ten-pager:

- What does the player first see when they start the game?
- What emotions/moods are meant to be invoked by your game?

- How is music and sound used to convey your game's feel?
- How does the player navigate the shell of the game? Include a simple flow chart diagram of how the player would navigate this interface. (You'd be surprised how many games have lousy interfaces because the team never thought about it!)

PAGE 7: GAMEPLAY MECHANICS

Terminology time! Learn these two valuable terms to sound like a real game designer! They are: mechanics and hazards. What's the difference?

A **mechanic** is something that the player interacts with to create or aid with gameplay. Here are a few examples of mechanics to get you started: moving platforms, opening doors, rope swings, slippery ice.

A **hazard** is a mechanic that can harm or kill the player but doesn't possess intelligence. Here are a few examples of hazards: electrified platforms, spike pits, swinging guillotine blades, jets of flame.

Describe some (you don't need all of them; I find that three are sufficient at this stage of your outline). What kind of unique mechanics are in the game? How do they relate to the player's actions? How will they be used in the environment?

A **power-up** is an item collected by the player to help them with gameplay. Examples include: ammo, extra lives, invulnerability, and so on. While not all games use power-ups, you can still find them in many different genres of games from platformers to racing games. Provide some examples of your power-ups and what they do.

Collectibles are items that are collected (well, duh) by the player that don't have an immediate impact on gameplay. These can be coins, puzzle pieces, or trophy items. What does the player collect? What is the benefit of collecting them? Can they be used to buy items, access new abilities, unlock material later in the game? Will they earn the player trophies or achievements?

If your game has an economy system, then briefly touch on that as well. Describe how players will be able to collect money and buy things in the game. Briefly describe the shopping environment (is it via a store or a peddler, and so on).

PAGE 8: ENEMIES

If a hazard uses **artificial intelligence** (or **AI**), then it qualifies as an **enemy character**. What enemies do we find in the game world? What makes them unique? How does the player overcome them?

Boss characters are larger, more fearsome enemies usually found at the end of levels or chapters. Bosses are different because many of them have unique personalities. They are the villains of the story. Who are these boss characters? What environments do they appear in? How does the player defeat them? What does the player earn for defeating them? Your readers will want to know! Boss characters are fun and make for great visuals in your document. Show 'em off!

PAGE 9: CUTSCENES

Does your game have movies or cutscenes? How will they be presented to the player? Describe the method by which they will be created including (but not limited to) CG, Flash animation, puppet show[7]. Describe when the player will be seeing these—during the game, at the header and footers of levels, and so on. Make sure to mention any attract mode movies.

PAGE 10: BONUS MATERIALS

Hooray! We've reached the last page of our ten-pager! Here's where we talk about any bonus materials or unlockables that will encourage the player to replay the game. Give some examples of things the players will be able to unlock. What is the player's incentive to play your game again? This is where you would mention things like multiplayer, downloadable content, episodic content, and so on.

[7] Don't fear, we will be covering all of these terms later on in the book.

If you need to see an example of what a ten-pager looks like in action, then just jump over to "Bonus Level 3" at the back of the book. Don't worry; I'll be waiting for you.

THE GAME DESIGN DOCUMENT (AND THE AWFUL TRUTH ABOUT WRITING THEM)

Welcome back. Now that you have some meat on your game design's bones, it's time to flesh it out with a GDD. A GDD outlines everything that will be in the game. It's a very important document that the entire team will refer to during the production of your game.

Some people confuse a **game bible** with a GDD. Don't make this mistake. A show bible is a term taken from television production. The show bible's emphasis is on the rules of the world and the backgrounds and relationships of the characters. This is an important document to create, especially if information about your world and characters is going to be shared with other individuals (like those working on marketing materials such as websites, comic book adaptations, and merchandising) but remember that the game bible has nothing to do with gameplay. That's what the GDD is for.

The horrible irony is, even though it takes lots of time and effort to write a GDD, no one on your team wants to read it. Why? Because most GDDs are very long and intimidating documents filled with information ranging from the useful to the arcane. When I was writing GDDs, I found that everyone was interested in them, but no one wanted to take the time to read them. So, if no one wants to read my design, then why am I spending all of my time writing it?

Well, eventually YOU will need to read your own GDD. Creating documentation will help you as much as your team mates. If you keep the game "in your head" I guarantee there is going to be a moment when you have too much to keep track of and you will get overwhelmed or even worse, you will forget about your great idea like the gun that shoots fire ants.

Unlike scriptwriting for movies, there is no "official" form of what a GDD looks like. Each game designer usually finds what works best for them. For example, because I like to draw, I illustrated my design documents. I found that my team mates understood concepts quickly when I drew pictures for them. This is what a single page from my GDD looked like:

MAXIMO III: Merged Grim Form

Maximo 3 starts with Maximo and his band in **bad shape**. In their quest for Sophia, the heroes have encountered the **Cult of Chut**; death-worshipers who find "a man who walks with Death" an affront to their beliefs. As a result, **Baron has been killed**, **Tinker maimed** (she now sports Zin parts) and **Maximo and Grim have been merged** into one, thanks to a **curse**. Maximo and Tinker have been hunting down cultist sects when they arrive in **Mashhad**, seeking revenge and a cure to Maximo's condition.

Maximo is covered in **tattoos**, which are actually the external manifestation of the **cultist's curse** that has trapped Grim within him. With the press of a button, Maximo transforms into **Grim**, allowing him several **abilities**.

As a result of the curse on Maximo, turning into Grim **drains Maximo's health**. Stay as Grim for too long and Maximo will **lose a life**. Only by collecting the souls of the evil cultists can Maximo sustain himself in Grim form.

As a phantom, Grim can **slide up walls, flow like a shadow along walls** give an little extra distance to a **jump** and **glide down** from long drops.

At some point in the game, Maximo will use Grim's form as a disguise to **infiltrate** the cult's tower during the **Chut Holy Day**. Gameplay will have the player **switching** between the two forms.

In addition, the player can perform several attacks with his scythe. Grim attacks **do not always kill**, rather they are used to "**prep**" an enemy for Maximo's attacks; such as **breaking a** cultist's **protection spell** or "**mortalizing**" ghostly foes.

Grim "preps" enemies

The **High Priest's plot** is to lure Maximo to their temple and transfer Grim into their own vessel: **Sophia**.

While in Grim form, the player cannot talk to innocents (they are too scared). However, Grim's attack will **free innocents of the cult's influence**. Turning them from enemies to **normal innocents** that Maximo must rescue from other enemies.

Remember, this is the way *I* created my GDD, because I found it easy (and fun!) to create and it effectively communicated my ideas to the other team members. Not all designers will want to work this way, and finding your own way is always best. As a starting point, there is a GDD outline in Bonus Level 4.

However, it doesn't matter how you communicate your ideas, just as long as you are clear. There are plenty of techniques that you can use to get this information across:

- **Storyboards.** Just like movies, gameplay can be storyboarded. It doesn't matter if you can draw detailed images or stick figures, there is truth to the old saying "a picture is worth a thousand words." If you are having trouble coming up with ideas, you can use published movie storyboards, comic books, or even the gameplay diagrams in this book for inspiration.
- **Diagrams.** If you are worried about your art skills (you shouldn't be; even a stick figure conveys information) then you can always diagram out your gameplay examples. Use consistent shapes and colors to represent elements of your game. Make sure you include a legend so readers know what your icons and shapes mean.
- **Animatics.** Using your storyboards or diagrams as a starting point, you (or an artist friend) can animate them with programs like PowerPoint or Flash. While this takes more time, seeing your gameplay examples in motion leaves very little room for misinterpretation.
- **The beat chart.** A beat chart is a document that covers the entire span of the game. The advantage is that it allows readers to grok[8] a lot of information on one page, and to compare and contrast the flow of information within the game. Hold on to your horses, cowboy; we will be talking more about beat charts in a moment.
- **The team Wiki.** Rather than killing trees, why not publish your GDD electronically on a Wiki? It's a great way for your team members to be kept up to date on the latest and greatest game material, especially since they can contribute to its creation. But be careful; as preproduction moves into production, a Wiki can very easily become neglected by the design team and become out of date.

A GDD is first and foremost about gameplay. How the character interacts with the world rather than relates to it; a subtle difference, but an important difference nonetheless. I find bibles important, especially when

---

[8] Grok means "to understand completely" and is a slang term created by sci-fi writer Robert Heinlein. Now do you grok?

communicating your game's universe to other interested parties, but it really should be done *after* you have started to flesh out your GDD.

While writing the game design document, always keep this **very important thing** in mind:

EVERYTHING IS LIQUID

This means that game designs are living things. Game designs change, they flow, they mutate and evolve. If you don't let your game idea simmer (like chili!) you may not think of a great idea or you may miss an opportunity to create some truly great gameplay. Eventually, many of the things you write in your document will become obsolete. At a certain point, writing things down becomes counterproductive and it all becomes about finishing the game. But you need a starting point and a GDD gives you that launching pad from which to soar.

Just like with your ten-pager, you need to know who your audience is. This is a bit easier as your primary audience are four types of people: the producer, the designer, the artist, and the programmer. Knowing how these different disciplines think and work and prioritize information is very important to getting your point across. Remember, the MOST IMPORTANT PART OF A GAME DESIGNER'S JOB IS COMMUNICATION. Take the time to talk to your team mates to find out what they are most interested in about the design. If you have to adjust some information in your GDD's format then do so. In the long run, your team mates will appreciate your effort.

Speaking of communication, remember that words are very powerful. Make sure you provide very specific examples and terms for the elements in your game design document, especially when referring to characters and game mechanics. If an accurate term doesn't exist, then go ahead and make one up!

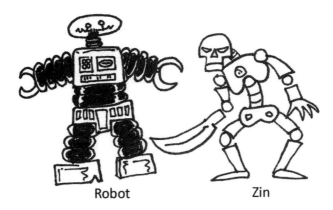

Robot   Zin

For example, when I was first working on *Maximo vs. Army of Zin*, I first referred to the game's enemies, the Zin, as robots. I quickly learned that everyone on my team had a different mental image of what a robot was, ranging from C-3PO to the Iron Giant. I realized that my team would be on the wrong page unless I provided a clearer description for them. The image I had in my head of the Zin was of a metal skeleton made out of riveted brass with turning gears for guts. I started using the term "clockwork undead" to describe the Zin. I found that by focusing my language to something very specific, my team mates were able to better visualize the image I had in my head.

You also need to be specific when thinking about how the gameplay unfolds to the player over the course of the game. How this happens is called **progression**.

GAMEPLAY PROGRESSION

Introducing gameplay to the player can be a tricky thing. Here are several suggestions on how you can start your game:

- The player starts from ground zero (or level 1) with no skills, gear and abilities.
- The player has several skills that are presented to them at the beginning of the game but have to be unlocked over time. The gating mechanism can be experience, money or some other factor.
- The player has several skills, but has no knowledge of how to use them … yet[9].
- The player has significant power that they can use immediately … only to lose it after a boss fight or initial confrontation.
- The player has significant power that they can use immediately … only to have to "start back at zero" as the game story is structured as a flashback.

Just as you need to know how your game begins, you also need to know how it ends. This is where the beat chart comes in extremely helpful.

---

[9] The character with amnesia is one of the oldest cliches in video games. Unless you have an exceptionally clever way to use this story point, I highly recommend not using it. Nothing makes gamers' eyes roll faster. Except for maybe the character realizing that "it was all a dream."

THE BEAT CHART

The **beat chart** is a handy-dandy tool that can not only help you develop the content of your GDD, but also provides a "map" of the structure of your game; this is extremely important when examining the gameplay progression. Every beat chart requires the following elements:

- Level/environment name
- File name (level/environment designation)
- Time of day (in context of the game)
- Story elements for level
- Progression: gameplay focus of the level
- Estimated play time of level
- Color scheme of level/environment
- Enemies/bosses introduced and used
- Mechanics introduced and used
- Hazards introduced and used
- Power-ups found in level/environment
- New abilities, weapons, or gear introduced/unlocked
- Treasure amount and type the player can find
- Bonus material found in level/environment
- Music track(s) to be used in this level/environment.

Here is an example of a beat chart of a couple of levels from *Maximo: Ghosts to Glory*. Italics designate a new gameplay feature:

Level: World 1-1
Name: Grave Danger (Boneyard)
TOD: Night
Story: Maximo enters the graveyard, fighting his way through undead creatures that bar his way
Progression: Player taught basic movement, combat and defensive moves. Player learns how to collect and map abilities
Est. play time: 15 min

Level: World 1-2
Name: Dead Heat (Boneyard)
TOD: Night
Story: Achille's drill has cracked open the earth, causing lava pits to open up throughout the graveyard
Progression: Player masters hazardous jumps and more intense combat
Est. play time: 15 min

Color map: Green (trees), brown (trees/rock), purples (tombstones)

Enemies: Skeleton (basic), sword skeleton (red), skeleton (axe), ghost, zombie (basic), wooden coffin, chest mimic

Mechanics: Holy ground, breakable tombstone, breakable torch, breakable crypt lid, breakable rocks, Achille key statue, key lock, opening gate (door), opening gate (cave), prize wheel, treasure chest, locked chest, hidden chest, end plinth

Hazards: Unholy ground, Achille statue, fall-away ground, skull tower, breakaway bridge, deep water, lava pit

Power-ups: Koin, koin bag, diamond, death koin, spirit, life up, flametongue, shield recharge, sword recharge, half health, full health, iron key, gold key, armor up

Abilities: Second strike, mighty blow, magic bolt, doomstrike, foot cheese

Economy: 200 koins, 2 death koins

Bonus materials: N/A

Music track: Graveyard 1

Color map: Red (lava), brown (trees/rock), purples (tombstones)

Enemies: Skeleton (basic), skeleton (axe), sword skeleton (red), sword skeleton (blue), skeleton (guardian), zombie (basic), raven, ghost

Mechanics: Holy ground, breakable tombstone, breakable torch, breakable crypt lid, key statue, key lock, opening gate (door), enemy coffin, floating platform, prize wheel, treasure chest, locked chest, hidden chest, end plinth

Hazards: Unholy ground, swinging gate, skull tower, flame jet, lava pit

Power-ups: Koin, koin bag, diamond, death koin, spirit, life up, flametongue, shield recharge, sword recharge, half health, full health, gold key, armor up

Abilities: Second strike, mighty blow, magic bolt, doomstrike, throw shield

Economy: 200 koins, 1 death koin

Bonus materials: N/A

Music track: Graveyard 2

When you compare two or more columns of a beat chart together, certain patterns start to emerge regarding the introduction of new enemies, mechanics, items, and abilities. You can then identify deficiencies in the design and start to move elements around. Filling in holes here, shifting bloated areas there.

Here are a few things to look out for:

- "Clumping": too many new enemies or mechanics being introduced at once. Spread these out over the course of the game. Remember, the first level of the game is always going to have several elements, so it technically doesn't count.

- "Samey-ness": too many identical combinations of enemies and mechanics. You want to mix things up to keep interaction fresh.
- Alternate your time of day and color schemes. If you have too many of the same lighting or color schemes in a row, things are going to feel and look repetitive.
- Alternate your music tracks. The player is going to get bored listening to the same music over and over again.
- Problems in game economy: make sure players have enough money to buy items to use in the world. Make sure the player doesn't have so much money that it becomes worthless.
- Mechanics and enemies should be introduced in conjunction with the items and abilities required to defeat them.
- When will the player have "everything" in the game? All weapons, all skills, all vehicles, all armor upgrades, etc.? Make sure the player has time to play with them. I try to make sure the player has everything by 75% through the game so the last quarter lets the player use all of their cool stuff.
- As a rule of thumb, I try to introduce two or three new mechanics, enemies, and rewards per level.

There is some debate as to which is better: a shorter, "bite-size" play experience or a longer, more involved one. With the rise of casual gaming, it seems that most players prefer shorter gameplay sessions (averaging around 15 minutes a session). However, this trend may change in a few years if gamers' tastes swing back to the hardcore market. What I believe matters the most is that you give your players their money's worth.

I usually advise teams to aim for a minimum of 8 to 10 hours of gameplay time for action-based games. This doesn't include replay time or time spent watching cutscenes or reading dialogue. Remember, it never hurts to have more content. If the worst comes to the worst, you can always cut content if you run into production delays. We talk about some tricks to help determine playing time in Level 9.

ABOVE ALL, DON'T BE A SCHMUCK

Creating all of these design documents is important but your designs mean nothing if you aren't a responsible game designer. Some of the following advice may seem like common sense, but I've also learned that common sense isn't always that common:

- **A good idea can come from anywhere.** I have seen many teams suffer from what I call "**not invented here syndrome**", a belief that any idea from someone who isn't on the design team isn't valid. Pardon my French, but only a colossally arrogant idiot would believe that. A good designer always has his/her ear to the ground for great suggestions from others. Always share your ideas and designs to others. They may disagree with you, but you don't always have to take their advice either.

- **Make a decision and stick with it.** While game designs are always changing, the worst thing you can do is keep redoing and redoing work. It's no crime to be a perfectionist, but there are many design issues that can be thought out and designed on paper first before a single pixel is rendered or a line of code typed. I have seen many projects drain away time, resources, and team morale when design leads are unable to commit to a direction.

- **Update often.** Send out e-mails, make comments on documents, and use different systems like comments or page colors to make sure your colleagues are kept up to date when changes occur.

- **Tackle the tough ones first.** Talk to your art and programming leads ahead of time about how they work and what issues in your design they think are going to be trouble spots. Don't leave these difficult design issues until the last minute. Sort them out first. If they don't work out, then you will still have time to make course corrections with your design.

- **Trust your instincts.** There are moments when you are going to have an idea for something in your game that no one else is going to believe will work. Sometimes you just have to dig in and fight for it. Pick your fights though. You don't want everything to become a drama. That will just turn off your team mates and you'll get branded as a prima donna. However, don't be afraid to fight for a good idea. You may be right in the end.

- **Respect the abilities of your peers and be mindful of their limitations.** Certain team members are better at certain things. Work with your producer to find out who would be the best person for the job. The last thing you want is a team mate working on an aspect of your design that they don't have the talent for or an interest in. Conversely, talk to your team mates about what they'd like to work on. You will always get better results if your team mate is into what they are working on.

- **Save often and always.** Accidents happen, vacations are taken, babies are born during the course of production. Any of these things can cause designers to not be around at a critical moment in production. Make sure your designs are accessible to all the pertinent team members, especially your producer. Use programs like Perforce, Alien

Brain or Subversion to store documents on a drive that is backed up regularly. Don't keep the contents of the game in your head. Write those things down. Make sure you have some system of filing so you can find your work too!

- **Stay organized.** When creating files and documents, use naming conventions that humans can understand. For example, if you have a forest level, then make sure the word "forest" or at least the letter "f" is part of the name. I find that using the "European" method of dating a document (DAY, MONTH in text, YEAR; for example 27 JUL 09) is a lot easier to decipher, especially when multiple documents exist. Naming files by date is helpful, especially when your project spans longer than a single calendar year. Make sure you use consistent naming of everything in your game.

- **Be prepared.** Eventually, you will need ways for others to get around your game. Have your game include level skips, a flexible cheat camera so others can take screenshots of your gameplay and cheat codes that enable invulnerability, grant power-ups and money, and so on. Talk to your publishing/marketing partners about their needs early on in the development of your game. Sometimes they will want additional content like extra levels, costumes, bonus materials to market and sell the game. Be prepared to create this material; don't leave it until the last minute of production. Be aware that you may have to make a demo of your game. Think about what you would want to have in your game demo to show it off in its best possible light. Earmark potential content such as specific levels or experiences that may be used for a demo later down the line.

Arm yourself with this advice, and I guarantee you, your project will go a lot smoother in the long run.

Now that we have some good habits and documentation examples, let's dig into and talk about one of the pillars of game design, something I call the Three Cs.

Level 4's Universal Truths and Clever Ideas:

- A game is like chili: it needs the right recipe, tools, ingredients, and time to come out right.

- A game design document should be just long enough to describe the action in a game.

- Know your intended ESRB target rating and design towards it.

- Work your way up from one-sheet to ten-pager to game design document.

- Use tools like beat charts to help find problems early on in your game design.

- No one likes to read long design documents, so find the best way to communicate your design ideas to your team.

- Everything is liquid; your game design WILL change over the course of production.

- Give your player their money's worth.

- Be smart when naming and organizing documents and files.

LEVEL 5

THE THREE CS,
PART 1—CHARACTER

While much of your game design is always changing, there are three fundamentals that need to be established early in your preproduction. I call them the "**Three Cs**":

1. Character
2. Camera
3. Control.

If you change any of the Three Cs during the course of your production, you risk massive problems with your gameplay, which may require extra reworking, and you risk endangering your game. Don't give me that look. I know this sounds dramatic, but so many game elements hinge upon the Three Cs that changing one thing will have a ripple effect through your entire game. I have seen teams catastrophically screw up and cancel their game because of their failure to stick to the plans of their Three Cs.

While we talked about writing a character in Level 3, I am now using the term in a different context. I will be talking about how the character is presented to the player and the activities the player does with that character. The **very important rule** about character design is:

FORM FOLLOWS FUNCTION

Let this rule be your motto when designing anything. It will come into play more importantly later on in the book, but should be your guide especially when designing your game character. There are several great books on how to design a character visually[1], so I won't go into great detail about this, but let me pass on some of the high level things to keep in mind.

As you are creating your character, you want to think about his or her personality. What are the three personality traits that you would use to describe your hero?

Mario: courageous, bouncy, happy
Sonic: fast, cool, edgy
Kratos: brutal, vicious, selfish

Apply these traits to your character's physical appearance. Animators have known for decades that the shapes you use for your character's design will help communicate their personality. Circles are used to make a character feel friendly. Squares are often used for strong or dumb characters, depending on just how big your square is. Triangles are interesting, a point-down triangle is often used to give a heroic character a powerful frame. However, use that same point-down triangle for a character's head and they seem sinister. Try rotating, mixing, and matching shapes to create compelling characters.

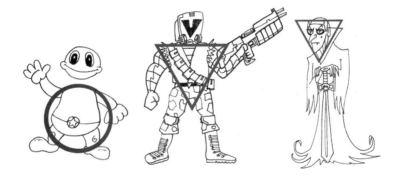

Another old trick that all professional character designers and animators use is the **silhouette**. A strong, clear silhouette of a character is important for many reasons:

• Tells us the character's personality at a glance.
• Helps distinguish one character from another.
• Identifies "friendly" or "enemy" characters.
• Helps the character stand out against background and world elements.

[1] Some of my personal favorites include: Disney Animation: the Illusion of Life by Thomas & Johnston (Abbeville Press, 1984), The Art of Star Wars (Episodes I–VI) series (Del Rey, 1976–2007), and Ben Caldwell's cartooning series (Fantasy! Cartooning and Action Cartooning) (Sterling Publishing, 2005).

For example, let's look at the silhouettes of the player characters of *Team Fortress 2*.

Due to their unique silhouettes, you can immediately distinguish one character from another. In the image above, the Heavy is clearly distinguished from the Pyro from the Spy. Body language plays a huge part in creating unique personalities. Not only does their silhouette give you a snapshot of their personality, but it provides the player with a quick way to recognize the character. This is important during gameplay so you know who is gunning for you and can adjust your strategy—or more importantly, who is in your sights. Boom. Headshot.

If you're designing several characters that appear on screen at once, like in multiplayer games, design them together. Use their silhouettes to make your characters "fit together" even when they are standing apart. This is an especially useful trick when creating "duo characters" like Jak and Daxter (tall and short) or Spongebob Squarepants and Patrick Star (square and pointy) or Mario and Luigi (fat and thin).

Other ways to distinguish your characters from each other is with color and texture. Super heroes in early comic books usually wore bright patriotic colors like red and blue, while villains were dressed in darker, "opposite colors" like greens and purples. In the original *Star Wars*, the heroes (Luke, Leia and Han) wore black and white clothing. Darth Vader and the Stormtroopers also wore black and white, but their costumes were hard edged and metallic: fitting for the villains.

Of course what determines whether your character is good or bad, noble or evil, is their personality.

PERSONALITY: DO WE REALLY NEED ANOTHER BADASS?

I have found that there are three types of video game characters. The first two are humorous and heroic. Here are a couple of tips on creating these types of characters:

Humorous character

- Says funny things: Writing funny dialogue is hard. If you can't write something funny, hire a professional writer.
- Does funny things: Do me a favor and try not to resort to farting or burping. Not only is it puerile, which makes you look like you couldn't think of anything funny to write, but all that gas flying around impacts your ESRB rating.
- Funny doesn't always mean jokes: Remember the 1960s *Batman* TV program? Batman was a funny character, not because Adam West was goofy, but because he played the character deadly serious; as if wearing a bat-costume and driving around in a bat-shaped car and pulling bat-shark repellent out of his belt were the most normal thing in the world. It was the contrast of this absurdity that made it so funny.

Heroic character

- Does heroic things: Saves the princess, the world, the day. Whatever your hero does, make sure it matters. But you can also make sure your character is good without becoming sappy.
- A hero is always good at something: Lara Croft is good at finding treasure. Sonic is good at running. Simon Belmont is an expert with a whip. Make sure your hero has a specialty, whether it's a weapon or a skill.
- However ... no one is perfect: A good hero is relatable and that means they have problems just like us. Phobias, unrealized ambitions, relationship issues: they all make the character more real. But it is one thing for a character to have these problems and it's another thing to make it part of your gameplay. Indiana Jones is afraid of snakes. What happens when he comes across a chamber full of them? It can't just be business as usual. The hero of *Trauma Center: Under the Knife* (Altus, 2005) lacks self-confidence in his own abilities, which adds to the drama of the story. In the MMO *Champions Online* (Atari, 2009) players may choose disadvantages, such as a vulnerability to fire or cold attacks. I guarantee that these disadvantages will end up inspiring some memorable moments in your game.

Go back to your three character traits. Let them guide your character's creation and everything he does in the game. How does he walk? Fight? Open a door? Celebrate? What does he do when he's bored and waiting for you to continue playing?

There is one other kind of character that is very prevalent in video games nowadays: the badass[2]. Remember, video games are all about wish

---

[2] The badass is known in more scholarly circles as the "anti-hero."

fulfillment. And like you, I wish I were a badass. To stride into a smoky bar room full of bikers—not that I have anything against bikers … on second thoughts, let's make that criminals—to stride into a smoky bar room full of criminals and gain their immediate respect with nothing more than narrowed eyes and a crack of my knuckles. Of course, I would have to kill them all, because they are bad guys. But you get my idea.

Anyway, like a humorous or heroic character, a badass has to be carefully created—otherwise you just end up with a lame character.

Badass character

- Does badass things, no matter if it is killing enemies or opening doors. Does it with style.
- Isn't a nice person. Sure, just about everyone in video games kills and steals[3], but badasses seem to enjoy it a little bit more. They go out of their way to add insult to injury and then revel in the results.
- Says cool things, but they (almost) never shout. They are so badass, they never need to. Just be careful: a stoic character can be easily mistaken for one without a personality.

The general public often gives video games a bad rap for teaching kids bad behavior. True, there are some game characters that I don't think are great role models. Unfortunately, beating the audience over the head with morality is generally considered bad form. If you have an issue with this, don't fret—there are subtle (read: sneaky) ways you can steer your character towards being good. Good doesn't always have to equal dumb.

If you are like me, and like your good guys to be good, here is a trick I pulled in *Maximo vs. Army of Zin* to sneak a little morality into the game. In the original game, the main character Maximo was just in the adventure for himself. He wanted to rescue the princess, defeat the bad guy, and collect as much treasure as possible. But to me, he didn't really come off as a heroic character. So in the sequel, I wanted him to act like a hero and do good things. (Keep in mind this was in the days before the "morality-driven character pathing" you find in games like the *Fable* series and *Star Wars: Knights of the Old Republic*.) But I couldn't force the player to do good things. That just didn't feel right.

---

[3] I think that Link from the Legend of Zelda games is about the worst person around. This adorable little elf (or whatever the hell he is) runs around chopping everyone's gardens to bits, breaks into their houses, steals anything that isn't nailed down and breaks all of their valuable crockery! And yet everyone is so happy to see him!

Instead, we created victims that the player encountered being
menaced by the Zin enemies throughout the levels. It was up to the player
to rescue them or not (sometimes they had to go out of their way to do
so)—there was no penalty for not saving them, but if you did save them,
they would give Maximo a reward: a few coins here, an armor power-up
there. When play testing the game, players immediately started to
become concerned about these villager characters and would feel bad if
they didn't rescue them in time. While progression was still the player's
primary objective, they would make sure to try to save the villagers. After the
session, they would mention that they liked being a "hero"; exactly the
feeling I wanted them to experience.

Of course, the other side of the coin is presenting the player with bad
deeds to avoid. In *inFAMOUS* (SCE, 2009) the player doesn't have to be
bad, but if he chooses to do bad things (like steal from NPCs or kill
civilians) and becomes "evil", the locals start to shout abuse and throw
bricks!

LET'S GET PERSONAL

Remember when we talked about naming characters back in Level 3? First
of all, make sure your character's appearance matches his name. Which of
the following characters do you think looks like a "Dirk Steele"?

I learned an important lesson about naming characters while playing the
classic computer game *X-Com: UFO Defense*. In the game, you command

an international military team that battles an invading alien threat. The team members you recruit are given rather non-descript names. Then I learned that you could rename them. All of a sudden, my team of previously generic soldiers suddenly gained a personality. And something funny happened … I started to care about them. Whereas I previously didn't care whether they died or lived, I now wanted to give them good weapons, heal them and make sure they returned safely from each mission. What this taught me was the power of customization.

If you aren't using a licensed character, then why not let the player name him/her themselves? Heck, even though Link is one of the most loved characters in gamedom, the designers of every *Legend of Zelda* game allow you to rename him. Anything you can do to let the player customize their character furthers their feeling of ownership.

Many games are now offering the player greater and deeper customization tools to allow them to make just about any character they want. *Champions On-Line*, *Saints Row 2*, and *Oblivion* all offer incredibly deep character customization tools to build very detailed heroes; you can spend hours before you even start "playing" the game. *Grand Theft Auto: San Andreas* (Rockstar Games, 2004) allowed the player to customize their character's physique. If you ate nothing but fast food, eventually your character would get fat.

Spore's (EA, 2008) creature creator goes even further: players have used it to build a staggeringly creative array of fantastical creatures from gorgeously detailed dragons to living game controllers! No matter what you build in the editor, the anatomy and physical traits of your character affect the way your creature moves and acts within the game. You don't even need talent to create your hero in the *Drawn to Life series* (THQ, 2007), which allows you to draw your character from scratch even if you can only draw a stick figure.

The level of player customization will only increase as time goes on. *Graphitti Kingdom*'s (Taito, 2004) deep customizing tools allow you to insert your own sounds and choose your character's animations. *LittleBigPlanet* (SCEE, 2008) even lets you "customize" your character's emotional state! Did you grab the prize bubble before your friend? Make your Sackboy smile. If your friend got it first, you can make him frown ... or scowl and "reward" your friend with a slap to the head!

Customization doesn't begin and end with the player character: it extends to choosing costumes, picking weapons, or decorating their home base. As I always say "Every player likes to play house."

Give the player options for personalization. Allow the player to customize any of the following:

- **Name:** not just of character, but of weapons, vehicles
- **Appearance:** hair/skin/eye color, ethnicity, height, weight
- **Clothing, armor and gear:** style, color, texture
- **Vehicles:** paint job, weapon and tech load outs, decals, hubcaps, even the thing that hangs from the rear view mirror
- **Home base:** furnishing, lighting, decorations
- **Weapons:** appearance, decoration, ammo loads, special effects

Speaking of weapons and equipment, give your character a signature weapon and gear/appearance. In this case, they shouldn't be customizable. These weapons are part of the character's identity. Most licensed characters use these signature weapons and gear to keep them unique. Can you imagine a Ghostbuster without his proton pack? Dante without his trenchcoat? Cloud Strife without his humongous sword?

Think about how the player is going to be using these items for gameplay. Make them appropriate to the action. While I advocate form following function, sometimes these items can help inspire the design to determine the player's actions.

Because most video game characters are viewed from behind, it's important to have something that creates the feeling of movement. For example, many characters have an object swinging from their back. With Lara Croft it was her ponytail. With Batman it was his cape. These both required unique code to create. Talk to your art and programming leads to make sure these visual markers are feasible.

While video game character design allows for a wide variety of stylization, the goal of many video game art directors is to create realistic characters. But be aware of the phenomenon called the "**uncanny valley**", where a character doesn't look quite right to the viewer. It can be distracting for the player, especially during cutscenes, if this occurs. Here are a few tips to remember when creating realistic-looking characters:

Facial proportions. Realistic human characters look odd if given features used to enhance personality traits. Watch out for features like large eyes, exaggerated chins, and wide mouths that can make characters look inhuman.

Movement. The more realistic the model, the worse animation tends to look precisely because of the uncanny valley. Be careful of stiff-limbed movement in the arms and shoulders. Hands can be particularly troublesome as most game art can't support jointed fingers and treat the hands as simple objects, which end up looking like hams. A human is a very flexible being, so make sure your character moves realistically. Put the effort into rigging your character's skeleton to be so.

Humanity. If a character looks extremely human (especially a non-human character, like an alien or robot), people will expect it to do human things and have a human personality. However, R2-D2 from *Star Wars* is a great example of playing against this expectation.

Now, for the other side of the coin, here are some tips to remember when creating stylized characters:

Facial proportions. Enlarge facial features such as eyes, chins, and mouths to convey greater expression and range of emotion. You find this all the time in Japanese games and anime.

Movement. If you don't have the time and money to spend on fancy inverse kinematics, motion capture and dynamics, you might be better off choosing stylized representations for your characters. The more stylized your character, the more exaggerated the movements can be. Watch and learn from old Tex Avery cartoons (for example) to see just how far you can go with exaggerated character movement.

Humanity. The great thing about stylized characters is that they don't have to be human. Anthropomorphic characters like Ratchet (and Clank), Sly Cooper and Aero the Acrobat can provide just as much emotion and player investment as human ones can.

Realistic or stylized? It's a choice that comes down to: what is best for your game? For example, the *Team Fortress 2* team started building their game with realistically designed characters and then did a 180 with character designs inspired by artists J. C. Leyendecker, Dean Cornwell, and Norman Rockwell by way of Pixar. It was a great choice; one that changed the tone of the entire franchise for the better.

FINALLY, WE TALK ABOUT GAMEPLAY

We've discussed what the player looks like, now let's talk about what he does. All gameplay flows from the main character. You have to think about the player's relationship to the world. How tall is your character? How tall or short are all the other characters and enemies in relationship to the main character? How long is the character's reach? If your character is a quadruped or a vehicle, how long and wide is it? As you create your character, you determine these proportions. These proportions become the basis of the character's **metrics**: the cornerstone of your gameplay and design.

But before we dive into metrics, let's talk about fencing.

When you fence you learn how far you travel when you step forward, how far your weapon goes when you extend your arm. A fencer learns that those distances get greater as you lunge at an opponent. It's important to know these distances to help you gauge how far away you are from your opponent and how close you have to be in order to score a touch on them. The fencer gets accustomed to these distances and adjusts their fencing style to compensate for them.

Video game players do the same thing. Metrics are especially important to players as they use them to gauge movement and jump distances "by eye", whether they know it or not. When playing, they get a feel for what is and isn't obtainable and anything that changes that constant will throw off the player and feel wrong.

Determining metrics start with the basic height of the character, the speed that character travels, and the height that the character can reach. I always use the hero character as a yardstick for the rest of the world. For example, in *Maximo: Ghost to Glory*, our measurement was called "1 Maximo unit", which was obviously based on the height and width of the main character. All game distances, widths and heights were expressed in this way.

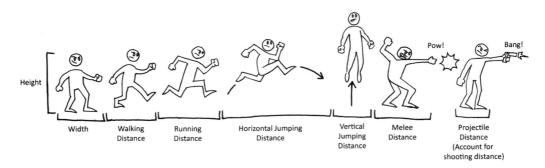

Use metrics to determine:

- **Height:** the height of the player character
- **Width of passage:** usually wider than the player character
- **Walking speed:** how far the player travels per second or unit of time
- **Running speed:** same as above, but faster
- **Jump distance:** usually farther than a walk, but not as far as a run; can also be based on the player's width (such as 5 player units across)
- **Jump height:** based on the player's height—a jump is half the player's height, while a double jump can be twice as tall as the player
- **Melee attack distance:** usually not much farther than the length of the player's arm and weapon
- **Projectile distance:** this can be as short as the player's reach or width to as far as the player can see

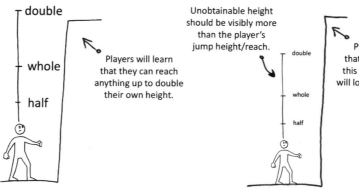

The cliff ledge shown in the above graphic is obviously completely unobtainable with a normal jump/double jump distance. The player will know that they won't ever be able to reach this height and will look for another way to get to their destination.

When determining metrics, you will have to work with a programmer to determine where and how the character is going to interact with the world. This is done by determining collision—the code calculates where and how the character is interacting with the world. The more collision points have to be calculated, the slower the code runs. In some cases, collision is determined from a primary point on the character model. There are generally three locations on a character from which the player can interact with the world: the head, the feet and the center of the body.

The head: while useful for attaching hats, treating the character's head as the main collision point can cause problems, especially when determining ground collision. The player character can appear to not be rooted to the ground, giving the appearance of slightly floating.

The feet: while detecting collision from the feet seems like the logical location, it can cause issues if it is used to determine where a power-up is collected (for example if it is in mid-air, the player will have to jump to collect it).

The torso: IMHO, this is the best place to determine the character's collision with the world. It provides enough coverage for both halves of the body and feels "right" when the player runs or jumps through an item for collection.

WHY WALK WHEN YOU CAN RUN?

Let's talk about bipedal characters for a moment. Every character walks. But many gamers will complain if a character walks too slowly. Instead, trying making the walk work for you. If you really want to screw with your players, here is something I have learned.

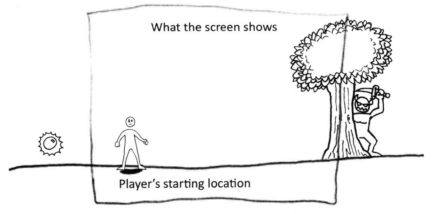

Use the screen to hide surprises and secrets.

Westerners are used to reading things left to right. You can use this impulse to get players to go where you want them to go. In the image above, players will usually go towards the interesting object on screen (in this case the tree) rather than going to the left where I have hidden a goodie.

Why have I done this hateful thing? Because making the player walk to the left makes people feel "ill at ease" and can be used to psychological effect. If you really want to mess with your player's head, make them travel to the left for the entire level. Most of them won't be able to figure out what is "wrong" about the level, just that something is (quite literally) not right.

While it is fun to mess with the player's head, there is something that many designers forget when designing their levels. If you are describing the action in your level walkthroughs[4] and you find yourself telling your colleagues "and then the character walks through here", this should set off very loud klaxons. Why? Because:

[4] Which we will talk about in Level 9.

WALKING IS NOT GAMEPLAY!

Don't fall into the trap of assuming your player will find gathering collectibles as interesting as you find placing them. While alternating the pace of your action is good, having your player travel for long stretches, no matter how much beautiful art they look at, is just boring. Keep it interesting even if they are just walking. Why have this:

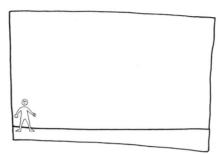

When you can have this?

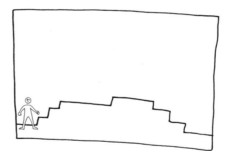

They both do the same thing: get the player from point A to point B. However, the second path is more interesting as it allows the player to use a variety of moves to traverse the terrain rather than just walking.

I often ask the developers I work with "do you really need a walk?" While it would seem unusual to not have a walk cycle for your character, I have found that a player will always choose a faster move over walking, be it jumping, rolling, or dashing. For example, when we were making *God of War*, Kratos could do a tumble/roll move. More often than not, the designers would roll their way around the levels even though it looked stupid. We did it because it felt faster than walking.

What I'm ultimately getting at is that if you are going to have your player walk, then make sure it is fast enough to be useful.

Where a walk *does* come in useful is when navigating edges and ledges. I have found that most players will walk to an edge because they are afraid that they may fall off. There are other tools that you can use in conjunction with the edge—such as a teeter and hoist (more on those in a moment)—but the walk is what the player will use most as it makes them feel safe and in control. There is a trade off to the teeter. Players can't attack during a teeter state (at least, I've never played a game that has allowed you to) and a teeter reduces the player's movement to zero, which is useful when keeping the player from falling to their death, but not so useful for getting away from that fast-approaching enemy! So maybe having that walk cycle isn't such a bad thing after all.

If your character is a vehicle (as in a driving, flying, or rail shooter), or rides in a vehicle, remember that driving (or flying or jet-skiing or whatever) should always move faster than the player's standard walk. When dealing with larger than normal characters such as cars, hovertanks, motorbikes, etc., you will have to deal with weight if you want to make them feel realistic. A car, for example, swings its back out as it goes around a curve. If you don't have this weight built in to your basic movement and metrics, a vehicle is going to feel "floaty" and not realistic.

Weight in general makes a character, be it a car or a person, feel like they are connected to the world. But with weight comes sliding and skidding. These need to be compensated for in the player's metrics. In some games, particularly platformers, the skid is part of the player's movement. In *Little Big Planet*, a player can very easily skid off of a platform or ledge if they don't land in the right place.

I'm torn about the usefulness of the skid. I find them to be very frustrating, but without them, the character movement feels stiff and artificial. Ultimately, you need to choose what is best for your own game[5].

Whether your game character is a person or a vehicle, a question you should ask yourself is: what is the speed of my gameplay? Fast or slow?

If your game is fast, then the majority of your gameplay should be fast. This includes:

- Running
- Jumping
- Flying
- Driving
- Shooting
- Bouncing
- Fighting
- Spinning
- Falling

Slow-moving moves include:

- Walking
- Ducking
- Crouching
- Sneaking
- Swimming
- Hiding
- Hoisting
- Climbing

[5] Which seems to be a running theme in this chapter, doesn't it?

I find it best to alternate between fast experiences and slow ones to keep the game's pacing interesting.

When thinking about running, ask what is it being used for? I prefer gameplay where the run speed is drastically different than the walk. The *Resident Evil* series uses the run not only as a way to move fast but as a way for the player to push through and escape from slow-moving zombies.

The **dash** is the run's cousin. A dash is usually a faster run that expires after a time limit. It is often used to get through timing puzzles such as closing doorways and fire jets, or as a combat move either to escape an enemy's attack or drive home an extra-powerful blow. To prevent your player from exploiting a dash, give it a **cool down**: a short period of time (usually a few seconds) before the player can use the dash move again.

Let's slow down and talk about "slow walking", aka **stealth**.

I admit I have mixed feelings about characters moving stealthily in games. As a general rule, I don't like the player to move slowly, unless the entire game (or a whole experience, like a level) is based on stealth gameplay. Whenever I have played games with stealth mixed in (not dedicated) I always end up running around blasting away at the enemies because I get tired with moving so slowly when I could be moving quickly instead. As this isn't the intention of the game, I usually lose a lot of lives playing like this[6]. But I know my frustration comes from the character moving agonizingly slowly.

---

[6] When you are designing a stealth game, make sure your character looks, or at least acts, stealthy. I once played a really well made game that featured a burly barbarian hero as the main character. I fully anticipated the game to be a brawler, since the hero was armed with several huge weapons that allowed me to cut the enemies up into messy chunks. However, as I played the game, I continually found myself dying in battle after battle. I got so frustrated with the game that I stopped playing it even though I really wanted to like it. I mentioned my regret to a coworker and he said, "You aren't playing the game correctly." Before I could make him take back such a dire insult, he said "It's not an action game, it's a stealth game." Armed with that information, I replayed the game stealthily and eventually finished it. Which I may have never otherwise done due to the mixed signals the game gave the player.

When you make your character move stealthily, make it a significant difference in speed. It's the same principle as walking vs running. A **creep** is useful if the player is ducking or is behind cover, is getting into position to snipe, or for humor such as when the character is trying not to wake a sleeping dragon. The creep move should be a mode that the player can activate at any time, but a creep works best when it is given some context.

But creeping aside, I think that the instinct to make stealth gameplay automatically equal a slow-moving character is incorrect. Have you ever seen a SWAT team member or ninja move around? They don't really creep as much as move in short bursts. Stealth comes into play when they have to wait or hide as something happens or some clueless guard with a very slitable neck passes by. This is where the tension that defines good stealth gameplay comes from. The gameplay of waiting. We'll talk more about stealth combat gameplay later.

THE ART OF DOING NOTHING

Even slower than stealth gameplay is no gameplay. However, just because the character is standing still doesn't mean he has to do nothing. An idle is an animation that plays while a character isn't moving, triggered after a few seconds of the player being **idle**. Did you see that? How the word describing the player's in-action is also the *name* of the move? Pretty clever, those early video game designers.

While idles were probably in other games before, the first idle that made an impression on me was in *Sonic the Hedgehog*. When the player stopped running, Sonic would look out at the player with an annoyed look on his face and tap his foot impatiently. That guy wanted to run! Pretty soon humorous idles were a staple of platform games through the 1990s. But they aren't just for laughs; an idle can convey personality and even a little narrative to the player. At the very least it provides some movement on the screen even when nothing else is going on. Keep in mind, other than adding character or humor, idles (usually) have no gameplay benefit whatsoever. You don't gain ammo, experience or money by being idle[7]. That's ok, some things should just be for fun.

Remember, when creating idles you don't want to create long and involved animations, as the player can press a button at any time and interrupt the idle. In fact, any idle that creates a poor transition into the player's moves will cause a problem, no matter what the length. Keep them short and snappy. Don't have any ideas for idles? Here are a few to start with:

[7] Some more recent games do allow you to gain back health for being idle, but that's just a by-product of not being shot at and has nothing to do with the idle itself.

- Twirl, reload or "shoulder" weapon
- Stretch and jog in place
- Glance around or be startled at an imagined noise
- Shiver with cold or wipe sweat from their brow
- Knock dirt from the soles of their shoes
- Adjust armor or pack
- Crack neck or pop knuckles
- Play air guitar or do a little dance
- Check a map or guide or talk on a cell phone
- Whistle and rock on heels as if waiting
- Eat or drink something
- Scratch self in embarrassing location
- Check watch
- Yawn or fall asleep.

MIGHT AS WELL JUMP

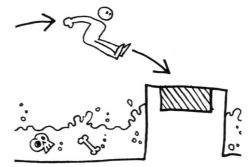

Of all of the basic moves in video gaming, the **jump** is the most mysterious, the most majestic, and the most misunderstood. In order for us to fully understand the jump, let us take a look at one with the help of my patented "slo-mo" graphic.

1. The player is at rest: this is when the player is walking, running, and so on.

2. The player presses the action button. The jump has to happen immediately, as so many jumps are the player's response to danger. In some cases, the jump may need a brief animation to sell the anticipation of the leap, but this animation should be kept as short as possible.

3. Make sure the jump rises to the maximum height quickly.

   A. Should the player be given the opportunity to do a double jump, allow them to do so before reaching the apex (top height) of the jump. Any time after the apex feels weird.

4. Falling is like jumping in reverse. Don't make the fall last too long or it will feel "floaty", which is a negative sensation to the player and screws with the player's sense of metrics—unless the player has some sort of power-up or ability that allows them to glide or float down to safety.

5. The landing can take a little longer than the jump, but it needs to "stick" to make it feel good and solid. I am not a fan of jumps that end in skids or slides as it is easy for a player to make a jump and still slide off the edge of a platform. This is one instance where I have found that "game physics" works better than "real world physics."

Let's take a second to talk about physics. Should you model your game physics on the real world or use "game" physics? Or should you abandon the laws of physics entirely? Good questions! And you better know the answer!

Since Sir Isaac Newton did all of the hard work back in 1687, one would assume this would be easy, right? Real world physics are based on the laws of physics we live with every day. But a certain fidelity to real life is necessary to sell real world physics, and trying to create something that precisely emulates real world physics usually ends up inferior to something tweaked. For example, gravity in games is not $9.8 \, m/s^2$ no matter what the real world says. In fact, some games even use different gravitational constants on different objects!

This is where game physics come into play. The programmers "tweak" the real-world values to fit the gameplay needs. Running speeds, jumping heights and distances, and collision bounciness always feel better when adjusted. Most people in the real world can't jump higher than their own waist, while the average platform game character can easily double their own height in a single bound.

What if your game takes place in space? Or occurs on a planet with low or high gravity? Or you can make exceptionally powerful jumps like *Jumping Flash*? You'll need to work all of this out ahead of time to make sure your metrics match your physics. Tackle this early and don't change it, or you will cause huge problems.

OK, let's jump back to jumping. As platform games were the most popular game genre in the 16-bit days, you can understand how the art of jumping has been taken to its furthest limits; more than any other player character movement. By my count, there are five major ways to jump:

- **Single jump:** The player jumps once—either vertically or horizontally.
- **Double jump:** a second vertical or horizontal jump that is chained after the initial jump.
- **Triple jump:** a third jump that can be done after the second jump, usually requiring something for the player to bounce off of and most often horizontal.
- **Contextual jump:** an "automatic" jump that happens when the player approaches a pre-tagged area such as a ledge.
- **Wall jump:** a special case jump that is performed after the player jumps "into" or towards a wall. If the player presses a button as they collide with the wall, they will jump off of the wall in the opposite direction. The player can gain altitude by chaining wall jumps which allows them to "climb walls" by wall jumping between two opposite facing surfaces. A wall jump can be treated as either a "natural move" that the player has from the beginning of the game (like in *Prince of Persia*) or it can derive from an earned skill or equipment (as in *Ratchet and Clank*).

Even as the player hurtles through the air, there are design decisions to be made. Some games treat jumping realistically and don't allow the player to change their trajectory after they jump, while others allow the player to course correct the character. Other games will allow the player to jump higher and further depending on the amount of time the button is depressed.

After years of making "hoppy-skippy" games (as I call them) I have discovered some curious things about jumping. Players usually do not jump from the edge of a ledge, but from a little way back. Edges make players nervous. They leap from an area I call the "**jump zone**", which can be up to half a jump's distance to the very edge of the platform.

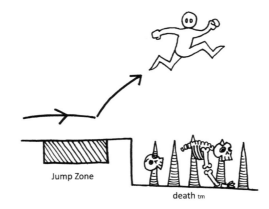

The target the player is trying to hit is a safe spot about half a jump length away from the edge of the opposite ledge. However, landing right on the edge makes a player nervous! This means when you create your jump, make sure to add one more jump length to your distances to make the player feel confident and secure when landing.

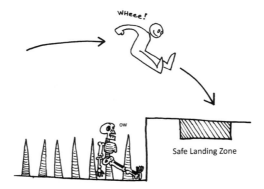

For smaller and floating platforms, the target should be the dead center of the platform—make sure there is enough space for them to land. There's not a lot of room on most floating/single platforms, which is why I don't recommend having a post-landing slide animation to your jump.

When a player gets nervous, they tend to jump again. If their target is too small, they will usually jump themselves to their death. Save the really small platforms for expert jumping puzzles. (Usually found late in the game.)

HOISTS AND TEETERS

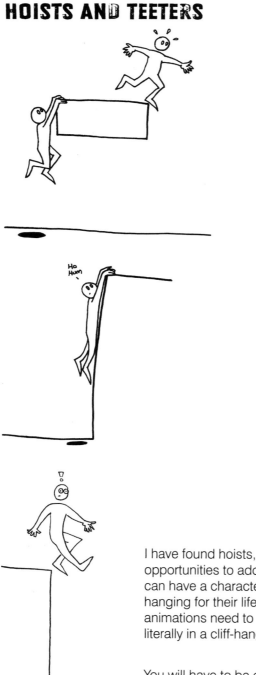

Hoists and **teeters** are two very useful tools for players to help them get around and avoid dying. The hoist allows the player to reach a height slightly higher than their jump allows. The teeter acts as a warning to the player that they are too close to an edge and may fall.

Not all games have or need hoists and teeters. However, if you are going to use these moves, make sure you account for them when creating your player metrics. A hoist generally adds anywhere to a full body length of the character to their jump height.

When a player is in a hoist position but hasn't moved back up onto the ledge or dropped down to the ground below, it is called a **hang**. Some games will bypass this state entirely by having a player automatically hoist themselves back up, while other games use the hang for gameplay, allowing players to hang from objects and surfaces while waiting for timing puzzles and other hazards to pass on by.

I have found hoists, hangs, and teeters really good opportunities to add character to your player. For example, you can have a character react humorously to the fact that they are hanging for their life or about to fall off a cliff! Remember, these animations need to cycle as the player may leave their character literally in a cliff-hanger!

You will have to be careful of what I call the "Wily E. Coyote effect." Remember in those old Chuck

Jones[8] cartoons where Wily E. Coyote chases the Road Runner off of a cliff? And then he stands on thin air for a beat before he plummets down into a little poof of dust at the bottom of a canyon?

WHAT GOES UP, MUST FALL DOWN

Speaking of **falling**, let's talk about it. Using the power of the slo-mo graphic, let's examine a typical fall off of a cliff.

1. The player will usually approach an edge with caution. If they plan on jumping, they will usually do it from the jump zone.
2. Does the character teeter? This acts as a warning to the player, but it can also disrupt the player's control.

---

[8] Charles "Chuck" Jones 1912–2002, director and animator of some of the best cartoons in existence including What's Opera, Doc?, Duck Amuck and How the Grinch Stole Christmas. He created the characters of Road Runner and Wily E. Coyote among others. Shame on you for not knowing this.

3. Give the player a chance to jump out of a teeter so they can get to where they want to go. If the result of missing a jump is death, let them see the bottom/death zone as they make the jump. Blind leaps of faith make players very nervous.

4. Does the character have a hoist? If so, the player can use the hoist to abort a jump or as a "last ditch effort" save option to keep from falling to their death. As some games use distance to ground as a variable to determine whether the player will take damage upon falling from a great height, a hoist can make the difference between a safe drop and death.

5. When the player is falling, do they have control over the fall? Many games allow for course correction and some allow for flat-out in-air maneuvering. Make sure the animation of the character falling communicates whether they have control or not. An out-of-control fall may have the character flailing about or screaming in terror while an in-control fall may re-use the same animation at the end of a jump.

6. Can the player "air jump" out of a fall? How will this ability be communicated to the player? Make sure there are plenty of gameplay situations that capitalize on this move.

7. What happens to the player when he hits the ground? Does he land on his feet like a cat and take no damage? Does he land hard on the ground and have a longer recovery animation, which would make him vulnerable to approaching enemies? Does he bounce off the ground like a rag doll and die? Make sure the player knows early on in the game whether or not there is any penalty for hitting the ground.

8. Whether or not your player take damage from hitting the ground, let them recover quickly so they can get back in control of their character and get moving again. Nothing is worse than waiting for a "get up" animation to finish playing.

ME AND MY SHADOW

As you are building your character in the game, it is important not to forget the player's **shadow**. Having a shadow provides several benefits to the player:

- A shadow acts as a reference point in 3-D space for the player— particularly important when gauging jumps.
- A shadow grounds the player in the world; it adds to the illusion that the character has weight and mass.
- A shadow helps players with edge detection. If their shadow doesn't "lie" on ground, they will get one more hint that it's not meant for them to stand on.

- A shadow conveys lighting and mood. In some survival horror games, the shadow can be a disquieting distraction to the player, literally making them "jump at their own shadow."
- A shadow can be used for gameplay: some games are starting to use shadow detection as part of their enemy's AI. Especially important for stealth gameplay.
- If you don't have a shadow, you don't have a soul! (At least according to Egyptian mythology!)

There are many ways to technologically represent a shadow in video games. It can be a complex shape that matches the silhouette and motions of the player character, it can be a rough form that follows the player, or it can be a simple black shadowy spot (or **drop shadow**) on the ground.

While a drop shadow looks less realistic, it is very effective as a device to let the player know precisely where they are in the level, particularly while making jumps, where the player can use the drop shadow to determine where they are going to land. However, some gameplay mechanics, like small or moving platforms, can make using the drop shadow as a guide tricky—just one more instance where visual realism can be at odds with gameplay.

No matter what your character's shadow looks like, you should still get one in, preferably during the early stage of your production. A few things to keep in mind about shadows:

- Watch out for your character's shadow being in two places at once. While this phenomenon does happen in real life, it will look like it is a bug in a game.
- Watch out for your shadow "casting" itself through surfaces, especially onto platforms that are above other geometry.
- Shadows react in different ways under different lights and on different surface textures. While you don't have to adhere to reality, it may seem weird to a player if a shadow shows up underwater.

THE WATER'S FINE... OR IS IT?

Speaking of water, swimming can still be a difficult thing to design gameplay around. In the earlier days of game design, water traversal was avoided altogether, resulting in a long tradition of "water = death" in video games. If you choose to go that route, keep your messaging consistent otherwise the player will get confused. Don't expect players to be able to differentiate between water that is safe and water that is deadly. My rule of thumb is that water within a single environment should be one or the other. There is no deep end to the pool. It's either all shallow/safe or deep/deadly. If you must have transitional water, give your player adequate cues and warnings of the danger of swimming too far. One game I worked on had a shark fin appear and swim near the player when they strayed out too far. If they ignored the warning and kept going, they got chomped on by a great white!

However, water gameplay can be quite interesting as it lends itself to exploration and exotic environments. But you must always consider several gameplay rules when considering swimming:

- How does the player enter/exit water? Always make sure water entrances and exits are clearly marked for the player. This can take the form of clearly marked ledges, sloping ramp geometry, or those little pool ladders—just as long as the player can tell "this is where I get out."
- Can the player swim under water or just on the surface? Sometimes the ability to dive isn't given to the player until later in the game. Sometimes not at all.
- If the player can swim underwater, can they stay underwater for an extended period of time? Is there some sort of a timer that gauges air supply or pressure that prevents the player from staying underwater for extended periods of time?
- Does air matter? Can a player die due to lack of air? Do they need to collect power-ups or have some other method to sustain their air supply?
- Can the player attack underwater? Do they carry their weapon and swim at the same time? A typical swim stroke may look strange or cause sorting issues if the player is carrying a weapon at the same time.

- How does the player react when they reach the bottom? Can they glide along the bottom? Or do they bob back towards the surface?
- Can the player do any actions underwater that they can do on land? Can they pull switches, or operate those submarine hatches you always seem to find in underwater levels?
- Does the player travel at a consistent speed or can they "swim faster?"
- Changing directions or elevation underwater can cause problems for the camera as it attempts to match the player's orientation. Quick underwater moves can cause a camera to flip around as it struggles to keep up with the character.

BE KIND TO OUR FOUR-LEGGED FRIENDS

Not every game features a bipedal character. The beauty of video games is that a player can be a dog, a spider or a spider-dog … just about anything. But when creating non-bipedal characters, there are a few things to keep in mind:

- Quadrupeds need a wider turning radius: build these wider-than-normal lengths and turning times into your metrics.
- Four legs generally means a character can move faster than a bipedal one. Take into account the character's acceleration and deceleration.
- A longer character means more body mass to hang off of an edge or fill up an environment. Adjust your character to world metrics accordingly. Be doubly mindful of the Wile E. Coyote effect.
- Many quadruped characters are shorter than average human height. Make sure you account for this difference when having characters perform attacks or simple tasks like opening doors or chests.

Let me reiterate: the key to avoiding problems with a quadruped character is to make sure your metrics are built around them.

USING ALL OF THE PARTS

As you are designing your character, try using him or her to communicate information to the player. Think about it: a player spends the majority of their time looking at the character. What better way to display their in-game status? Personally, I like this method as I find it extremely clear as to what the player's status is at all times. All aspects of the player can be treated visually. Here are some other ways to communicate information through visuals and animation:

Movement

- Give subtle clues, like the character's head turning to look at interesting and interactable items in the world.
- Make a character automatically reach out for pickups or door handles.
- Make your character respond positively to favorite things, negatively to perilous things. Maybe go as far as to refuse to go into sure death situations.
- A player's health can be reflected by their movement. In the *Resident Evil* series, wounded characters will limp and move at a reduced speed.

Appearance

- Make a player's health be reflected by their appearance. Many games have the player's physical appearance become more battered and bruised the more damage they take. In *Batman: Arkham Asylum*, the more often the player "dies" the more tattered Batman's costume becomes. Taking a cue from the *Ghosts N' Goblins* series, we had Maximo lose armor and clothes the closer he reached zero health.
- Make status part of the character design. Isaac, the main character in *Dead Space*, wears a space suit with a glowing spine that doubles as a health meter, as well as readouts that show oxygen and weapon status.
- Use visual effects to represent state. Have wounded characters bleed out, leak oil, or shoot out sparks.

Inventory

- Player's gear can be part of the character, rather than hidden within an inventory screen. When designing *Maximo: Ghosts to Glory*, we had inventory items like keys appear on the main character's belt. This allowed the player to always know what they had without having to check their inventory system.
- Any major ability upgrade should have a model and/or animation component to it. An evolving character keeps thing interesting to the

player, who is looking at the same character for the entire game. Even better, take a page from *World of Warcraft* and allow players to dress up and customize their characters whenever they gain new gear and abilities.

Weapons

- Rather than just adding a +3 upgrade to a weapon, give it a physical manifestation of that new power. Have it glow, gout flame, add runes, sights, nozzles or other "bits" to reflect the weapon's new capabilities.
- If you don't want to change the weapon's appearance, consider changing the animation of the player character. A more powerful gun requires a different shooting stance than a lighter one.

In short: keep it clear, expressive, and visual and you can't go wrong.

WE ARE NOT ALONE

In early video games players were a single hero battling against computer enemies or a human opponent. Games like *Double Dragon* and *Teenage Mutant Ninja Turtles* allowed a friend to help out, as long as you didn't mind them bumping into you as you played. While cooperative gameplay with multiple players has advanced greatly in the MMO and FPS space, console games have pushed the envelope in the other direction; the **second character**. When creating gameplay with a second character, you have to decide whether the character is **playable** or a **companion**.

OY!

Howcum he always gets
the sexy companion
and I always get
the talking squirrel?

A second playable character (or SPC) lets the player swap between controlling multiple characters. When control is relinquished on one character, the second becomes controlled by artificial intelligence. This concept originates from Japanese RPGs where the player can "control" each of the party members to battle enemies during the combat sequence. The idea quickly spread across the Pacific to American action and sports games like *The Goonies* (Datasoft, 1985) and *Speedball* (Imageworks, 1988) and over the Atlantic to the UK with *Head over Heels* (Ocean, 1987). However, control would revert back to a single character for navigation purposes during the rise of consoles like the Famicom (aka the Nintendo Entertainment System), partially due to hardware limitations.

In *Mario & Luigi: Superstar Saga* (Nintendo, 2003), the player can control either Mario or Luigi for the duration of the game; though there isn't too much difference between them. However, the characters in *Lego Batman* (WBI, 2008) have unique abilities used to solve puzzles. Keep the "player zapping[9]" to a single button press to allow players to quickly jump to the other character. If the player can swap with more than one SPC, determine the method by which the player will be able to make the choice quickly:

- Player chooses the SPC positioned closest to the player.
- The player cycles through a preset list of characters.
- Use a "compass-style" selection window which allows the player to select directly rather than in a cyclic order.
- A predetermined location in the level automatically switches characters.

The difference between a SPC and a companion character is that a companion is controlled by the game's AI. In some cases, a companion is the second player character, as in the *Lego Star Wars* games or *Army of Two*.

Originally, AI-controlled characters were a bit of a pain—standing right where you wanted to be and being pretty useless in a fight. But thankfully games have evolved. Companions can be useful in combat (*Resident Evil 2, F.E.A.R. 2*), provide navigational support and advice (*The Legend of Zelda: The Wind Waker, Darksiders*), can aid the player in puzzle solving (*GoldenEye, Mark of Kri*), or even heal or help the player when they are in physical danger (*Ghostbusters, Gears of War 2*). They don't even have to be human; like the canines Shadow in *Dead to Rights 2* (Namco, 2005), Dogmeat in *Fallout 3* (Bethesda, 2008), or the weighted companion cube in *Portal* (Valve, 2007).

---

[9] "Player Zapping" was the charming term used for SPC switching in Resident Evil 0 (Capcom, 2002).

While companion characters are helpful in gameplay, be aware that creating a companion character is often a significant dedication to game assets as they require complex AI and animations as robust as the main character. However, the more varied and intelligent these characters are, the more real these characters will become. And the more real the companions are, the more the player is going to care about them.

When creating these companions, remember that **opposites attract**. Give character abilities, strengths, and limitations that complement and contrast each other. A perfect example can be found in *Resident Evil 2* with Claire Redfield and Sherry Birkin. The two characters couldn't be more different: Claire is a capable fighter and Sherry is a scared and defenseless little girl. Claire wields two guns to take out zombies while Sherry can crawl into hiding places and access areas to find puzzle pieces and items. Each character couldn't survive without the other, and that's the feeling you have to convey with a companion.

A game's puzzles and progression can be designed around how to utilize the companion to help both characters progress. *Ico* and *Army of Two*'s heroes **need** their companion's help to complete the game. As the player is going to be spending the entire game with the companion character, you want to create a relationship early in the game so you don't have to do much AI programming to sell the companion's personalities later. Sully in *Uncharted: Drake's Fortune* and Captain Pierce in *Call of Duty: Modern Warfare* are two strong examples of companions with well-written personalities and motivations.

Sometimes two characters aren't enough. *Mortal Kombat: Armageddon* (Midway, 2006) has 63 unique playable characters! Games with large casts can be found in many game genres: fighting, car combat, RPG, RTS, FPS, and survival horror games.

Start your character creation process by creating a stereotype: the old "fighter, magic-user, thief, cleric" class/profession model, for example. Wait a second, what about creating unique, compelling characters? Yeah, yeah, that stuff's all great, but sometimes a player will need to judge a book by its cover. At the beginning of many games, the player doesn't have the luxury of a storyline—they're just gonna pick the character that looks the coolest or that they identify with the most.

But that doesn't mean your characters have to be stereotypes, particularly in the way they play. Your characters should have something significantly different to offer to gameplay. It helps to build an abilities matrix to compare and contrast your characters so none of them have abilities that are the same. The characters in *Team Fortress 2* live in one of three classes: offensive, defensive, and support. They have three categories that impact gameplay: health, speed, and attack. Let's see how they stack up:

Offensive Class	Defensive Class	Support Class
Soldier	**DemoMan**	**Medic**
High health	Medium health	Medium health
Mid to strong attack	Slow to mid speed	Medium speed
Medium speed	Strong attack	Medium attack
Heavy	**Pyro**	**Sniper**
High health	Medium health	Weak health
Slow speed	Medium speed	Medium speed
Strong attack	Strong short-range/weak long-range attack	Medium attack (headshot does instant kill)

Scout	Engineer	Spy
Weak health	Weak health	Weak health
Very fast speed	Medium speed	Fast speed
Weak to mid attack	Medium attack (gun turret can be improved from weak to very strong attack)	Weak attack (backstab does instant kill)

As you can see, the characters in *TF2* are very finely balanced. No two characters share the same attribute specs, and weaknesses are counterbalanced with strengths. Where the heavy is slow, he has the strongest attack. Where the scout has a weak attack, he is very fast. Even the most statistically average character in the game, the medic, can heal and grant temporary invulnerability to the other players; an ability that is totally unique to the other classes in the game. This balancing act is like a game of "rock, paper, scissors", where each character has a weakness and a strength. These characters also support different types of gameplay: the sniper, heavy, and engineer all work best when they root themselves in place—notice how there are one of these types in each class? Your characters will become more balanced the more classifications there are to gauge them against, such as:

- Movement speed
- Movement type
- Attack speed and rate
- Attack strength
- Attack range and duration
- Armor strength
- Health
- Encumbrance
- Advantages (like health or puzzle solving).

Be careful to make sure these values and traits are easily editable; if you need to make a global change in your game, you don't want to spend all your time tweaking values.

WHO ARE THE PEOPLE IN YOUR NEIGHBORHOOD?

The general. The hooker. The innkeeper. The service robot.

Non-player characters (or NPCs, as the kids call them) come from all walks of life: kings that assign quests and award trophies for completing them, blacksmiths that craft new weapons and armor. You know what the great thing is about them? YOU (as the player) are the center of their universe! They solely exist to help (or hinder) you! How's that for stroking your ego? That's why, in some way, every NPC needs to provide the answer to this question:

WHAT DOES THE PLAYER NEED TO SUCCEED?

What *does* the player need to succeed? Good question. I'm glad you asked. Every NPC needs a role. A job. A reason for living. All NPCs should provide one or more of the following:

- Objectives for the player
- Access to new locations where objectives await (anything from keys to maps to pointing in the right direction)
- Methods for the player to travel to said locations
- Rewards for completing objectives (can be economic or pride rewards)
- Tools to defeat enemies
- Gear to protect players from said enemies
- Answers to puzzles and problems
- Backstory about the world and its characters—just don't be too long winded

- Players' instruction on gameplay (though never tell the player something they already know)
- A compliment to your hero on their awesomeness (or suitably quake in fear if your hero is a badass)
- Humor.

While your NPC is waiting to provide help to the player, give them something to do. NPCs are the "extras" in the video game universe, and just like extras, they need to be given "business." In movie-making lingo, business is what extras do in the background of a scene to make it look like life is going on regardless of what the actors are doing: eating, talking, chopping wood, washing the floors. Simple animations are a good start. Complex activities are even better. In some games NPCs perform different activities depending on the time of day[10]. Just don't make the player have to chase the NPC around to talk to them.

When putting NPCs into your game worlds and levels, be sure to place them within eyesight of where the player is traveling. Make them easy to find. Place them on the game's mini-map if you have one. Don't make the player have to hunt them down. Unless your story calls for it, don't put them

---

[10] In life simulators like Harvest Moon and Animal Crossing, NPCs will go to bed if it's late enough. That means that many players will not be able to interact with some characters because they're sleeping. Make sure you take this into account, as you don't want to waste production time creating assets that the player will never see!

in strange locations either: an innkeeper should be found in the inn, the police captain in the police station, and so on. If needs be, put a large arrow over their head.

Have your NPCs be physically distinct in dress and body language. A soldier is going to look and act very differently to a gang member. Use as many visual cues as possible to help the player remember which character has what information or which guy is gonna sell them that phase plasma pistol for a good price.

If having unique NPCs isn't possible due to budget or time, you can still distinguish them with different "voices." This can be done via text as well as voice acting. The lead designer of *Bioshock* told a story of how players had trouble distinguishing the NPCs from one another until they spoke with strong international accents. Not all NPCs tend bar, dispensing advice in outrageous accents. Try making NPCs gameplay function surrogates like the game's store or save file system. Replacing a gameplay mechanic like a switch or crate with an NPC makes your game feel less contrived and predictable. Just be aware that talking to an NPC will slow down the pace of your game as the player will have to actually have a conversation to open a door rather than just turn a handle.

Interaction with an NPC can also initiate a puzzle, activate a mechanic, or start a countdown clock. Protecting an NPC on escort missions or in battle arenas is another common gameplay mechanic. Or if you don't want your NPC to be so helpless, have them taunt and spur your player into action. In *Darksiders*, a counter pops up when the smith Ulthane challenges War to see who can kill the most enemies. Not only does this indicate the start of the contest, but it changes the player's mind set into one of competition.

Study other games and see what they do with their NPCs. Use any good ideas you find and create your own. Making your NPCs less predictable will keep the player on their toes and curious to see who they will meet around the next corner. And around the corner of this book is the next of the Three Cs: the camera.

Level 5's Universal Truths and Clever Ideas:

- Form follows function: your character's actions and personality should determine their appearance.

- Give your characters distinct shapes, silhouettes, colors, and textures.

- Name your hero appropriately.

- Customization will increase player attachment.

- Use the player character to determine game metrics.

- Walking is NOT gameplay.

- Use the player character to reflect their in-game status.

- Companions and SPCs require a fair amount of work to get right. Make them compliment the player character.

- Balance multiple player characters to maximize effectiveness.

- Give your NPCs gameplay functions.

LEVEL 6

THE THREE CS, PART 2—CAMERA

Do you hear that crashing sound? That is the sound of a video game controller being thrown through a 50″ 1080p HDTV plasma panel with a 600Hz subfield drive. And why was this fine piece of technology utterly pulverized? Because your game has a really bad camera.

Did you know that over 1 billion TVs are destroyed a year because of really bad game cameras[1]? Nothing will cause a player to stop playing your game faster than a poor camera. This is why it is so important to get it right.

GET IT RIGHT: CAMERA VIEWS

Choosing the right camera for your game is not only very important for determining how to program the camera, but it also impacts how you design your game, map your controls, and create your

---

[1] This is a completely made-up statistic.

artwork. It's pretty common for a game to have more than one style of camera, but you should stick with one "main" camera style for the majority of your gameplay and only use other camera views for specific gameplay situations.

Static camera. A static camera does not move position and stays fixed onto a single screen, location, and image. The earliest video games used static cameras because (a) they hadn't invented the scrolling camera yet (duh!), (b) it allowed the player to keep their eyes on several game elements at once and, in the case of early 3-D games, (c) it allowed teams to maximize the game's artwork by creating art that would only be seen "from certain angles." An item in a game world that is only viewed from one angle doesn't need a backside, which saves on production and processing time.

Even though they're old school, static cameras can still be found in use today in many Flash-based arcade/puzzle games like *Peggle* and those "find the object" games that your mom likes to play. Another advantage to using a static camera is that you can use it to set the mood. A clever use of the static camera to help mood can be found in early survival horror titles like *Alone in the Dark* and *Resident Evil*. These developers not only used the static camera shot to represent a single room, but also used it to set up the camera for maximum effectiveness. Another advantage is that you can easily use it to set up events in your game world, because you don't run the risk of a player looking the other way when it happens. However, you have to be careful with a static screen because they aren't very dynamic. Make sure to compensate for this problem with lots of animation and effects to keep your screen lively.

If you aren't satisfied with a camera that stays put, you can always ask your programmer nicely to make it into a scrolling camera instead.

Scrollable camera. Pretend you are looking down at a desktop. Or use the above picture if you are bad at pretending. On this hypothetical desktop you can interact with all of the elements on the desk, but hey—you just can't find your pen. In the picture, what you can see is represented by the gray box. By moving or "scrolling" the camera (in this case your eyes) to another part of the desk—voilà! You find your missing pen beside a book. Amazing!

A scrollable camera offers all of the advantages of static screen but with the added advantages of (a) movement, which keeps the player engaged in the act of moving the camera, and (b) allowing you to hide stuff off screen or reveal it in a big dramatic way. This is why you will find it being used in many old-school adventure games like *Day of the Tentacle*. If you use a scrollable camera with a God-mode camera or in isometric view (which I'll be talking about later), then you can simulate a table top to simulate miniature games. This is why a scrollable camera is used in RTS and dungeon crawl games like *Dawn of War* and *Diablo III*. Make sure your controls for moving your camera are simple and relative to the player's controller. You don't need anything fancy to move a camera around.

Work with your programmer to **tune** the **hydraulics** of your camera: the speed at which the camera accelerates/decelerates. A scrollable camera that moves too fast will overshoot the player's target, which gets very frustrating as the player goes through a process of overshooting back and forth, a condition that eventually leads to insanity and/or a destroyed monitor. Conversely, don't make your camera scroll too slowly. This can be particularly catastrophic in a game where your little army's platoons are in danger of being wiped out by enemy tanks and your damn scrolling camera is too slow to get to them in time. Oh the humanity!

You can always let the player decide what speed they want the screen to scroll at. Just make sure they know where to find this option in your game and give them several speeds to choose from. Just "fast" and "slow" won't cut it.

In the beginning, there was the static screen. The static screen was fine for *Invaders from Space* and the *Kongs of Donkey*. But that was in 1981 when no one knew any better. And then game players cried out for more. So in 1982, the great Irem descended from the heavens in a purple moon buggy and introduced parallax scrolling to the video games world.

Parallax scrolling. As a parallax scrolling camera moves, the world moves with it. This camera view revolutionized video games, allowing game developers to create longer and deeper game worlds in which to play. There are two different ways you can treat parallax scrolling. First is plain ol' scrolling. The camera is controlled by the player's movement—the player essentially stays in the center of the screen as the world moves past them just like in those old-fashioned western films. Giddyup!

When using this type of scrolling, be careful to play out how your game level loads as your player may be able to "outrun the load." Always play your game level backwards to make sure that your player can't break your game.

The second type of parallax scrolling is the **forced scroll**. The player is forced to "keep up" with a scrolling camera, which is why it was first used on driving and flying games like *Moon Patrol* or *Scramble*. It became popular with first person shooters like *Operation Wolf* and third person rail shooters like *Panzer Dragoon* and was later used for "chase" sequences like those found in *Crash Bandicoot*. More often than not, if a player fails to keep up with the camera, something horrible (such as death) happens to them. This makes a forced scroll camera great for gameplay where you really want to put pressure on a player, but keep in mind that you don't want to use it consistently in a game; that is, unless your whole game is based on this idea.

Parallax scrolling games dominated home video games throughout the 1990s (really—I was there). There were tons of them! When you have a bunch of people making a genre of game over and over again, innovation eventually sneaks in. And it happened. Twice, in fact.

The first was **Mode 7**, named after the 7th (out of 8) background layer on the Super Nintendo entertainment system[2]. Artists drew the background layer in perspective stretching to the horizon. Scrolling the artwork (which was drawn to look like the ground), created the illusion of a background infinitely moving towards or away from the horizon. Add a forward-facing or rear-facing sprite and you would create the illusion of a car or character travelling towards or away from the screen. Excellent examples of Mode 7 can be seen in *Mario Kart*, *F-Zero*, and *Super Star Wars*. However, designing a level for Mode 7 gameplay can be tricky, as your level has no true back wall; the effect only works with an infinite background. While technology has advanced to allow programmers to easily create 3-D worlds without any special graphic mode, the term still remains in use by some (albeit ancient) game developers.

[2] The camera effect called "Mode 7" actually existed before the SNES. Racing games like Night Racer (Micronetics, 1977) and Pole Position (Namco, 1982) were some of the first games to feature a scrolling ground plane that gave the illusion of 3-D space.

In addition to scrolling the camera along the parallax, programmers found inspiration from the **multi-plane camera** used in traditional animation. This camera gives the illusion of depth by zooming the camera towards and away from the screen. By having a camera that tracked in and out of the **Z-axis**, developers were able to create level designs with parallel paths. Games like Disney's *Hercules Action Game* (Virgin Interactive, 1997) used the multi-plane camera to create **bi-dimensional** gameplay; the forerunner to what is known as **two and a half D**. A side effect of the zooming effect in bi-dimensional games was severe pixilation that occurred when the camera zoomed in on a non-scaling sprite. You can still find this effect being intentionally imitated in "retro"-style games.

FIRST PERSON CAMERA

As gameplay moved into the Z-axis, game creators explored more cinematic camera views. While a few games in the 1970s featured a **first person camera**, it wasn't until *Wolfenstein 3D* (Apogee Software, 1992) and its successor, *Doom* (id Software, 1993) that the camera view became popularized. The camera is used in a variety of game genres, from racing to platform; it became most associated with the **first person shooter**. Despite its popularity, it's hard to discern if the first person camera is really the best camera for gameplay. Here's a quick comparison of the pros and cons of the first person camera:

Advantages	Disadvantages
Easier to aim weapons at targets	Hard to gauge jump and movement distance
Player views character as "self", allowing for greater immersion in game world	Players can't see their character and can lose emotional connection
Easier to create atmospheric situations (like horror)	Player is not always looking where the designer wants them to look
Player gets close look at weapons, world objects, and puzzle items	Game objects (like pickups) have to be exaggerated in scale to compensate for distance

As you can see, the arguments for and against the first person camera are pretty darn even. But regardless, there are some pretty fun visual effects you can pull off when using a first person camera.

- **Blood splatter:** many current FPSs use a blood splatter effect on the screen to show that a player has taken damage. You can also have the screen start to "grow dark" or dim to represent the player dying. Some games use this effect heavily and some games do it light, but I feel it's pretty unfair to punish a dying player with the additional disadvantage of not being able to see the gameplay (or where the damage is coming from!).
- **Raindrops/mist/lens flare:** based on, for example, images seen on TV news camera lenses, the effects of weather can be shown. Some driving games even include windshield wiper controls to clear away these effects.
- **"Predator vision":** based on the thermal camera effect seen in the movie *Predator*, you can simulate these effects in a first person view to make the player actually feel like they are using high-tech or alien gear, such as night vision goggles. Just make sure the effect actually gives the player a gameplay advantage in addition to looking cool.

- **Blurry/drunken cam:** first person view gives the designer a chance to put the player in the character's shoes. As long as the altered state doesn't interfere too much with the player's control of the game for too long, there's no problem with giving the player a good whack in the head now and then—or at least an awful simulated hangover.

Those make the first person camera view sound pretty fun, right? Remember, many of these effects can be used with a third person camera too, but using them with the first person camera really makes you feel like you are "in-the-action." But wait, before you pass judgment, let's "toss" one more "chunk" of information into the "pot":

DIMS stands for **Doom-induced motion sickness** and it is a very real thing. It's what happens when your eyes register movement and your inner ear (responsible for balance) doesn't. Motion sickness is heavily influenced by the field of view of the game's camera. So, the larger the field of view, the more people will feel motion sick[3]. Victims of this form of motion sickness can suffer from clammy skin, sweating, dizziness, headache, and nausea.

To avoid having your players vomit all over your game, try the following remedies: get the game's frame rate as close to 60 frames per second as possible. Avoid bobbing foreground elements, like your player's weapon. Keep your level's floor as flat as possible[4]. Add large stationary objects to your environments which give the player something to focus on. Don't whip the camera around too much. Try not to have your player change their elevation view (looking up and down) too quickly or often.

And while I am not a doctor, and don't even play one on television, I recommend getting some fresh air, drinking a glass of water, and taking non-drowsy motion sickness medicine if you have to play an FPS for long periods of time.

---

[3] This is the reason why I never sit closer than the seventh row from the front when I go to the movies.
[4] This is what killed me when I played Goldeneye on the N64. Don't get me wrong, this is a brilliant game, but there was one level with an undulating floor that, after I played it for a half hour, I threw up like it was Christmas.

THIRD PERSON CAMERA

Another good way to avoid turning your game into a puke-a-rama is to pull the view back into the **third person view**. Now remember, this isn't a solve-all solution, but I have found that when the player has something to focus on, the effects of DIMS seems to reduce. A third person camera also lets the player get a better view of the world, the action, and what's coming up behind you. Watch out War! That skeleton's got a sword!

Pulling the camera back behind the player offers many advantages over the first person view. First off, you get a clear view of your character ...'s butt[5]. Well, that can be fixed by allowing the character to turn around and run towards the camera. But then you have to make sure the camera can track backwards with the player. Does that mean the controls become camera relative or player relative? And how does the player restore the camera back to its original position? Hmmm. This may be more complicated than I first thought.

Getting a third person camera to work correctly may be the biggest challenge a team has to face. While there are many things that can go wrong with your camera, let's try to work through them to get them right.

Camera movement. When I was in high school, I had an after-school job of videotaping sporting events. As I concentrated on filming the game, I lost track of everything else that was going on around me. As a result, I tended to back into the coaches and trip over the gear lying on the sidelines, which

---

[5] The story goes that Toby Gard, one of the designers of Tomb Raider (Eidos Interactive, 1996), made his lead character a woman because he didn't want to spend the entire game's production staring at a guy's ass.

(a) didn't result in great footage, and (b) generally pissed off the coaching staff. To solve this, I recruited a friend to act as a spotter as I filmed to make sure the collisions were kept to a minimum.

Having that experience made me realize that every camera needs a spotter—even ones that live within video games, which is why I say "treat the camera like it's a person." As you program your camera and build your world, give the camera room to maneuver and the player a way to manipulate it. This style of camera is commonly called a **follow cam** because it follows after the player. After years of working on 3-D follow cams, here's what I've learned to watch out for:

Sorting. Sorting is what happens when a camera moves through a character or geometry. Nothing breaks the illusion of a real world faster than this. What's worse, in many cases, the sorting camera will show the background layer of the world, which in most cases is a sky or flat color layer. It looks crappy and great pains should be taken to make sure this doesn't happen in your game.

You can avoid sorting by paying attention to the camera and the geometry. One way is to give your camera a detection radius so that it can avoid passing through world objects by moving over, under, or around objects. If you don't want your game to process that much collision detection (which causes the game to slow down), have world objects turn transparent. It works pretty well with objects within the confines of the walls, but shouldn't be used for perimeter walls. Avoid having objects in the world disappear completely as players get disoriented when elements in the level flicker in and out of existence! (And it looks bad.)

Controls. Think about how your camera is going to operate in regards to controls. Many games won't work properly if the player is pointing the camera straight up or straight down. Another annoyance for me is the great "airplane controls vs. player-relative controls" debate. Personally, unless I'm flying a plane, don't make me push up on the analog stick to make my character go down. Many FPSs do this and frankly, it's just stupid since in most FPSs you are playing a character, not an airplane. If you have to have this camera-relative control option, at least give me the option of changing it. Even better, make the character-relative controls the default and make the airplane controls the option.

Corners. The number one cause of **camera flipping** (when the camera tries to find a good place to come to rest but ends up bouncing between two or more objects) are corners. Rather than trying to come up with an overly complicated camera system to combat flipping (and believe me, it usually ends up being overly complicated), just keep players out of corners in the first place. But rather than creating invisible geometry (oh how I hate invisible geometry; more ranting on this later), build blocking geometry like small retaining walls, shrubberies, boulders, or fencing which tell the player to "stay out!" of corners. Don't invite trouble: keep your collectables out of corners. Keep your enemy's AI path/detection zones out of corners. Move your gameplay elements to the middle of the room. Stay out of corners! I mean it!

OK, so you didn't listen to me. You HAVE to have that one power-up nestled in the corner of that room. Then, as your character walks into the corner make sure your camera goes up. Imagine that the Amazing Spider-Man is your camera man. What does Spidey do when he reaches a wall? He climbs up. Have the camera scoot up along the surface of the wall to look at the player from a bird's-eye view (or would that be spider's-eye view?). But avoid having the camera show the player from a direct top-down view. Not only does it look bad, but it just invites flipping once the camera tries to decide where to look at the player.

Position. A topic of disagreement among the world's greatest designers is whether the camera should strictly follow the player as if it were attached to a stick stuck to the character OR whether the camera should be more laid back and follow the character around freely. Don't stress it dude, the camera will catch up with the player when it feels like it. (Or when the player chooses to reset it.)

Maybe it's because I grew up in Southern California, but I am definitely in favor of the second method for the following reasons: there are fewer chances for obstruction, you see the character's face from time to time, you can set up gameplay where the player has to deal with enemies that sneak up behind them, and it's easier to orchestrate "chase"-style gameplay. Why this is such a contentious topic is not because the world's greatest designers are against such concepts but because they have to give up control of the camera.

GIVING UP CONTROL

Bad things happen when players are given control of the game camera. They start sticking it in places they shouldn't be sticking it. They find ways to get the camera stuck into geometry. They generally screw things up. And I can tell you that nothing pisses off a game designer faster than watching some idiot screw around with the camera. So you, the game designer, have three choices to solve this issue. Loosen up your sphincter and let the player take control of the camera or screw 'em, take the control away, and make that camera all yours! Or you could decide when they need control and when they don't. You are the designer, you call the shots!

Make your choice, adventurer!

TURN TO PAGE (133) to let players have control of the game camera.
TURN TO PAGE (135) to take control of the game camera away.
TURN TO PAGE (137) to let the player sometimes have control and sometimes not.

SO YOU'VE DECIDED TO LET THE PLAYER CONTROL THE CAMERA

In the past I've used three methods to give the player control over the game camera.

The first method is to allow the player complete control over the follow cam. By using the analog stick (or a mouse for PC games), the player can move the game camera to look around 360 degrees at any time; while running, standing still, while in combat, whatever. The disadvantage of this is that players can get quickly disoriented, miss interesting and important level events and clues, or suffer DIMS.

The second method is a **free-look camera**. This camera allows the player to stop and look around the world (effectively a first person view). The free-look camera is usually initiated by a button press, which activates a mode in which the player can use the analog stick (the one that is usually used to move the player) to rotate the camera around 360 degrees. I have seen versions of this camera where the free-look cam is restricted to a little less than 180 degrees in an attempt to mimic the natural rotation of the human neck. When the player presses the button to return back to the third person view, they are usually reoriented in the direction that the free-look cam was facing.

Reorientation. Speaking of reorientation, giving the player the option to reorient the camera to its default position (behind the character in the case of a third person camera) is usually appreciated by the player. It comes in particularly useful during combat and platform jumping scenarios. Reorientation is usually achieved with a quick, single button press by the player.

Speed. Be mindful of the speed of your third person camera as it is rotated around by the player. A good camera feels like it has hydraulics; it never stops dead, but rather slows down slightly as it decelerates. This will keep the player from suffering from DIMS. As a player character is usually in motion, another trick I learned is to have the camera slightly overshoot its target when the player stops and creep back to center on the player if they stay still long enough. Just remember, you NEVER want the player to get out of the camera's view.

The third method is to give the player selective control over the camera. Like with the first person free-look cam, this mode is activated by a button press which brings the camera in for a closer look at an object's detail or into a special mode like a sniper's scope. The difference between selective control and a free-look camera is context.

With the free-look camera, you are simulating the turning of the character's head. With selective control, you are simulating a piece of equipment, like binoculars or a telescope. Any limitations this camera may have should mirror the limitations of the object the character is using. This realism sells this view, so let reality be your guide.

Some game designers find the transition from third person to first person to be jarring, and feel it risks taking the player out of the carefully constructed atmosphere they've created. *Resident Evil 4* created a unique solution for their shooting gameplay. As the player aims their firearm, the camera viewpoint shifts down to hover behind the character's shoulder.

Another infrequently used alternative is to use **second person view**, where the camera mode is given to an entirely different character. In the *Mark of Kri* (SCEA, 2002), the player "sees" through the eyes of Kuzo, a bird that can be flown on spy missions. In *The Darkness* (2K Games, 2007), the player can control a "tentacle cam" to see around corners and further than the player's POV. When the player has seen what they want, a button press returns the view back to the third player view.

SO YOU'VE DECIDED TO NOT LET THE PLAYER HAVE CONTROL OVER THE CAMERA

Good call. The last thing you need is someone screwing around with the camera making your game look bad. You will realize that there are many benefits to taking away the player's control over the camera.

- Removing camera control gives the player one less thing to worry about. If they aren't wrestling with the camera, the player is free to concentrate on what's important: playing your game.

- More visual bang for your buck. A camera where YOU determine what it's looking at means that game art can be built to maximize polygon and texturing limitations. In *God of War*, the environments were built like theater sets, not in full 3-D. Why build the back of a building if you are never going to see it?

- You can treat your game like a dark ride. Disneyland's *Haunted Mansion* is the perfect real-world example of a designer-controlled camera, as its omni-mover carts[6] always have the guest looking at the most interesting scenes in the ride. You commonly find this kind of **rail camera** in first person shooters like *Time Crisis* (Namco, 1995) and *House of the Dead*. (Sega, 1996).

- Your game world simply looks better. Taking away camera control means you can set up shots. Want a worm's-eye view to make the boss look more menacing? No problem. Want to skew the camera to make the world look demented or creepy. Go right ahead. No one is going to be able to screw it up.

- What did I miss? Have an important clue or event happening in your game world? Want the player to be able to see the Tower of Doom looming in the background or that giant spider that is creeping up on them? No problem. Without camera control, you don't risk the player missing anything important in your game.

- Want to have the camera do a barrel roll? Zip in and out between columns? Move around pillars or over or under objects? Match the player's movement as they crawl under obstacles and through narrow passages? Go right ahead and go nuts with those complex camera moves. Using a rail camera you can set up elaborate and cinematic camera angles. You don't have to worry about the player wrestling to regain control of the camera. Just make sure your gameplay controls remain consistent during any of these fancy camera moves.

- If you decide to obstruct or let the character get out of the player's view, make sure that your character-relative controls let the player guide the character back into view. For example, if the player moves the character behind a fence, the player should be able to keep pushing the control stick in the same direction with the assumption that the character will eventually emerge on the other side. Don't place hazards

---

[6] Which they call "doom buggies." Heh.

behind the obstruction or widen the path in these areas, which would allow for movement in the Z-axis: the player could get unjustly hurt or lost when not in view. These situations, however, are great places to hide goodies.

But the most important thing to remember when removing the player's control of the camera is to make it clear they don't have control over it. Once this is established to the player, they can focus on the gameplay and not worry about the camera.

2-D vs 3-D? In the end, all that matters is that you use the camera that is best for your gameplay.

SO YOU'VE DECIDED TO LET THE PLAYER SOMETIMES HAVE CONTROL OVER THE CAMERA

You are a fair and balanced individual who knows the meaning of moderation. Now go back and read about the other two options so you can actually learn something, you know-it-all.

TWO AND A HALF D

Crash Bandicoot (SCEA, 1996) was one of the first games to take two-dimensional platform gameplay and move it into the third dimension. Unlike bi-dimensional gameplay which uses sprites for the game world and characters, two and a half D uses three-dimensional character and world models but limits the camera movement in the same manner as a bi-dimensional game: up, down, and in/out on the Z-axis.

When making your two and a half D games just follow the same rules as with a parallax scrolling camera, with the guidelines of taking control away from the player as listed above.

ISOMETRIC CAMERA

Introduced with *Zaxxon* (Sega, 1982), the isometric camera gave the player a new way to look at the playing field. Not quite side view and not quite top down, the end result creates a rather toy-like view of the world. This, and the smooth scrolling 3-D world on a 2-D display, contribute to why the isometric view is popular with building and simulation games.

There are some advantages to an isometric (or iso) camera. Players get a quick snapshot of an environment's layout and the relationship of items within it, which makes it good for environmental puzzle solving. Hordes of enemies seem more impressive when seen from this camera view, as exhibited in games like *Diablo* and *Starcraft*. That said, elevation can cause some problems in iso view. Determining whether something is higher up and closer than something farther away and lower can be difficult, as they both appear to be in the same spot on screen. Regardless of how small their subjects look compared to their first and third person cousins, iso games can still be quite detailed and beautiful. However, if your gameplay is less concerned about getting a detailed look at the inhabitants of your world, then go ahead and steps into the sandals of the divine with **God view**.

Because details aren't as important in God view you will find it in games that are concerned with controlling cities or dominating land masses like *Spore* or *Supreme Commander*. God view is essentially an isometric camera but where the player is given a wider field of vision over the world, sometimes as high as low orbit.

TOP-DOWN CAMERA

Considered to be an "old-fashioned" camera view, you can still occasionally find action arcade games presented in a **top-down view**. Classic games like *Smash TV* and *Gauntlet* are examples of games that used this camera view. There are some disadvantages to this view, such as not being able to get a good look at the game character or the game world, and concepts like depth should be avoided from this perspective.

An interesting variation on the top-down camera view is the **top-down/side view** camera. While some elements in the game level are presented from a top-down view (usually world elements and power-ups), other elements (like characters) are presented from a side view. This view has a certain charm to it, similar to how characters in Egyptian tomb art are always shown from the side view. Games like *Snake* and *Tower Defense* are some of the more recent types of games that use this quirky camera view.

SPECIAL CASE CAMERAS

OK, so you've decided on what camera to use for your game. You're ready to go, right? Wrong! What about the camera for special instances? Designing a camera to work underwater or while flying adds another layer of complexity.

Here are a few red flags and tricks to keep in mind when adding these extra layers to your own game:

- Make sure your camera is always moving along with the player while flying or swimming. Don't let the player rise or fall off screen.
- If your player flies or swims straight up or down, make sure your camera doesn't sort through floor geometry.

- While swimming, keep your camera underwater with the player. Don't have it pop out of the water unless the player is swimming on the surface. Try to keep a clear distinction between "in water" and "on land."
- Try to resist the urge to have your camera realistically bob while underwater. It's effects like this that make players suffer from DIMS.

TUNNEL VISION

Another tricky camera angle is when the player is moving through environments like caves, sewers, or dungeons. Low ceilings, narrow passageways, and tight doorways can cause all sorts of trouble to the camera.

I find that if you restrict the movement of the camera using a rail camera in these troublesome locations, not only do you alleviate any camera problems, but it also helps maintain the feeling of claustrophobia. Avoid low angles, rather keep the camera at the character's shoulder height or slightly above the player—but watch out for low-hanging stalagtites that will cause camera sorting issues.

CAMERA SHOT GUIDE

Now that we've seen all the ways a camera can present the game, let's go to the 5-second film school and find out how to set up your camera to get the best shot—just like those Hollywood professionals!

Extreme wide shot (EWS). This shows a character or location from a very far distance. This shot is perfect for showing castles looming in the distance or a planet-killing space station in orbit.

Very wide shot (VWS). Closer than an extreme wide shot so that you can make out some details. Usually used for establishing shots of buildings or other large things like space ships or to set the tone that the player is stranded out at sea or in a desert.

Wide shot (WS). The entire subject (be it a car or person) can be seen in frame on a wide shot. Usually used when first establishing a main character or vehicle so the player can get a good look at it in its entirety.

Medium shot (MS). About half of the figure of the subject can be seen in frame: usually your character from the waist up. Which means your character doesn't need to wear pants that day.

Medium close up (MCU). Also called a "head and shoulders shot." This view is most commonly used when a character is talking. Make sure to animate hands to keep the character on the screen lively.

Close up (CU). Also called a "head shot": the camera is tight into a character's face to show expression. When you get this close to a CG character model, you start to see flaws (such as in the interiors of mouths or close views on textures). I recommend using this shot sparingly.

Extreme close up (ECU). Wham! Right up the nose with this one. It's great for focusing on the expression in eyes like in spaghetti westerns and old horror movies. Or you can use it to show details on objects such as puzzle clues, or even the puzzles themselves.

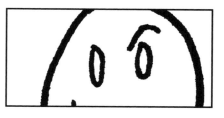

Cutaway. You know when the hero says "I need to get that magic sword" and the next shot is a magic sword? That's a cutaway. A cutaway can be used for a character reaction shot too.

Cut in. Here, our hero says "I need to examine this clue" and then the camera shows a close-up detail of the clue. That's a cut in.

Two shot. This is called a two shot because it features two elements (usually talking characters) shown on screen at the same time.

Over the shoulder shot (OSS). A shot taken from over the shoulder of a character. It's a good opportunity to show hidden things too, like characters revealing that they have a gun strapped to their back or are crossing their fingers as they promise not to kill the bad guy.

Noddy. A shot in which a character is reacting to what someone else is saying (they are "nodding" in response to the speaker). You see this shot a lot with news interviews.

Point of view shot (POV). A shot from the perspective of someone or something. Usually shown from the eyes of the player, but can be from the point of view of a watching enemy, a floating power-up, whatever you want!

CAMERA ANGLE GUIDE

Now that you know what kind of camera you are using and what your shot is going to look like, let's place the camera to make things look as cool as possible.

Eye level: the camera is aiming level at the eyes of your subject.

High angle: the camera is above the subject, looking down on it. This can make things look less impressive. A good shot for showing elements in relationship to each other.

Low angle: the camera is below the subject, looking up at it. This makes things look more menacing or impressive. Great for boss fights.

Worm's-eye view: the camera is literally on the floor looking up, as if a worm were watching the action.

Bird's-eye view: a shot taken from high up in the sky, as if a bird were watching the action.

Dutch tilt: we did this trick in *Maximo: Ghosts to Glory*. We wanted our in-game camera to feel slightly creepy or wacky, like shots you see in a Sam Raimi horror movie or the 1960s *Batman* TV show. Tilt the camera so everything seems to be

cockeyed. If you do a Dutch tilt subtly, it has a great effect on the player who realizes something is wrong, but isn't sure what. If you do it severely, it really makes things feel screwed up.

CAMERA MOVEMENT GUIDE

Moving the camera is an art all unto itself. Here are the most common ways to move a camera. See if you can incorporate these moves into your game camera to make it feel more cinematic.

Arc: where the camera follows or dollies around a subject in an arc. A common technique is to have the camera arc around the player for 360 degrees if something amazing or wondrous is happening to the character (for example, they've just gained a new power).

Dolly zoom: the camera adjusts the focal length but is moved forward or back to keep the subject the same size on camera. You see this shot a lot in Steven Spielberg movies where a character is amazed by something or comes to a realization that something bad is going to happen.

Follow: the camera moves with the subject. Depending on the style of your cutscene, you can try to make your follow a little shaky as if it was taken by a hand-held camera.

Pedestal: moving the camera up to match the subject. Like a tracking shot but vertical. Having the camera pedestal past objects in the foreground helps add to the illusion of speed, especially if you are trying to show something rise up suddenly or powerfully.

Pan: when the camera moves to the left or the right. Play around with your pans: move them around and past objects. Place items in the foreground to make more interesting shots.

Tilt: where the camera's focus is moved up or down but the camera's position stays the same. Effects like lens flare can make a tilt more interesting.

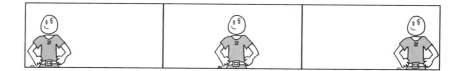

Dolly: where the camera is moved smoothly towards or away from the subject. This is also called a tracking or crab shot. Speed can really make a dolly more interesting; a slow crawl if something is mysterious or suspenseful, or really rocket forward if something is dangerous or dramatic. Play around with starting and ending your tracking before your subject starts moving to make things feel more dynamic.

Zoom: the focal length of the lens changes, giving the illusion of the camera moving. Be careful not to zoom in through items (sorting) or zoom too close to characters or world objects that aren't very detailed. Seeing textures go from fine to pixilated breaks reality for the viewer.

OTHER CAMERA NOTES

Now that you are an expert cinematographer, let's work on your directing skills.

Nothing kills a good shot faster than having unappealing composition. The most basic guideline for composition is called **the rule of thirds**.

See in the above image how the screen has three imaginary lines running through it? The rule is that you want to put the item of focus either a third of the way up or a third of the way to one side or another. Of course, once you have mastered the rule of thirds, you will want to break it. That's OK too. After all, you are an ar-teest.

Another tried and true rule is called **crossing the line**. Just like in the rule of thirds, there is an imaginary line that cuts through the middle of your scene or environment. Let's say you have your hero running away from a deadly trap.

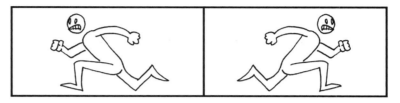

The hero has just crossed the line, which makes it look like he is running first to the right and then to the left, which just looks weird and doesn't convey that our hero is running in the same direction. Instead, add a shot of our hero from the front to show that this is the same guy in the same place.

You also want to apply crossing the line when you have two characters talking to each other, otherwise they'll look like they are talking to someone else off screen.

ALWAYS POINT THE CAMERA TO THE OBJECTIVE

An excellent rule of directing your shot, whether it is in-game or in a cutscene, is that the camera should tell the player what they should be looking at. For example, you enter a mysterious, underground chamber. The player can be told any number of things by the camera's movement: where puzzle elements can be found, the appearance or location of enemies, a dramatic reveal of a beautiful piece of architecture, or where the exit is. Or even better, all of the above. Playwright Anton Chekhov said "If in the first act you have hung a pistol on the wall, then in the following one it should be fired. Otherwise don't put it there[7]." In other words, show everything that the player needs for the entire room or scene. You can spool clues out to them, but don't make them blindly guess.

Even if the objective can't be seen by the player, give them tools to find another way to see it. *Batman: Arkham Asylum* uses a "detective mode" (literally a pair of X-ray specs) that allows Batman (the player) to see hostiles as well as points the way to secret paths. *Heavenly Sword* (SCEE, 2007) displays a picture-in-picture view to show puzzle clues and "beauty shots" of the enemies during boss fights.

NEVER LET THE CHARACTER GET OUT OF THE CAMERA'S SIGHT

Oy. I can hear all of the kvetching now. "How can I keep my camera on the character ALL of the time? But what if my character goes behind a wall or hides behind a very dense shrub?" Feh. Not a problem. There are several tricks you can do to help the player keep track of where they are in the game. Observe:

- Show an arrow, name tag, or "ghost image" outline of the player through geometry.
- Have the screen react as if it were an X-ray or thermal imaging device and show the player's skeleton or heat signature while they are behind the object.
- Make the wall or object turn transparent to show the character behind it.
- If your character gets off screen (this can happen in multiplayer mode[8]), have an arrow or icon point to where they are.
- Zoom into first person mode to show the character's POV.
- Build your geometry to make sure you can always see a little bit of the character; tinted windows, arrow slits, grating with gaps all goes a long way to show the movement of the player behind it.

While the player is in this obscured view, the camera should NOT act any differently: the last thing the player needs is to have to wrestle with the camera when they can't see their character.

---

[7] *Anton Chekhov: A Life*, Donald Rayfield (Henry Holt and Company, 1997).
[8] But it won't because you aren't going to let your main character get out of the camera's sight, right?

MULTIPLE PLAYER CAMERAS

Keeping a camera on a player is tricky enough but what if you have more than one player? I have seen many a game designer go mad trying to determine a workable camera scheme for multiple players. Fortunately, I have done all the hard work for you and will save you a trip to a padded cell.

Split screen: *GoldenEye 007* (Nintendo, 1997) had a great four-player split screen mode that worked pretty well as long as you didn't expect to make out any detail on the screen. *War of the Monsters* (SCEA, 2003) used a split screen that only engaged when the two combatants were far enough away from each other to trigger it. Now, in the age of giant plasma screens, split screen works better because each player can actually see what is going on.

Zooming screen: *LittleBigPlanet* zooms out whenever there is more than one character on screen. If any of the characters get off-screen, they use an arrow to keep track of the player's location. If they stay off screen for too long, the player is "killed" until the next checkpoint is reached. *Power Stone* does something similar, but dynamically scales in and out as there can be up to four players on screen at once. The characters get pretty tiny at times, but coupled with an indicator arrow system you can keep track of your character pretty well.

Camera in picture: You can also go with the camera-in-picture route. A main character is represented on the "big screen" with additional characters shown on smaller insert camera views. It's not the best solution for some types of multiplayer games like FPSs, but it works pretty well for sports titles.

Whew. I think we've exhausted the topic of cameras. Time to move on to the last of the Three Cs … Controls.

Level 6's Universal Truths and Clever Ideas:

- Choose the right camera for your game.

- Prevent DIMS by minding frame rate, speed of camera movement, and level topography.

- First person camera allows for greater player immersion.

- Third person camera allows the player to get a good view of their character and the world.

- Treat the camera like it is the player's "spotter."

- Remove camera control whenever it becomes a problem.

- When removing camera control, make sure the player knows it.

- Use Hollywood-style camera angles and shots to heighten game visuals and drama.

- Never let the character out of the camera's sight.

- Accommodate multiple players using the game camera.

LEVEL 7

THE THREE CS, PART 3—CONTROLS

Once upon a time, I joined the team of a console game that had been in production for three years. I was asked to take a look at the current state of the game and report back any issues I had. Overall, the game was really good but there was one thing that bothered me. One of the enemies could only be defeated with a quick time event (see Level 8 for more on these), and even though I'm awesome at playing action games, I just couldn't seem to press the button fast enough to win the contest and kill the monster.

I went to the creative director and told him that I thought the controls for the minigame were too hard. He asked me "How did you hold the controller?" This is what I showed him:

He said "Oh, no wonder. You are holding the controller wrong." Whaaa? As far as I knew, there was only one way to hold the controller. Keeping things respectful, I asked: how did *he* recommend I hold it? This is what he showed me:

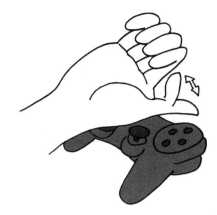

I wasn't sure if he was joking. "I don't believe that players would change their hand positions midway through the game. It just doesn't seem very natural." He became insulted and proceeded to tell me that not only was it the proper way to hold it, but that *everyone else* on the team held it that way as well. "Hmm. Did you *tell them* how to hold it that way?" I asked. "Yes." He replied. I gave his way a try but still didn't win the fight. If anything, the new hand position made things worse. I returned to his office and told him "Sorry, but I think players are going to have difficulty playing this." Pointing his finger at me, he said "You are 100% WRONG!" and stormed off.

Three months later, after testing revealed that the quick time event was too hard to play, the controls were adjusted. What **very important thing** did I take away from this experience?

ALWAYS REMEMBER THAT HUMANS ARE PLAYING THESE GAMES

Not six-fingered mutants or multi-tentacled squid men from Praxis Prime. It's Homo sapiens who play video games; most of them possessing short if not stubby fingers and mediocre motor skills coordination, which is why it is important to consider ergonomics when creating your control schemes.

Ergonomics is the study of fitting equipment to fit the worker. Great pains are made by hardware developers to see how the player holds and uses the controller. Which is why it never made any sense to me that a developer would create a control scheme that forced the player to twist up their hands like pretzels. To help with this, I created this rule of thumb (BAA DUM! TISH![1]) that I call the "**Gamers' Guide to Flex-O-Fingering**."

---

[1] Thankyou, thankyou. I'll be here all week, folks. Try the veal.

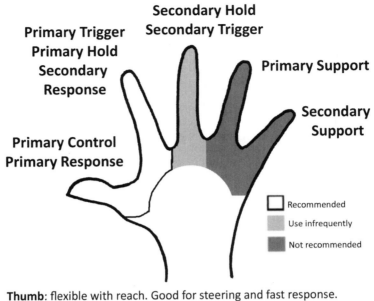

Thumb: flexible with reach. Good for steering and fast response.

Index: strong and fast. Used for response or hold moves.

Middle: weaker but usable for hold moves. Decent reach.

Ring: weak with poor reach. Better for stabilization

Pinkie: poor strength, reach requires hand support.

When you are designing controls, try establishing design rules for your controls schemes based on hand placement (for example, in FPS games it's common to use the keyboard for character movement and the mouse for aiming and shooting). Not only is it helpful when determining what controls go where on the controller, but the player will begin to associate muscle movement with a certain action even if they don't realize they are doing it.

Speaking of keyboards, just because you have a whole keyboard available for use, doesn't mean you have to use every single key. Keeping your keyboard controls localized around commonly used key groupings like QWERTY or ASWD makes it easier for players to adapt to.

Another way to assign controls is thematically. In *Tak and the Guardians of Gross* (THQ, 2008) the motion-controlled Wii Remote was used for all of the player's magic powers while the analog stick/nunchuck controlled all Tak's real-world abilities like interacting with objects and fighting. If the player had any question on how to perform a move, they would usually try the thematically related controller first. Just make sure that you don't cross signals and start intermingling your themes. That just leads to confusion and sadness.

The tricks above are really no big secret; it boils down to this: you just need to understand the control needs of your audience. Here are a few more tips (exclusive to buyers of this book[2]!):

- If you are designing for younger players, keep the button presses simple. Don't create complex combinations as these younger fingers just can't make them. Or if you are designing a kid's game using the keyboard, try not to spread out your key commands too far as most kids tend to "hunt and peck" the keys—which isn't good if you want them to make quick actions.
- MMO and FPS players often create hotkeys and macros to chain attacks or spell effects. Give them the option to customize their controls. You never know when you'll need to cast "Combustion, Icy Veins" and "Fireball" to boost your dps. In addition, customizable controls have the benefit of being disabled gamer friendly.
- Fighting gamers, like fans of the *Street Fighter* series, pride themselves on mastering ultracomplex control schemes, but remember, not everyone can pull off the dragon punch move in *Street Fighter II*. If you want to keep your game accessible to other types of players, don't go nuts with the ubercomplex controls.
- *Track and Field* (Konami, 1983) was a very popular game that required manic button pressing to make the little athlete character run. However, it was impossible to accurately do this move without the aid of a pencil (see image), resulting in what us kids called the "**pencil trick**." However, the pencil trick destroyed game controllers. While I'm sure that controller manufacturers loved the pencil trick, it's unfair to your players to make them resort to it.

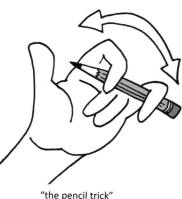

"the pencil trick"

[2] Please do not use these tips if you are just looking at this page in the bookstore. Thanks.

- While it's fine to experiment with unconventional control schemes, make sure the player has the option to revert it back to a more traditional one.
- On that note, offer the player several control options. Or, even better, let the players map their own controls in the options screen.
- For Zeus' sake, don't reverse your flight controls! Pulling back on the stick should make the plane go up and pushing forward should make the plane go down. Nobody likes those reversed controls and anyone who tells you otherwise should be forced to play the super-awful *Superman 64* and fly through rings for a week straight.

DANCE, MONKEY, DANCE

A good designer will think about how the game is played in the real world as well as in the game world. Think about how the player is going to move those fingers over the controller. Avoid repetition and strive for an uncomplicated control scheme. If you get it right, you create what I call the "dance of the buttons" for the player. If your controls get too complex or repetitive, you end up with the players resorting to **button mashing**.

Button mashing is a derogatory term to describe when a player isn't sure how to control the game, resulting in them wildly and/or rapidly hitting the buttons randomly to get any sort of positive result. This usually happens in action and fighting games when either the control scheme is too complex or they aren't getting satisfactory feedback.

Button mashing contributes to player fatigue and "gamers' thumb" (otherwise known as "occupational overuse syndrome"), characterized by stiffness, burning or cold sensations, numbness or weakness. The American Physical Therapy Association[3] recommends the following exercises and advice:

[3] Exercises courtesy of the APTA website (http://www.apta.org).

- Keep your wrists straight (don't let them droop) as you hold the controller.
- Sit comfortably in a chair with good back support.
- Stretch every 20 minutes to give your head, neck and shoulders muscles a break.

- Tap each finger with the thumb of the same hand. Repeat five times.

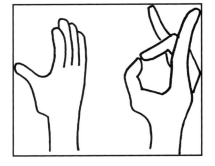

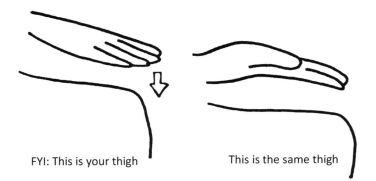

FYI: This is your thigh   This is the same thigh

- Alternate tapping your palm and the back of your hand against your thigh as quickly as you can. Repeat 20 times.

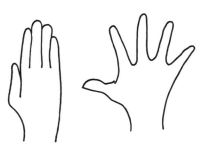

- Open your hands and spread fingers as far apart as possible. Hold for 10 seconds. Repeat eight times.

- Clasp your hands together and turn your hands away from your body and extend your arms forward. Hold for 10 seconds and repeat eight times.

- Fold your hands together; turn your palms away from your body and extend your arms overhead. You should feel the stretch in your upper torso and shoulyders to hands. Hold for 10 seconds. Repeat eight times.

However, not all button mashing is bad; you may be able to use it to your advantage. I have observed that the first thing a player does when they start a game is to press all of the buttons on the controller. This is because (a) players want to see what happens and (b) no one ever reads the game manual. So how do you get a player to learn if their first instinct is to just mash buttons?

Simple. Have the character do something cool whenever they press a button, even if the player doesn't understand how they're doing it. *God of War* does this fantastically well: Kratos pulls off some awesome attack moves even when you just mash buttons—and it's completely intentional. Once the player sees these moves happen a few times, they will slow down to try to dissect how they pulled them off.

Never have a button do nothing when pressed. Here are some ways to deal with this:

- Play a "negative response" sound effect or animation to make it clear to the player that this control isn't available. I always liked that the character in *Dark Castle* shrugged his shoulders if he was out of ammo or missing a key.

- Make it clear during your training mode that a button is inactive. Then make a big deal when it is unlocked. *Brütal Legend* stops the game dead and shows a full-screen graphic whenever the main character gets a new move. Just remember (a) not to teach more than one new move at a time, and (b) don't jam new moves down the player's throat too quickly. Players tune out if they get overloaded with information.

- Assign a redundant but related function. If the triangle button is slated for a projectile attack that the player doesn't have yet, assign the melee attack to the button until they find that kill-o-zap blaster. The player will mentally equate the triangle button with combat until the "true" move is unlocked.

With the advent of motion controls like the **Wii Remote** and **Project Natal**, designers now have an opportunity to recreate real-world controls for moves. But before we get into that, let's talk about how to get the most reality out of traditional controllers.

One of the best examples of recreating real-world moves using an analog stick can be found in *Pitfall: The Lost Expedition*. (Activision, 2004). In the game, water is health and the player carries a canteen to hold water. Whenever the player comes across a cistern, he pushes the stick forward to fill the canteen. When he pulls back on the stick, the hero Harry takes a drink from the canteen to replenish his health. The clever combination of intention and animation makes this feel very satisfying. Mapping the moves to logical control locations helps immerse the player into the game world. In *Maximo: Ghosts to Glory*, the goal was to create an "out-of-game" correlation between Maximo's moves and the real-world Playstation 2 controller.

Maximo's overhead swing is performed by pressing the triangle, the button at the "top" of the controller—echoing the swing from high to low, while the horizontal swing is mapped to the square button on the horizontal plane of the buttons. The jump, which starts on the ground, is mapped to the X button, the lowest button on the pad; while the shield throw is mapped to the circle button—the shape of the button icon matching that of the shield.

Some genres of games like FPS, RTS, and platformers have widely accepted control schemes. For example, the space bar, X or A button usually makes the character jump in a platformer. The more your control scheme resembles that of other successful games in the same genre, the more easily your player will embrace it.

Shoulder buttons can be found on most modern console controllers but consider the actual button size when mapping controls. For example, on an

Xbox 360 controller, the left and right shoulder buttons are physically smaller than the left and right shoulder triggers. You should assign "quick move" functions to the shoulder triggers such as shooting, braking, and acceleration or melee attacks. Why? In the heat of combat or as the player skids around a corner, the player will want to quickly respond to the situation. With the smaller shoulder button, there is a risk of the player's finger slipping off. Use these smaller buttons for "slow move" functions, such as precision aiming, looking at a map screen, or swapping inventory.

Speaking of "quick moves," I can't believe I've gone this far into the chapter without mentioning this **very important thing** about controls:

AS THE BUTTON IS PRESSED, THE ACTION SHOULD HAPPEN

Don't get me wrong, I love beautiful character animation as much as the next guy, but nothing pisses off a player faster than pressing a button and then having to wait for the gorgeous animation to finish playing. The only thing that happens quickly in these situations is the player dying due to misjudged timing or stray enemy attacks. Save the nice animation for the finish of the move. Or in other words, when the player presses jump, the game should say "how high?"

Long animation and controls do have their place, as long as there is a balance between the risk and reward. *Mark of Kri* has some very long wind-ups for attacks, but they are the most powerful attacks in the game. When you hit an enemy with one of those suckers, they aren't getting back up again. The risk is the wind-up; the reward is the high damage or instant kill.

CHARACTER OR CAMERA RELATIVE?

A common snare that game designers can get into is creating controls that alternate between being **character relative** and **camera relative**. Because of the frustration it can cause to the player, the designer needs to pick one control scheme or the other for the duration of the game and STICK WITH IT.

With a camera-relative control scheme, the controls change depending on which way the character is facing the camera. Say we are playing a survival horror game: "*Terror Zombie Death Mansion 3*", and our stalwart hero stands in a hallway.

When the player presses left on the analog stick, the character walks to the left. The room he enters has the camera pointing at our hero—in the opposite direction from the shot in the hallway[4].

[4] Tsk, tsk! Someone has "crossed the line" with their camera. Didn't you read Level 6?

Now when the character presses the stick to the left, the character walks to the right—because the controls have been mapped to how the game camera sees the character, rather than from the character's orientation. Unfortunately, thanks to the backwards controls, our hero has walked right into the arms of a zombie, who proceeds to chew out his brains.

This is why I'm not such a big fan of the camera-relative control scheme. I much prefer a character-relative control scheme. In a character-relative control scheme, the game controls are always relative to the player character. If the control stick is moved to the left, the character will always move to the left no matter where the camera is facing. The game compensates for the player's movement even if the camera turns 180 degrees around.

There's no need to get fancy with the controls ... unless you are designing for one of those new-fangled motion controllers.

SHAKE, RATTLE AND ROLL

Most modern game controllers are outfitted with **actuators** and **gyroscopes**. They are the devices that make most motion controllers like the ones found on the Wii or the PS3 possible.

An actuator gives feedback to the player in the form of vibrations. Like with control schemes, make sure the language of your actuator usage is consistent. Rather than blasting the thing off all of the time, limit it to when a player takes damage or when they earn a reward. You can have a lot of fun with actuators, if you take the time to play with them.

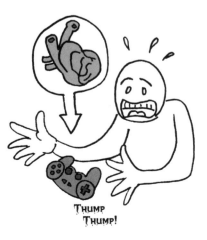

THUMP
THUMP!

My favorite use of an actuator was in *Silent Hill* (Konami, 1999). The developer figured out how to vibrate the two actuators at different frequencies to simulate a heartbeat. Whenever the character was scared or hurt, the controller's "heart" would vibrate, telling the player that they were in trouble. It was really creepy and effective.

A gyroscope allows the player to rotate the controller as another way to manipulate an on-screen element. The control applications for gyroscopes can be quite robust. I have played games that allow the player to nudge arrows while in flight (*Heavenly Sword*), maneuver falling characters (*Ratchet and Clank: Tools of Destruction*), or even flip over an entire level (*Super Mario Galaxy*).

The most important thing to remember about having the player use gyroscopes is to clearly communicate the direction they have to turn the controller in. As the gyroscope is "hidden" within the mechanism of the controller, it's easy for a player to forget that this is a control option; make sure to remind the player that this function is available.

Whatever the action, I find that players respond best when the moves match a real-world action. If you tell players to swing the controller like a sword (or a tennis racket, or a bowling ball, or a conductor's baton …) they get it. The trick is to design and tune your in-game sword to *feel* like a sword through animation and physics. Game animations with the right timing, speed and feel of friction in the world will make them feel less "floaty" and "gamey"—a feeling which is always less desirable to the player.

The fun thing about gyroscopic controls is that you can get away with silliness. No game plays with the user more than *WarioWare: Smooth Moves* (Nintendo, 2006). While there are only about 20 "moves" (and half of them are button presses) that the Wii Remote/nunchuck combo can do, the designers of *WarioWare* encourage players to hold the controller in bizarre ways to play their microgames. But it's all part of the fun; the goal is to make the user look stupid, whether it's placing the Wii Remote on your head like a Mohawk haircut or flipping it like a spatula tossing a pancake.

True motion controls are still in their infancy, especially in the home market, but here are a few things to keep in mind as we march forward into the future:

- Many players don't play video games to exercise. Unless the goal of your game is for players to lose weight, don't forget to build in breaks and changes in control motions to keep players from wearing out or suffering repetitive stress injuries.
- Always account for **lag**: the time it takes between performing an action and when it happens on screen. As most games are based on timing, nothing is more frustrating than an action not happening when the player does it. This is especially true for rhythm games like *Rock Band* and fighting games like *Street Fighter*, where lag issues can screw up the

player's timing and the game becomes too frustrating to play. *Guitar Hero* even allows the player to adjust the lag to match the player's skill level.

- An issue with on-line games is **latency**: a communication delay in the time it takes for game data to be received and decoded. Latency can cause lag or in worse cases, control lock-up, sound distortion, game freeze, or crashes. This is less of a design issue and more of a programming issue, as tightly written code prevents unnecessary transmission of data that can cause latency issues.

- Keep your player's movements broad. Precise and subtle motions tend not to register on the game cameras.

- When drawing shapes or glyphs, keep the shapes simple, like circles, triangles, and lines. Even seemingly uncomplicated shapes like figures of eight and squares can get misinterpreted by motion-detecting controllers.

- Don't overdo it. Already many motion-controlled games are getting dinged for being "**waggle-fests**", where the designers make every game action use the motion control for the sake of it. Make your game controls a mix of traditional analog stick, button press, and controller motions.

Congratulations! You've mastered the Three Cs! But how are you going to communicate these newly minted design ideas to the player? Come with me to the remarkable Level 8 …

Level 7's Universal Truths and Clever Ideas:

- Let ergonomics play a role in designing control schemes.

- Consider assigning control functions thematically.

- Consider emulating control schemes of other games in the same genre. Familiarity relieves confusion.

- As the button is pressed, the action should happen.

- Use negative responses as well as positive ones.

- Give your player a break to avoid "gamer's thumb" and other health problems (take a break yourself while you are at it).

- Camera-relative controls or character-relative controls? Pick one and stick with it.

- Avoid creating controls that are contrary to the game's visuals.

- Use the game controller's special features to make your controls more intuitive to the player.

- Beware of lag and latency issues.

- Player's movement with motion controllers should be broad and mimic reality.

LEVEL 8

SIGN LANGUAGE—HUD AND ICON DESIGN

Picture, if you will, another dimension balanced between game and the real; a dimension of sight and sound, a realm of things and ideas. No, it isn't the *Twilight Zone*, but the zone known as the **HUD**.

Named after the **heads-up display** found in modern aircraft, the HUD is the most effective way of communicating with the player. The HUD refers to any visual element that communicates information to the player. The mini-screens and icons found in a HUD are some of the best tools in a video game designer's bag of tricks. They can communicate information, emotion, even tell the player where to go and what to do. Let's look at some of the HUD elements found on an average game screen:

1. Health bar/lives
2. Targeting reticule
3. Ammunition gauge
4. Inventory
5. Score/experience
6. Radar/map
7. Context-sensitive prompt.

HEALTH BAR

A staple of action, adventure, platform, and shooter games, the **health bar** represents how close the player is to death, or having to restart for some other reason. Health bars are the most flexible of the HUD elements and come in a variety of forms and imagery depending on the game:

- Many health bars are bars "filled" with color (often red) or icons. As the player takes damage, they lose a percentage of the bar or the color empties from the icon. When the bar is gone, the player dies …

- or vice versa, you can have a damage bar. When this bar is full, the player dies.

- The health bar may represent the status of some sort of on-board defense system, as seen in the *Metroid* games.

- Health can be represented as shields. When all of your shields are gone, the last hit destroys the player, as seen in *Star Wars: X-Wing* (Lucasarts, 1993). Shields can also be represented as a numeric percentage.

- Health can be represented as a story device. In *Assassin's Creed* (EA, 2007), the health bar represents the game's narrative. Stray too far from the "correct story" and the narrator says "that's not the way it happened." Then the character is "reset" back to the proper point in the story.

- Just because a player loses health, it doesn't mean they can't get it back. If *Halo* players find cover and wait, their health bar eventually recharges back to full. This "wait for health" technique is becoming increasingly popular in action games and I think it's a pretty good compromise in lieu of a game over/death screen, which pulls the player out of the game.

- Recently, health bars have become replaced by first person style effects which are also used in third person view. In *Uncharted 2: Among Thieves* (SCEA, 2009), damage is indicated by blood smears or a red blur effect that "point" in the direction of the source of damage. Just don't obscure the player's view so much that they can't see the action.

- In *Metroid Prime* and *Batman: Arkham Asylum*, if the player is hit by an electrical attack, the screen "fritzes" for a brief moment.

- As the player takes damage in the *Call of Duty* titles as well as *Uncharted 2,* the screen darkens, accompanied by heavy breathing and a heartbeat sound effect. In *Silent Hill* the controller's actuator simulates a heartbeat as the player is dying.

TARGETING

sights can be simple or complex

A **targeting reticule** helps players locate and/or lock onto ranged targets. They can vary from as simple as the "dot" of a laser sight to a complex lock-on system that also provides target information such as health and range.

- A reticule shouldn't dominate the screen, but don't make it so small that it's hard to see.

- I have seen many reticules rendered in white, but this can make them hard to see on some surfaces and backgrounds.

- Reticules are commonly activated in a zoomed-in mode, such as a sniper's scope. Some reticules change size to allow for more precise targeting when zoomed in, as seen in *Red Faction: Guerrilla* (THQ, 2009).

- Have the reticule change color or "sharpen focus" when over a target. This gives the player a clue when to fire.

- Give your reticule some "stickiness", also known as "aim assist." When aimed at a target, make the reticule gravitate towards it, allowing for faster targeting. This works great for vehicular weapon targeting.

- Build in gameplay to your reticule. *Team Fortress 2's* zoomed-in sniper's reticule also projects a laser pointer spot. Enemy players see this spot and can make efforts to avoid being shot.

AMMO GAUGE

Whether your **ammunition gauge** displays bullets or a simple number, it will be one of the most watched gauges onscreen. As some games  sparsely distribute ammo (*Resident Evil 2*, I'm looking at you!), placing this gauge in an easy to see location is particularly important.

- If you have the screen space, display both clips and individual bullets, like in *Operation Wolf* (Taito, 1987).
- If the player has to track multiple types of ammo, such as grenades or rockets, make sure that they can be brought up with a button press (as they are in *Ratchet and Clank: Tools of Destruction*).
- I know this one seems like a no-brainer, but always display the ammo gauge of the weapon currently armed by the player.
- Even if your player's weapon has infinite shots, you can still display it to let them know what weapon is armed. (The *Metal Slug* games do this.)

INVENTORY

A staple in adventure and RPGs, **inventory** allows players to track and manipulate objects collected during the game. Keys, potions, puzzle items, and weapons are common inventory items.

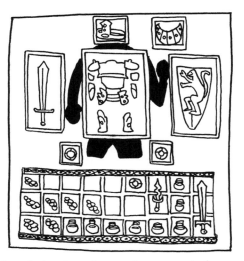

- Players need quick access to items like potions and spell components. Hotkey or drag-and-drop systems will help players grab items quickly.
- Allow the player a location to see their inventory items in all of their glory. *Tomb Raider* (Eidos, 1995) shows the items in Lara's backpack on a larger scale for easier inspection.
- *Diablo* has a limited inventory where each item has a specific size. Inventory becomes a bit of a puzzle where the player has to fit as many items as possible into a limited space.

- Inventory items can be represented either realistically or as icons. Whichever graphic style you choose, make sure that they have clear silhouettes and use simple color schemes.

- If you are going to create a restricted inventory system, allow the player to expand it later in the game. For example, start with a pouch; expand to a backpack and eventually a magic bag of infinite holding.

- Make sure the player has another permanent location in the game (like their home base) where they can store their items. No one likes losing what they found or bought.

- Why not use a "magic box" like in *Resident Evil 2*? Whatever items are stored in the box appear in boxes found further in the game. That way the player never has to run back and forth through the game world.

SCORE

 Achievement Unlocked
10G - You have reached Chapter 8

In the beginning, there was **scoring**.

Can you believe the earliest video games only had single-digit scores (*Pong* and *Computer Space*)? It quickly jumped to four (*Space Invaders*), then six (*Galaxian*), and by the time the arcade boom started in the early 1980s the high score was king. Entering your three-letter handle into a game's high score table was the sign of true mastery—provided the arcade owner didn't reset the machine and wipe it out!

As the home market grew, high score became less important and stat tracking started to replace it. Text-based **combo meters** replaced score bars in games like *Devil May Cry* (Capcom, 2001). However, with the increased popularity of online gaming **leaderboards**, scoring has returned to live harmoniously alongside combo meters, stats, and achievements.

Scoring indicators can take a variety of forms. They are still most commonly found in arcade-style games and Japanese RPGs like the *Final Fantasy* series, but scoring is starting to creep into western-developed RPGs like *Borderlands*[1] (2K Games, 2009).

Whatever form your scoring takes, make sure that when it happens, it's big and flashy. Video game developers are great at making players feel

[1] Borderlands' developers call it a RPS—a role-playing shooter—but would that qualify as picking nits?

unskilled and stupid, but bad at making them feel good. There's no such thing as overdoing it when congratulating the player. *Zack and Wiki: Quest for Barbaros' Treasure* (Capcom, 2007) does a great job of making even the worst player feel like the smartest, most skilled player in the world. Every little successful action results in a shower of fireworks, congratulatory text, and happy pirate rabbits flipping through the air! And let me tell you, nothing stokes your ego more than back-flipping bunnies!

Here are a few pointers to make your rewards feel rewarding:

- Use voice and sound effects to call attention to whenever a player gets a reward.
- Freeze gameplay to allow for the player to savor the moment of reward or have the hero celebrate along with the player with victory animations, sounds, and effects.
- You can never have too many particles, especially when celebrating an achievement or awarding a high score.
- The player needs to see a clear "cause and effect" for scoring, so they understand how they achieved their score. For example, as the player collects a gold coin in the world, the coin "travels" up to a tally. Don't forget the cool "Las Vegas-style" sound effects. Cha-ching!
- Choose an easy to read font. Ornate fonts (like medieval script) with heavy stylization or even serifs can be hard to read. Watch text length as you may run out of screen space!
- Fill up as much of the screen as possible with your celebratory effects, but don't interrupt or cover up gameplay.

RADAR/MAP

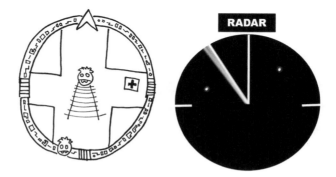

The first game **radar/map** was found in *Rally-X* (Namco, 1980), which allowed players to see the location of power-ups without seeing the game map or enemy cars. Since then, map screens have provided much more detail to players, from outlining the playfield to revealing secret clues.

- Make your map large enough to be legible, but not so big it fills up the whole screen; if you must have the map fill up the whole screen, do your player a favor and pause the gameplay.
- Make it easy for the player to move/travel and look at the map at the same time. It's too much of a chore to open a map, memorize the locations, and then close the map to return to the game. The smart designers of *GTA4* let the players add markers onto the map, which lead the player right to the objective!
- Create a legend for your map's icons so the player can easily identify and find checkpoints, doorways, quest items, traversal goals, or story points.
- Be sure to indicate changes in elevation on your map if you have them in your game world. It's too easy for players to get confused when dealing with levels with multiple elevations. Use a color code or an "onion-skin" effect to show what layer the player is currently on.
- Show the player's direction using an arrow or some other icon. This way the player will know if they have to reorientate themselves in relationship to goals.
- The **fog of war** is when a map is obscured until the player actually "clears the fog" from an area by moving through it. You can always give your players ways to expose the whole map. Avoid refogging areas as the player will get confused and turned around on the very thing that is supposed to help them navigate.
- Add other information to your map to aid the player. *Batman: Arkham Asylum* provides a distance-to-goal counter while the *Metal Gear* series shows the "detection cone" of enemy guards. *Harry Potter and the Order of the Phoenix* (EA, 2007) displays the names of NPCs on the "Marauder's Map."
- Incorporate visual themes into your mini-map. Fantasy maps look good on parchment, use a high-tech holographic display for a sci-fi game, and so on. Even the map can add to the game's gestalt.

CONTEXT-SENSITIVE PROMPT

The **context-sensitive prompt** is an icon or text that appears when the player is next to an object or character with which it interacts. The most common context-sensitive prompt displays the icon of the button or control that the player has to use to have the event happen. For example, in *Grand Theft Auto 3*, an icon of the "Y" button appears whenever the player stands next to a car they can hijack.

In *Maximo: Ghosts to Glory*, we created a variation of context prompts called "**plings**": emoticons that told the player when they couldn't do an action as well as when they could. Need ideas for when to use these guys? Here's a short list of suggested uses for context prompts:

- Doors, gates, and/or hatches.
- Mechanics such as cranks, levers, and pushable objects.
- NPCs: not only for talking anymore, you can use plings and emoticons to show their emotional state. Catch them in a good mood and you'll get a better response/reward than if they're angry, scared, or sad.
- Items and weapons that can be collected by the player.
- Use of vehicle or minigame. There are numerous games that allow the player to man a machine gun turret during the middle of regular gameplay.
- Jump locations: *The Legend of Zelda* games do this.
- Quick time event prompts, as seen in the *God of War* series: a preset sequence of events that progress if you press the right button (see the quick time event section further on in this chapter).
- Combat notification: icons that show when an enemy is vulnerable to a certain type of attack.
- Secret treasure items: have your icon appear when the player is close to a hidden item.

In addition, there are HUD elements that are self-explanatory, like fuel gauges, speedometers, and countdown timers. Just like the others mentioned above, keeping it clear, clean, and simple is the winning formula for making a successful HUD system.

THE CLEAN SCREEN

Ah reality. It's a double-edged sword. You want your game to look like a ... dare I say ... *cinematic* experience ... but you still need to communicate gameplay and controls to your player. What to do, what to do?

Well, the first step in keeping your screen clear is to make your HUD elements move or fade off screen while they are inactive. Of course, they need to reappear whenever they are valid (such as when the player is taking damage or collecting treasure) and always make sure that the player has a quick and easy way to bring them back up if they need to know the information. A simple shoulder button press usually does the trick.

Some games strive to remove HUD elements altogether. Peter Jackson's *King Kong: The Official Game of the Movie* (Ubisoft, 2005) utilized a few prompts at the beginning of the game, but mostly conveyed game information via sound, animation, and visual effects. The result made for a very cinematic and immersive experience. If you want to go this route, here are some suggestions:

- Have characters react to things in the world to indicate function or interaction. Have them look at collectable items, reach for places they can get to, comment on things in the world that they are supposed to interact with, and so on.
- Opt for full-screen-sized effects over smaller or subtle ones. It never hurts to overemphasize. Use whatever you can to get your point across—sound, voice, visual effects, color, and lighting.
- Use glows or other attention-drawing effects on items to make them stand out. Or use what I call the "Scooby Doo effect[2]."
- Use cinematic characters to lead your players through the world. If you don't want to do that much work, have a big ol' glowey arrow or path markers show the way.

If video game interfaces were a galaxy of planets and on one side of the galaxy was the planet "No Interface" then all the way on the other side of the galaxy would be the planet "Gobs of Interface." I might add that both of these are very dumb names for planets, I mean what do the inhabitants of these planets call themselves? "No Interfacians?" or "Goblings?" But I digress … This is where the RPGs, RTSs, simulations, adventure games, and some slumming shooters all live. Hello there friendly life forms of planet Gobs of Interface; let's examine your interesting markings and plumage.

ICON HAS CHEEZBURGER[3]?

---

[2] The "Scooby Doo effect" is named after a by-product seen in Hanna Barbara cartoons of the late 1960s and 1970s. While the background image of the cartoon is beautifully painted, the animated elements (such as a character or prop) are more flatly colored (usually lacking shading), making them unintentionally stand out against the more detailed background.
[3] Yeah I know, that was a really really bad pun. Sorry.

The first thing you'll notice on many RTS and adventure games is that there are a lot of **icons** on screen. Icons for tracking stats; icons for weapons; icons for magic spells; icons for the contents of bags of holding and whatnot. I believe part of the allure of these icon-heavy games is that the player makes lots of choices, has lots of things to build and collect. That's OK—not every game needs to be like one made by Oscar winner Peter Jackson[4].

So as you are making icons for your game, here are 157[5] things to think about.

- Pick the right image for your icon. If pressing your icon builds tanks, then guess what picture should be on the icon[6]?
- Make sure the image that you use is current and accurate. I was working with a team who had an icon for a stamp function (like an ink stamp) that looked like a postage stamp. Many of the younger testers didn't even know what a postage stamp was!
- Color-code your icons. Fiery punch? Make it red! (Or at least orange.) Chilling hand of frost? I'll give you one guess (blue). You can take color coding one step further and make the image or background of the icon a representative color. For example, all the icons that advance the player to the next screen could be green, and your sword combat icons could all have a red background or feature that color in the artwork (make sure it's a different shade of red than the one you are using for fire attacks!). The goal is for the player to understand similarities between icons and be able to choose the correct one at a glance.
- If color isn't enough, then use shapes as a differentiator.
- Try and avoid text in your icons. Not only will you have to change them for localization, but they may be too small to read.
- If you are going to use text (like a word) as an icon, make sure it is legible and looks more like a button than straight text.
- Never, ever combine several visual elements (like text and a character and a logo) on one icon.
- Surround your icon with a strong black or white outline to make them "pop" off the background.
- Look at all of your icons together to make sure you aren't creating any similar-looking ones. Try to make each of them as individual as possible.
- A good trick is to have text of an item's name (spell or whatever) appear if the player moves their cursor over the icon. A reminder from time to time never hurts!

---

[4] In 2004 for The Lord of the Rings: Return of the King. He did that HUD-less King Kong game too. Weren't you paying attention?
[5] Give or take 150 or so.
[6] I can't believe you are actually looking down here for an answer!

- Don't leave creating icons to the programmers. They only care about the functionality, not the design or the art.
- Learn from the experts. Apple, Adobe, and Microsoft have dedicated icon artists that create clear and clever icons for their software and operating systems. You can find great graphic design books and font sets that incorporate icons. Games that use lots of icons like RTSs and sims are great sources of inspiration. When we were making Maximo's ability icons we were inspired by the designs on Boy Scout merit badges. Icons can be found everywhere, don't feel you have to reinvent the wheel.
- When the player selects the icon make it do SOMETHING. Change color, make a clicky sound effect—anything to register user interaction. I would avoid using a voice effect though, as no one wants to hear "Good choice, commander!" every time they press a button. If you need voice, then only repeat it once every three or so clicks. And make sure to record a few extra voice cues to avoid repetition. So, to make this clearer[7], think of it this way: click no. 1, "Yes sir!"; click no. 2, "Right away!"; click no. 3, "I'm on it!"; click no. 4, "Yes sir!"; click no. 5, "Right away! … you get the idea.
- The most important button on the interface should be the biggest. This goes for the most-used button as well.
- Make the most-used buttons easy to reach from the middle of the screen or wherever the player's cursor will spend the most time.
- Make your icons a little "sticky" so the cursor will easily gravitate towards the buttons.

Ultimately, the rule of thumb when creating icons is:

KYSS = KEEP YOUR SYMBOLS SIMPLE[8]

Today's audiences are very familiar with icons, from comics and cartoons[9] to the desktop of their computer, so take advantage of it! Over the years, video games have developed their own vocabulary of icons. Here are a few classic examples:

[7] Or possibly to make this understandable at all.

[8] That's Your with an "I".

[9] Icons in comics and cartoons? Sure! From stars and tweeting birds over Daffy Duck's head to Pow! bursts when Batman throws a punch, to scratchy marks over Charlie Brown's head to show that he's mad to those swirly circular "rootbeer-ootles" coming out of Opus the penguin to show that he's tanked on A&W, you can find icons all over comics and cartoons.

- Red cross: used to designate healing items[10].
- 1 Up: universal video game-ese for an extra life. Also the head or little "doll" version of the character works well for this.
- Heart: can be used as a replacement for red cross or 1 up.
- Food/soda can/pills: energy or healing. As in "Elf needs food badly[11]."
- Exclamation point: put one above enemies' heads to show surprise. Put it above your hero's head to show they can interact with something.

- "No" symbol: which means that the player cannot use or does not need this. Also used for busting ghosts.
- Skull: poison, death, danger. And sometimes pirates.
- Coin: money, gelt, dough-rey-mi. Howabout a nice big sack o' cash lusted after by bank robbers?
- Controller icons: used as a shorthand to prompt the player to press the specific control for a specific action. You find these a lot in quick time events, which we'll come to next. And here we are!

DON'T GET QTE

Quick, press the button!

Now press it again. Too late! You died. Congratulations. You have just lost the first book-based **quick time event**.

A quick time event, or **QTE**, is a prompt that forces the player to make a split-second action or suffer usually painful or fatal consequences.

---

[10] The Canadian Red Cross has contacted game developers about using the red-colored cross image in "violent video games." The organization interprets the use of the image as a misuse of their trademark. The video game industry as a whole has not officially addressed their complaint.

[11] I wonder what game has "Elf needs pills badly"?

Dragon's Lair (Cinematronics, 1983) first featured QTE gameplay—hell, the entire game is a quick time event—but after a brief spurt of similar arcade games (*Cliffhanger, Space Ace, Thayer's Quest*) QTEs almost went the way of the text adventure. *Shenmue* (Sega, 1999) brought them back and christened them QTEs at the same time. They've become a gameplay staple since *Resident Evil 4* and *God of War* made them popular.

Players either love or hate QTEs, but they are here to stay. There's no need to hate them though; they're just one more gameplay tool in a designer's tool kit. The trick is to use them responsibly:

- Never use a QTE for something the player can do for themselves in the game. I prefer to use them as shortcuts to cinematic sequences. Save QTEs for big exciting moments and nigh-impossible actions.
- Timing is everything. Give the player a "beat" to process the appearance of a QTE icon and another "beat" to press the appropriate button.
- Don't string them out for too long; as most QTEs need to be repeated if the player fails the sequence, there is nothing worse than having to repeat the QTE over and over and over again.
- There's something worse than repeating a QTE, and that's a QTE that doesn't play fair. While random QTE icons sound like a good way to introduce variety, this is the one time you want predictability in your game. Once the player memorizes the pattern, they can concentrate on watching the cool actions. Now I know what you are saying. "Wait a second! There are video games with random QTEs in them." And I'd say "You are correct." However, I just don't like them. They make the player feel like they won because they were lucky, not by their own skill.
- Keep your QTE controls to a single set of controls. Most games use the buttons or sometimes a stick. Try not to use the harder-to-reach shoulder buttons.
- Make sure the QTE icons are big and easy to see. Keep their placement consistent: don't move them around.
- Try not making the QTE mandatory. Both *Uncharted 2* and *Batman: Arkham Asylum* offer QTEs as options for dispatching enemies, however, if the player misses that opportunity they still have plenty of other ways to take the bad guys out.

- When using motion-controlled QTEs, keep the waggling short. And if you are going to make them waggle the controller, don't do it too many times in a row. Gamers want to play your game, not get wrist injuries.

HUDS, AND WHERE TO STICK 'EM

Now that you have created a whole mess of beautiful icons, what are you going to do with 'em? Why slap 'em up onto the screen, of course! But before you are going to display them willy-nilly, let's see where they can go. Our zombie friend is going to help us out with this one.

This part of the screen is sometimes known as the "safe frame" because screen objects almost never get obscured out here in the middle. Since the middle of the screen is where the action is, please refrain from putting your HUD there. (Unless it's for targeting, a reticule, or id'ing game objects.) If you have to bring up a full-screen display, consider making it translucent like the holographic screen in *Dead Space* (EA, 2008). This way, the player doesn't get disjointed from their environment and "lose their place" in the game world.

The upper left side of the screen is traditionally used for the most important information: health, score, and so on. As the (westerner's[12]) eye travels from left to right when reading information, putting icons to the left so the eye can travel back "into" the game on the right usually feels pretty good to the player.

[12] While many Asian and Middle Eastern languages read right to left, I can't think of a single video game that displays information on the screen in this way.

Displaying icons along the bottom of the screen works well too, as long as you watch out for **clipping** that can occur if a player is using a monitor or TV screen that isn't calibrated for your game. Assume at least 50% of your audience has a crappy television set; heck, even gamers with excellent HD LCD rear projection sets still can get clipped images on the sides of their screen. Get that information as close to the safe frame as possible (and always offer screen calibration options).

If you are going to use the right, left, and bottom of the screen, be careful of the "bracketing effect" that happens—this will make your game screen seem smaller and claustrophobic. I've seen some RTS screens so filled with HUD elements, it felt like I was looking out of a mail slot!

If you are going to have lots of icons on screen, why not consider letting the player choose which ones they want and prioritize where they should go. This way, the player can choose what they feel are the most important icons for them. Just make sure you don't give them the option to obstruct the main gameplay field.

Some icons open up other screens, like inventory lists. Make sure the player has a quick way to get back to the game. You may want to consider allowing the player to pause the game so he/she doesn't get bushwhacked by an enemy while they are trying to find their +6 rod of killing. Of course, you could be like the designers of *Dead Space* and intentionally allow enemies to attack while your character is rooting around in their holographic space backpack for another air canister. According to interviews with the team, this was an intentional choice: they wanted the player to not be able to rely on the "gamey" mechanic of the world freezing (as happens in, say, *Resident Evil*) while looking for inventory items. It really conveys the sense of dread as necromorphs are bearing down on you when you realize that you just don't have time for a break.

When you are dealing with interface, there is one **very important rule** I never, ever try to break. Pencils out?

YOU SHOULD NEVER HAVE TO PRESS A BUTTON MORE THAN THREE TIMES TO REACH ANY GAME SCREEN

Why? Because the player doesn't want to spend the entire game pressing buttons to reach interface and inventory screens! They want to play the game! Let them play the game! Why aren't you letting them play the game? Think of the children! Oh, the humanity!

Sorry. Lost it there for a moment.

Seriously, don't make the players dig to find the options and get to the gameplay. Make everything in the game reachable within a button press or two. Consolidate screens if you have to. On one game I worked on, it took 16 button presses just to reach the game play. After some thought and re-conjiggering, we managed to get it down to four button presses. Not too shabby if I do say so myself.

THERE ARE OTHER SCREENS THAN THE HUD

Oh, video game screens. There are so many of you. Where to start? With a list of course!

- **Title/start screen.** The first thing your player sees (other than the box cover[13]), so it's important to set the right mood. The problem is, there are so many styles to choose from! Let's see:

---

[13]OK, technically, the player also sees a warning screen, a publisher logo, a developer logo, and the logos of the companies of any technologies leased by the development team, but starting with those wouldn't make for a very exciting list, would it? Stop making me get ahead of myself!

- The "movie poster" title screen that mirrors the cover of the box.

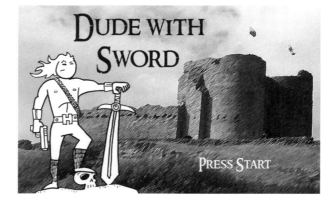

- The "heroic pose" title screen where the hero is standing on some high bluff, long hair blowing in the breeze, giant sword and/or gun at the ready …

- Why am I in a jungle? What is that monkey statue doing there? Is it a relic I will be raiding? These are all questions brought up by the "enigmatic image." The image is something important to the game, but the player has no idea because they haven't played the game yet. When they finally learn the significance, their minds will be blown!

- The "logo" screen, where a large image of the game's logo is displayed. Not very exciting, but effective. Make it more exciting with strobing colors, rotating effects, bouncing text, anything to get some motion in there.

Title screens often feature menus that offer selections such as save/load, number of players, options, bonus features, and difficulty. It all depends on how many button presses you want the player to make before they get into the meat of the game; however, I find that players just want to get to the good stuff so keep the button pressing to a minimum (no more than three screens "deep" right?, not counting your front-end logos and legal). And remember, you can always put many of the start/title screen functions on your pause screen.

THE PAUSE THAT REFRESHES

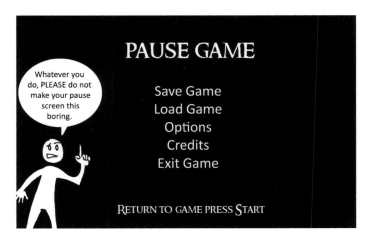

Pause. The well-designed pause screen can do more than give the player a break. It can be used to save a game, access the options screen, game map or inventory screen, or even exist to be enjoyed as with *Banjo-Kazooie's* (Nintendo, 1998) lovely acoustic version of the theme. Whatever you do, just make sure that the player doesn't feel like they are missing any of the game by pausing. Remember, most people use pause screens to take bathroom breaks. Of course, you can always skip the pause screen altogether like in *Dead Space*, but God knows when you'd get a chance to take a whizz.

When designers create pause screens, they have this bad habit of making the first choice "resume" and the next one down something like "options." Usually the map and save game is a few more choices down. This makes no sense to me. Let's say you use the start button to bring up the pause screen. Think of all the times you are going to have to press the start button, then d-pad down the list to the "save game" selection, and then save the game and then return back up to the resume button? Why not use the start button to close it again? Why do you even *need* the resume option? If the save button is the most common selection the player will be making, then make it the first thing they can select. If it isn't, make it the map or the inventory. Plan your pause screen out as carefully as you do your level! Your players will thank you for it.

Wow. Look at that graphic below. Those are all the options that can stem from a pause screen.

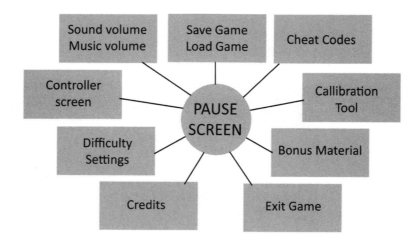

Options. Like the ancient labyrinth, the option screen usually leads to more screens. But don't lose your player in a maze of choices. Think of the option screen as a hub, with the choices the spokes that radiate from it. Sound and music volume controls, controller settings, difficulty settings, and even bonus and cheat codes can be placed under the options heading.

Calibration tool. If your game is particularly moody and dark in theme and visuals, then I suggest having a screen calibration tool. A calibration tool allows the player to adjust the screen's contrast on a dark-colored image or set of color bars. While it's fine for this to live in the options screen, I prefer to have the player adjust it before starting the game, to see the game in the best light … er darkness possible.

Save/load game. One of the most important aspects of your game, keep it simple and automate the process whenever possible. Always start a new game with creating a new save file. Don't make the player hunt around for this and make sure they quickly pick up on where it is—even in the tutorial if possible.

I highly recommend allowing for several (at least three) save files. Players often restart new games after completion, want back-up files in case they make catastrophic choices during gameplay, or even just to let someone else concurrently play the game.

Customization goes a long way when creating a save file. Let the player name their own files. Store playtime, titles of game levels or chapters, and even inventory items like lives or gear to help the player remember their progress. Show icons or images to help jog the player's memory further. Everything helps.

Autosave is a useful function that acts as a backup if players are too engrossed in playing. Give the player the option to load a game from a saved file or the autosave. You can always give the player the option to turn autosave off, though I'll be damned why you'd want to.

Be careful when designing the save system that it doesn't become a "reset system." There have been many games where it is easier and faster for the player to reload a game than to die and start again. Don't let the player use the save system as a gameplay mechanic, as it breaks the immersion of the play experience.

Just a few ways to hide a load...

abnormally long corridors   very slowly unlocking doors   microwaving popcorn

Loading screen. Many players consider loading screens as a necessary annoyance, but that's just because developers fail to treat them as part of the game. More recent games strive for a "seamless" loading-screen-free experience by disguising the loading screen with slowly opening doors, long elevator rides, or dissipating fog. If you must have loading screens, here are a dozen ways to spruce them up:

- Show concept art
- Ask trivia questions
- Have a playable minigame[14]
- Display the game map
- Display a character bio
- Provide tips on gameplay or control (though be careful not to repeat these—even the most useful tip becomes annoying after several viewings, so don't display control tips that the player has already seen)

[14]Unless you work for Namco, you may want to avoid this one as they own the US patent (#5,718,632).

- Fill in gaps in the game story
- Play a short video briefing the player on the upcoming mission or location
- Have the player fight endless waves of enemies or destroy a large object
- Provide "beauty shots" of your character or items in the game
- Have the player manipulate an interactive object like the game's logo or an item.

Hardware manufacturers require that there be some moving image on a loading screen so the player knows that the game hasn't crashed. No matter what your loading screen displays, you should provide a progress bar or percentage loaded indicator so the player knows how long they have to wait.

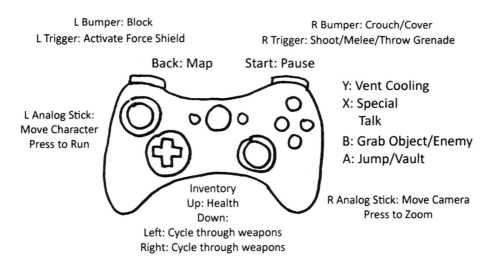

Controls. When showing the control screen, first and foremost, you need to display an image of the game controller as shown in the above image.

Some games show the character that performs an action when you press the appropriate button. At the very least, display text explaining the control.

Make sure this screen is easily accessible from the game for quick player reference. Also, consider allowing the player to customize the controls or at least give them several options to remap controls schemes.

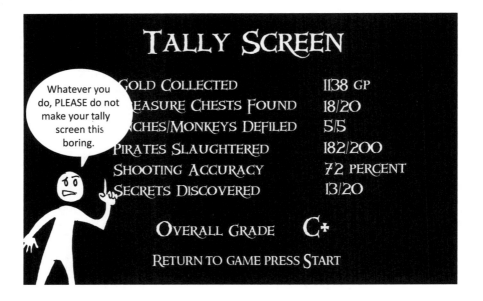

Scoring/stats. Otherwise known as a "Tally Screen", this screen appears at the end of a level. It displays the player's progress and performance in the game. You can tally just about anything on a tally screen. Here are just a few:

- Score
- Time of completion
- Accuracy of shooting
- Enemies slain
- Money remaining/collected/spent
- Number of lives
- Rating (can be an A, B, C grade or a "word" rating, like "Awesome dude" or "Master of the Universe")
- Objectives reached/completed
- Secrets found (usually expressed as a X/Y value)
- Gallons of blood spilled/distance travelled/chests smashed ... you get the idea.

Legal/copyright. These screens are required by publishers and hardware manufacturers. Make sure that they are legible and more importantly, accurate. And for Thor's sake, make them skippable.

Credits. Allow me to pull out my soapbox for a moment. People work very hard on games. Too many people in the video game industry get screwed out of the credit they deserve due to egos, politics, and old-fashioned neglect. I am a firm believer that if you work on a game, you should get a credit. That credit should be what is on the person's business card. Sadly, it doesn't always happen that way: it's something in the gaming industry that needs to change.

Regardless, credit screens are an important part of the game. They are a celebration of the people who made and contributed to the final game. They deserve to be seen, but they should be as entertaining as possible. Some games get it—*LittleBigPlanet* for example has an amazingly entertaining credit sequence. *Typing of the Dead* (Sega, 2000) has a playable minigame where the player can type the credits! It's simple:

GIVE CREDIT WHERE CREDIT IS DUE (AND NEVER, EVER BE BORING).

If you want to find more inspiration for great looking screens, take a look at most movie DVDs. DVD designers do a great job at creating a **gestalt**[15] built around the film. This level of attention to detail takes a lot of time and effort on behalf of the art director and designers, but it's always worth it[16].

There are other screens that fall under this category as well, such as the **game over**, **bonus materials**, and **store** screens. Don't worry; I'll be covering these screens in greater depth later in the book.

A FINAL WORD ON FONTS

As you make HUD and display screens, you are going to need to think about fonts. I find that fonts follow many of the same rules as icons when it comes to legibility and clarity. However, they do present some of their own issues:

- Theme your font to your game, but don't use overly ornate fonts that are hard to read.
- Be mindful of the color of your font and your background. For example, never place red text over a black background, as it usually blurs on many TVs, particularly older ones or ones where the console is hooked up on composite cables.

---

[15] Die Gestalt is the German word for "whole." In the context of games, it applies to the overall feel of an experience.
[16] Some excellent examples of gestalt in games include Twisted Metal Black (SCEA, 2001), Brütal Legend (EA, 2009), and House of the Dead: Overkill (Sega, 2009).

- With the rise of HDTVs, developers can display higher resolution fonts. However, I have found that any font size under 18 point is very hard to read on a standard definition television. Remember that not every player has a state-of-the-art screen[17]!

Remember, the goal of all of these screens is to communicate clearly and efficiently to the player. Now let's move on to the good stuff: the game itself! But first, the obligatory Universal Truths and Clever ideas section …

Level 8's Universal Truths and Clever Ideas:

- The HUD communicates game concepts to the player.

- The player should be able to access the HUD information quickly.

- Keep HUD elements away from the sides of the screen and closer to the safe frame.

- Design easy-to-see and read icons.

- Make QTEs fair and easy to perform.

- You should never have to press a button more than three times to reach anything in the game.

- Don't make the player dig through screens for important information.

- Fonts should be easy to read: don't make them too small or too fancy.

- Even the most "boring" screens can be exciting and interesting.

- Give credit where credit is due.

---

[17] The text displayed in Dead Rising (Capcom, 2006) was so small that players couldn't read mission objectives—rendering the game unplayable to those with standard definition sets.

LEVEL 9

EVERYTHING I LEARNED ABOUT LEVEL DESIGN, I LEARNED FROM LEVEL 9

You can't expect a book called *Level Up!* not to have a chapter on level design. But what do I mean by **level**? Much like the word **score**[1], its definition changes when used in different contexts. Observe:

Level: an environment or location where game play occurs. "If you are on the Death Star level then you are near the end of the game."

And

Level: a term favored by developers that describes how to break up physical space based on a specific gameplay experience. "I must have died a dozen times on the mine cart level."

And

Level: a unit of counting the player's progression, especially, when repetitive gameplay is involved. "I'm up to level 20 on *Tetris*."

And

Level: the rank of a player based on their earned score, experience, or skills. A term for marking character progression and improvement as in: "I finally leveled up my third *WoW* character to 70." The most common use of level in this context can be found in RPGs.

---

[1] Score: (1) To gain something (as in "I scored a battle axe off that weapon drop"), (2) to calculate a total (as when a high score is tallied), (3) to cut without cutting all the way through (like scoring metal with a lightsaber), (4) to "get lucky" with a ... but hey, this isn't a dictionary.

A possible explanation for **level** having four definitions in the video game industry is that video game developers have extremely limited vocabularies.

Another reason for the multiple definitions is that developers have used the term "level" in different contexts for so long that it's too late to get everyone to agree to call it something else like a **floobit** or a **placenheimer**. So level it is. But why level? Most ancient game designers believe that the term came from *Dungeons and Dragons*, when players would travel down many dungeon levels (like floors of a building) to reach the dragon. (Hence the title of the game.) Why no one thought to call it "floors" is beyond me.

In fact, to complicate things further, there are many times a level isn't even called a level. I've played games with rounds, waves, stages, acts, chapters, maps, and worlds in place of where I would use the term level, but even these have their specific definitions. Let's review:

Rounds can be found in games where you play the same action, if not similar gameplay, over and over again. It can be used for sports games like a round of golf or boxing where the activity is the same, or there can be variation in the gameplay like rounds of *Peggle* or *Diner Dash*.

Waves usually refers to combat, as in "wave after wave of enemies assaulted the stalwart heroes!" Pretty exciting stuff, but you are still doing the same thing—beating[2] the crap out of bad guys. Whole games can be

---

[2] And by beating, I mean punching, stabbing, shooting, karate-chopping, decapitating, rocketing, and exploding.

made of waves of enemies like in *Plants vs. Zombies* and *Defend my Castle*, or it can be a sequence of play like those found in *Gears of War 2* or *Uncharted 2*[3].

Stage is usually interchangeable with the term wave, but it's often used when describing an experience that has clear separations that relate to the activity—much like the separate stages of a rocket[4]. Stage is often used when referring to the actions of a boss enemy. We'll talk more about this later in the dreaded Level 13.

Acts and **chapters** are often used when the developer wants the player to concentrate on the story of the game. These titles make a game feel classier. They're not fooling anyone; they're really just game levels.

Levels are often referred to as **maps** or by the location of the environment (like "Power Plant" or "Insane Asylum"). This is most common in FPSs, where players associate the location with a style or method of gameplay.

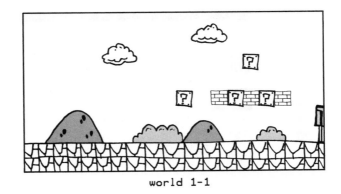

world 1-1

The term **world** is often confused with level, but I blame this on its origin. World was first used in *Super Mario Bros.* with the famous "World 1-1." The game was extremely successful and the term became immediately embraced by developers. However, by my own definition, World 1-1 should actually be called Level 1-1. And here's why:

World: a video game location that is distinguished primarily by its visual or genre theme and may be comprised of multiple locations that share this theme.

---

[3] It can be in any action game, not just ones with "2" at the end of their names.
[4] Remember, these terms were first created and used by early game creators: the same guys that made up your high school rocket club. Sorry cool kids, the nerds have taken over the world.

In early video games, players would refer to the levels as worlds; as in "Fire World", "Ice World", and so on. However, as the home market demanded longer play experiences and developers wisely learned to create multiple levels using the same texture sets and/or mechanics, worlds gained additional sequences—most famously seen in *Super Mario Bros.*'s World 1-1. However, World 1-1 is just the first of four levels of the first world[5]. There needed to be a term to define these separate sections of play, hence the term level.

Because there have been so many game worlds over the years, some of them have become hoary clichés. Most developers run screaming from these, but they still have their uses. I therefore present to you:

THE TOP 10 CLICHÉ VIDEO GAME THEMES

1. **Outer space.** One can easily see how a black television screen may have served as inspiration to early game developers as the perfect stand-in for outer space. Brightly displayed vector-drawn stars looked great on those early CRT screens. Player-controlled spaceships meant no animations. Spaceships could be rendered in simple geometric shapes. Gameplay could be based primarily on physics: an important advantage to those early programmers during the days prior to game designers and artists. As the earliest game genre—the shooter— evolved, outer space continued to be a popular locale for video game battles to be waged. Outer space also allows for all the tropes of sci-fi:

---

[5]World 1-1 is grassland, 1-2 is an underground cavern, 1-3 are mountain-like platforms, and 1-4 is the interior of a castle. These levels are all part of a world known as the Mushroom Kingdom. And now you know.

aliens, spaceships, computers, and futuristic weapons. All things beloved by the geeky game developer community.

2.   **Fire/ice.** These levels swiftly became popular for three reasons: first, fire and ice levels created hazards that were easy to program—flames and low friction surfaces. These hazardous terrains created perfect timing puzzles that caused the players to "break their rhythm", making the level more challenging. Secondly, fire and ice environments lent themselves towards a wide array of deadly inhabitants, from lava men and flame-breathing dragons to snowmen both of the abominable and frosty varieties. And third, fire and ice levels added color (red and blue) to the palette of gameplay worlds, especially important to distinguish screenshots on the back of home console boxes in those early 8-bit days. Today, fire and ice levels are camouflaged as snow-bound train wrecks and lava-filled temples, but as long as the color, feel and mechanics are represented, they'll always be fire and ice levels to me.

3. **Dungeon/cavern/tomb.** The connections between *Dungeons and Dragons* and Tolkien's *Middle Earth* run strong and deep in the DNA of video game developers. Dungeons are laden with traps to avoid, puzzles to solve, and mechanics to circumvent. Dungeons offer up waves of enemies (without a whiff of explanation as to why they live there) and of course, there was always lots of collectable treasure to be gleaned. Even when the game world isn't themed to medieval fantasy, players still thrill in raiding uncharted dusty tombs. Technically, dungeon locations offer game artists many advantages: great opportunities for dramatic lighting, and intricate carvings and statues. Even in the early days of gaming, cave wall textures were made from easily repeatable (or "tiled") art.

4. **Factory.** Factory levels became a staple of platform games, especially as the platform game genre exploded on home gaming systems. The dynamic mechanics offer game developers easily created, combined, and repurposed hazards that can be tuned to a wide variety of difficulty levels. These adaptable factory mechanics quickly spread to other locations too: moving platforms, conveyer belts, and turning gears were present in the tombs, circuses, and space stations of just about every action and platform game[6].

---

[6] I consider it a triumph of the video game industry that Star Wars creator George Lucas, at the last minute, added a factory level to his 2002 movie Attack of the Clones. The movie's heroes ride conveyer belts and make timed jumps through smashing presses worthy of a sequence right out of a Nintendo platformer.

5. **Jungle.** The jungle theme allows video game designers the flexibility of the dungeon but without the dull colors and right angles. With its exotic traps (like quicksand and pongee knife-lined pits) and exotic creatures (such as crocodiles, snakes and scorpions) set in a colorful outdoor environment, jungle levels quickly became a prevalent video game level theme as game art became a focus. Jungle levels lend themselves to robust mechanics: swinging vines, tree branch platforms from which to leap, and rivers with moving logs à la *Frogger* that keep a player's heart beating like a jungle drum.

6. **Spooky/haunted house/graveyard.** Spooky environments are great when your game requires mood and story. Players slowly explore creepy environments, punctuated by unsuspected "scares" in the form of play mechanics or enemies that seemingly spring out of nowhere. But scaring people is an art; you must build pacing into your levels.

Allow moments of quiet, followed by moments of distraction, before you scare your player. Music and sound design are critical to the spooky theme; it goes hand-in-hand with encounter and puzzle design. But be careful you don't tip your hand too much. You can easily give away your scares if you don't choreograph things correctly. After years of making haunted houses in my garage, I find the best scare is one the player expects but doesn't know where it's coming from.

The spooky theme is also the most adaptable theme of the video game tropes. There have been spooky adventures, platformers, RPGs, FPSs, and even puzzle games. Everything's more fun when it's scary!

7. **Pirate (ship/town/island).** The spiritual brother to the spooky level is the pirate level[7]. The pirate theme is perfect for high action gameplay, melee combat and of course, lots and lots of treasure. Many pirate levels capitalize on the pirate's natural form of transportation: the pirate ship. And then there are the pirate skeletons. Who doesn't love these guys? Like the spooky theme, the pirate theme is treated as a "catch all" that can be applied to almost any genre of game to increase its sales.

[7] The only reason I can fathom why pirate and spooky levels are often found in the same game is the designer's love for Disneyland where the "Pirates of the Caribbean" and "Haunted Mansion" attractions are found in the park's "world" of New Orleans Square. I know that's the reason why we had them in Pac-Man World.

8. **Gritty urban.** No matter if it's populated by criminals, punks, mutants or supervillains, the gritty urban theme allows for fantastic action in a realistic and relatable setting. That relatability is part of the genre's appeal. Artistically, it's easier for artists to create the world outside their door. Densely detailed environments just keep looking better and better as system processors and game polygon counts rise. While it's ironic that players would want to play in a world that mirrors the one right outside their door, they get a choice that most people never do: to improve or destroy it.

9. **Space station.** The space station has become the stand-in for the dungeon in sci-fi games (especially in the FPS and survival horror

genres), all strongly influenced by the 1986 film *Aliens*. In video games, most space station halls are infested with horrible aliens and malfunctioning robots. The space station theme lends itself to a variety of tech-based mechanics including laser-based force fields and factory-style moving platforms. Space stations allow the art team to show off when creating spectacular visual effects, whether it is holographic computer displays or stunning starscapes.

10. **Sewer.** While you could eat off the floor of Mario Bros.'s sewer, video game sewers got more disgusting as game graphics improved. This modern analog for the fantasy dungeon[8] grew more complex and deadly with hazards ranging from giant rats and albino alligators to fetid water that caused instant death upon immersion. You can also find the harmonious addition of factory-level mechanics in sewers, such as whirling ventilation fans and sinking platforms to challenge players. Just be glad that smell-o-vision never caught on.

Just because the above themes are considered clichés it doesn't mean that they are unusable. To give them a twist, just apply the **Mexican pizza** technique.

Back in the 1990s Taco Bell introduced the "Mexican pizza": a pizza-shaped snack made with Mexican food fixings. To me, it sounded vaguely disgusting. However, curiosity got the better of me and I tried it. It wasn't bad. But what I learned was that you can combine two things you wouldn't think go together to get something surprisingly good and, more importantly, completely original.

---

[8] Didja know that early D&D players would play live-action sessions in sewer and drainage systems? The forerunner to today's live-action roleplaying (or LARPing).

While designing *Maximo: Ghosts to Glory*, we applied the Mexican pizza technique. Instead of just a graveyard, our graveyard was cracked apart by volcanic eruptions that blasted out gouts of fire. A fire graveyard, if you will. We also made a pirate level that was enshrouded in ice—you get the idea. We took hoary level themes and breathed new life into them simply by combining them with each other.

THE NAME GAME

Now that you have your level's theme, give it a name. However, a level always has two names: one for the programming team and one for the player. The level name is a file name, created to be referenced with the game's code. Here are a few things to remember when creating file names:

*   Keep it to eight characters max as (a) it's easy for team members to remember and (b) takes up less space in the code.
*   File names aren't the name that the player sees, so you don't have to be witty. For example, "factory 01" succinctly lets your team members know the most important info: location and order.
*   For more complex titles, use abbreviated text: for example, fac01s01 would stand for "factory 1, section 01."
*   Make sure your naming conventions don't overlap. If "sec" stands for section in one area, don't use it for "secret" in another.
*   Organize your levels. Keep files in folders where it is easy for other team members to find them. Use file-sharing software to make sure changes aren't made without the other team members knowing about them.

In the context of the game, the level's name is a different matter. Just like with naming characters it's important to give your level the right name: one that fits its feel. There are a few schools of thought to naming levels:

*   **Functional.** A straight-up number system is a hallmark of retro gaming. It cuts to the chase and gives the player an idea of progress. However, as most players aren't exposed to the highest number in advance there's no way for them to accurately track overall progress. Another disadvantage to functional naming is that it lacks personality.
*   **Location.** Police station. Sewer. Science lab. What's good about using the location names is that you immediately get an idea of what the

player will be seeing and/or encountering. However, these expectations are based on the player's knowledge: something that may not match what you are going for. Using the right words is important when naming a location.

- **Descriptive.** "A nasty surprise", "on the road again", "death from above." Descriptive level names read more like chapters of a book. This is great for providing foreshadowing or tone. Be careful not to tip your hand too much and ruin any surprises your plot or level may hold. Or you can be tricksy like the *Dead Space* designers and have the first word in every level spell out a secret message!
- **Punny.** If you are feeling particularly creative, then try writing a punny title for your game level. Punny titles were all the rage in the late 1990s, starting with *Crash Bandicoot*. Usually you want to reserve this type of naming for games with a sense of humor.

Remember, level names are your level's first impression so put your best foot forward!

EVERYTHING I LEARNED ABOUT LEVEL DESIGN, I LEARNED FROM DISNEYLAND

↑
The world is the best narrator.
Ken Levine[9]
↑

I believe that it is within a game's level where the story should actually be told. Using space to tell a story isn't a new concept; it's been used in architectural design for centuries. When I first started designing game levels, I found that theme parks held the answers to many of my questions on how to tell a story as well as inform the player. I pored over theme park maps[10] and studied how they were laid out. I found that theme parks are designed to move guests from one adventure to the next in the most effective way possible, much like a well-designed game level.

---

[9] Ken Levine was the creative director of Bioshock, a highly rated FPS whose fully realized undersea world of Rapture has become the gold standard for level design.

[10] I used to love to collect theme park brochures during family road trips to other more educational destinations; souvenirs of places I never actually visited. Who knew they'd come in so useful in the future!

Disneyland, in particular, proved to be a source of great inspiration. I read about Walt Disney's imagineers and how they went about designing their own world. Walt Disney had a deep love of miniature railroads and Disneyland was structured around a train track. The imagineers needed something to fill in the middle of the track, so five "lands" were created, each inspired by Disney's passions: history, progress, nature, his animated movies, and nostalgia for his childhood hometown. These became Frontierland, Tomorrowland, Adventureland, Fantasyland, and Main Street.

The imagineers filled these lands with attractions; themed adventures that allowed guests to "ride the Disney movies." These attractions were built as storytelling experiences within a physical space, and detailed attention was given to each scene as the guest passed through it.

I noticed that the creation and structure of Disneyland bore a strong resemblance to creating and structuring a video game world. The basic progression of creation is this:

Disneyland: *world* to *land* to *attraction* to *scene*.

Video game: *world* to *level* to *experience* to *moment-to-moment gameplay*.

The world of Disneyland contains many lands. Within each themed land are attractions, each with their own story. The "story" of the attraction is composed of scenes.

The world of the video game contains many levels, each with their own part of the story. Within each themed level are experiences to move the player through the level. Connecting these experiences is the moment-to-moment gameplay which keeps the player engaged.

This notion of working from the "top down" helped me approach a game world and determine what the confines are and what lives within it; to determine that, you need to make a **game world map**.

Some designers really got into creating their world map and loved to share it with the player. A common pack-in with early computer games were lovingly rendered maps printed on parchment, cloth, and even faux leather. But you don't need to create anything so fancy. Your world map can be something as simple as a flow chart created in Visio. It only needs to chart out where the player is going and what he'll find there. A map can also define the spatial relationships of locations in the world: this can help the designer determine how the player is going to get around and in what order.

The game world map is important not only to help your team understand the connection of all the levels to one another, but offers the player several advantages as well.

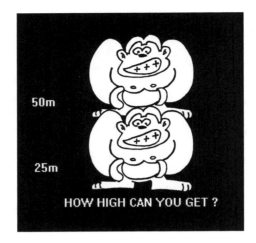

One of the earliest arcade games to expose the player to a map of sorts was *Donkey Kong*. It was a simple graphic of several Donkey Kongs stacked on top of one another with the challenge "how high can you get?" Challenging the player and letting them know ahead of time how many levels they have to climb in order to win the game whets the player's appetite. It gives them a goal to work toward.

The next great advance in mapping came with the arcade game *Ghosts 'n' Goblins*. Before starting play, a map was displayed with a little icon of the player at his current location. "You are here." The camera then panned over the entire world, teasing the player with everything that was to come. I remember seeing this and thinking "I wonder what's in that ice level at the far end of the map?"

Even if your characters don't physically travel anywhere in your game, you can still use a map to show progression. The fighting game *Mortal Kombat* displays a screen full of characters' headshots, with most of them "locked up" at the beginning of the game. But by showing all the locked windows, the game's map provides foreshadowing that there will be many characters that the player will eventually fight. As more opponents are unlocked, the player is then compelled to "collect them all."

Foreshadowing is a powerful tool to get a player excited about the activities and dangers found in a level. Building anticipation is just as important as delivering on it. In all my years of making haunted houses, I've found that a scare is bigger and better if the victim knows it's coming. It's waiting for the scare to happen that drives them nuts.

You can use lighting, sound effects, and geometry to make a level look foreboding. And remember, nothing says "beware" like skulls and skeletons strewn around an environment. You can never have too many skeletons[11].

---

[11]While I believe that you can never have too many skeletons, I think it is possible to go overboard with filth and gore. Some horror games levels are splattered with blood and grime. Maybe it's just me, but I never find these environments scary. What is scary is a befouled bathroom—but what makes it so scary is the smell and that you may have to touch something: two senses that are completely absent from a video gamer's "vocabulary." And by the way, having a room decorated with corpses strung up like Christmas ornaments doesn't make it particularly scary. It just looks ... festive.

Another lesson I learned from Disneyland is to provide foreshadowing with **posters**. The guest passes by posters advertising attractions as they enter the park. While the guests don't understand the significance of the images they're seeing, the posters provide foreshadowing to future adventures. In games, one of the best use of posters is in *Bioshock* when the player, first entering Rapture, sees posters advertising the superpower-giving plasmids. Only once the player learns about plasmids and what they can do, is their significance understood.

Much like a game map, the level itself should help transport the player through the level from story point to story point. The always eloquent imagineers of Disneyland describe it this way:

⬆ *When we began designing Disneyland, we looked at it just as we do a motion picture. We had to tell a story, or in this case, a series of stories. In filmmaking, we develop a logical flow of events or scenes that will take our audience from point to point through a story. If I were to 'leapfrog' from Scene One to Scene Three, leaving out Scene Two, it would be like sending the entire audience out to the lobby for popcorn in the middle of the film[12].* ⬆

Disneyland's attractions tell four different stories to their guests. I have found these stories have parallels with the player's goals within a video game level:

- Escape/survive
- Explore
- Educate
- Moral.

With the **escape/survive** goal the player has to survive being in a place they have no business being in; whether it's a ghost-infested manor or a crazy factory where one misstep means being ground up into cat food. Storytelling is shown through **action** and **location** which moves the player along quickly, using gameplay centered on movement and combat.

---

[12] Disneyland The First Quarter Century, Walt Disney Productions, 1979.

The **explore** goal allows the player to discover the story at their own pace. The island village in *The Legend of Zelda: The Wind Waker* and city of Megaton in *Fallout 3* let the player explore the environment and create the story in their own order. **Freedom of mobility** and **conversation** are important storytelling tools when exploring is the player's goal.

While there are many *educational* games, the **educate** goal has yet to make the full transition into entertainment games. Educational games carry a stigma that they are only for younger or "non-gamer" audiences. There are exceptions. *Assassin's Creed 2* exposes players to the history and characters of the Italian Renaissance. The developers of *Guitar Hero* promise their next title will teach players how to actually play a real guitar. Emphasize **observation** and **imitation** when determining the player's goals and gameplay.

Examples of a **moral** goal can be found in many of Disneyland's attractions. Mr. Toad's Wild Ride's moral message is: "drive like an idiot and you'll crash and go to hell." Quite a statement for the happiest place on Earth! Games like *Star Wars: the Force Unleashed* and *Fable 2* that allow the player to experience a "good" or "bad" endings have been around for a while, but such moral cause-and-effect rarely exists within the game's levels. Well, except for *Bioshock*. An early level is a horror show that warns the player of the dangers of using plasmids; ironically, the very thing you are injecting into yourself to give you superpowers. Use **choice** and **consequence** to deliver your level's moral goal and then make those choices impact gameplay.

In addition to these goals you need to ask "what is the player's objective in this level?" Some levels exist to teach a specific gameplay move such as jumping, combat, driving, or how to play the game. Answering this question will guide and focus how you design the player's moment-to-moment gameplay within the level.

THE BEAT CHART

Now look at all the useful tools you have to help you: character, character actions, story, level themes, a world map. These are all you need to build an entire universe! In order to help organize my thoughts, I like to create a **beat chart**. A beat chart is a tool often used by Hollywood writers and directors to help organize and plan their movie's production. At the very least, your beat chart should contain the following information:

- Level name
- File name
- Player's objective
- Story beat
- Play style
- Enemies

- Mechanics
- NPCs
- Bonus materials
- Time of day
- Color mapping

Creating a beat chart helps the designer determine gaps and clumping in your game. You can reorganize the game elements to spread things out and make the game feel more organic. Let's pretend we are making a game called *Relic Raider*. Our hero, Jake Hunter, travels the globe looking for lost treasure. We've developed our story and have brainstormed the gameplay and the game's environments and enemies.

Take a look at this sample beat chart and see if you spot any problems:

Relic Raider beat chart

Game Element	Level Name/File Name				
	Shanghai/ Roof01	Jungle 01/ Jung01	Jungle 02/ Jung02	Temple of the hidden skulls/ Jung03	Mountain Escape!/ Road01
Location	Shanghai rooftops	Jungle	Jungle	Ancient temple (int)	Mountain pass
Gameplay	Stealth, shooting, jumping	Shooting	Fighting	Platform, jumping	Driving
Objective	Find crime boss Wu-Fan	Jungle part 1	Jungle part 2	Reach chamber of skulls	Car chase
Story beat	Jake steals medallion, is caught by Wu-Fan	Jake explores jungle	Jake finds temple of skulls	Jake places medallion in statue, Nazi general Hauser shows up	Jake steals truck, flees Nazis
New weapon	.45, machine gun	Machete	No	No	No
Enemies	Tong thug, axe man, machine gunner	Jaguar, native (spear)	Jaguar	Jaguar, Nazi soldier	Nazi truck, Jeep w/ machine gun
Mechanics	Swinging rope, zip line	Swinging rope, zip line	Zip line	Spiked pits, blow darts, crushing walls, fall-away floor	Falling rocks
NPC	Wu-Fan	Guide	None	Hauser	None
Bonus materials	Art gallery 1	Art gallery 2	Art gallery 3	Alt. costume	Art gallery 4
Time of day	Night	Night	Night	Day	Day
Color mapping	Blue/red	Green/ brown	Green/ brown	Green/gray	Tan/sky blue

Did you spot all of the issues the beat chart exposed?

- Level naming is inconsistent. Rather than have generic titles like "jungle 01" find a way to give them more descriptive names like "temple of the hidden skulls."

- Roof01 and Road01 could be mistaken for each other. Name the Shanghai level "Shang01"; the more distinct, the better.

- Since Jung03 doesn't seem like it shares too many assets, I would call it "temp01" to show that it's a different place than the other jungle levels.
- Do you need two jungle levels back to back? Perhaps the activities in Jung01 and Jung02 would be better combined to make one improved jungle level?
- The driving seems to get introduced a little late in the game. Before that seems to be four "on-foot" levels. Find a way to bring the driving in sooner, or lose a walking level.
- While the other levels are very specific, the jungle objectives seem unfocused. Give the player more of a purpose.
- Introduction of weapons seems to ramp up quickly and peter out fast. That's a warning sign that you need more interesting things for the player to do and toys for the player to use.
- The enemies are clumped up at the beginning of the game. Enemy AI could be repurposed for more effective use. Jungle 02, while listed as a fighting level, doesn't seem to have any enemies that would work well with fighting.
- Repurpose mechanics like you would enemies. There are a lot of unique mechanics in the temple that will take time and effort to create. Can any of these be re-used in other ways?
- Art galleries are a pretty basic reward. What other bonuses can you give the player rather than just the same thing over and over again?
- There are three night levels in a row. Break some of this up with morning, evening, atmospheric effects like rain or snow, and so on. And the interior of a temple is going to be dark, so it doesn't make a difference if it's day.
- There's a lot of green in that color map. Make sure that the visuals offer a more diverse palette, otherwise all the levels are going to feel the same.

Just by spending a few hours creating and observing the patterns created by a beat chart, we were able to make significant improvements to production, gameplay and art before we built a single asset!

RE-USING RE-USE

While looking at the above beat chart, I noticed that there are several different gameplay systems: platforming, shooting, driving, and stealth. These different systems add diversity to a game, but when it comes to creating them they have nothing to do with each other. One of the most important design decisions you can make is how and when to re-use gameplay systems over the course of the game.

If you use a game system less than three times over the course of the game, then it's not worth having. This doesn't mean that you have to have the same gameplay section over and over again—you can be smart with your art assets and repurpose them.

For example, a vehicle system can support a jeep, a hatchback, and a sedan. Creating the vehicle system costs more time and money than it does to build the three different cars. But remember, there is only so far you can stretch your recycling: the same system we use for our cars can't support a hovercraft or motorcycle. Although they are both ground vehicles, they behave quite differently.

There is always a trade-off between design and programming. Learn the limitations of the game system and craft your game accordingly. Create a small number of gameplay systems that you can re-use over and over again throughout your game. This will maximize your game as well as your schedule and budget. Use the limitations to your advantage. If you need examples, take a look at any game created by the Japanese developer Treasure Co. Ltd (*Gunstar Heroes, Dynamite Heady, Ikaruga*) who really knows how to milk a small palette of mechanics. When you are creating your beat chart, make sure you don't use the same gameplay systems back to back. Unless your game is specifically a driving game, don't follow a driving level with more driving.

You can work with your artists on how to best re-use art assets as well. Simply re-coloring and re-texturing game items will make them look different from level to level.

THE GARY GYGAX[13] MEMORIAL MAPPING SECTION

There are many ways to start building level maps. The designers of the original *Metal Gear* built their levels out of Lego blocks. Many developers do rapid level prototyping in 3-D tools like Maya or 3D Studio Max. One designer I know liked to model his levels in clay. Myself, I like a ream of blank paper, a very sharp #2 pencil and an eraser. I like making maps on paper because it reminds me of the good old days of creating *Dungeons and Dragon* levels.

---

[13] Ernest Gary Gygax (1938–2008) along with David "Dave" Arnenson (1947–2009), created the first role-playing fantasy game, Dungeons and Dragons. Creating dungeons and adventures for D&D served as the springboard for many a young game designer's career, myself included.

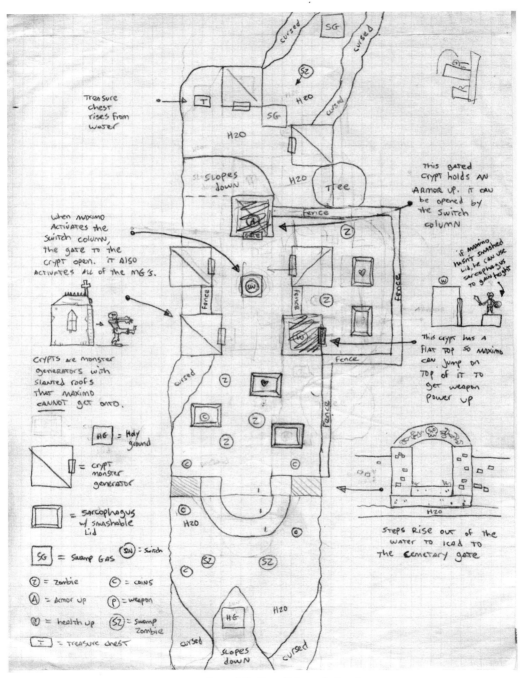

An example of "alley" level design

I have found that there are two types of three-dimensional video game level design: **alleys** and **islands**.

Alleys create a directed gameplay experience; the player has a goal to reach and the level is built to help them reach it. Your alley can be narrow like those found in *Portal* or it can be wider to give the illusion of freedom and space, as seen in *Call of Duty: Modern Warfare 2*.

Alleys offer the following advantages to designers:

- It's easier to place camera trigger zones when you know where and how the player will be entering and moving through the level.
- You can get dramatic with your camera movements to inform the player, or enhance the action and drama.
- You can remove the camera controls from the game, allowing the player to concentrate on gameplay.
- You can create scripted, triggered gameplay events, since you know where the player is looking.
- It's easier to choreograph combat and other gameplay events like traps.
- Bottlenecks can be created to prevent backtracking.
- The designer can use illusional narrative to tell the level's story.

The island level, in my opinion, is a bit more challenging to design and build. The game camera has to be flexible enough to accommodate a wide variety of widths and elevations. Scripted events are tough to execute, as there's no guarantee that the player will be looking in the right direction. Combat encounters can be completely circumnavigated by players. Even stagecraft-style tricks like façades are useless, as level geometry can be viewed and interacted with from all directions.

Despite these limitations, island level design offers expansive space that allows the player the freedom to choose the order in which they want to experience the gameplay. *Mario 64* is one of the earliest examples of island level design in which the player could choose to climb mountains, explore hills, or swim into underwater grottos in any order they liked. Islands allow for unparallel freedom for the player. In fact, an entire genre—the **sandbox**—has emerged as island level designs have grown bigger and bigger. *Grand Theft Auto 4, Burnout Paradise*, and *Halo*'s multiplayer levels are just huge island playgrounds.

When creating these sandbox worlds, you should divide them up into distinct areas to aid the player's navigation and orientation, much like the "lands" of Disneyland. Disneyland goes through great pains to make each land visually distinct. Take Frontierland: It has everything you would expect in the old west; watering troughs, wooden cigar-store Indians, wagons,

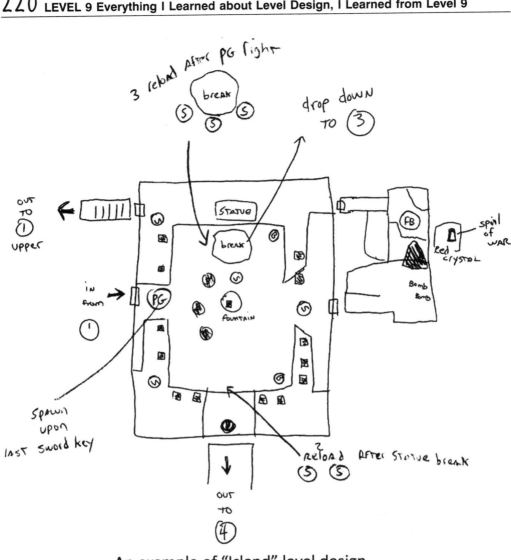

An example of "Island" level design

cactus, and even those old video game standbys: crates and barrels. (Frontierland's main thoroughfare was originally dirt road until guests complained about dusty pants and shoes.) Disneyland even themes the trashcans! For example, Frontierland's trashcans are painted to look like wood, while Tomorrowland's are futuristic silver. You always know where you are even when throwing out the trash.

The game *Crackdown* uses this technique throughout their sandbox world of Pacific City. Not only is each zone themed to aid navigation, but the themes match the criminal gang that the player has to overthrow. The Shai-Gen Corporation runs Chinatown while the tech-using Volk inhabit gleaming skyscrapers.

Disneyland's imagineers pioneered these types of architectural landmarks like Sleeping Beauty's castle, the Matterhorn and Space Mountain, which they call **weenies**[14]. Weenies are used to get the interest of guests and draw them in their direction. Weenies don't have to be giant castles or mountains. They can be interesting architectural elements like statues, bridges and buildings, or even natural elements like a distinct tree or rock. Theoretically, you want to string your weenies along your path to keep the player moving from one to the next. When creating 3-D maps, make sure the path is clearly marked with weenies. I once created a map that looked like this:

Top View

[14] Walt Disney himself coined the term after the frankfurter that off-screen animal trainers would wave at their dog actors to get them to walk past the camera to where they wanted them to go.

When I play tested this part of the level, players would travel down the road, see the path leading behind the house, and walk around the back of the house looking for treasure. When they emerged onto the road, they turned around and walked back down the way they came!

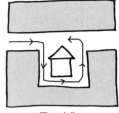

Top View

I realized that the area needed a landmark (marked on the map) so when the player came out they were able to re-orient themselves.

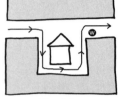

Top View

This brings up to an important truth about designing games: the player will ALWAYS find a way to break your game, whether they are doing it intentionally or not. Tackle this head-on by making the player play the game the way YOU want it to be played, but provide plenty of help to show them the way.

Islands work particularly well for multiplayer games as you can accommodate many different styles of playing. Do you like to sneak around the back of the map? Islands provide a back to sneak around. You can still charge up the front if you want, or you can camp over on that hill and snipe to your heart's content[15].

But like ebony and ivory, alleys and islands can live together in perfect harmony. Islands can still have alley-like sections. *Red Faction Guerrilla* and *Team Fortress 2* have interior spaces that feel like alley level designs, but their freedom of approach and wide perimeter edges mark them as islands. *Uncharted 2: Among Thieves* alternates between using alleys and islands frequently. *Darksiders* and the *Maximo* games use alleys for their dungeon levels and islands for their hubs and battle arenas. Whether to use island or alley all depends on the gameplay.

Islands have the following advantages:

- They give an extraordinary feeling of space and scale. It's quite an experience the first time you realize a level goes on and on.

[15] Not that anyone reading this book would stoop so low as to be a camper. And remember, there is a special place in hell for spawn campers.

- Islands promote exploration, and encourage designers to fill in "in-between spaces" with secrets, additional missions, and objectives.
- Gameplay options are laid out in front of the player like a smorgasbord.
- Vehicle gameplay (like racing and car combat) feels better in wide-open spaces than in tight alleys.

Sandboxes are tricky things because I have found that no matter what a player tells you, a world where the player can choose to do anything at anytime can be intimidating and confusing. Despite the freedom that the sandbox world promises the player, they should still get some prompting on what to do next even if they don't want to do it. There's a reason why your annoying cousin is always calling you in *Grand Theft Auto 4*.

THE DAVE ARNENSON MEMORIAL MAPPING SECTION

Let's get cracking and get our game design down on paper with a map.

When creating a map, you first must determine a scale. When drawing a **top-down view map** on graph paper, the size of the player usually equals one square. All other elements, such as treasure, mechanics, enemies or objects, are drawn in relation to the size of the player—much like how you determine player metrics. Represent these elements as icons on your map. Create a legend for the icons on your map so readers can determine what they are looking at. You will want to include:

- Player's starting point
- Enemy starting locations
- Doors, teleporters, gates
- Puzzle mechanics (like levers and switches)
- Treasure chests and power-ups
- Traps, and their areas of effect
- Significant landmarks (like statues, pools, pits, and so on).

I start my level map creation process by roughing out the major locations where I want big events to happen: a treasure chamber, a battle arena, a puzzle room, a mechanic that you want the player to learn, a spectacular view, and so on. Then I start to think about what I can use to connect those rooms together: hallways, mazes, chasms, or passages. Then I usually move on to graph paper, which helps me communicate the scale of the level to the level artist. Often I will draw in elements such as the tombstones, crypts, mechanics, and enemies.

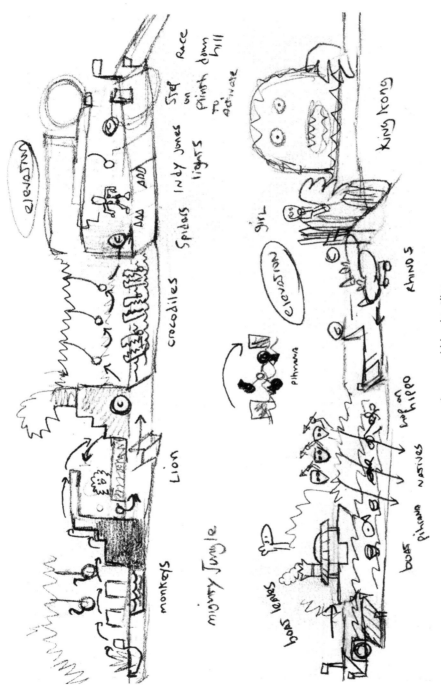

a (very rough) level outline

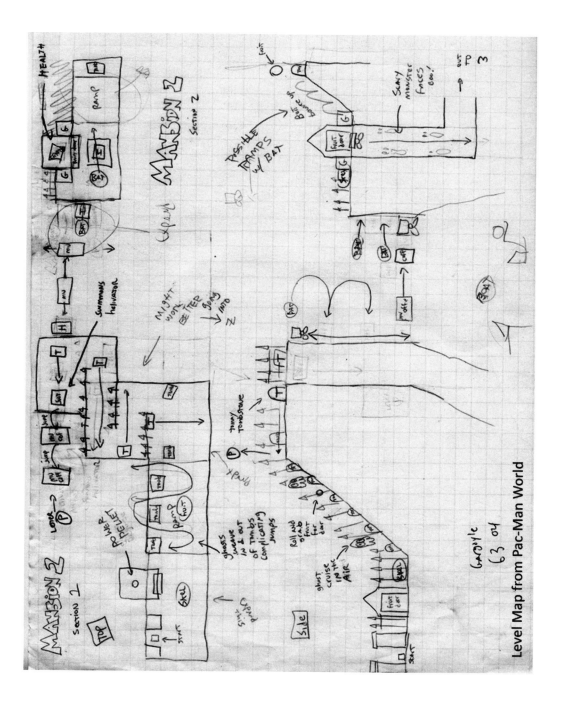

Level Map from Pac-Man World

When creating passages for a top-down view map for a 3-D level, I recommend making it five squares wide: that's the width of the player plus two more widths on either side. It provides enough room for the player to navigate, for combat to occur, and the camera to have some room to maneuver. However, I can guarantee that your first few efforts at level design will usually end up too small and too cramped, so don't be afraid to be generous with your proportions.

Use geometry and lighting to help move the player down the path. Players are drawn towards light, while they tend to avoid or overlook dark places. You can use shapes like diagonal lines to draw the player's eye in a specific direction. I learned my favorite trick from the designers at Naughty Dog, the creators of the *Crash Bandicoot* and *Uncharted* games. They use a trick they call the **squint test**. Take a look at the image below and squint your eyes until they are almost closed.

What's the brightest thing on the screen? The main path. You can do the same thing in your game using color and lighting. Even if the player doesn't consciously notice this, they will still be able to see which way to go. If the player has someplace to go, don't waste their time with needless wandering. Never intentionally try to get the player lost. Instead, find ways for them to get quickly to the main objective. A good trick is to talk your way through a level design. Describe to someone else what the player will be doing. If you ever find yourself saying "then the player walks over to here", cut that section out of your game. Because a **very important thing** is:

WALKING IS NEVER, EVER GAMEPLAY!

Only **lazy designers** consider walking to be gameplay. You're not a lazy designer, are you? Of course you aren't. You are an **active designer**. An active designer who creates active things for your active character to do. Actively.

Prevent the player from walking for too long. Look at all the other things the player could be doing instead of walking.

- Jumping
- Fighting
- Collecting
- Climbing
- Swimming

- Swinging
- Flying
- Escaping
- Sneaking
- Exploring

Speaking of exploring, let's talk about multiple paths. Which one to take? The one that leads to the harem of 1000 delights or the one that leads to the lava pits of Overfiend? Decisions, decisions.

No matter how you slice it, multiple paths are a tricky thing to deal with, regardless of whether you are designing an alley or an island. They work better for some genres of games than others. The wide-open worlds found in FPSs, RPGs, and driving games require multiple paths just to keep traversal from getting boring.

But multiple paths raise multiple questions that need to be addressed: Which path will the player choose? What can you do to entice a player to go down one path over another? What can the designer do to promote the player to use that alternate path? Hidden power-ups or cash prizes? Provide an achievement for all secrets discovered? Some producers balk at the idea of designing and building a part of the level that the player may never see. Whatever the answer you decide on, make sure that it provides something significant to your level.

Some designers don't like **backtracking**, when a player has to go back to a part of the level they've already been to. I don't mind it. I think it's a good way to get the most out of your level. I like to use backtracking for puzzles. I always say "show the player the door first and then let them find the key." Just don't make the player go back and forth too many times. If you need to make the player go to a location more than twice, do something to it to make it different: add gameplay like (new) combat or collectibles, change the topography by having an earthquake change a flat spot into jumpable hills. A nice natural (or unnatural) disaster can work wonders.

Conversely, you should design alternate ways for your player to get around your level and game world. These are unlocked as the player exposes more of the world. Anything is preferable to having to plod through the same terrain over and over again. Give the player a car or a horse to get through those slow spots, let them ride a train or get a lift in a zeppelin, or, if your fiction supports it, there's always the ever-popular teleporter.

Just be aware that traveling in vehicles can really chew up the real estate. You'll want to build that space into your levels. But it's a double-edged sword. Don't make the experience last too long, especially if it's something you will be doing often. Just remember the **very important thing** when it comes to traveling through levels:

IF IT EVER FEELS LONG OR BORING, THEN IT IS

Avoid boring levels! But how? Variety is one way. **Fingers** are another way of making a world feel deeper and fuller without having to build lots of complex geometry and multiple paths that the player may never take. Picture a linear path.

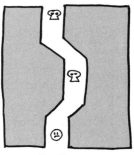

Top View

Not too exciting, huh? You can place all type of hazards and enemies along the way to make things challenging for the player, but it's just going to feel like a straight path even if you crinkle it up and bend it around.

However, if you start to add fingers off of your path, little dead ends for the player to explore and go down, it makes the player feel like they are exploring the level and not just promenading down it. It expands the life of your level and you can promote the player exploring it. Let's take a look at our level now that we've added a few fingers off of the main path:

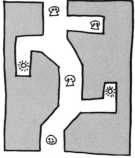

Top View

Now you have interesting places for the player to explore as they work their way through a level. While I wouldn't suggest putting something down a finger that is important to the critical path, you can place whatever you want down a finger: combat, treasure, bonus materials, or just something visual or fun. Remember this simple yet **very important thing**:

**EVERY FINGER SHOULD HAVE A REWARD AT THE END,
EVEN IF IT'S JUST A TRASHCAN**[16]

WRAPPING UP MAPPING

Creating elevations on a top-down view map can be a bit tricky. You can draw levels in different colors, but I find that gets visually crowded. Use tracing paper or paper and a light board to layer the elevations of your level, and break them up by the height of the player. Be sure to clearly mark which elevations are what so viewers can read them in the correct order. While you are at it, number the consecutive map pages or tape them together into one big map so they are easier to read. Just because a sheet of paper is square doesn't mean you have to design to a square shape. Cut, fold, extend—do whatever you have to do to make your map accurately represent your design.

If you are drawing your map from the side view, determine the height of your character first and then draw the map to scale. It's a lot easier to show vertical gameplay from a side view. Sometimes you are going to need a combination of side and top view maps.

You don't need to be working on a game with an isometric camera to use an isometric map. They're a little trickier to draw, and they require some artistic skill to create, but they work great for showing things like elevation.

---

[16] Whether that trashcan has trash or treasure in it is up to you.

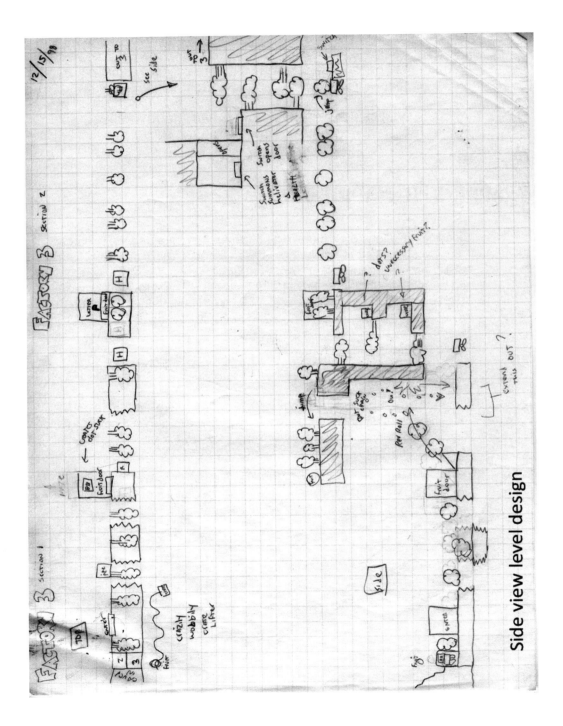

Side view level design

Isometric level design

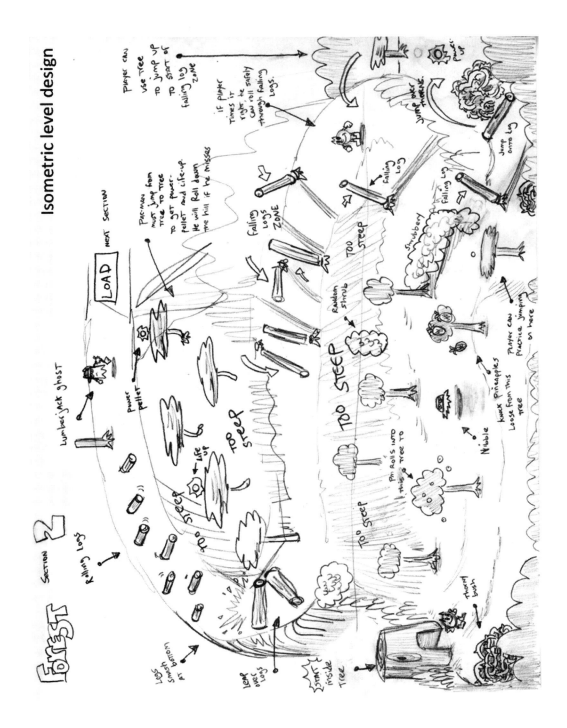

Isometric maps work best when representing games using a 2.5-D camera. If you need to show depth or a part of the level that is obscured by geometry on your map, you can show the missing information using a cutaway or X-ray view. Or you can create a flap that can be lifted by the viewer to see what lies underneath. Make as many layers as you need to convey your idea for your level. Some of my levels have had so many panels, they started to look like an advent calendar!

Other information to include on your level design maps:

- Enemy spawn locations and detection/aggro radius.
- "Bread crumb" collectibles (like coins or *Pac-Man* dots) that lead the player through the level.
- Secret entrances/breakable walls or other concealed locations.
- Obstacles and barriers like walls, trees, tombstones, and so on.
- Be sure to clearly mark specific terrain like cursed earth, swampy water, slippery ice, and hot lava.

ILLUSIONAL NARRATIVE

Illusional narrative is a storytelling trick I first observed when riding the Peter Pan's Flight attraction at Disneyland. Having flown over London and to Never-Land, we have reached the part where Peter Pan and Captain Hook are engaged in a pitched sword duel on the deck of the pirate ship. The Darling children have been captured by the pirate crew and watch the battle.

The guest's ship flies around a corner (cleverly disguised as the sail of the pirate ship) and now. Peter Pan is victorious, the Darlings are freed, and Captain Hook is keeping himself from being eaten by the crocodile.

Illusional narrative is the video game equivalent of what happens in the gutter of comic book panels or between edits in a movie: the player fills in story when given two or more images or environments. With the proper transition and presentation, you could convince a player that a train has crashed, a world has become overrun by aliens, or a character has crossed a room without animating a single element. The cost to production is significant. Real-time animations take time to produce and have to be ripped up and redone if the designer decides to change something in the level.

Just make sure that the elements are viewed in the order of your story, and use gating mechanisms such as bottlenecks, camera views, checkpoints, turning elements on and off, or even plain ol' doors to keep the player from "turning back the page."

GRAY MATTERS

Armed with your level maps, you are now ready to start building (or have an artist start building) your game levels. But hold on there, tiger! Before you even start thinking about enemies, mechanics or even detailed geometry, you will have to flesh out your level in **gray box** form.

A **gray box level** is created within an art tool (Maya and 3D Studio Max are the two most common industry art tools, though others exist). The gray box level shows the scale, size, and relationship of basic elements pertaining to camera and character metrics. It is pivotal in determining scale, camera, and pacing. Spend time running your game character around the gray box level. Have others play the level to find confusing areas and trouble spots. Iterate on your level while it's still easy to make big sweeping changes. You may find that a level works better if you rip out an entire section and stitch the remaining pieces together. A straight hallway may be more thrilling with plenty of twists and turns to transform "boring old" enemies, mechanics, and treasure into unexpected surprises.

As you are building your level, you might be wondering how long should a level be? Early in the production process, you should **pace out** a level to determine its overall length. Start your character at the beginning of your gray box level, then start walking. Don't worry about hazards or combat or collecting every music note in the level. Just walk from the start to the finish. Whatever time it took for you to get from point A to point B is roughly half the time it will take you in the final game. So if you need your levels to average a half-hour each, then it should take 15 minutes to pace out the level. While it seems weird to do this, remember that many publishers and reviewers are concerned with the overall length of a game. I tell developers that a single-player action game should last at least 8 to 10 hours. Going longer than that is great; just make sure your production schedule and team plans for it.

Another pacing technique is to change the player's emotion every 15 to 20 minutes. Sadly, the gamut of emotions experienced in most video games is pretty limited[17], but you can make a player go from mystery to fear to panic to wonder using geometry alone.

---

[17] I would go as far as to say that most video games let the player experience only five emotions: aggression, fear, surprise, joy, and disappointment. And some games only disappoint.

Divide your gameplay between "big moments" and "small moments." Don't stack too many big moments next to each other—you'll wear your player out. Conversely, small moments of calm and quiet will only feel boring if there are too many of them in a row. *Shadow of the Colossus* successfully balances the big moments of battling giant monsters and quiet moments of traveling through the expansive game world.

Time of day and weather can be used to emphasize events and elements in your level. How would the player traverse the level if it were covered in snow or took place during a blizzard? How would a fairy village look differently if it were set at night? Make sure that any weather effects extend to the player character, the mechanics, the enemies, and other elements in the level. If one element isn't affected by the weather, it will ruin the entire effect. Give your game levels a variety of atmospheric effects and times of day to keep things interesting.

Variety should be applied to the level geometry as well as to gameplay. Alternating interior and exterior spaces keeps your level from feeling like too much of the same physical space. You don't have to alternate the spaces in between every room but break it up according to what feels natural. Players usually feel safer in large spaces. Tighter spaces feel more mysterious and dangerous. Be mindful of your camera placement throughout your level design. Allow enough room in tight spaces for the

player and camera to move around or just resort to a fixed or rail camera. When staging combat, larger spaces allow you to throw bigger and larger groups of bad guys in, while narrower spaces work better for one-on-one battles.

Verticality is very important when designing levels. Alternating elevation makes an environment feel natural, provides much-needed variety, and allows designers to set up "Kodak moments" of any impressive visuals like statues, vistas, and horizons. As a player walks or climbs up, they feel like they are making progress and heading towards a goal.

However, as a player travels downwards, they may try to skip elevations by jumping downwards. If the player can be killed by very long drops, make sure that the player has a way to look down to gauge the metrics of the drop. There's nothing more annoying than falling to your death if it looks like you can safely make the drop. If you don't want the player to drop down, then corral them in the direction you want them to travel with switchbacks, ladders, or other climbable surfaces.

My golden rule of level design is this **very important thing**:

IF IT LOOKS LIKE THE PLAYER CAN GO THERE, THEN THEY SHOULD BE ABLE TO

Establish a visual language within your level to establish where the player can and cannot go. Use low walls, shrubbery, or rock walls to indicate impassable areas in the level to the player. They will learn that these visual cues mean "you can't go there." Whatever you do, please don't be a lazy designer and use **invisible walls**.

Nothing breaks immersion faster and makes a level feel less like a real place than smacking headlong into a big fat wall of nothing.

Want to screw with your player's head? Have your character travel from right to left, particularly if you are making a 2-D game. Western audiences are used to reading and viewing information in a left to right orientation. Making a character walk from right to left can make a player feel uneasy, even if they can't articulate why[18]. I find this works best when the character is entering the boss's lair at the end of the game.

Another fun way to torture your player using level geometry is to force them to walk across very thin platforms over great heights, boiling lava, or swirling whirlpools. Increase the danger by using a bird's-eye view camera to view the action. I call these perilous situations **sphincter twitchers**, and use them in all of my level designs. Even if the player is never in danger of dying, they sure will feel like they are!

When working with your artist, unless the surface is specifically designed like a ramp, stairs or natural incline, make sure any geometry that the player

---

[18] I have no idea if this trick works on Azeri-reading players.

can stand on (like platforms) is relatively flat. Most characters are not programmed to adjust their body to uneven surfaces and, even if they are, they can "stutter" or misstep as they are playing their walking animations. Try to have smooth transitions between even small elevations to avoid this problem.

While making a level feel like a real place helps the designer create the level, remember that you shouldn't be bound by realism: this is a game after all, and you are only limited by how real you want to make it.

However, here is a cautionary tale about realism. A friend of mine was a designer who joined the team of an action shooter. The levels had already been created by the artists, who were extremely proud that they had created architecturally accurate buildings. These buildings had realistic nooks, stairwells, in-scale hallways, and even bathrooms on each level. The buildings were almost completely unusable in the game as the spaces didn't allow for gameplay or work well with the game camera. Think of it this way: in the movie *Star Wars* we never saw the toilets on the Death Star. I'm sure they were there just off camera, but because we didn't need to see them, we didn't *have* to see them. Omit any parts of your building, temple, city, and so on that doesn't help support telling the story that you want to tell.

Stop! Wait, you haven't built your gray box levels yet have you?

Good, because you will want to create a **playground** first. A playground is a gray box level not intended to be used in the game. It is a separate testing ground for game mechanics and hazards. All mechanics and hazards should be tested and tweaked in the playground until they feel right, then you can use them in your levels. Here are a few things to test in your own playground:

- Create ground angles to test basic walking, running, inverse kinematics (IK), and other technology to make sure the player looks good while moving even when not on level ground.
- Build several simple boxes at a variety of elevations to test the player's metrics with jumping, hoisting, teeter, etc. You should create any specific length and height geometry to test double and wall jumps.
- Test mechanics and hazards to determine distance, timing, and lethality.

The sister to the playground is the **combat arena**. This is just like a playground but used by the dev team to test combat systems, cover systems, and enemies. Have a way to quickly spawn and test combinations of enemies to create the best combat experiences. I'd rather hold off on talking about this because—SPOILER ALERT—the next two chapters are all about combat and enemies!

LEAVE THE TRAINING LEVEL FOR LAST

The **training level** is where the player learns all of the basics of gameplay. It teaches the player the game's basics. It is the player's first impression of gameplay. It stokes the player's enthusiasm[19] for the rest of the game. You'd think that this is the most important level of the game.

You'd think!

Unfortunately, the training level is often left until the end of the game's production. Now, I know why this is done. Developers will argue that you won't know the most important lessons of the gameplay until everything is in the game. They state that by the end of the game's production, the art team is capable of creating the best-looking art and effects for the training level in order to give the first level of the game the biggest bang for the buck. Sometimes they claim the player will learn the basics over the course of the game. The reality is, production schedules get tight and priorities shift, resulting in the training level usually not getting the love and attention it deserves.

You may want to consider creating the training level first. Sure, it may not look as pretty, but your team can always go back and polish up the art. The advantage is that you, along with the player, will be learning the basics, and can accurately determine what the player should learn before the designer blinders kick in. A training level always benefits from a pair of fresh eyes.

Even better, don't have a training level at all. I have found that in the best games, the player is always learning new moves, gaining new gear, experiencing new gameplay, and constantly learning. Why not make your **entire game** the training level?

Now that we've started to create our levels, what are we going to fill them with? I have a sneaking suspicion we'll find out in the next chapter …

[19] Hey, I think I found a sixth emotion!

Level 9's Universal Truths and Clever Ideas:

- Even a cliché can be made compelling.

- Use the "Mexican pizza" technique to make level themes unique.

- Level names can help convey mood and info to your player.

- Design from the top down: world, level, experience to moment-to-moment gameplay.

- You can never have too many skeletons.

- Use level maps and posters to give information and build anticipation.

- Determine the theme of your levels: escape/survive, explore, educate or moral.

- Use the beat chart to point out weaknesses in your game's overall design.

- Design your games using a tight set of gameplay systems and mechanics: maximize play through re-use.

- The player will always find a way to break your game.

- Make the player play the game the way you want it to be played.

- Is your level an alley or island? Design to each style's strength.

- Map and gray box your levels to plan camera placement, prevent architectural issues and gameplay problems.

- Walking is never, ever gameplay.

- If it feels too long or too boring, then it is.

- Every finger should have a reward at the end, even if it's just a trashcan.

- If it looks like the player can go there, then they should.

- Use playgrounds and combat arenas to test metrics and systems.

- Leave the training level for last (or not).

- The entire game should train the player.

LEVEl 10

THE ELEMENTS OF COMBAT

Every action is seen to fall into one of three main categories, guarding, hitting, or moving. Here, then, are the elements of combat, whether in war or pugilism.
B.H. Liddell Hart

British military theorist Sir Basil Liddell Hart may have died before video games became popular, but his quote neatly covers the basics of video game combat. Combat is a popular and major component of a video game player's moves and activities. A good combat system requires much thought and work from the development team in order to get it right. But before we dive into combat, we need to open and look into the messy can of **violence**.

The simple truth is this: many video games are violent.

Let me amend that.

Video games are about **action**. Some of those actions, like hitting, shooting, stabbing and killing, are violent.

However, anyone who assumes that all video games are violent obviously knows nothing about video games. A large number of video games don't rely on violence, from the first video game, *Tennis for Two,* all the way to the latest iPhone puzzle game. I could fill this entire book with a catalog of non-violent games. But somehow, it's always the *Dooms, Mortal Kombats*, and *Grand Theft Autos* that get all of the attention. Why? Because:

1. Violence in video games is graphic, dramatic and visceral.
2. As a result of the above, it offers a player the quickest positive response feedback loop.

The player does an action (hitting, shooting), sees the immediate result (enemy is killed by attack), which grants a reward (experience, money, power-up). This elegant feedback loop allows for quick and frequent player-to-world interaction. It's Freud's pleasure principle[1] in practice. Ring the bell, a reward is gained. Why stop ringing the bell?

Another reason why violence is common in video games is that other human interactions like conversation, romance, comedy and manipulation are hard to recreate in games! The result is (a) alternate methods of gameplay aren't explored by development teams as often as violent ones. (b) Because game players tend to buy the same types of games over and over, (c) publishers find that newer styles of play are harder to sell.[2] (d) Parents and other social groups who mean well don't always find out all of the facts before leaping to the assumption that all video games are violent.

Let's avoid all of this stress by doing our part as responsible members of society and keep mature games out of the hands of younger gamers. There are plenty of alternative games out there. You wouldn't take a little kid to a R-rated movie, so why would you let them play a M-rated video game?

As mentioned back in Level 3, the ESRB reviews and provides ratings for game content. At their website[3] you can find their descriptors of violence found in games:

- **Comic mischief.** Depictions or dialogue involving slapstick or suggestive humor.

---

[1] The fact that a developer called "id" created the FPS, a genre that directly adheres to Freud's pleasure principle, is almost too delicious to ignore.
[2] EA's marketing team tried to cancel their best selling game, The Sims, during its entire development; they thought no one would buy it!
[3] http://www.esrb.org/ratings/ratings_guide.jsp

- **Cartoon violence.** Violent actions involving cartoon-like situations and characters. May include violence where a character is unharmed after the action has been inflicted.
- **Fantasy violence.** Violent actions of a fantasy nature, involving human or non-human characters in situations easily distinguishable from real life.
- **Violence.** Scenes involving aggressive conflict. May contain bloodless dismemberment.
- **Intense violence.** Graphic and realistic-looking depictions of physical conflict. May involve extreme and/or realistic blood, gore, weapons and depictions of human injury and death.

When designing violence in games you should realize that it's all about context. The more violent activities the player does themselves, the higher the rating. Ask yourself these following questions to help determine the proper rating for your game:

- Does the player do the violence themselves? Do they use realistic weapons?
- How frequently does the player perform the violent act?
- Does the game reward the player for performing violent acts? Does the game show that violence is "not appropriate" in any way?
- How graphic is the violence? Is there dismemberment? Do the game visuals linger on the violence?
- Is there leftover residue like bloodstains or gibs? Better graphics equal more realistic graphics equals more realistic violence.
- Is the violence against "bad guys?" Do the enemies suffer as they are being killed/defeated?

Now that you know how violent your gameplay will be, let's start to design how it is going to happen.

400 QUATLOOS ON THE NEWCOMER!

When designing combat moves for your character, first consider your character's personality. Is your character acrobatic like the Prince of Persia? Is your character jumpy like Mario? Stealthy like Solid Snake? Brutal like

Kratos? Each of these characters has a uniquely different combat style because they have uniquely different personalities.

What genre is your game? What kind of gameplay experiences do you want the player to have? These questions will help determine your character's weapons. Or maybe you just have your hero carry a laser scimitar *and* a phase-plasma pistol. Either way is fine.

Study real-world fighting styles to make your character's attacks feel more realistic and distinct. Give your character a signature weapon. It will help quickly define their personality to the player. Can you picture Cloud Strife without his huge sword or Bayonetta without her guns? Your character's weapon is going to dictate how they fight. Rygar's throwable shield creates a different combat experience than a Big Daddy's melee drill. Even if your hero uses an unconventional weapon like a giant spatula or bubble wand, brainstorm all the different uses to which the player could put them. The more original, the better!

Now that you've chosen your weapon, let's fight!

In combat, the attack used totally depends on the player's distance to the target. Check out the four ranges of combat: close range, medium range, long range and area effect.

Knowing what your character's combat range (or ranges) is going to be makes a huge difference in how the player approaches combat during gameplay. A *Mario* game is almost exclusively close/medium range combat whereas *Contra* is a long range combat game. As a result, Mario must come into close contact with enemies in order to defeat them, while in *Contra*, the player's goal is to keep away from enemies and keep them from ever getting close by shooting them at a distance.

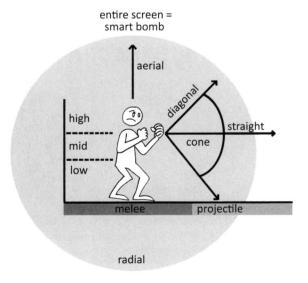

Close range combat consists of grapples, punches, strikes, sweeps, tickle fights, and quick burst moves like head butts and upper cuts.

Medium range combat consists of weapon swings, flying kicks, and dash attacks.

Long range combat consists of shooting or throwing projectiles or spells at enemies.

Area effects, like **smart bombs** and "super" attacks will affect enemies at long range or on the entire screen.

In addition, attacks can be delivered from four different elevations to give combat variety: standing, low, high, and aerial. While you don't have to use all four of these elevations in your game, you will have to make each of these elevations have their own set of attacks as they make the player deal with combat in very different ways:

Standing position is the basic shoulder height of the player. Man-sized and larger opponents can be struck at this elevation.

Low position strikes are at the waist height (or lower) of the enemy and delivered from a crouched or kneeling position.

High position attacks are delivered over the head of an average height enemy. They can only be done by jumping then attacking. High attacks are used against flying or large enemies like bosses.

Aerial position is when a player has jumped or flown into the air to attack. Aerial attacks can be extended jumps like those found in *Devil May Cry* and *Dante's Inferno* or they can be true flying like in *Marvel Ultimate Alliance* or *Dark Void*.

Attacks from any elevation and range can be delivered both **vertically** and **horizontally**. In *Maximo: Ghosts to Glory* we designed enemies that could only be defeated by one of the two attacks.

A skeleton guard wore an armored helmet that deflected Maximo's overhead vertical attack. Another skeleton warrior used a shield that blocked Maximo's horizontal attacks. The solution was to use the opposite direction attacks to smash the skeletons.

Attack	Control	Range	Speed	Direction	Damage	Special
Slash	Square	Close	Med	Horizontal	Medium (10 hps)	Can be blocked by shield
Overhead strike	Triangle	Close	Med	Vertical	Medium (10 hps)	Can be thwarted by helmet
Thrust	Forward on stick, Triangle	Close	Fast	Forward	Strong (25 hps)	Knockback to target
Jump strike	X, down on stick, Triangle	Close/ medium	Slow	Downward	Strong (25 hps)	Stun to any target in two-unit radius

An **attack matrix** like the one above is useful to track important information about combat moves. An attack matrix should include the following data:

- Attack name
- Control scheme
- Range of attack
- Speed of attack
- Direction of attack
- Damage—in terms of strength as well numeric damage (usually expressed as a value or percentage)
- Special—anything that distinguishes the attack from other attack moves

Feel free to add as many columns as you might need to your attack matrix to accommodate degrees of severity, defensive items/moves, and so on.

You can use an attack matrix to track combat moves and compare and contrast values for maximum variety. Each attack should be distinct and usable in a specific combat situation.

Timing is one of the major keys to great combat. When the player presses a button, the character should quickly perform the attack. If you want your combat animations to feel smooth, then you must strive to have your game run at 60 frames per second. While many games run satisfactorily at 30 fps, lagging and stuttering that can happen at these lower frame rates will really impact your player's combat experience. Don't waste time with long and elaborate wind-up animations. If you do this, it will throw off the player's timing and they may end up missing or striking when they don't want to. Quick moves can be rapidly done in succession, but they tend to lead to button mashing.

Lunges are more fluid thrusts that return the player back to his original standing position. By combining quick strikes and lunges you can create a **combat chain** that will keep the player's basic attack from feeling boring.

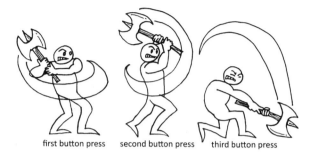

first button press   second button press   third button press

To create a combat chain, create three or more attack moves that will run one after another. If the player presses the attack move once, play the first animation. If the player presses the button again within a short (usually within a second) time period, the player goes into a second attack move. Usually, this second attack move deals more damage, so there is an advantage for the player to "chain" these attacks together. A third attack will do even more damage, and so on.

If the player is allowed to land multiple hits in a row, make sure that your animation (or game code) also moves the player character forward; otherwise, when the enemy is knocked back, the player won't be able to land the next attack in the chain. The hero in the image below misses because he doesn't translate forward. His attack only succeeds when he shifts forward.

OK, remember when I told you back one page ago that you shouldn't do elaborate wind-up animations? I meant it—but only on that page. Elaborate wind-ups are awesome because they lead to powerful attacks that can chop a player in two! These moves work great when the player is wielding an oversized or heavy weapon. Because of the long wind-up, the player is forced to risk the wait for the reward of landing a more powerful attack! Risk vs reward. Remember it. It's gonna be big.

Speaking of rewards, use particle and visual effects to make attacks feel more dynamic and rewarding; from "slice streaks" on sword attacks and speed lines for dash moves like those seen in the *Onimusha* games, or resort to those old standbys of fire trails and blood splatters like in *Madworld* (Sega, 2009). Be big, be dynamic, and be dramatic! Give big action moves like ground pounds and smashing uppercuts big screen effects that fill the screen with debris, dust, lightning bolts and other eye-catchers. The more spectacular the better!

So what happens when you actually hit something? A strike without a reaction animation from the enemy doesn't feel like the player has hit anything. It's like the attack is merely skipping off the surface of the enemy. If you can't afford to have the enemy  have reaction animations (due to memory limitations, for example) at least have effects and sound effects that indicate that a successful hit has landed. Powerful sound effects make attacks feel more rewarding. Vocal reactions such as a big "Oof!" from enemies are always satisfying!

Exaggerate the impact of a powerful hit to heighten the feeling of strength of the attack and increase drama. The enemy should react to wherever they've been hit. Got cracked in the coconut? The enemy's head (and some teeth) should fly. Kick out their  leg and a bone should splinter or they should at least topple to the ground. This kind of animation is getting easier to do within the game code using rag doll physics systems like Havok and PhysX, but sometimes nothing beats good old fashion key frame animation.

If conflict is drama, then combat should be a freakin' opera complete with flying spear-carrying valkyries and a glass-shattering fat lady! Hype up that drama! A particularly powerful strike should be accompanied with a camera shake, a rumble from the controller's actuator or combat  slowing down to show off the power of the hit. *Batman: Arkham Asylum* uses slow motion to indicate that the player has defeated the last of the enemies in a combat encounter.

Before I forget, here's a pearl of wisdom: close battles are more exciting. Don't get me wrong, kicking hordes of enemies' asses can be quite satisfying, but just make sure that your player is evenly matched to his skill level for the majority of the game.

You can really pull out all of the stops if you use a **cinematic finishing move** where the action slows or freezes and the camera pans around the action. These finishes are frequently seen in fighting games like the *Soul Calibur* and *Street Fighter* titles, but they've crept into other action games since they just look so darn cool! This is because of this **very important thing**:

PEOPLE WANT TO PLAY GAMES THAT MAKE THEM LOOK COOL

And nothing makes a player look cooler than a **QTE**. Just look at the Mighty Bedbug in action below. You have to admit that pressing button prompts to create a choreographed combat sequence makes the battle look spectacular.

Case in point: Batman's combat in *Batman: Arkham Asylum* relies on QTEs to choreograph combat moves rather than leaving the player to flounder around on their own. Why? Because Batman is a badass. He'd never miss a punch. Why should the player? The result? When the player successfully does an attack using a QTE, the player feels like an expert of combat—just like Batman.

While QTEs have been around since *Dragon's Lair*, they can be found in some of the most recent action games. They are combat-oriented minigames that are activated within combat when an enemy or boss has reached a certain level of health. The player has to press a certain button or complete a certain move (like waggle a motion controller or analog stick) within a very short window of time. If the player is successful, they are rewarded with an animation of the hero performing an elaborate attack on an enemy. Most QTEs require several button presses for the player to reach the end of the sequence, which ends in the death of the enemy or boss.

Here are some tips when designing QTEs:

- Reserve QTEs only for the most bombastic and elaborate attacks. Since control during QTEs is limited, ask yourself "is this something the player can do instead?" You can always use single button QTEs like those found in *Darksiders* or *Batman: Arkham Asylum* as finishing moves.

- Always position the button prompt in the same location on screen. Otherwise the player will get confused about what button they have to press.

- Allow the player time to recognize the button prompt and then press the button. This recognition usually takes most players a **beat** (a "one-one hundred" count).

- If the player fails to press the correct button in time, then try to get the player back to that QTE state quickly. For example, if it took three different sets of patterns to reach the QTE, don't repeat those three sets if the player fails. Have the player repeat one set before the QTE is activated.

- I'm torn over instant player kills for failing QTEs. On the one hand, it allows for some very bitchin' animations of your hero getting ripped apart by the boss monster. On the other hand, I'm against instant kills in general. I recommend the player taking substantial damage from failing a QTE sequence, that way they can survive to try again. If they are on their last bit of health, you can still have that bitchin' animation play ...

Dude, c'mon, be cool!

I have played targeting systems that allow the player to choose enemies in front or behind them by selecting a specific button or direction with the analog stick[4]. Other games treat targeting like a QTE, where the window of opportunity to attack lasts as long as the enemy is in view or nearby.

Melee is hand-to-hand combat. Pretty much all the rules of combat apply but remember that those hands can be lethal weapons and hold impromptu weapons found in the world: props or objects such as lead pipes, chairs, or even cars! Make it easy for players to pick up and drop these items— provide on-screen prompts if you have to.

[4] The Mark of Kri (SCEA, 2002) had an innovative lock-on system that had the player use the DualShock controller's analog stick to do a "radar style" sweep to target a sequence of enemies that could be programmed by the player. The technique was patented by the game creators.

When designing weapons, think about their speed, their range, the damage they do and what other effects they may have, such as fire or poison. If a weapon is upgradable, then make sure the effects are seen on the weapon. Merely adding a +3 to the stats doesn't provide the player with the gameplay information and visual rewards that they deserve.

While swinging a weapon around, be mindful of it sorting through objects. That just looks bad. Instead, have weapons respond to the world, such as rebounding off of stone or metal surfaces or blades sinking into wooden ones. Be aware of the flipside of this, that the player's weapon will rebound off of any non-breakable item in the world. Carefully design your combat environments to use this to the player's advantage and disadvantage. For example, a hero would learn he couldn't swing his giant axe around in an arena filled with unbreakable stone pillars lest he risk rebounding off of them, which would give the skeletons a chance to attack.

Stealth kills are quick attacks used to kill or disable an enemy in one move without alerting other enemies nearby. They are usually performed from a crouch or cover position or by positioning the player behind their target. They often use QTE style prompts to activate and reward players with dramatic enemy kills. Make sure that stealth kills can only be done under certain conditions (in the right position, while under cover, while in shadow), otherwise players will constantly use them over regular attacks as an exploit. Don't let a cool move become stale to the player.

Grapples are similar to stealth kills in that a player can activate them under specific circumstances. Grapples are rare in most games with the exception of the fighting and wrestling genres (for example, *WWE Smackdown vs. Raw 2010* (THQ, 2009)). It's difficult to program two-character collision as it requires the main character and the enemy to be animated together so the moves look natural and sorting doesn't occur. However, if you take the time and effort, you can have your hero pull off some pretty devastating attacks and slams. Just like with grabbing items, make it easy for players to grab and release their opponents. Many games make this a context-sensitive move.

What's another way to make the player look like an expert? Use a **lock-on system**. The later *Legend of Zelda* games have a particularly good lock-on system in which the player can lock onto the enemy closest/in front of them with a button press and flick the analog stick to select the next one over to the right or left. As long as the button remains depressed, the player is locked on to an enemy. As each enemy is dispatched, the targeting system latches onto the next available enemy. Lock-on systems require HUD visuals to help the player track their targets. Here are some examples:

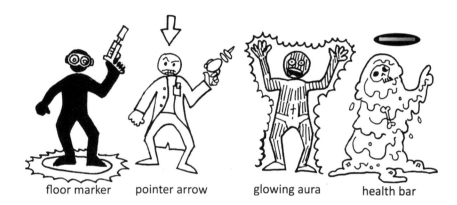

floor marker   pointer arrow   glowing aura   health bar

NOW YOU HAVE TO KISS ME

Letting the player miss isn't such a bad thing. The player will be forced to become more skilled with their attacks, which will make them feel like more of a badass as they master combat timing. Or if the player just doesn't get it, you can always increase an enemy's collision dynamically if the player misses or dies too many times in a row. Or you can offer to drop the game down to a lower difficulty setting. Do whatever you can to keep your player playing.

ON MOVING

If you take any martial art, you quickly learn that moving is just as important as attacking. The goal in a real-life fight[5] is NOT to get hit. Why should video games be any different? Allow your player moves that give them options for retreating or avoiding damage, and also ones that can be combined with combat moves for quicker or more powerful attacks.

Dodges and **rolls** allow players to get the heck out of dodge and quickly move out of the way of attacks. They should be quick and easy to perform too: a button press and single control stick move. Mind your metrics. Make sure your dodge lets the player get completely clear of wide-range attacks and longer-reaching weapons like halberds and huge swords, or radius-based attacks like explosions and magic spells—otherwise you might be doing what they call in *WOW* "the graveyard hustle."

After the player does a dodge, there should be a beat to allow the player to get back on their feet. Not only does it give the player a chance to reorient themselves, but it keeps the player from using it as a movement exploit.

Allow players to use dodges and rolls to get past hazards. They add a nice moment of tension when dashing through a closing door or rolling under a swinging blade. But be careful. During a roll or dash, the camera has a tendency to collide with whatever the player is trying to avoid. I don't suggest having the camera to pass through the hazard (that looks sloppy) or have the camera dip down with the player (as that gets disorienting.) Consider the camera locking in place as the player dodges and then have it "catch up" with the player when they've cleared the obstacle.

---

[5]Not that I'm advocating fighting in the real world: remember, the first rule of fight club is ... oops, I've already said too much.

Dashes are forward moves that can be used for defense or attack. Like dodges, dashes should be very quick to perform. Many action games like *Devil May Cry* (Capcom, 2001) and *Darksiders* (THQ, 2009) have dash moves that can be upgraded with more powerful sword or punch moves. Even your basic dash move should do something besides move the player. You want a dash to feel quick and powerful. And fast. And dare I say, dashing?

The player should be able to use the dash to ram into enemies or smash breakable objects. Even though a dash targets one enemy, you can have the player's momentum continue to have him hit several enemies at once or create a "sonic boom" to send bad guys flying! Whee!

While generally used for traversal, **jump** moves can be combat moves too. Where would Mario be without his famous "**butt bounce**" attack? The collision zone should be like a good pair of pants; there should be plenty of room in the butt. Don't make these pixel-perfect attacks. After the attack hits, apply **recoil bounce** to move the player a short distance away so the player doesn't land on or next to the enemy and take damage. If the enemy hasn't been killed by the butt bounce, minimize risk to the player by putting the enemy in a stunned state.

Many games allow the player to maneuver during this recoil bounce to let the player chain bounce attacks off of the heads of multiple enemies! Make sure you award an escalating bonus for each additional bad guy bounced. Make it a big moment for the player—they've just done something cool!

You don't have to be a short Italian plumber to do jump attacks. Weapon-wielding tough guys can do these moves too. Just make sure you follow these guidelines:

- Make sure the player's maximum jump is taller than the tallest enemy you can jump attack. Otherwise you'll be colliding with the enemy's head or shoulders, which will look strange.
- When the player lands, apply the same rules as an attack impact: stop the action for a beat by freezing the enemy or world's action, generate explosive effects, rumble the controller—anything to make the attack feel more powerful.
- Even if the player misses, the strike could generate some radial effect; a stun or knock back for nearby enemies, for example.
- Allow the player a quick recovery—they'll want to get back into action immediately.
- Then again, you could give the player a delay as part of the risk/reward of performing the attack. For example, Mario firmly plants his butt into the ground after a butt bounce. If he misses an enemy, he's vulnerable for a beat to getting hurt by an enemy.

If jumping is a little too frivolous for your big bad space marine or soldier, you can have them **vault** over obstacles to add variety to battlefield movement. Vaulting works well with cover systems (see below) and ducking.

Gears of War 2 (Microsoft Games Studio, 2008) provides players with a prompt to notify them when they can vault over a low wall.

ON GUARDING

WATCH OUT!

That's how fast you have to respond to an attack, so you'd better make sure your **block** is quick to pull off! Blocks can be either general or positional.

General blocks are found in action games; a single button press to cross weapons, arms, or lift a shield to block an incoming attack. They're an all-purpose block for any situation and enemy. It doesn't matter if your shield is a one-handed buckler or Roman Scuta, the function is still the same: the player blocks an attack with the press of a button, holding it aside during the rest of combat.

Don't underestimate the use of sound effects in conjunction with a block. A nice loud CLANG! lets the player know they've successfully executed a block. Or have sparks or some other effect (as long as it's not blood) visually clue the player in. Some blocks displace the player back a little bit to make the player have to move back in to hold his ground. Giving a successful block a disadvantage is a bit douchy, but if you want to, then go ahead—it's your game.

Nice buckler!

Sweet scuta!

Positional blocks correlate to a particular elevation and require a stick move and/or button press to block at the appropriate height, whether it's a high or low. You find these blocks most often in fighting games. You'll have to decide whether a player can hold a block or not. Arm blocks are usually quick and drop down after a second or so. Other fighting and action games allow the player to hold the block indefinitely, or at least until an enemy does an attack that breaks the player's block or knocks them off their feet. Shield blocks can last longer, allowing the player to "hide" behind the shield for an extended period of time. Some designers don't like letting the player camp a block, but that can be circumnavigated with breakable shields or giving enemies knockback attacks. Oh, and don't forget to prevent your shield from sorting through the ground when the player crouches to block low attacks.

As a designer, you need to decide whether your shield is breakable or not. It will make a big difference to how the player uses it. In the first *Maximo* game, we had a breakable shield. The player was able to upgrade it to a stronger shield through the course of the game. However, as it was still a limited resource we found that players were reluctant to use it, preferring to jump and dodge out of the way of attacks instead. In the sequel, we wanted to promote shield usage, so we made it unbreakable. Players were much happier to block now that the worry of breakage was taken away. But shields aren't just for blocking anymore:

- Combine with dash move to clear obstacles
- Smash enemies at close range
- Throw a shield as a short-range projectile
- Use the shield as a sled down steep inclines
- Place shield over head to protect from falling debris or lava
- Use shield as a crowbar to move large objects
- Keep shield on back to protect from back-stabbing enemies.

Heck, attach a shield to a chain like in *Rygar*, and it becomes a whole new weapon!

If a shield isn't enough protection, then **armor** will do the trick. There are several things to consider when giving the player armor. **Encumbrance** is one. The more armor the player wears, the slower (and noisier) the player becomes. You usually find encumbrance in RPGs, not often in action games. It's fine if you are trying to be "realistic" but if your game's emphasis is on action and combat, it may be better to not use it.

Perhaps your game makes a distinction between different parts of the body in combat? If so, you can use the "paper doll" approach to armor. The player has to armor his head, torso, arms, hands, legs and feet. This feels more realistic and gives your player more items to buy and collect. However, it does require an interface—usually quite large, as it has to show the entire body. Make sure it's easy for players to find, select and change their armor. And discard or sell unwanted armor as well.

Your hero has finally defeated the first boss and won his prize: a new suit of armor. But don't cop out and just give your player a +2 chainmail shirt. Whenever the player earns an armor upgrade, make it look dramatically different. For example, full plate looks substantially different (and cooler) than a leather jerkin. By visually improving the player's armor, the player can tell their "rank" at a glance.

Give it a unique name too, like the "Holy Armor of Protection" or "Dragon Scale Armor." This will make the player feel like they've won something important and worth having.

But armor is not just for protection. Isaac's spacesuit in *Dead Space* has a health meter right down the spine. Players can check their status at a glance without the need for a HUD.

Ghosts 'N Goblins also shows health status but in reverse: as the armor pops off, the player gets closer to death. This is a good trick for enemies too, as it lets the player know how many hits are left to defeating a foe.

Armor upgrades are a great way to give a player a new ability. Can't move that heavy block? This hydraulically powered armor can help you move it. It doesn't even have to be a "suit of armor." Mario's Tanooki[6] suit not only added protection, but let him fly, grow, and turn into an invincible statue.

Nice jammies.
Did Mom pick them out?

Ha-ha.
Does that tin can
make you invincible?
I didn't think so.

What's great about armor is it's an easy way for the player to customize their character without changing the base model. *World of Warcraft* does it right. You can find, buy and even make custom gear—and when another player sees your pimp helmet, they're gonna want one too. It's a great way to motivate players to spend more time in your game. It doesn't have to be armor; it can be hats, unique weapons or mounts. The more customization you allow the player, the better.

STATE OF THE ART BANG BANG

↑   *Ooooh! Guns, guns, guns!*
Clarence Boddiker (RoboCop)   ↑

Shooting is simple. Aim the gun, pull the trigger. Right? But let's look at some of the most popular multiplayer shooters and see how wide they vary from each other:

Quake has maps that promote linear action and predictable looping movement patterns. Weapon and armor pickups can change the dynamics of the action in a heartbeat.

Halo is played more like a sport, with game-like modes of play. The rhythm of the action is slower than many shooters, partially due to the player's

[6]Tanuki are Japanese raccoon dogs. Mario wears Tanuki footie pajamas with raccoon ears. It's adorable. Really.

regenerating health, promotes "attack then retreat" strategies. Vehicles play a big part of the gameplay as well.

Call of Duty: Modern Warfare has a multiplayer mode that concentrates on short-range combat with intense action. Players can concentrate on upgrading their weapons and characters like in an RPG.

Team Fortress 2 resembles an RPG but the players assume widely varying skill-based roles. The game modes promote teamwork over single player actions.

Left4Dead is also all about teamwork; in fact, you can't win without it. While most multiplayer shooters match opponents one-to-one, Left4Dead pits a handful of players against an endless horde of zombies. Game modes resemble stories more than in other shooters.

Even in games where shooting isn't the main focus of play, **ranged combat** can immediately change the dynamic of the game. This is why I recommend that if a game isn't a shooter then guns should be saved until later in the game. Let the player get used to their moves and attacks without a gun first. When you feel like they've learned all they can, then go ahead and arm them.

Creative Director Hardy LeBel, who has designed many successful shooters like *Halo: Combat Evolved* and *SOCOM 3,* says that ranged combat is about building a distinctive rhythm. There are several factors that influence that rhythm such as targeting methods, reload times, weapon fire rate, weapon accuracy, rate of fire and lethality, the availability of ammunition, the availability of area-of-effect weapons like grenades, player health mechanics, and so on. Even level design, AI behavior and mechanics all contribute to that rhythm. Whew! That's a lot to digest at once, so let's start with the **three As**: action, aiming and ammo.

Action is the loading, firing and unloading of a gun. Here are some questions you need to ask about a weapon's action:

- How quickly can the player reload their gun?
- Does the player need to reload with a button press or does it occur automatically? You can create some great risk/reward gameplay around reloading a gun, as the player is vulnerable during loading (such as in *Gears of War*, where a properly executed manual reload is faster, but a botched one is even slower and leaves the player defenseless for longer).
- Is there a limit to the ammo? Does the player even need to reload the gun at all?
- What is the gun's rate of fire? A faster firing gun is going to use ammo quicker than a single shot weapon. Can the weapon be fired one shot at a time or in bursts?
- Does the firing bloom obscure the player's view?
- Can a shot take out more than one target at a time?

Aiming is how the player sights a target. Aiming is a huge issue in games. It can make or break a shooter. Early shooters relied on the player's reflexes and skill in positioning the cursor over the target and pulling the trigger at the right time. Until *Halo: Combat Evolved* (Microsoft, 2001), most successful first-person shooters were played on PCs—partially because of the ease of aiming with a mouse. To help players manage the tricky task of aiming with the Xbox's analog sticks, the game used aim assist.

No matter what type of aiming method you use (aim assist, auto-aim, free aiming, and so on), you need to design and implement targeting mechanics for the tastes of your target audience.

- How does the player aim? Is there a scope? How much of the player's view does the scope obstruct?
- How does depth of field affect aiming? An effective visual trick is to have far-away objects that are blurry suddenly become clear when viewed through a long-range sight.
- Is aiming manual? Does the gun have drift? Can the player steady their shot? From how far away can a player make a shot?
- Is aiming automatic? Is there a quick-fire mode? Is there an auto-aiming/ lock on system?
- When you fire the gun, does it kick, throwing off the player's aim? Does it rise like a Thompson submachine gun?
- Are there systems to improve the player's aiming such as laser pointers, bullet time or heat-seeking ammo?
- Can the player move while aiming? Are there limitations to where the player can aim, like diagonally or overhead?

- Does the scope detect other ways of seeing the target such as IR, motion detection or heartbeat? Can the gun be modified in any way to become silenced or have additional add-on weapons like grenade launchers or bayonets?
- Can the player use shooting for puzzle solving, or trick shooting? Shoot targets? Shoot locks off of doors? Shoot the gun out of the hands of enemies? Ricochet a bullet into an enemy?
- Can the player disable the targeting mechanism or replace it with another style?

The targeting reticule and/or the iron sights on your weapons should be one of the most sophisticated feedback mechanisms in your game. They will likely need to communicate aim, bullet spread, recoil, jamming, overheat, ammo, successful hits vs near misses, friend or foe, and the list goes on and on. And it will need to accomplish that while remaining useful and unobtrusive to the player. A great deal of time and writing could be dedicated to designing the targeting reticules for shooting, but suffice it to say this **very important thing** applies:

PLAY THE BEST SHOOTERS AND STUDY THEIR SOLUTIONS

Taking some time to deconstruct the mechanics and behaviors of the best-in-breed games will add immeasurably to your own gameplay.

Ammo is what the player shoots. Ammo raises it own questions:

- Where and how is ammo carried? Is there a limit to the amount of ammo carried by a player? Do you need the right ammo for the right gun?
- Does ammo have any special effects like incendiary, poisonous, heat-seeking, or armor-piercing properties?
- What happens when a shot misses a target? Does it impact against something in the environment? Does it affect that item? Break glass? Chip plaster? Ricochet off of metal?

SPA-CHOW!

Put that thing away!
You're gonna get us killed!

Here are a few more tricks to make your gunplay more effective:

- Accentuate the excitement and danger of a gunfight with sound: weapon firing, bullet impacts, enemy gunfire, whizzing bullets, and so on.
- Play the SFX of the gunshot and bullet impact at full volume regardless of the target's distance to the player. This will let them know whether they scored a successful shot. Don't forget to let the player hear the voiceover of the character, too.
- Don't forget the weapon visual effects. Muzzle flash, spent shells kicking out and smoke from the barrel all make the experience more realistic.
- In general, players like gunfights at shorter ranges, as they are more exciting.
- Regardless of how graphic your weapon hits are, show some sort of impact effect when a bullet hits its target—from sparks to explosions to spraying gore.
- Needless to say, level design IS game design when it comes to building the rhythm of ranged combat. If you design spaces that are long, open corridors and you have a high lethality combat model, players will play cautiously. If you have lots of cover and break line-of-sight frequently PLUS you have a regenerating health model, then gunfights will feel like swirling dogfights as players engage and disengage to heal.

Mr. LeBel leaves us with this important thought: "in general, players expect ranged combat to feel powerful and satisfying. It's an easy mistake to try and make ranged weapons weak to help offset the perception of too much power in the hands of the player; fight that impulse and try to remember to be "generous" to the player, and they will thank you for it."

THE BEST GUN FOR YOU

When designing guns, even if you are creating made-up weapons, it's helpful to start with their real-life counterparts; after all, weapons are built for particular roles that can directly apply to their use in your game. But that will only get you halfway there. You should consider thinking about them in terms of effectiveness:

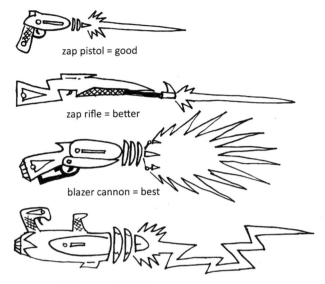

zap pistol = good

zap rifle = better

blazer cannon = best

kill-o-zap = freakin' awesome

But balancing weapons can be tricky, especially if basing them on real-world equivalents. There are gun-nut players that have their own opinions about which gun is better and how they should perform. You could go crazy trying to please everyone, so base your weapons on what fits the needs of your game first. Here are some guidelines to get you started:

- **Pistols** fire in a straight line (unless you are that guy from *Wanted*), which will dictate where you can shoot and who you can shoot. One enemy at a time unless your ammo pierces several enemies at once! That's going to keep the pace of shooting slow. Pistols usually require frequent reloading too, as their magazines carry from 6 to 15 rounds.

- **Rifles**, especially sniper rifles, mean the player has to aim and shoot. You usually can't fire from the hip with a rifle. That means the player is going to be vulnerable and usually looking down a scope, which means tunnel blindness. Sounds like a good opportunity for an enemy to sneak up… Many rifles carry large quantities of ammo: some have drum magazines that hold up to 100 rounds.

- **Shotguns** and **flamethrowers** fire in a cone, rather than a straight line. The cone is a shorter range than a pistol or rifle but can hit several targets at once. Both weapons do high damage to targets when hit at close range. Shotguns carry less ammo than guns or rifles, and flamethrowers go through propellant at a fast rate. A flamethrower's blast can be maintained for an extended time and does residual damage to an enemy.

- **Automatic weapons** allow you to fire quickly, but accuracy goes out the window. This high rate of fire also uses up ammo fast, regardless of larger magazine sizes. Designing your machine gun to have a little kick, drift or spray will not only make it feel real, but push the player to master using the weapon accurately. Are your automatic weapons one handed or two? Can the player use two at the same time? This will determine what other actions the player can do while shooting.

- **Heavy weapons** pack a big punch, but usually take a while to warm up or cool down. The Heavy's **minigun** in *Team Fortress 2* takes a few beats to start spinning, but the player has a way to keep the gun spinning even when they aren't shooting with it. The disadvantage is enemies hear you coming a mile away… **Grenade launchers** are also harder to aim, but do big damage. The *Call of Duty* games change the targeting on their grenade launcher to make it feel different and less accurate. The result is a very different "shooting" experience than a pistol or rifle. Magazine sizes vary from a dozen grenades to hundreds of rounds for fast-shooting miniguns.

No matter what the weapon, think about the range, speed and strength of the weapon. You can use an attack matrix like the one below to track these values and compare and contrast your weapons for maximum variety.

Weapon	Range		
	Short	Medium	Long
Dual pistols	Strong	Weak	N/A
Assault rifle	Strong but slow	Very strong	Weak
Shotgun	Very strong	N/A	N/A
Sniper rifle	N/A	Medium	Very strong

Notice how there is very little overlap in weapon attributes, and any overlap that does exist has a disadvantage like shooting/reloading speed. Keeping the weapons distinct will help in making the game feel well rounded.

Ranged combat weapons aren't always guns. Fantasy games, for example, have a wide variety of projectiles from arrows to magic missiles to cones of cold. Regardless of the genre, as long as you design your ranged combat with the guidelines set down for guns: range, damage and the three As, you should be fine.

One last question to ask is in a multiplayer game, should you allow **friendly fire** or not? It totally depends on the gameplay mode. It seems much more logical to have friendly fire in a player vs player mode than in a cooperative mode. Whatever your choice, allow the player to turn it on or off.

Oh no. You've just run out of bullets. Now what?

Players feel incredibly powerless when they're playing a shooter and have nothing to shoot with! So give your player a melee weapon that is always available. It can be a knife, fists or even a pistol whip or clubbing attack with a rifle butt. Giving the player this option to bash the baddie allows things to feel fair and realistic. The *Gears of War* games don't mess around in this department: they give you a chainsaw mounted onto your gun!

They say you can never have enough guns, but you don't want your player to be carrying around a golf bag full of firearms. Many games limit weapons

to a main gun and a side arm. But if you do that, you'll need to be able to switch between them quickly; preferably with a single button press.
Call of Duty: Modern Warfare 2 allows you to draw your side arm faster than you can raise your rifle; helpful for those situations requiring a quick shot.

"I was going to wait for him to empty it before I said anything."

Gears of War and *Uncharted* use a **cover system**. This not only allows the player a way to take cover against surface or barricade to avoid being shot, but to also fire "blindly" or in a limited manner at the enemy. The player is often penalized for avoiding risk by not being able to aim while under cover. Cover systems usually require a button press or command by the player to place them in and out of this mode. Be careful that your cover system doesn't become too "sticky", otherwise the player may be going into cover when they don't want to.

RUN AND GUN

There are many, many ways to shoot at things in video games: from a plane, from a train, out of a box, at a fox—you name it! Here are the main elements of a shooting gallery screen:

1. Turret showing weapon and player
2. Shootable object containing reward or powerup
3. Ground-based target
4. Visual element that indicates why the player can't shoot "past the screen"
5. Aerial target (note the clear indication to the player that it has been hit)
6. Smaller aerial target (generally worth more points)
7. Smaller ground target (also worth more points).

Mounted ranged combat is a shooting gallery style gameplay where the players defend against waves of incoming enemies. Players will tend to fire constantly if the weapon has unlimited ammo, or in short bursts if it doesn't. You can also get the player to fire in bursts if the weapon needs a cool-down time. To help the player aim, add tracer bullets. Not only does it look cool, but it will help players get "leads" on fast moving enemies or ones with erratic movement patterns. Let the player know the range of the weapon. If the player can't reach a target, then create a good visual justification as to why there are areas of the screen the player can't hit.

As both the target and the weapon move during **aerial combat** and **vehicular combat**, give the player opportunities to line the target up in their sights. If the player has a chance to see the target coming, line up the target and fire at the target they will feel in control. If too many targets whip by the player without giving him a chance to react, the player will resort to firing blindly which will make the experience seem mindless and frustrating. Adjust the speed of the targets or the craft either naturally or artificially to give the player ample shooting opportunities.

Rail shooter gameplay happens when player movement control is taken out of the equation. Games like *House of the Dead: Overkill* (Sega, 2009) and *Star Fox* (Nintendo, 1993) are rail shooters. You can also find rail shooter sequences in titles like *Red Faction Guerrilla, Uncharted 2* and *Wet*.

A unique advantage of rail shooters is that the game developer has complete control over the game camera and the sequence of events. This allows the developer to create scares they know the player will experience, furious shooting sequences and dramatic scripted events.

In fact, some rail shooters bear more resemblance to a theme park **dark ride** like Disneyland's *Haunted Mansion*[7] than a video game. In fact, interactive dark rides have started to appear in theme parks around the world[8], completing the circle of inspiration from dark ride to video game to dark ride.

NOT JUST SHOOTING

You don't really need a gun or melee weapon to defeat enemies. There are so many ways; one hardly knows what to choose! The more variety you introduce into your combat, the more fun the player will have:

---

[7] This reminds me of the time Disneyland's Haunted Mansion literally became a shooter. In the summer of 1974, a Disneyland guest wielding a .22 pistol took a shot at one of the duelist ghosts in the Ballroom scene. The bullet made a hole in the giant pane of glass used to create the scene's pepper ghost illusion. The management was frantic. It had taken a helicopter to originally install the giant sheet of glass and they'd have to rip the ceiling off the ride in order to replace it. However, a clever imagineer took one look at the spider-web cracks in the glass and slapped a rubber spider over the bullet hole. Voilà, problem solved! The spider is there to this day.

[8] On your next vacation, why not travel the world playing interactive dark rides? Buzz Lightyear's Space Ranger Spin (Walt Disney World, Florida), Men In Black: Alien Attack (Universal Studios Florida), Laser Raiders (Legoland Windsor, UK), Challenge of Tutankhamen (Six Flags, Belgium), Labyrinth of the Minotaur (Terra Mitica Theme Park, Spain) and Toy Story Midway Mania (Disney's California Adventure); all dark ride rail shooters.

Grenades. When throwing grenades, allow the player to predict the arc. *Gears of War* and *Uncharted* both have "throw path" targeting aids to assist the player. Don't neglect the effects when those suckers blow.

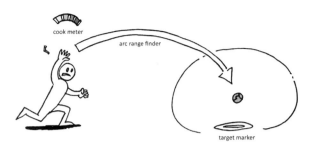

Kick up dust, debris and blow props sky high to really sell the explosion.

Throwing a grenade should always carry the risk/reward of having it accidently go off if held for too long, or even bounce back at the player. Soldiers "cook" their grenades by holding on to them after pulling the pin to make sure it goes off where it lands. *Call of Duty: Modern Warfare* not only uses a HUD element to warn players of an incoming grenade, but allows players to pick it up and throw it back! Remember that grenades can also be shot from rifles and launchers for greater accuracy and range.

Since many players duck back under cover after throwing a grenade, make sure you provide enough sound, visual and controller rumble cues to inform the player when a grenade detonates, even if they aren't looking at where it landed. If a player gets too close to an exploding grenade, don't hesitate to blow them up as well.

Sometimes you just need to blow up **everything**. It doesn't matter if you are calling in carpet bombing or a magical meteor storm; **smart bombs** are great one-shot solutions to keep the baddies off your back, if only for a few seconds. Show the player the controls for a smart bomb so they don't confuse it with a regular attack. When activated, smart bombs should

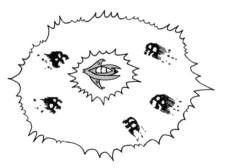

destroy everything on screen save the player. If there are destructible items, they should blow up too.

You have a few options to how the player can activate a smart bomb, depending on how much tension you want to create. In *Defender*, the smart bomb is immediate while in *R-Type*, the player has to charge up the smart bomb before firing it. Let them know what they are working toward so they can make an accurate decision as to when to use it. Be careful that you don't let it charge up too fast or be used too frequently, otherwise all the bad guys in your carefully designed combat encounters will be wiped out in the blink of an eye!

Wherever there are explosions, there is **fire**. Sometimes there's fire even without the explosions—things just need to be burned. Fire creates great-looking visuals and lingering damage to enemies and environments. But fire takes no sides: players should get hurt by fire if they stray into it. The fire should eventually burn out so the player doesn't paint themselves into a napalm-colored corner.

Fire also means flamethrowers. The closer you are to your enemy, the more damage a flamethrower should do. Flamethrowers are the weapon of choice for players who don't like to aim. Allow them to "fire and forget" or "hose down" enemies with flame.

Don't forget to use fire-based weapons as a gameplay mechanic too. Flaming swords and other weapons don't just do extra damage to ice-themed enemies, they can ignite braziers, detonate explosives, burn through rope, illuminate dark areas, cauterize wounds; the gameplay possibilities are vast.

Another lingering indirect attack is poison. Make sure you have an associated visual for poisoned items. A green gassy effect, a dripping blade, a hovering "death's head" effect are all traditional video game indicators of poison. Players should be able to tell when they are wielding a poisoned item or have poisoned an enemy—make the visual unique and distinct. As a poisoned character loses health, make sure each increment that the poison takes has a clear sound effect and visual effect associated with it. You are creating a timer in which the focus of the player will shift from regular gameplay to "find and administer the antidote." If the antidote is an inventory based item, don't make it too hard for the player to retrieve it. Even if poison is uncommon, make the antidote more common. There is no worse feeling in a video game than making the player feel like death is inevitable. Always give them a fighting chance.

stunned   knockback   knockdown   grabbed   transformed   off-balance

Another horrible feeling for players is to take control away from them. While **stunning**, **knockback**, **transformation**, **loss of balance** and **sliding** are worthwhile tools to use in lieu of taking damage, they should be used judiciously by the designer.

- **Stun.** When hit by a stun, the player loses all control of the character for a short period of time, usually leaving the player in danger of being hit by an enemy attack or finishing move. Stuns are usually accompanied by visual (like cartoony stars or "tweeting birds") and sound effects.

- **Knockback.** The player is knocked back through the air a short distance then falls to the ground. A knockback (or KB) can be lethal if a player is on a platform or next to a ledge. Be careful not to put the player into a situation where they can be "double bolted[9]" by KBs.

- **Knockdown.** The player is knocked to the ground, which requires a second or two to get back up. While on the ground, the player is vulnerable to additional attacks. In some games, getting back up is automatic, in others it requires button mashing, stick waggling or a QTE.

- **Latching on.** An enemy grabs or latches on to the player, pinning their arms and restricting their movement. Enemies can cause damage for

---

[9]The term "double bolting" comes from the Ratchet and Clank games when a player is hit by an enemy and loses bolts, the game's unit of currency. The bolts disappear if not collected after a period of time. However, there are some situations where the player is knocked by an enemy into another hazard or enemy which causes more bolts to fly out of the player. The player is stunned by the attack and cannot regain control fast enough to collect any of the first bolts before they disappear, let alone the ones that were just knocked out of them. Thus they lose double the bolts from the initial attack.

every second they are latched on. Enemies can be shaken off by waggling the controls, or performing jump or spin moves.

- **Transformation.** The player has been hit by a magic spell that transforms the character into some other form. In *Ghosts 'N Goblins*, Arthur turned into a frog. In *Maximo*, the hero could be transformed into a zombie, an old man and a baby. In all cases, the player's move set becomes limited; they cannot attack or jump and in some cases, lose almost all control. During a transformation, game controls can be reversed to sow player confusion (for example, push controls left and the player moves right). I recommend ending the transformation quickly. Reserve for special occasions as the player will tire of it if used too often.
- **Loss of balance.** This animation is used as a teeter move. The player briefly loses complete control as the character reacts to losing their balance. This works well as an indicator rather than a disabling move.
- **Sliding/skidding.** After a run, dash or jump move, the character slides to regain their balance. While this adds quite a bit of personality to the character, it can be annoying especially when it happens several times in a row as the player struggles to bring the player to a stop. Like a KB, a skid can slide a character right off the edge of a narrow platform.

Don't let enemies have all of the fun! Design enemy-disabling attacks to give your players the advantage in combat. Use caution when creating attacks with these types of results. Consider what it is adding to the gameplay. Ask yourself this **very important thing**:

ALWAYS STRIVE TO ENABLE THE PLAYER, EVEN WHEN YOU'RE DISABLING THEM

Remember, don't let enemies have all of the fun! Design enemy-disabling attacks to give your player the advantage in combat. They'll thank you for it.

DAMMIT JONES, WHERE DOESN'T IT HURT?

In order for all this combat to mean anything, the player has to have something to lose. That means **health** and **lives**.

To calculate the player's starting health, I suggest calculating in terms of the maximum damage the player can take. For example, at the beginning of the game, your hero can take 20 hits from enemies before losing a life and without replenishing health. Next determine how much damage an average enemy's attack does. In this example, a normal hit will cause 10 **hit points** of damage. That means the player's starting health should be 10 x 20 hit points = 200 health.

There are many ways losing that health can be represented to the player. **Numbers** are simple and transparent but boring. They stand out against cluttered HUDs like those found in MMOs and RPGs. Just keep the font legible.

A **health bar** doesn't take much space running along the top or side of the screen. They can be framed with themed artwork to make them look more interesting and part of the HUD. However, it can be difficult to tell when small amounts of damage have been taken. A health bar can be segmented for readability.

If you are feeling artistic, **icons** can represent the player's health with simple visuals: human outlines that go from green to red (*WWE Smackdown*), crystal globes of blood (*Diablo*) or hearts (*Legend of Zelda*).

Some platform games use a **companion character** as the player's health meter. For example, *Crash Bandicoot* is followed by a tiki head that loses feathers with each hit the player takes. The problem with this system is that it cannot support a large amount of health.

Things are more direct with **character-based health** systems. *Ghosts 'N Goblins* represents health with armor that pops off the player. *Dead Space* and *Ghostbusters* have status meters as part of the character's armor or equipment. The characters of *Resident Evil* clutch their midsections and limp when they've taken

(That Elf needs food badly!)

damage. Many car combat and driving games show visible damage to the vehicle. You know your car is close to death in *Grand Theft Auto* when you are dragging a bumper and your engine is smoking! Whatever method you use, you need to have some sort of feedback: the player can't always keep their eye on the health bar, so these character-based feedback mechanisms make it possible for the player to gauge how close to death or restart they are. They can then adjust their strategy (retreat, heal themselves, etc.) based on this knowledge. Just make sure these systems don't interfere with the player's movement or attacks.

Many modern games have moved towards a **HUD-less health system**. As the player takes damage, the screen becomes splattered with blood which gets thicker as more damage is taken. More dramatic effects, like turning the whole screen blood red, monochromatic or blurry, can be used too. Sound and music can drop off and be replaced by heavy breathing and a heartbeat. In *Batman: Arkham Asylum*, whenever the player is hit by a taser attack, the screen's video "short circuits."

Other systems that defy classification have shown up over the years. In *Sonic the Hedgehog*, as long as the player holds one collectable ring, they cannot be killed. Or at the other end of the scale, *Bushido Blade 2* featured so many one-hit kill attacks that the health bar was completely dropped.

Players can regain health with the aid of power-ups, increases in level or experience and even time. *Halo: Combat Evolved* pioneered the concept of regenerating health in first person shooters. As long as the player wasn't taking damage, the health meter would refill at a slow but steady rate. The *Ratchet and Clank* games ditched health altogether as the developer wanted the player to reach the end of the game, not constantly see a game over screen.

Whatever method of displaying health is used, the player should clearly know when they are getting hurt and losing health. Don't skimp on the dramatic animations and particle effects. Both a **hit sound effect** and a **vocal reaction** ("ow!", "oomph!", and so on) should play. Health should deplete in a very obvious manner, because with every hit the player is closer to losing their life.

DEATH: WHAT IS IT GOOD FOR?

Let's face it, **lives** and the **game over screen** are an outmoded concept.

When video games first arrived, their goal was to suck quarters as fast as possible out of the player's pocket. The best way to achieve that was to make the player want to keep playing despite being killed as often as possible. Additonal lives became a good short-term goal for the player to keep in the game. When game characters became little people in lieu of blips and spaceships, the concept of dying came with them. (After all a spaceship doesn't die, does it?) The emotional impact of the finality of dying (Unless … Quick! Get that next quarter into the slot!) was too good to pass up.

When games moved to home systems, lives followed—but the players had paid for their game and there were no more quarters to gain. So why kill the player? Why not let them finish the game they've paid for?

Another problem with killing off a player often is that it discourages the player from continuing the game fairly. For example, players of Doom (id,1993) found that it was easier to restart the game from a saved file than it was from an in-game checkpoint. By using this exploit, the player ceased to worry about death and never even saw the game over screen.

Many developers have caught on to this and abandoned the concept of player lives. Instead of killing the player and ending the game, players are reset to checkpoints within the level, where they can keep trying over and over until they succeed. In *Prince of Persia: the Sands of Time*, the player can "rewind time" to a point where the player is safe. This type of mechanic has to be carefully implemented though: it is possible for a player to get into a situation where they can't rewind far enough to avoid death and would die all over again. A narrator tells the player "that's not how the story happened" before the character restarts from a checkpoint. In *Batman: Arkham Asylum*, the player is given a chance to save the caped crusader from a fall to death by pressing a QTE button. If successful, Batman climbs back up to safety.

However, some genres like action and survival horror still utilize **lives** and **game over screens**. If you *have* to kill your player, remember the following:

- Let the player know that they have lives and that they will be lost. Players become protective of their character and will fear for their safety.
- Display lives clearly in the HUD. Make it clear when the player is losing a life.
- Allow the player plenty of opportunities to regain lives. They can happen during level ups, be power-ups, or rewards for collecting objects.
- When killing a player character, do it quickly. Don't create a long, drawn out death animation that the player has to watch over and over again when things get hard in the game.
- The same goes for game over screens. Don't make the player sit through long death sequence cutscenes. Make the path to restarting gameplay after death as quick as possible.
- When killing a player, make it as violent as your rating allows. Let the player really feel some pain when it happens. Empathy toward the game character will motivate the player towards self-preservation.
- If the player earns something during one life, don't double punish them by taking it away from them when they lose that life.
- If killing the player during a boss round, don't make the player have to play the whole sequence all over again. Why not let them continue on with the fight as if nothing ever happened, or only punish them with a little bit of boss health regained?

- That said, the threat of death is a great motivator for the player to do better and learn that skill or control. Just use this power judiciously, okay? I trust you.
- If using alternate death systems, like the player dies if their NPC partner dies, make it clear that (a) the player needs to protect the partner character with their lives and (b) they will die if they don't.

Think very carefully about using lives in your game. If you don't think killing the player will make the game experience better or more exciting, or think it will actually be more frustrating, then don't do it. Because this **very important thing** applies:

YOU WANT TO KEEP THEM PLAYING

Never give the player a good reason to stop. Once you've lost them, you may never get them back. Instead of a game over screen, why not create a **"keep going" screen**? When the player dies or leave the game, show them a preview of the next level, the next story point or the next treasure item, weapon or powerup? Give the player a sneak peek to get them so excited that they won't want to stop playing!

Now stick close, we're moving into dangerous territory in the next level: one populated by hordes of enemies!

Level 10's Universal Truths and Clever Ideas:

- Be mindful of ESRB guidelines when creating violent gameplay.

- Violence is all about context: a violent act is going to feel more violent if it is the player who does it.

- Give your character a signature attack or weapon.

- Create an attack matrix to track your combat moves and reactions.

- People want to play games that make them look cool.

- Use a lock-on system to enable the player during combat.

- Close battles are more exciting.

- Use QTEs to heighten combat drama but don't overdo them as they get old.

- Fighting enemies is supposed to be fun.

- Be aware of the three As when designing projectile combat.

- Use attacks to hamper and incapacitate the player rather than kill.

- Make it clear to the player that they have taken damage.

- Always strive to enable the player even when disabling them.

- Keep the player playing.

LEVEL 11

THEY ALL WANT YOU DEAD

Video games are populated with a plethora of beings that want to kill you: aliens and androids, pirates and parasites, mercenaries and mushroom people. However, I realize not every video game features slobbering, sword-wielding enemies—often they use guns too!

Yes, yes. I realize that there are plenty of other video games that use other forms of conflict, such as time, human competitors, or even the player's own skill, to challenge the player. But we are not talking about those types of games[1]. As I flip back to Level 3, I am reminded of three types of conflict found in stories: **man vs nature** (like a hurricane or a giant white whale); **man vs self** (where the hero is struggling with an internal problem issue like "where to go for lunch[2]") and **man vs man**, or in the case of video games, man vs zombie, or man vs ninja pirate, or man vs hideous-alien-creature-made-from-the-skins-of-your-dead-crewmates.

[1]Yet.
[2]I have seen large groups of full-grown people completely paralyzed by this internal conflict.

Those are the type of enemies we are going to be talking about. While zombies and ninja pirates and alien thingee enemies are great fun to design, you first need to follow this **very important** golden rule:

FORM FOLLOWS FUNCTION

Hey! I saw you trying to design that winged skeleton enemy[3] without thinking about how he's going to attack. Put down the pencil as I repeat myself; because **THIS REALLY IS VERY IMPORTANT**:

FORM FOLLOWS FUNCTION!

You *need* to (not "would kinda like to") determine the function of an enemy first. So many things are resting on the decisions in your design; how it will be coded by the programmer, how the rigging model will be built by the animator, how it will be textured by the artist. These important enemy attributes are:

- **Size**
- **Behavior**
- **Speed**
- **Movement**
- **Attacks**
- **Aggression**[4]
- **Health**

---

[3] He does look pretty awesome though.

[4] I realize that aggression is considered part of behavior, but since combat is often treated by designers as its own system, it deserved its own heading.

All of these attributes, along with your level's theme, will allow you to determine who your enemies are, what they will end up looking like and how well they will work together when they are placed in the game. Having to redo an enemy character again and again and again is a big morale killer for your team and a huge waste of time and money[5].

short   average   large   huge

Speaking of huge, enemies come in a wide range of **sizes**:

Short enemies are no taller than the character's waist.
Average enemies are roughly the same height as the player character.
Large enemies are several heads[6] taller than the player.
Huge enemies are at least twice the player's own size.
Gigantic enemies are so large that they can only be completely seen from a distance.

The size of the enemy will determine how the player will fight it. For example, a short enemy can only be fought by crouching, or with a low attack like an upward sweep or radial spin attack. On the other end of the scale, a huge enemy with a vulnerable head can only be reached with a jump attack. Design your combat so the player "fights their way up" the enemy: an average enemy should be able to be hit by a low and medium

---

[5] And irresponsible. Please do not be an irresponsible designer.
[6] Artists measure characters in terms of "heads"—literally the height of one average human head. For example, an average six-foot human is seven heads tall, while a heroic character is eight and a half heads tall.

attack, a huge enemy should be hit by a low, medium and high attack, and so on.

Size also influences health. Larger enemies traditionally have more health (are harder to kill) than smaller ones. This might account for why many bosses are so darn big. Size will also dictate the enemy's reaction to attacks. Hit a short enemy with a knockback attack and they should go flying. Hit a large enemy with the same attack, and it may not even budge. You'd be lucky if a gigantic enemy even notices your attack, let alone reacts to it.

Hey!
Quit it, you
big bully!

They say variety is the spice of life. I don't know about spice, but I do know it is variety that keeps a player from getting bored. Size can influence a player's emotions too. Defeating a huge enemy can make a player feel heroic while defeating a short one can make them feel like a bully.

Now that you've determined size, ask yourself, what is my enemy's **behavior**?

- How does my enemy move?
- What does my enemy do when in combat?
- What does my enemy do when it is hurt?

Answer these, and you will have the foundation to a robust enemy. The goal when designing enemy behavior is to not repeat behaviors. Even better, design your enemy's behaviors to complement each other.

A **patroller** moves back and forth or up and down in a mechanical fashion. The path of movement can be more involved than this, but its movement is always predictable.

A **chaser** pursues a player if they are approached or some other condition is met. In many games, patrollers can turn into chasers when they see the player or the player attacks them.

A **shooter** is an enemy that fires a projectile. Shooting patrollers and chasers will fire at the player once they've been spotted. Due to the nature of the attack, this enemy will try to keep distance between itself and the player rather than engage them.

A **guard** is an enemy whose AI priority is to guard an item or location (like a doorway) rather than actively pursue the player. Guard behavior can be easily combined with chasing or shooting if the player manages to steal the item or get past the guard.

A **flyer** is an enemy that, well … flies. They are aerial patrollers but because the flying adds another dimension (literally) to the movement, they deserve their own classification. Flyers can swoop down to attack players or you can have them fire projectiles from a safe distance. Flyers are more advanced enemies, as their movement and attack patterns are more difficult for the player to predict. Players trying to attack flyers usually stop to target or make a jump attack.

A **bomber** is a flyer that attacks from above rather than from the side. Bombers are common in 2-D games as it is often difficult for a player to use a 3-D camera to see an enemy above them.

A **burrower** is an enemy with an invulnerable state that allows it to get into an advantageous position to attack the player. The player must wait for the enemy to emerge before they can attack it.

A **teleporter** is an enemy that can change position around the playfield. The player must attack quickly lest the enemy teleport out of harm's way. The teleporter varies from the burrower in that the teleportation is instantaneous, giving the player no time to attack. Give your player a way to disrupt the enemy's teleportation, such as a stun or another disruptive attack.

A **blocker** is an enemy that defends itself against the player's attack with a shield or other defensive device. The shield can either be circumnavigated with an attack from another direction or elevation (such as from down low or from behind), or the player can disarm the enemy with a specific move or attack. Shields can make the enemy temporarily invulnerable, requiring the player to break the shield with a specific move or action, or wait around until the invulnerable state passes.

A **doppelganger** is an enemy that looks like the player and has moves, attacks and uses AI that mimics the player's own. Doppelganger enemies force the players to use moves or weapons in an unusual manner in order to defeat "themselves."

The goal of having all of these different behavior types is to have enemies that complement each other. Enemies should "live harmoniously" with each other, creating interesting combat puzzles for the player to solve.

Once you create enemy behavior that works well together, it will create gameplay. The player will learn how to perform **threat analysis**. This forces the player to ask themselves: "Which of these two enemies is going to be the bigger threat? I must kill that one first and figure out how to defend against the other one(s) until I do."

Here are a few interesting enemy combinations that I've found work well together:

- A blocker with a shooter positioned behind him. As the player tries to whittle down the blocker, the shooter is taking pot-shots at the player.

- A big chaser and a group of smaller flyers. While the player goes after the big guy, the little guys attack. However, if you leave the big guy alone and go after the flyers, you're gonna get thumped.

- A teleporter and a chaser. As the player tries to catch the teleporter, he leaves himself open to the chaser's attacks.

- A guard and a bomber. While the player is tied up with the guard, the bombers attack from above.

Depending on **speed** and **movement**, an enemy can be more dangerous, harder to target and more frightening. Use the different speeds: **non-mobile**, **slow**, **medium**, **fast**, and **quick** for your enemies.

TK-421
Don't just stand
there, get him!

The difference between a hazard and an enemy is mobility and AI, but every rule has its exceptions. Just because an enemy is **non-mobile** doesn't mean it can't move. Movement = character and life. A humongous tentacled Cthulhu-esque creature may be immobile due to its sheer size or even technology limitations, but a player would still consider it an enemy. Non-mobile enemies like a robotic wall-mounted laser-sighted machine gun can still have enough AI to make life difficult for the player. Design ways to keep the player engaged as they attack non-mobile enemies, whether it's a timing puzzle that stands between the enemy and the player, or even a puzzle that's part of the enemy itself.

The speed, size and strength[7] of an enemy are inversely proportional: small enemies are fast but not strong, big enemies are strong but not fast. Medium-sized enemies can be either strong or fast, but if you give them

[7] Hey! It's the three Ss!

both attributes they end up feeling "**cheap**" as they've been given an advantage that the player cannot match. Whenever an enemy is extremely overpowered or too perfect at making attacks, it feels like the player is fighting a computer rather than an actual living creature.

But I digress.

A **slow** enemy works best when there are lots of them. One zombie isn't very threatening, but a dozen of the slow-moving undead can make even the most stalwart hero a little nervous. Often a slow enemy packs a big wallop: if the player gets hit, it's their own damn fault. Or you can give a slow-moving enemy a fast attack to keep the player on their toes. Slow enemies often have built-in defenses, allowing them to brace themselves against a player's attack or casually swat them aside. If you want your enemy to feel powerful, have them move slowly like the Tyrant, Nemesis and Dr. Salvador from the *Resident Evil* series. The inevitability of the bad guy advancing on the hero can make the player panic and make fatal mistakes.

Medium speed is just what it sounds like: the speed of the enemy's movement and attacks will likely match the player's own speed. Medium speed may be a little predictable, but useful for most situations. I've found it's helpful to make medium-speed enemies run slightly slower than the player, especially when chasing them. This allows the player to retreat at their running speed if necessary without fear of getting cut down from behind. The player can then reorient themselves and face the enemy in time to deliver an attack or effectively defend. It's OK to tweak speed values here and there to get the effect you want. There's no hard and fast rule when it comes to this; you've just got to do what feels right and fair.

Fast enemies either dart forward to quickly strike and back away, or they move quickly around and then jump in to do multiple attacks. A fast enemy works great in horror and action games. The player will have less time to react to an incoming enemy and may panic and make dumb mistakes—until they learn to keep their cool. However, don't make a fast enemy constantly attack the player, as they get frustrated by getting hit by something they can't hit back—unless this is the strategy you want. The smaller the enemy, the quicker they are. Give fast-moving enemies an erratic movement pattern to give your players a real challenge.

A **quick** enemy moves in bursts. They can move blindingly fast—so fast that it may seem unfair to the player, but you can balance that by limiting their attacks and moves. Help the player see quick moves coming by playing a warning animation. This will allow the player to dodge, block, or strike before the enemy completes its quick move.

What is your enemy's **movement style**? Does your enemy charge the player like a bat out of hell? Does it zigzag erratically to avoid taking fire? Does it make a beeline and then retreat? Does it jump from cover to cover? Does it crawl on the walls to ambush the player from above? Does it run away and never fight at all[8]? Knowing your enemy's movement styles will not only determine their attacks but also their personality.

Determine whether your enemy moves randomly or predictably. Avoid extremes and insert variety. Too random and the player might feel the enemy moves too arbitrarily. Too predictable and an enemy feels too "game-y."

The best solution doesn't include unpredictability. For *Crash Bandicoot 2*, Naughty Dog tried creating more behavioral AI with less simple patterns. Focus groups found them inferior. The players liked the challenge of figuring out the enemy's patterns. On the flipside, players like unpredictability in sports games. Predictable patterns become "holes" for the player to exploit, which ruins the experience.

Coordinating several enemies' movements adds complexity. Consider how your enemies behave and group together during a fight. Some enemies can use flocking behavior to create realistic group movement.

Look at the movement behaviors of different animals, birds, and insects for inspiration. Humans usually move in straight lines. Predatory mammals like wolves and tigers move in looping arcs as they circle their prey. Crabs move sideways rather than in straight lines. Birds fly in swooping patterns as they catch updrafts to aid their flight. Insects zigzag as they course correct during flight.

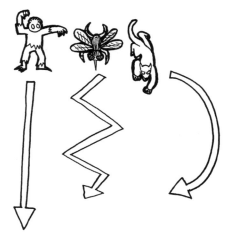

---

[8]Personally, I think enemies are more fun when you can fight them.

This might go better
if we all went at once...

Let's consider how the bad guys in a Bruce Lee movie fight scene behave. Bruce Lee is surrounded by dozens of karate experts, but they never attack him in more than groups of ones and twos. They are very polite, those kung fu villains. This strategy works well in games too. It allows you to create the illusion of a group without overtaxing your game or the player.

Work with your programmer to create **pathing AI**. Determine the needs of your enemies to figure out how they are going to move around. Here are some questions that should be addressed when creating pathing and behavior AI:

- How mobile are your enemies? Do they have more than one movement speed? Can they can break into a run or slide to a stop? Do they leap over obstacles or use doors?

- How aggressive is your enemy? Fast-moving frothing berserkers or slowly advancing stone-cold killers? Enemies can even be cautious or cowardly, afraid to get hurt or die. Giving an enemy a sense of self-preservation makes them feel like real people.

- How much of a team player is your enemy? Do they raise the alarm and alert other enemies to assist them? Will they try to keep a player pinned down while another closes in for a melee attack or better shot? Will they try to flush a player into the open where another enemy will have the advantage? Will one grab and grapple the player while another attacks them? Do they have a "partner", like a guard dog or attack drone?

- How defensive is your enemy? Do they crouch or duck behind objects? Do they use cover or hold the line? Do they act stealthily when they spot a player? Do they try to attack from behind and sneak up on a player? Do they have defensive items like shields or defense systems?

- How versatile is your enemy? Can they pick up and use dropped weapons or health? Do they drive vehicles or man weapon emplacements? Can they take over functions for other enemies if they are killed? Can they fly or use non-ground-based movement?

Most AI characters use a **waypoint navigation system** to move around. A grid or path is laid out by the designer that determines where the AI moves. As the AI moves, the programmer can determine what movement and animations are played to create specific AI behavior. Areas can be designated as "go" or "no-go" areas based on world geometry or to achieve a specific AI behavior.

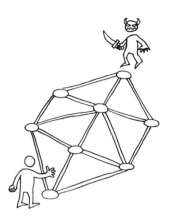

All this means is that your bad guys either travel along a preplanned network of paths or wander around within the confines of an invisible box (or sphere).

This allows the designer to choreograph a world event with an enemy—like crashing through a wall or reaching a specific spot at a particular time. However, placing waypoints can be time-consuming and they don't always meet all of the AI needs.

Because most waypoint-guided enemies are programmed to determine the shortest and quickest path to the player, be careful of enemies clipping corners and objects. You can fix this by tweaking your waypoint paths. Pull the waypoints in a bit at corners or near objects to compensate for this movement.

BRING ON THE BAD GUYS

You are walking through a graveyard winding your way through the tombstones when you see a skeleton blocking your path, ready to fight.

Wait a second. Rewind. There's a much more dramatic way to introduce this bad guy into your world.

You are walking through a graveyard, winding your way through the tombstones. One of them shakes as you pass by. Suddenly the camera zooms in on the player as the screen shakes and the controller rumbles. The camera whip-pans around to a grave as a hand thrusts itself out of the ground. The tombstone shatters into a million shards as a skeleton bursts from the grave, its eyes glowing evilly and bony fingers clenched, ready to fight! Now that's exciting!

Enemy introductions are a really effective way to tell the player that they've encountered something new, exciting, and dangerous:

- Freeze the camera or zoom in on the creature: let the player get a good look at what's about to kick their butt!
- Display the name of the enemy on screen—players like to put a name to an enemy.
- Foreshadow: *Resident Evil 2* provides a great "what the hell was that?" moment when a licker enemy runs past a window right before you encounter it. It builds up suspense for when the licker actually appears to the player. Make it an event!
- *Devil May Cry* does a great job of introducing all of its enemies in a very dramatic way. Have them smash through a window, kick down a door, blast into the world in an explosion of special effects—anything to give your bad guys a good first impression!

Spawning an enemy into the world is just as important as removing them. You want to make sure that the player isn't able to slaughter the enemies before they get a chance to arrive on the scene. Some games make enemies invulnerable upon spawning or have them spawn from off screen where the player can't reach them. You may consider creating a hazard or mechanic that allows the enemy to spawn on the playfield without getting killed.

In *Maximo: Ghosts to Glory*, we created coffins that burst through the ground to deliver enemies into the world. If the player collided with them, they would be knocked backwards. If they swung at them, they would shatter the coffin, but the enemy inside wouldn't be hurt and would go right into their attack routine. Why go through all of this trouble? Because of this **very important thing**:

FIGHTING ENEMIES IS SUPPOSED TO BE FUN!

In an action game you are going to be fighting a lot of enemies, so do whatever you can to make it **awesome**! Explosive effects, funny or dramatic hit reaction animations, cool and/or gory kills and, of course, lots of feedback and rewards[9].

When the enemy is defeated or killed, what happens to the enemy? Do they vanish in a puff of smoke or pop like soap bubbles? Do they dramatically clutch their hearts and die an agonizing death? Do they explode? How is treasure delivered to the player after the enemy is defeated[10]?

Determine how the enemy model is removed from the world. Do they fade away, leaving only weapon pickups where their bodies once were? Do they dissolve into a pile of goo that then melts away? Or do bodies stay on screen as a gory reminder of your combat? Remember, what happens to your enemy affects your ESRB rating.

Every action game I've worked on has had one enemy that does this attack behavior: step 1: enemy sees player; step 2: enemy charges player

---

[9] We'll talk about how to make the most of rewards in Level 13.
[10] Looks like Level 13 has its work cut out for it!

like a madman; step 3: when said enemy gets close enough to the player, they explode. While this sounds exciting, the execution always causes problems.

Some days you can't get rid of a bomb!

Third person cameras tend to flip around to show the back of the player and first person cameras only show the player's POV from the front, the player never sees the exploder pursuing them and therefore never gets an indication that they are about to get blown up real good. Sure, you can give the player a warning by calling out that special enemy on a mini-map or have some sort of grenade detector HUD element like in *Call of Duty: Modern Warfare 2*, but odds are that guy's still gonna catch up to you and then your head is going to fly one way and your giblets the other. What I'm trying to say is, no matter how you make it easier for the player to avoid getting blown up, this still isn't a very good enemy design. Why? Because of this **very important thing**:

ENEMIES SHOULD BE FOUGHT, NOT AVOIDED

I'm not talking about the type of avoiding where the enemy is a whirling dervish and you have to dodge out of its way before it hits you. No. I'm talking about the "this enemy is too hard, too cheap, too much of a hassle to fight I don't want to fight him" type of enemy.

As a designer, you should strive to make the player WANT to fight the enemy. Your job is to make the player realize that there are plenty of advantages in risking life and limb to fight the bad guys:

They have the loot. Gold, bolts, experience points, health—it doesn't matter what it is as long as they have it and you want it.

They block the path. This is a lot easier to pull off in a 2-D game. You can block the player artificially to force a fight, like a battle arena …

They have the key. And you need that key to get through the gate that leads to the next room, section or level. I've always wondered: why is it the last enemy you fight is always the one who is holding the key?

You need to take their power. Tired of getting shot at? Defeat that enemy and take their bigger, better gun! Want to upgrade your +1 mace to a +2? Then kick that orc's ass!

They're making fun of you. Taunts are a great way to motivate players into fighting. Having an enemy taunt or challenge a player if they're standing still for too long not only can force a player into attacking, but is a great way to get some character into the enemy. Taunts work great in multiplayer fighting games like *Street Fighter* where the player takes a risk by taking a break from combat or defense to mock their opponent.

It makes you feel like a badass (aka it's fun to fight). Nothing will keep a player fighting more than having a solid combat system. To achieve that, see Level 10.

Don't forget to let enemies have a chance to be a badass too! Give your enemies some sweet attacks like these:

Melee attacks: Do they use hands/ claws/tentacles/feet? Do they have raking attacks or punches? Do they know martial arts? Can they grab or ensnare? Can they perform throws? Can they "ground pound" or cause earthquake attacks?

Weapon combat: Do they use weapons? One-handed or two-handed weapons? Are they a barbaric or skilled fighter? Can they disarm or be disarmed by the player? Can their weapon be used by the player? Can the weapon extend, be thrown, or boomerang?

Projectile combat: Do they use guns/magic spells/ranged weapons? How accurate are they with their attacks? Will they blindly fire or wait for the perfect shot? Do they track movement or lead when aiming? Do they need to reload? Is their projectile explosive? Can they be disarmed? Do they have a close range melee attack if engaged or disarmed?

Persistent damage: Does your enemy's attack have a side effect like acid/ poison/fire? Does it do damage with the attack or as a lingering effect? Can it be healed by the player or does it wear off over time? Can it be countered by player equipment/gear?

Telegraphing attacks is important for effective enemy combat. An enemy should have a "tell" animation that informs an observant player that the enemy is about to go all stabby, shooty, or clawey. Tells include:

- Cocking a fist back to punch
- Growls or yells before swinging weapon or charging
- Part of anatomy (like twitching tail or reptilian fins) moves before attacking
- Weapon's laser sight has to acquire target before firing
- Weapon or spell "charges up" before firing.

Not every attack needs to do damage to the player. There are plenty of ways to give the player grief without doing them permanent harm:

Block/parry: the enemy can block or parry the player's attack, causing a stagger in the player's combat flow. This can break combat chains, reset combo meters, and cause the player's weapon to rebound or ricochet. Whatever the source of the block, be it a force field, an actual shield or a defensive grab, don't ever make the player wonder why it happened.

Knockback: rather than taking damage, the player is knocked backwards when hit. Putting distance between the enemy and player can upset any combat chain or disrupt any activity the player was engaged in, like spell casting or operating a mechanic. It is particularly effective when the player is hit while standing on a narrow platform knocking them off or to their death.

Stun: the player is stunned into a defenseless state. It can either be while standing or down to the ground. The player should lose momentary control; just as long as it doesn't last too long, which can be very frustrating for players. Circling stars and tweeting birds effect are optional.

Freeze/paralyze/capture: acts like a stun, but can be broken out of by performing button mashing or furious waggling of the control stick. Characters are often entombed with a freeze attack. The player may or may not take damage during this attack. Make sure you have a cool "victorious breaking free" animation and effect when the player finally regains control.

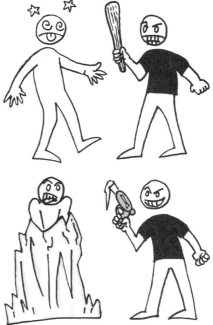

Repair/heal: the enemy regains health. I suggest using this infrequently as it can feel unfair to the player. This works best if the enemy has a healing animation as well as a health bar to show that they've returned to their fully (or partially) healed state. Consider allowing the player to attack the enemy to disrupt their heal.

Buff: this works like the heal, but the enemy is gaining power to charge an attack. Usually this can be found when charging magical attacks. You also find it in shooters when the bad guy is charging up their weapon to unleash hell on the player. The enemy can either be in an invulnerable state while buffing up or the reverse, which would cause the enemy to lose the advantage they sought.

This is just getting unfair.

Thief: the enemy steals money or equipment from the player, causing the gameplay dynamic to shift from "fight the enemy" to "get that bastard who just stole my chainmail!" Make sure the player has a fair opportunity to get back what's been stolen. Never steal anything the player has bought or won as part of progression: make it something that is (somewhat) easily replaceable.

Leech: the enemy drains the player's "charged up" resources. This can be super meter power, mana, shield power, fuel. Usually the player doesn't have an opportunity to regain the resource from the enemy that attacked it. Once it's gone, it's gone. Players will soon pick up that leeching enemies should be dispatched as soon as possible.

Unexpected behaviors: if the player is expecting a movement pattern or attack, having another up their sleeve adds a nice bit of variety to the encounter. The variety adds to the illusion that your enemy is learning to react and defend against the player. The player will have to adjust their battle plan as they go rather than falling into the same old routine.

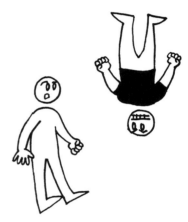

Vulnerabilities or **resistances**? Make sure they're clear to the player and follow logic. Of course, that murderous snow angel is going to be vulnerable to fire, just like that flaming pyre corpse is just going to laugh in your face when you wave that burning torch in front of him. Let the player make logical connections—don't ever let them wonder why something doesn't work. Enemy taunts are great for conveying that information. The smugger or more cutting the enemy's taunt, the better. Just don't overdo it; even the funniest or best-delivered line gets boring after the third time.

Even if an enemy has fierce attacks, nimble defenses and cool behaviors, there still has to be a way to kill them. Determining an enemy's health is done the same way you would for player characters. Balance your enemy's health in relationship to the player's attack. Start with how many hits you want your enemy to take before it dies. Consider all of the different attacks your hero has when determining this. Your goblin enemy may be able to withstand three normal hits, but a holy sword may be able to kill him in one stroke.

All of the notes about displaying player health applies to the enemy's health as well. Refer to Level 10 rather than making me retype it all here.

I LOVE DESIGNING ENEMIES

Enemies offer a designer a chance to really flex your creative muscle. It's fun to come up with horrible monsters and evil villains. Personally, I find adversaries to be the most interesting characters in a story. And not just the "big bad" bosses. Look at all of the great cannon fodder found in movies and comics: Imperial stormtroopers, orcs, Cobra troopers, death eaters, AIM scientists, parademons, Nazi soldiers, those henchmen in James Bond films that flip through the air whenever a grenade explodes.

But I'm proud to report that no one comes up with more creative cannon fodder than video games. In games, **anything** can be an enemy! An angry pickle! An irate toaster! Whatever the heck a goomba is! A whole glorious world of psychopathic possibilities is yours for the choosing… but rather than overwhelm you with a huge list[11], I've created the **Alphabetical Bestiary of Choices**:

---

[11] Besides, that's what books like the AD&D Monster Manual are for!

A is for arachnid, our pois'nous, crawly friend. Beware his webby legs or you'll meet a sticky end.

Battlemechs, huge and metal, with cannons all a-blazin'. Stand beneath their feet and you'll go squish just like a raisin.

C is for criminals, quite the cowardly lot. Better catch them quickly or you're likely to be shot.

D is for the dinosaur that's chewing on my rear. Who said genetic engineering was such a good idea?

Evil creepy children, blank eyes stare so sadly. They're easy to dispose of ('cept when guarded by Big Daddy.)

Flying devils bedevil you while climbing a wall. Give 'em a whack, knock 'em back, before they make you fall.

I hate those *G*hosts who chase me merely out of habit. But they'll run the other way if I eat a power pellet.

*H*enchmen, mercs and soldiers: they'll kill you for a buck. My advice? Shoot them first. If they shoot back, duck.

*I*rradiated Insects! It's my house they invade. Someone know where I can find a 10-foot can of Raid?

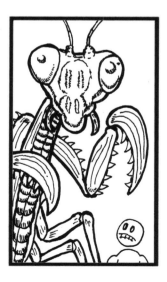

Do not shoot a Jungle Beast, treat with kindness instead. Even when they steal your gal, throwing barrels at your head.

Killer Plants may look pretty, but do not stop to smell. Shooting thorns and whipping weeds will send you straight to hell.

A Lich is just a skel'ton that has a fancy name. You should place a score or more of these into your game.

M is for mutant freaks, scarred by radiation. Their drippy flesh could use a little bit of lotion.

Red Ninjas vanish from sight, throwing stars at you.

If they do any other attacks, make sure to tint them blue.

Orcs, the standard foe of any knight or wizard. Can be fought by the score in any game by Blizzard.

P is for the pirates who sail the seven seas, in ships laden with treasure and crews full of disease.

Dragon, spider, alien: whichever type of fiend; they're always harder to defeat when they are called: "the Queen."

Robots are a paradox—they're s'posed to make life better. But when they're in video games, they always make me deader.

*S*paceships, as an enemy, come in many flavors. Try *Galaxian*, *Sinistar*, or plain ol' *Space Invaders*.

T is for treasure chest; their mimics should be banned. First you're reaching for the gold, but then you lose your hand.

Darn those *U*nholy cultists! Their demons are a blight. They're crazy; but without these guys, there'd be no one to fight.

Vampire bats are all a-twitter, flying rather quickly. Trying to draw a bead on them is making me feel sickly.

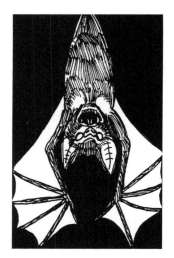

Werewolves have fearsome claws, sharp and ready to maul. But rendering all that hair makes games slow to a crawl.

Xenomorphs are nothing but an intergalactic pest! Infest your ship, eat your brains, and burst right through your chest.

Behold these enemies of **Y**ore! Gorgons and animal-men. (Lead designer's been watching Harryhausen films again.)

Zombies are the final foe, so with your gun take aim. They'd be so much scarier if not in every game.

If you don't want to use any of those traditional enemies, don't sweat it. Come up with your own foes! Here's how:

- **Start with your theme.** Brainstorm the types of enemies based on your game's environment. For example, an ice world can have killer snowmen, yetis, disgruntled skaters, snowball-throwing midgets, and penguins with machine guns.
- **… Or start with your story.** Who is the main enemy in your story? For example, in an original trilogy *Star Wars* game, I would expect to be

fighting stormtroopers no matter what planet I am on. Other villains can appear, but the player should be constantly reminded of their arch-nemesis.

- **Come up with a way to tie them together.** What's the one visual or behavioral cue that will differentiate your enemy from the others in your game? Or from other games? Within your game, you can create groups of enemies based on shapes, color, physical attributes, weapons, or uniforms.

- **Be economical with your enemies.** Re-use models, animations, and textures wherever possible to get the most bang for your production buck. When creating similar enemies with different behaviors and attacks, make them look different at a glance. I call this design mentality "**Red Ninja/Blue Ninja**" as a red ninja enemy may be set to hop and throw shuriken, while a blue ninja may use dash attacks with sai. Sub-Zero and Scorpion, two of the most famous characters from *Mortal Kombat* series, were originally just reskinned versions of each other[12].

- **Does the enemy belong in your world?** You wouldn't expect to find a cybernetic death-mecha in a *Super Mario* game; that world is too whimsical for such "serious" enemies. Conversely, a goomba would be seriously out of place in a realistic *Medal of Honor* style title.

- **Make your enemy look like an enemy.** Glowing red eyes, demonic horns, fangs, clawed hands, spikes, skull ornamentation, ragged capes, fearsome masks and helmets that obscure faces. Sure, this is stereotypical imagery but if your player sees a character in the world with any of these visual traits, they're going to shoot first and ask questions later. Stereotypes are stereotypes for a reason: they're easy for the viewer to understand. Don't be afraid to use them to your advantage.

- **… Or go against expectation and type.** You can go against "type" and juxtapose your enemy's visual with their behavior. How about a cute bunny that turns into a slavering killer? Or a hulking troll that will burst into tears when attacked? The more personality you can add to make your enemy feel and look unique, the better[13].

I HATE YOU TO PIECES

When introducing your boss to the player, do it in a memorable fashion. Who can forget Darth Vader's entrance in *Star Wars*? Make sure the player

---

[12] Of course, in the case of Sub-Zero and Scorpion it would be "blue ninja, yellow ninja", which doesn't quite have the same zing.

[13] Just remember not to violate the triangle of weirdness.

gets a good look at the villain, that they understand "this is the bad guy" they will eventually fight. You always want to give your main villain[14] their "Joker moment", where the bad guy executes a henchman or some other NPC to show what a truly bad guy (or girl or he-she-demon) he is. This can happen within the game or a cutscene.

Have other characters talk about how bad the boss is before you introduce him. Or give the player information in collectable form like audio clips or data files or letters to warn the player about the enemy. This works when dropping hints to the player on how to defeat the enemy or boss. Arm them with knowledge along with the firepower. Anticipation of fighting the boss will be greater if the player knows the fight is coming.

When I was working on a game based on the movie *Demolition Man*, the designers were presented with an interesting challenge. Simon, the movie's bad guy, didn't fight the hero until the very end of the game. But the designers knew that Simon had to be a recurring villain in the game so they came up with a clever solution.

At the start of every level, Simon would run out onto the screen, shake his fist at the player and then run off. The effect on the player was electric. They'd shake their fist back and say: "Oooh! That darn Simon! I'm a-gonna git him!" and then proceed to blast their way through a half hour of gameplay. By the time the player reached the next level, they were probably so heady from all the killin', they forgot why they were there until Simon would run out again, shake his fist and re-energize the player. This taught me a **very important thing**:

---

[14] If you can have other enemies than just the main villian have this "being bad" moment, then that's even better.

MAKE THE PLAYER HATE THEIR ENEMY

How? Simple. Make sure your boss does bad things! This is why villains are always killing off their own henchmen: so they have someone to kill if they can't kill the main characters! Have the enemy take something the player needs or cares about. Kill the hero's parents, kidnap the princess girlfriend, burn down their quaint village, you get the idea. Whatever your enemy does, make sure it impacts the gameplay as well as the story. Make the parent the blacksmith that gives the hero that magic sword. Does the girlfriend heal the hero whenever he visits her hut? Not anymore! The enemy just kidnapped her! And now that the village is burned to the ground, where is the player going to store all the collectables he's found? Japanese RPGs do this right—they kill off the player's girlfriend, who happens to be your best party member. Are those tears I see? Are they being shed for a lost love or because you can no longer heal every other turn?

When it comes time to design your boss fights, don't feel like you have to kill the boss at the end of each battle. In fact, it's better if you don't. It gives the player someone to fight later in the game. Because your player will have "history" with this bad guy, they will hate them even more! If you kill off your enemy in the first act, who is left for the player to fight? Unmotivated, your hero loses the will to live, starts drinking, moves in with his parents[15].

Pathetic.

And more importantly, not fun.

Taunts are a great way to get the player's Irish[16] up, but you have to be careful not to overuse them. To paraphrase Spider-Man, "With great power,

[15] Oh right, his parents are dead! Now you've turned your hero into a homeless person. Are you happy with yourself?

[16] I apologize to any Irish people reading this, especially Irish people who are prone to get angry at authors.

comes dialogue-the-player-is-going-to-tire-of-hearing-over-and-over-again." Taunt the player physically as well as verbally. You can even build them into your enemy's attack moves. For example, in *Maximo: Ghosts to Glory*, there is a sword-wielding skeleton that, every time he'd successfully hit the player, would do a little flourish with his sword, like a gunslinger spinning his guns before he holstered them. This flourish was created to give the player an opportunity to strike back and wipe the grin off that cocky little so-and-so's face.

Simple animations like idles and taunts go a long way in making an enemy feel smarter than they actually are and provide lots of character. Has the player retreated too far for the enemy to attack? Have it berate the player or make "come here" gestures. Did the player successfully elude the enemy with stealth? It should shrug its shoulders and mutter that they must have been seeing things. Some games have guard enemies taking smoking breaks or falling asleep at their post to make them easier pickings for the hero. But keep in mind you don't want every one of your enemies to act this way, otherwise you've just thwarted the uniqueness you were trying to achieve.

One last thing about enemies: sometimes you should let the bad guys win.

I don't mean killing off the player in order to give your enemies a victory, but don't baby your players either[17]. Let the enemy get in a hit (or a cheap shot) once in a while. Give the enemy a temporary invulnerable attack state. Force the player to run away or at least block an attack. Have your enemies outnumber the player several times over. Let them sweat it out as to whether they'll survive the encounter. The player should feel like they are actually in danger from the enemies. A bad guy isn't going to feel very threatening if the player doesn't have to struggle to defeat them. And the player's victory is going to feel hollow if the enemies don't provide a challenge.

NON-ENEMY ENEMIES

As mentioned at the start of this chapter, not every game has physical enemies that are to be overcome with hot lead and cold steel. There are plenty of ways to push and punish your player without resorting to fighting sentient beings.

Gremlin. This character looks like an enemy, but doesn't directly engage the player. Instead, a gremlin will disrupt the game by undoing the player's

---

[17] I'll be talking more about difficulty in Level 13, so hold your horses.

progress. For example, *SimCity* features a Godzilla-like monster that stomps through the player's city leaving destruction in its wake.

Tormentor. This enemy challenges and taunts the player throughout the course of the game, but never directly confronts or attacks them. The alien overlord of *Space Fury* and *Portal*'s sentient computer GLaDOS are examples of tormentor enemies. In the case of *Portal*, the player can "defeat" GLaDOS by tearing her apart but it is implied that - SPOILER ALERT!! - she is "still alive" at the end of the game.

Time. "Time pressure makes people think something is a lot more complicated than it really is[18]." Found primarily in skill-based games like driving/racing and puzzle games, a ticking clock is a great way to unnerve the player, creating pressure without using an enemy. Some games will allow the player to extend or slow the clock for temporary relief. If the player doesn't achieve the objective or finish the task within the allotted time, the player either loses a life or the scenario is reset. Time can also be used as an endgame, where the player has to escape a base before it blows up.

Human competitor. Player vs player, competitive or cooperative— regardless of the gameplay mode, I find the best and worst thing about multiplayer games is… the other players[19]. Your friends (and complete strangers) will always find new ways to torture, torment, and humiliate you during a game. As a designer, never underestimate the power of one-upmanship and revenge. Just give the players the tools they need to act on these and sit back and watch the fun unfold. As the old saying goes, keep your friends close and your enemies closer, because sometimes they are the same person.

HOW TO CREATE THE WORLD'S GREATEST BOSS BATTLE

↑ *Video game BOSS (n): a large and/or challenging enemy that blocks a player's progression and acts as the climax/ending to the game's environment, level, or world.* ↑

---

[18] A succinct quote from Portal designer Kim Swift from GDC 08: Portal Creators on Writing, Multiplayer and Government Interrogation Techniques, Chris Faylor, Shacknews.com (http://www.shacknews.com/featuredarticle.x?id=784).

[19] I am reminded of Jean-Paul Sartre's famous quote: "Hell is other people." As Sartre died in 1980, we'll never know whether he would have appreciated a good deathmatch.

At first glance, a **boss battle** may appear to be an encounter with a very, very, very large enemy with too much health. But this is an underestimation. Bosses are very complex creatures with many unique and separate working parts that should be thoughtfully designed.

Just like with enemies, boss characters are fun to create. But before you start designing your boss, you must first make sure that you have completely defined the player's move and attack set. Once that's set, there are three different ways to design a boss fight:

- **Learned moves.** The boss encounter is designed around the player's existing set of moves. You don't have to teach the player anything new and they feel like they've mastered those skills when they defeat the boss. The *Mario* titles design their bosses this way.
- **New abilities.** The boss encounter is designed around the player gaining a new weapon or new move. The player's learning curve is part of the boss round's difficulty. You find this in many of the bosses in the *Legend of Zelda* series.
- **Combination.** No one is saying these two design styles are mutually exclusive. Make sure to stage your encounter with emphasis placed on one style or the other—don't try to do both at once.

WHO'S THE BOSS?

Boss design is just like enemy design, where form should follow function. Knowing the boss' movement and attacks will determine the boss' appearance: if he can shoot, give your boss a gun (or a magic spell or a rocket launcher or a large nose to sneeze out nose goblins), and if he can defend himself, give him a shield (or a force field or protective cowling or a missile-deflecting karate move). In a nutshell, if they can do it, they should have it.

Next, consider how does the boss relate to the hero? No, I don't mean in a "Darth Vader is your father" way, but rather what does the boss represent? The James Bond movies of the 1960s and 1970s had a really good formula for bad guys. There were technically three "boss types" that Bond had to defeat.

physical   mental   global

The first villain was the arch henchman; the **physical adversary**. A muscle-bound goon that would beat the tar out of Bond until he turned the tables with one of his spy gadgets or a deftly executed judo move to throw the goon into a pool of piranhas. Physical adversaries in the Bond films are the classic henchmen like Jaws, Tee Hee, and OddJob. In video games, these characters are monstrously large, freakishly hideous, and very heavily armed.

The second villain type is the mastermind; the **mental adversary**. These villains are fought at the film's climax. Usually mastermind intelligence leaves the hero at a disadvantage and against overwhelming odds. In video games, this is when the boss gets into their robotic suit to blast away at the hero or forces the player to solve an environmental puzzle that, when solved, brings the cackling villain to his knees.

Even though the mastermind has been defeated, there is still one more "villain" to defeat: the **global threat**. This isn't a person so much as a threat to the hero's world. This can be the timer on Goldfinger's nuclear bomb, Hugo Drax's deadly spore bombs, or SPECTRE's space-capsule-eating rocket.

Some questions to consider when designing bosses:

- What makes the boss a worthy adversary? Most bosses have the upper hand on the player in size, strength, firepower, and defenses—make sure the player knows they are in trouble even before the fight begins.

- What does the boss represent to the hero? In many games and movies, the villain is merely an obstacle to the hero gaining true love (rescuing the princess) or a threat to peace. But don't be content with those tropes. Villains can represent the inner demons of the hero; in *Return of the Jedi*, Luke Skywalker must reject the dark side and become like his father in order to defeat the Emperor (or at least motivate daddy to toss the old bastard down a shaft.)

- What does the hero gain by defeating the villain? It shouldn't be treasure, weapons, or power. In most movies and games, the hero is content to merely save the world and restore the status quo. But in the classic "Hero's Journey" story structure, the hero returns from their adventure with knowledge. For example, in *Indiana Jones and the Temple of Doom*, Indy finds out that fortune and glory aren't the only important things in life.

- Every good villain has their own motivation and goals. Give your boss a more compelling motivation than "he's evil." I find "the seven deadly sins of man" (lust, gluttony, greed, sloth, wrath, envy, and pride) to be a great starting point for villainous motivations. The Joker lives to create chaos and amuse himself. Voldemort wanted to regain his corporeal form and power. Whatever the villain's motivations and goals, they have to come in conflict with the hero's own. The boss is the primary obstacle to the hero's success. Only once the villain is defeated can the hero truly achieve their goal.

- What's the boss' job? In video games, most bosses are guardians; the guardian of a magic weapon, of a captured princess, of progression. But by keeping it at just this, you are doing a disservice to your villain. Give the boss a motivation.

- Is your game based on a licensed property? Remember that these boss fights are the highlight of the fan's play experience. If you aren't a fan of the property yourself, research it enough to find out what the player would want to do. It's safe to say that a *Star Wars* fan will find a lightsaber fight against Darth Vader a lot more thrilling than shooting down his advanced TIE fighter.

Congratulations. You've done a great job giving your boss a believable motivation, clear goals, and an intriguing backstory. It looks menacing and has awesome attacks and behaviors. But the most common way to make a boss look bad and dangerous is to make it **huge**.

SIZE MATTERS

A bigger boss means a badder boss… and bigger camera problems. You can start to solve this by always focusing the camera on the boss. As the boss should completely command the player's attention, you should never let the boss, or the player, leave the camera view. Avoid placing your camera:

- Too high: the high angle de-emphasizes drama and the scale of the boss.

- Too low: the foreshortening that happens makes it hard to gauge the distance to the boss and see incoming attacks. It can also cause clipping issues if the camera drops through level geometry.

Use elevation in the level and with the boss to help rectify some of this. Allow the player to reach the boss by climbing geometry to higher elevations. Or you can bring the boss down to the player's level just in time for the player to give the enemy a good smack to the face. One thing you want to avoid is **crotch whacking**. This is when the height of the player is just tall enough to reach the crotch of the huge boss.

A big boss means big attacks. Why be content with the boss throwing rocks when you can have it throw cars? Why not buildings? Or entire city blocks? The more dramatic your attacks, the more memorable they are. Take inspiration from games with bombastic bosses like *Contra* and *God of War 3*. Regardless of how spectacular the attacks are, you will need to give the player an opportunity to fight back. The player needs to work out when it is safe for them to attack. They need to memorize the boss **attack patterns**. Patterns are at the heart of every traditional boss fight and are created when several attacks and behaviors are strung together into a predictable sequence. Here's a simple example to show how patterns can be created.

fig. 1.   fig. 2.   fig. 3.   fig. 4.

Let's say the player is fighting a giant mech armed with a laser cannon. The cannon's laser sight sweeps the arena three times (fig. 1). Once the sight has acquired a target (the player), the cannon will fire a stream of laser blasts—first to the right, then to the left, then in the middle of the arena. The mech's cannon then transforms into a larger weapon. This new form charges up for a second (fig. 2) and then fires a single thick beam that sweeps the ground of the arena which can only be avoided by jumping or ducking behind cover (fig. 3). When the attack is over, the mech's chest cowling pops open and vents steam (fig. 4). After a couple of seconds the cowling snaps back closed in a burst of electricity and the mech re-transforms its cannon back into its original configuration. The attacks cycle until there is a break in the pattern initiated by the player, such as the player taking damage, dying, or successfully attacking the boss.

This example shows the components of a boss fight: the primary attack, the invulnerable attack, the vulnerable state, and opportunities.

The **primary attack**, the laser blasts, create **movement patterns** for the player to memorize and follow (left, right, center). As long as the player knows that sequence, they'll be able to avoid taking damage.

Movement patterns should be easy to remember, but feel free to change the order of events to add some variety. Random movement patterns can be used, but I have found that many players find them difficult to determine and get frustrated if they don't "luck" into a favorable pattern.

The **invulnerable attack**, the charged cannon shot, is a dramatic, large-scale attack that forces the player to take avoiding action. As the player cannot hurt the boss during this attack, the player must act defensively, breaking up the play pattern.

The **vulnerable state**, the mech's chest cowling opening up, reveals the boss Achilles heel to the player and is vulnerable to the player's attacks. This should be the chance the player has to inflict the most damage on the boss. The boss weak spot should be visually designed to be obvious to the player: make it flash, glow, or highlight it in some manner. It should stick out like a sore thumb. You can prolong a vulnerable state by stunning or incapacitating the boss—it becomes very clear to the player that they have a chance to attack without the fear of being attacked back. Make sure you end the vulnerable state with an attack/event of some sort (in this case the electric burst), which pushes the player away from the boss and informs the player that their chance to attack the boss is over.

Opportunities, like the cannon changing form, are chances the player has to attack. The window of opportunity is usually shorter than the one given by the vulnerable state. Taunts work well for this too. Just don't overuse any vocal cues, otherwise the player will get tired of hearing them over and over again.

I like to think of boss fights as a dance between the enemy and the player. Alternate between offensive and defensive moves for both the boss and player. Get more mileage out of your boss attacks and moves by changing the timing, speed, and range; just make sure these changes escalate. Most bosses start out pretty easy and get harder as they go. This is why many bosses have several rounds of patterns—the boss gets  madder and the threats ramp up until the ultimate climax when the boss is defeated.

Even as your boss is trying to kill the player, make sure to do all you can to keep the fight going. Provide plenty of opportunities for the player to regain health or power during the fight. Tools like **dynamic difficulty** will programmatically determine what the player needs to succeed. You can apply dynamic difficulty to enemy AI, reaction times—in fact, just about anything. Delivering the right power-up exactly when the player needs it makes the boss fight feel exciting and dramatic.

I have a confession. While most games design the final boss to be the hardest, I have designed them to be one of the easiest. Why? Because I want the player to end the game on a high note and feel like the biggest badass on the face of the planet. They've already done the hard part—playing through the entire game.

When the player gives the boss their comeuppance, use animations, sound cues, and visual effects to show that the player is damaging it. A robotic enemy can shoot off sparks, a fleshy foe can spray out gouts of blood or ichor. Other bosses will limp or crawl as they are close to death. Work with your artist to build your boss to have parts of it get chopped off or use several models that show increasingly damaged states. No matter how your boss goes, remember this **very important thing**:

LET THE PLAYER ADMINISTER THE *COUP DE GRACE*

The last strike of the fight *needs* to be delivered by the player. It's very important psychologically for the player to feel that they have won. This is the climax of the encounter—don't rob your player of their victory with a cutscene or a canned animation. Once the boss is dead, let the player savor the moment with celebratory text, music, or effects.

Sometimes, due to story or licensing needs, your enemy will escape at the end of a boss fight. As the enemy escapes, do it with style. Having an enemy escape to fight another day shows to the player that they are a worthy adversary and another encounter is coming. But even if the boss escapes, you still need to make the end of the fight satisfying. You need the **false kill**. You must first knock the boss to his knees before he gets up and runs away. Hold camera on that defeated boss for a moment. Let him curse the player's good luck (because it's never skill that defeats a bad guy, right?) Make sure it's clear to the player that they've won the fight.

One more thing. Sometimes the player is going to die. When they do, make sure they return to a safe respawn point. The boss shouldn't attack until the player is ready to fight. Consider keeping the boss' game state upon the player respawn. This means picking up the fight where the player left it rather than restarting the entire boss fight sequence from the beginning.

LOCATION, LOCATION, LOCATION

Where a boss fight takes place is just as important as designing the fight itself. The level is an extension of the boss fight—and sometimes, the level IS the boss fight.

The basic boss fight takes place either in a circular arena or a linear screen-wide walkway. This allows the camera to stay focused on the boss who generally inhabits the center or back of the room with occasional trips to the side and outer edges. For more dynamic boss fights, add elevation to the arena. *Devil May Cry* had an interesting fight where the player kept alternating between fighting the boss on the walls of a castle and in the castle's courtyard.

Think about the boss in relationship to the environment. How will a boss use the level for movement or attacks? Having dynamic elements like collapsing statues or walls or break away floors can keep things exciting and surprising as the environment gets wrecked by the boss (and the player) over the course of the battle. Bust that joint up! Just be aware that if the player has to replay the boss fight, it may get a little stale seeing the event happen again and again.

Designing boss arenas with dynamic level elements is the best of both worlds. The arena contains dynamic objects and elements that will react to a certain boss attack or action. These can be breakable windows, smashable floorboards, crushable computer consoles, and so on. This way, no matter what order the boss interacts with these elements during the battle, interesting things will happen. It creates a different experience every time.

A **scrolling battle**, where the player and boss fight their way through several locations, makes for a dynamic boss fight. First determine the method of player locomotion during the fight. Are they fighting on foot (chasing each other?), on top of vehicles (like the moving train in *Uncharted 2: Among Thieves* or hopping from car to car as in *Wet*), or while piloting vehicles? (Maybe they *are* vehicles!) Just be careful as scrolling boss fights require as much work, if not more than a full level.

Another variation is the **puzzle boss**: a boss that is actually invulnerable and cannot be defeated by a direct assault by the player. Instead of fighting, the player has to survive the boss' attacks long enough to use objects in the level that will defeat it. Spidey can't actually hurt the Rhino boss in *Spider-Man 2* (Activision, 2004) but if Spidey can trick the Rhino into smashing into electrified machinery, he can defeat him. The most obvious (and hilarious) example of a puzzle boss is in *You Have To Burn The Rope* (http://www.youhavetoburntherope.net) where the Grinning Colossus can only be defeated by … well, I'll let you guess how to beat this one[20].

WHY NOT TO CREATE THE WORLD'S GREATEST BOSS BATTLE

Some designers believe that boss fights are too "old school"; that they grind game progression to a halt; that the time and effort to create bosses with their non-reusable artwork, hard-coded behaviors, and unique animations just isn't worth the production cost. They create a skill gateway; whenever someone has told me that they've quit playing a game, it was usually because a boss was too hard.

An alternative to these problems can be found in turning the boss fight on its head. Instead of making it about a big *creature*, make it about big *drama*.

---

[20]Spoiler alert: you have to burn the rope.

Make the fight personal to the player, and more about pivotal moments in the story.

My friend, designer Paul Guirao (*Dead to Rights*, *Afro Samurai*), created what I thought was the best boss fight design I had ever heard. During the course of his game, the player would learn to arm-wrestle in order to win cigarettes—the game's currency while the hero was in prison. At the climax of the game, the hero is knocked to the ground by the villain who attempts to plunge a dagger into the hero's eye! The player has to use his arm-wrestling skill to force the dagger away, and eventually turn it on the villain himself.

Paul's design really opened my eyes (groan) to what a boss fight could be. It sounded awesome and dramatic and very different to anything else I had seen in games. What I really liked about it was:

Emphasized drama over scale: it didn't need a rocket-firing colossus rampaging through a city to be exciting.

Intimacy creates urgency: because the camera view was to be very tight (only the faces of the two characters, their hands, and the dagger were to be shown), the impending danger was heightened to a degree not seen in most video games.

Better utilizes existing assets: all the assets for the fight—the hero, the villain, the dagger, the arm-wrestling HUD meter—were used in other parts of the game. Nothing new had to be created to make this boss fight playable.

Told story with boss fight, not cutscenes: video games are **interactive** entertainment—playing the story is always better than watching it.

SPOILER ALERT!

Years later, as I played the ending of *Call of Duty: Modern Warfare 2* I was reminded of Paul's knife-fight design. In *CoD:MW2*, your player character is stabbed in the chest by the villain who is now killing your commanding officer. The player has to (painfully) pull the knife from his own chest and hurl it into the eye of the bad guy (in very dramatic slo-mo).

Had the designers at Infinity Ward heard of Paul's knife-fight design idea? Or was it just a good idea for a boss fight whose time had finally come? All I know is it was as awesome and dramatic as Paul's boss fight idea had sounded to me all those years ago.

Level 11's Universal Truths and Clever Ideas:

- Form follows function.

- Design your enemies to complement and contrast with each other.

- Carefully balance the enemy's strength, speed, and size.

- Fighting enemies is supposed to be fun.

- Enemies are meant to be fought, not avoided.

- Not every enemy attack has to do damage.

- You always want the player to hate the enemy.

- Use dynamic difficulty to give the player some help.

- Watch out for camera issues when creating a large-scale boss.

- Where the boss fight takes place is just as important as who the player is fighting.

- The player has to give the boss the killing blow.

- There are other types of enemies besides big stompy monsters.

- Emphasize drama over scale.

LEVEↈ 12

THE NUTS AND BOLTS
OF MECHANICS

↑ *If you find a path with no obstacles, it probably doesn't lead anywhere.* ↑
Author unknown

There's nothing worse than an empty level you just walk through[1], so we need to start throwing things in the player's way. Good things, bad things, things that make the player cry with pleasure and weep with sadness. We need **mechanics**. Lucky for us, there are four types of these beauties to work with: **mechanics**, **hazards**, **props**, and **puzzles**.

Before we dig in, be aware that mechanics is another term that suffers from MDS: multiple definition syndrome. Board game designers say mechanics are the gameplay systems used to play a game. These are things like turns, action points, resource management, bidding, and even rolling the dice.

Video game mechanics are objects that create gameplay when the player interacts with them. They can be jumped on, activated with a button press, or pushed around. Combine them with interesting level layouts and enemies. Some of the more common video game mechanics include:

- Opening/closing doors
- Pushable blocks
- Switches and levers
- Slippery floors
- Conveyor belts
- Moving platforms.

Platforms are a beloved mechanic of action game designers. They come in a wide variety of styles and flavors that can be used to bedevil and delight players. Here's a suitable-for-framing chart that I've devised to help you identify platforms in the wild. Be careful, some of them bite!

[1] Because WALKING IS NOT GAMEPLAY!!

PLATFORM PRIMER

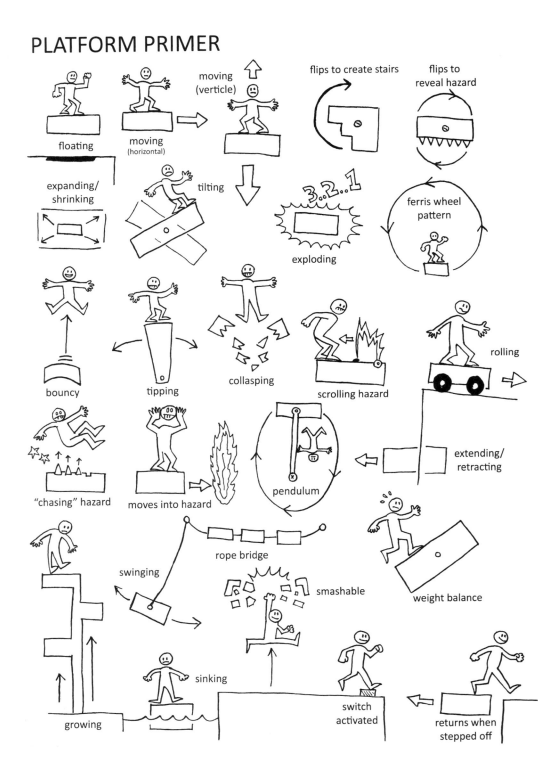

floating

moving (horizontal)

moving (verticle)

flips to create stairs

flips to reveal hazard

expanding/ shrinking

tilting

exploding

ferris wheel pattern

bouncy

tipping

collasping

scrolling hazard

rolling

"chasing" hazard

moves into hazard

pendulum

extending/ retracting

weight balance

swinging

rope bridge

smashable

growing

sinking

switch activated

returns when stepped off

You would think that something like **doors** would be easy to design; after all, we all have used them in the real world, right? But doors open their own set of issues. Think about how the player is meant to open a door. Normally? Carefully? Aggressively? Remember, the character's personality comes into play when thinking about this. Kratos kicks open doors. "Soap" Mctavish uses explosives to blow open doors. Jill Valentine opens doors very slowly and carefully. Does a player have to pick the lock before they enter?

Be mindful of which way your door opens. Does it open in? Does it rise up like a portcullis? Does it lower down? Does it swing out? All of these opening actions can lead to different gameplay scenarios. *Mappy* (Namco, 1983) used doors to whack and temporally stun enemies. A portcullis in an action game might lower back down after raised, requiring the player to dash under it before it drops down. Even a simple door in a survival horror game can be closed in the face of an enemy to buy the player the time to reload or escape.

Despite their benefits, doors can bring their own problems. Quickly opening doors can clip into the player or cause the player to get knocked back. Make sure your player doesn't get caught on doors and doorway geometry. It may seem like an insignificant problem, but after getting caught up in hundreds of doorways, your player will be pissed off. That's the reason why so many games make opening doors a canned animation sequence. The early *Resident Evil* games designed their level loading to correspond with the player opening a door. Not only did it mask the loading of the level section, but it built tension as the door slowly swung open.

Make sure you know the answers to these questions and then keep the method of entry consistent throughout your entire game.

Some doors are just not meant to be opened. Locked doors are perfect for getting players to find another route through a level, but just make sure it's super clear why they can't get through. Your locked door can look like it's made out of unbreakable metal, have a huge lock on it that the player doesn't have the key for, or it can be blocked with debris that the player can't move. Whatever the choice, the appearance needs to be obvious to avoid frustration. Locked doors are often (some say too often) used to introduce this common gameplay scenario: the quest to find the key[2].

Switches, **cranks**, and **levers** are another old standby in video game design. Some designers love using them, others avoid them like the plague. I admit that nothing makes my eyes roll faster than seeing a lever sitting in the middle of a room. It's something that screams "video game" to me. How many times in your life have you actually pulled a lever? But, they are very useful for a variety of gameplay mechanics. If you do use switches and levers, keep them visually simple. Now I know that one of the great pleasures in designing video games is creating fantastical things, but players will clearly understand the "cause and effect" if you keep things grounded in reality.

Whatever you end up doing with your switches and levers, make sure that:

- You consider placing a visual effect like a glow or an icon on your switch or lever. Because levers are usually shown as slender poles, the player might have a hard time seeing them.
- The player sees the effect of activating the switch/pulling the lever. That means using a camera cut, voice, and/or sound effect to make sure it's clear.
- The switch/button should change appearance to show that it is in a new state. Have it change color, position or shape. If the switch is a one-way switch (one that only operates once), play a nice meaty sound effect to indicate that it's permanently changed its state. If it's a resetting switch, then play a "timer" sound effect to indicate that that switch is going to revert back to its original state. You can even display a timer graphic so the player knows how much time they have left.

[2] We'll talk more about keys in Level 13.

Cranks are like levers and switches that take time for the player to activate. Some cranks are operated by pressing a button and holding it, while others require furious button mashing to open. Some games turn rotating a crank into a rhythm game where the player has to sync button presses with the animation of the character onscreen. You can even turn a crank into a combat puzzle like the ones in *Devil May Cry*. If turning a crank takes X seconds to activate, then spawn enemies to attack the player as they are turning it. If the enemies hit the player, he'll be knocked off the crank, which will unwind the crank's progress. The player will have to alternate between fighting enemies and turning the crank.

Need a little more help coming up with mechanics? I just happen to have a list in Bonus Level 6.

HOLY DEATH TRAP!

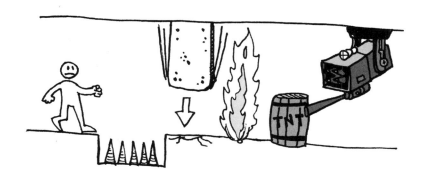

Hazards are the mechanic's nasty little brother who will slip an M-80 into your underpants when you aren't looking. They look like mechanics, they often act like mechanics, but they will kill a player just for snoring too loud. Hazards may also resemble enemies, but the key difference is intelligence and/or mobility. All hazards have predictable patterns and limited movement.

- Spiky pits
- Smashing blocks
- Blasting flames
- Exploding barrels
- Laser-guided missile launching turrets.

When you are designing hazards, the first rule is to make sure that they look dangerous. That means spiky, flamey, frosty, sparky, poison-y. Slap a big death's head on it if you have to.

When creating your mechanics, take inspiration from the theme of your level. Create things that look like they belong in the level. For example, in the dungeon level of *Maximo: Ghosts to Glory*, we had:

- Grabbing prisoner hands that pop out from grates
- Suit of armor wielding a chopping axe
- Spinning spiked iron maidens
- A toxic sewer filled with floating coffin platforms.

Get inspiration from dangerous-looking things in the real world; from spiny cacti to razor wire. Use shape, color, sound effects, and particle effects: anything to make it clear to the player that they WILL get hurt if they touch/collide with this hazard. And to demonstrate this point, there follows a great example of what I DON'T mean.

I was designing a hazard and took the design to the artist who was going to be building it. I suggested that the hazard be colored red, as many cultures associate the color red with danger. The artist said "that's too predictable. I think it should have yellow and black stripes." I was intrigued (I was thinking of the yellow and black hazard edging found on loading docks) so I asked her why. She replied "because bees have black and yellow stripes and everyone knows that bees are dangerous."

Epilogue no. 1: The hazard ended up red.

That story reminds of another story. A designer and I were reviewing level designs. This particular level featured a ship that would sail away as the player started the level. The player had to run to catch up with the ship, otherwise they would literally miss the boat. I told the designer that I thought that the player would stop and look around to get their bearings when they started a level. If the player took the time to do that, they'll literally miss the boat. What would happen to the player if that happened? He said "Oh, we can just drop a big rock on the player's head so they'll die and have to start the level over again."

Epilogue no. 2: We didn't make that level. As a result, I came up with this **very important thing**:

NO DROPPING ROCKS ON THE
PLAYER'S HEAD[3]

Instant death hazards just suck. They are cheap and mean-spirited. If the player is going to die because of a hazard, let them die because they didn't pay attention or get the timing right. Make them realize it was their fault they died, not because the designer decided they needed to die. Death is never a good way to educate the player. It just makes the player frustrated and sad.

The secret to balancing great video game design is knowing this:

Difficulty = promotes pain and loss.
Challenge = promotes skill and improvement.

A difficult game does whatever it can to punish the player. A challenging game confronts the player with obstacles that can be overcome with skill and knowledge. I believe a challenging game is much more rewarding than a difficult one.

Some gamers absolutely love difficult games. The list of ridiculously difficult games could fill this entire chapter: *Demon's Souls*, the *Ninja Gaiden* series, *Contra*, *Ikaruga*, *Shinobi*, *Devil May Cry 3*, the *Ghosts 'n Goblins* series, *Defender*, *Battletoads*. I admit, it is quite an accomplishment to finish a difficult game, but those that do are in the minority. If you want players to play your game to completion, then your game needs to be challenging, not difficult.

When I first started designing video games, I would refer to the balance between challenge and difficulty as the "**fun curve**." There is a point in the game where things have ceased to be challenging and drop straight into difficult and frustrating. The goal was to never "go over the fun curve." Years later, I learned there was an actual psychological theory about the fun curve called "**flow**." We'll get to flow in a moment.

My key to keep players from "going over the fun curve" is to create **ramping gameplay**. A designer must build one gameplay system upon the last, teaching the player a new move and how to master it against mechanics and enemies. These gameplay elements are combined and gently intensify as the game progresses. But I'm getting ahead of myself. If

---

[3]I mean that figuratively as well as literally.

we are going to talk about the timepiece, we are going to have to examine the clockworks first.

TIME TO DIE

Another important mechanic is the **timing puzzle**. Timing puzzles are mechanics that move. They are perfect for creating tense moments where the player has to wait for the right moment to dash through whirling blades or smashing pylons[4]. They cause anticipation for the player as they wait for the right moment to jump to a moving platform. A timing puzzle should have the following:

1. The hazard must have a discernable movement pattern. Back and forth, up and down, zigzag, circular, or figure of eight: it doesn't matter, just as long as the player can track its movement.
2. The hazard must have predictable timing. Random timing is unfair to the player, who needs to understand the pattern to be successful.
3. The window of opportunity must be tight, but not impossible. Allow leeway for the player at the start and close of the window's opening.
4. Use "tells" in the world to give the player clues to where it is safe to stand and where they will be hurt or killed. Bloodstains, grooves in the floor, lighting and shadows, sound effects, particle effects, geometry, decorative elements; players notice these things and will learn to use them as markers for success.

wait for it...   wait for it...   ...go for it!

Props are mechanics after a big Thanksgiving dinner; they don't move unless someone asks them to get off the couch and do the dishes. These

---

[4]To this day, I still get tense thinking about those spinning paddles in the Spectre chamber of Dragon's Lair; a scenario which may be the first video game timing puzzle.

items can be placed by designers and artists into the level to make it feel more like a real place. Sometimes they act as barricades or obstacles for the player to avoid, jump over, or take cover behind:

- Desks and chairs
- Parked cars
- Barricades
- Statues and gravestones
- Trees and shrubbery
- Fences and walls
- Potted plants and water coolers.

Thinking up props can be an entertaining exercise in free association and brainstorming. Start with the predictable items that you would find in your level and go from there. Here's an exercise—come up with as many items and props for the following level themes:

- Easy: the street of a Wild West town
- Medium: a supervillain's lair
- Hard: Chinese clothing factory.

Pro tip: if you find your brainstorming ideas getting silly or filthy, you know you've reached a good place to stop. Let it settle overnight or for a day or two before starting again. Or take a research break and look for more inspiration in books, games, movies, or the interwebs.

Don't be satisfied with merely thinking up items to decorate your world—allow your players to interact with them. Start with natural reactions. If you shoot a water cooler it should explode in a watery splash. Let players knock over light items or shove around heavy ones. Let players closely examine interesting pieces of statues, bookshelves, or paintings.

You can shoot or smash props to access new areas or yield treasure. In the Lego games (like *Lego Star Wars* and *Lego Batman*), you can pretty much destroy anything—all yielding studs, the game's version of money. There's nothing more satisfying than busting up junk to get tons of treasure, but try not to overdo it as it can turn your carefully designed gameplay into a mindless smash-fest.

Crates are breakable items that yield goodies and double as platforms, but they're also overused clichés that have become a joke within the gaming industry; visually boring and, frankly, a lazy fallback for designers and artists who don't want to burn the brainpower to think up more interesting breakable objects.

START TO CRATE TIME: 00:00:05

Now, that's just pathetic.

Gaming website *Old Man Murray*[5] created a review system called "**start to crate**" that gauges the time it takes a player to encounter a crate in a game. While the article is meant to be satire, I find it to be a good gauge to determine just how creative your game is. Rather than reinvent the wheel… err, crate, here is a list of 50 breakable objects you can populate your game with other than a crate:

Barrel, treasure chest, vase, urn, trash can, mailbox, newspaper stand, baby carriage, metal drum, cargo container, cardboard box, cage, lantern, lamp post, filing cabinet, fish tank, toy box, keg, hay bale, pile of skulls, dog house, bird house, Tiki idol, statue, fortune-telling machine, church donation box, suggestion box, ATM, hollow tree stump, attaché case, safe, suitcase, TV monitor, fuel tank, refrigerator, oven, breadbox, bureau, wardrobe, parked car, coffin, arcade machine, soda machine, fire hydrant, vending machine, oxygen canister, filled shopping cart, one-armed bandit, copy machine, and toilet.

There. You never have to have a crate in your game again. You're welcome.

There is one more type of mechanic, which is the rarest one of all. It's the mechanic that's "just for fun." This can be the player piano that plinks out a tune as you approach it or the toilet that flushes if you interact with it. Don't be afraid to include these just-for-fun props in your own game.

THE MUSIC OF MECHANICS

In the great chili pot that is video game design, hazards are the beans. Just like beans, they act as filler when you don't have enough meat to go around

---

[5] See http://www.oldmanmurray.com/features/39.html for the article in question.

and… they help the designer make "music."[6] The goal of good level design is to help the player achieve what psychologist Mihály Csíkszentmihályi[7] calls **flow**. (I told you we'd get back to it.)

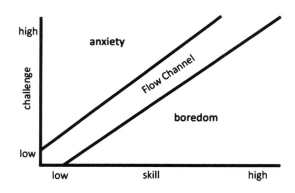

Csíkszentmihályi's theory proposes that there is a point between boredom and difficulty. A place where players become so engrossed that they become energized, focused, and unaware of time. But in order to create flow, you need to know how to orchestrate these elements together. Reaching the state of flow feels like making music; it's the rhythm of a great level. A natural rhythm of the player's movement and actions—or flow—starts to emerge as he traverses the level[8].

To me, game element placement is orchestrated like the instruments in Sergei Prokofiev's *Peter and the Wolf*. In this famous musical piece, each

---

[6] Yes, I went there.
[7] Pronounced "cheek sent me high-ee" You can bet your ass that I cut 'n' pasted that name.
[8] The ancient Greeks believed there was a correlation between music and mathematics. The Playstation game Vib Ribbon (SCE, 1999) uses musical beats from any music CD to generate gameplay mechanics and hazards. The same ideas shown here in my example can be applied from a mathematical persepective, where the gameplay elements and mechanics are combined to create a formula of successful gameplay. I am told that game designer Mark Cerny (Marble Madness, Crash Bandicoot, among others) works this way.

character (Peter, a duck, a cat, a bird, and the wolf) are represented by a different musical instrument. The piece starts out with Peter (represented by strings) walking through the forest. This musical theme gives the impression of movement, just like where the player is learning how to do the basics in a game: walking, driving, and manipulating the game character.

Then Peter is joined by the bird, which adds a higher register flute to the music. The two themes intertwine, adding excitement to the music; just like treasure and collectables keep the player excited and motivated to continue playing. The duck (represented by an oboe) joins in and the music speeds up and gets more complex, similar to the addition of complex movements and mechanics to your level design. When the lower register cat (a clarinet) comes in, the music picks up as the cat chases the bird, adding a little conflict to the piece—much like hazards in a level.

Once all the characters are together, the wolf's dangerous sounding theme comes in; this echoes the arrival of enemy characters in a game. The music in *Peter and the Wolf* intensifies as the wolf eats the duck, is attacked by the bird, and threatens and battles the heroes until they are rescued by the crashing arrival of hunters. (Represented by drums.)

Let's take a look at how we can introduce and orchestrate gameplay elements the same way that *Peter and the Wolf* adds instruments.

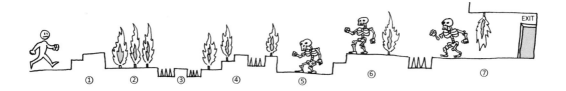

1. Start your player moving through the world with simple movement challenges: walking, jumping, and collecting goodies.
2. Then add one mechanic. Repeat it a couple of times so the player understands how it works.
3. Add a second mechanic, and let the player learn that one too. Then combine the first one with the second.
4. Make things exciting with a hazard. Let players get used to doing the things they would normally do in the game (traversal, collection, interaction with mechanics) but now with the hazard being part of the equation.
5. Now come the enemies! Give the players a chance to learn how to fight them.

6.   Combine the enemies with the hazards for more excitement.

7.   Finally, just as the player is getting used to all of these game elements, toss one of them on their head just to keep the player on his toes!

Well-designed enemies and hazards go together like peanut butter and chocolate! If you create them to complement each other[9], they'll end up being versatile tools when populating your level. Think about what order you want the player to do the activities and set up the scenario for the players to figure out. Here are a few examples of how to combine enemies and hazards to make life more difficult for your players:

The player has to jump over the hazardous pit with an enemy waiting on the other side. Place the enemy far enough away so he doesn't engage the player until he safely lands after the jump. To make this scenario more intense, have the pit have a timing element to it: pit opens and closes, a pendulum swings back and forth, fire gouts up, block slides down, and so on.

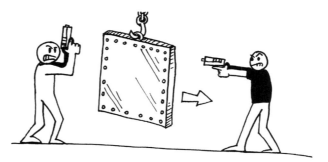

Here's an enemy that throws or shoots a projectile through the path of a moving hazard. Design the timing so that it passes through when the opening appears. The solution is for the player to dispatch the enemy (with their own projectile) before running through the moving hazard. Or the player can use the moving obstacle as cover to get in closer to the enemy.

[9] This is easy because form always follows function, right?

The whirling saw blade in this chamber will cut the player in half if they collide with it, which makes fighting these multiple enemies a challenge; the player has to dance between combat and avoiding the hazard. However, the blade should also kill the enemies, which makes the player feel clever when he lures them to their death by saw blade. Give the player plenty of opportunities to turn the death traps against their makers. It's all about the villains getting their comeuppance!

Fire pit, moving obstacle, whirling blade; there are many more combinations you can do with just these three mechanics. As these examples show, you really only need a few mechanics and enemy types to make a rich play experience. A well-designed game uses a handful of mechanics. The key is how you combine them. Play any game by developers Treasure (*Gunstar Heroes*, *Dynamite Heady*, *Ikaruga*) or Naughty Dog (*Crash Bandicoot*, *Uncharted*) to see some great examples of how to get the most out of your mechanics.

Be mindful that it is possible for players to get bored with mechanics if they are repeated too often, so think about the context in which they are used. Think of a good mechanic like a baseball pitcher. You need to rotate them in and out of your game to keep them fresh and effective.

A NICE LITTLE CALM SPOT

Now that we've gotten past the hazards with our lives, let's talk about a friendlier mechanic: **checkpoints**. Checkpoints are predesignated locations within the level where the player can save their progress, take a break, or reassess their choices of equipment, route, and so on. They can be invisible to the player or visible. You will want to determine which method is better for your own game.

Visible checkpoints offer the player a target in the level, provide a sense of security when they are activated, and can be an opportunity for an exciting or fun animation. The player feels a sense of accomplishment every time they reach and activate one.

On the other hand, visible checkpoints can look "gamey" and sometimes require explanation on how they can be activated.

Invisible checkpoints don't break the player's immersion while playing the game. However, as they are invisible, the player may not be sure when they are activating a checkpoint or where they will respawn upon death. This can be frustrating for the player as they wonder how far back in the level they will end up.

No matter which style checkpoint you use, here are a few rules of thumb to remember:

- Always face the checkpoint in the direction you want the player to travel in. Otherwise they'll get turned around or have to reorient the camera upon respawn.
- Never place a checkpoint next to a hazard or in the detection zone of an enemy. It's totally cheap to take damage when you (re)appear in a level.
- Players should respawn on the ground. That way they don't have to wait for the character to land on the ground. Also, avoid long respawn animations for the same reason.
- Place the checkpoint on flat, even ground to avoid any collision problems upon respawn.
- Make sure your game's saved data is retained whenever a checkpoint is activated. Don't make the player have to go into another menu just to save the game.

RIDDLE ME THIS

Puzzle mechanics can be tricky; not just because they can be difficult to design or because they often require unique assets to create. It's just that puzzles are tricky to classify. Here's one definition I've found:

↑   *A puzzle is fun and has a right answer.*   ↑
Scott Kim

While Mr. Kim has designed waaaay more puzzles than I ever will[10], this definition doesn't feel quite right to me. What bothers me is the use of the word "fun." Fun is completely subjective, like the words "funny" and "sexy." What I think is fun may not be fun for you. And frankly, I don't find many puzzles in video games to be fun. For me, there's nothing worse than a puzzle whose solution I just can't fathom. At least with a difficult boss monster, you can brute force your way through to victory. You just can't do that with a puzzle. So, with apologies to Mr. Kim, I have created my own definition:

↑ *A puzzle is a challenge that has a right answer.* ↑
Scott Rogers

The difference is the word "challenge." That's a puzzle's job (and the entire game for that matter!) to challenge the player. And the challenge of the puzzle is "solve me."

The player first needs to know what reward is offered for solving the puzzle. It can be to open a door, create a picture, or translate a message; just make sure the player knows "what do I need to do?" I always think this **very important thing** applies:

SHOW 'EM THE DOOR AND *THEN* SEND 'EM AFTER THE KEY[11]

When creating the puzzle, keep the puzzle's pieces simple and modular. You only need a few pieces to create many combinations. Work with as few moving pieces as possible to prevent the player from getting confused. Make sure that when a puzzle piece is adjusted, the player can see that it's

---

[10] Go to http://www.scottkim.com for loads of puzzley goodness, including free games!
[11] It doesn't have to be a door. And it doesn't have to be a key. I'm speaking metaphorically here.

been adjusted and a clear way to return it to its original position. Many times it's easy to lose track of progress. Keep the pieces uniform unless irregularity is part of the puzzle. Uniformity and consistency will keep it easy for a player to understand how the elements fit together. Let them concentrate on the puzzle, not the manipulation of the pieces. When the player interacts with a puzzle piece, a simple button press should show a result. It may not automatically lead to the solution, but they should get the idea that repeating the action will eventually get them there.

When I'm confronted with a puzzle in a game, I "check the puzzle" against every ability I have, every item I'm carrying and every object in the room. So I think about what the piece *is* and its relationship to the other pieces as well as to the entire puzzle. If the relationship of the puzzle pieces isn't clear, it's easy to get stumped. Make sure that you avoid cultural references or arcane or unusual uses of pieces to solve the puzzle.

For example, *Resident Evil 2* had a puzzle where the player needed to open a door in a police station. The puzzle required placing chess pieces into a control panel. Whaaaat? First of all, since when do you find chess pieces in a police station, let alone ones that operate a control panel? Now if it had been… I don't know… the ID cards of dead police officers found throughout the station, it would have made more sense. What I'm getting at is: tie the puzzle into the game's story and it won't seem so abstract to the player.

Players should have all the tools nearby that they need to solve the puzzle. It's not fair to make the player run all over the level, let alone the game world, wondering what works to solve the puzzle and what doesn't.

The layout of the puzzle is as much a clue as the pieces. If you present a board style layout, players can visualize movement and patterns using the board as a guide before they tackle the problem. If puzzle pieces move in a particular fashion, then players can visualize the consequences of moving the pieces. Just like with timing puzzles, movement and layout will help the player see patterns emerge which will help them reach their goal.

Puzzles in video games are essentially gating mechanisms. If you have lots of puzzles, then make sure there are multiple paths of progression. Eventually, they will have to come back to the puzzle that stumped them to solve it. But perhaps players will have figured out how to solve it in the meantime.

Tell the player whether they are close to finding the solution… or not. Remember that kid's game where you are searching for a hidden item and another player says, "you're hot" and "you're cold" depending on how close you are? Essentially, that's what the game designer needs to do for the player. Make your hints relevant to the puzzle. Ask yourself "what would I want to know at this point?" Remind the player what their goal is. Use camera cuts to show cause and effects that happen during the puzzle. Use voice and sound effects to give positive reinforcement. There are really only four ways to solve a puzzle: reason, knowledge, skill, or plain ol' dumb luck. The best puzzles allow players to use all four of these in some capacity to solve the puzzle. Granted you don't want the player to stumble onto the solution, but if that's what it takes, then a stumped player should at least be able to do that.

You need to give the player the "A-Ha!" moment (no, it's not the moment when you realize that "Take On Me" is a pretty catchy song). It's the moment when they realize how the puzzle fits together and the solution. They may still need to execute the puzzle, but that part should happen quickly; by that point, it's just a matter of getting the grunt work done.

However, if they don't get that "A-Ha!" moment and fail to solve the puzzle, don't make it a big deal. Find a way for the puzzle to be solved regardless of the player. Give the player hints or even the answer if you have to. Of course, getting the solution without solving the puzzle should cost the player something—a bonus or cash, as in the diminishing rewards in the *Professor Layton* games. Should you take hints or guess an answer wrongly don't make the punishment or payment something so severe as losing a life. Let the decision to pay-to-progress be the player's choice to pay the fine and skip ahead. Progression is a right, not a reward.

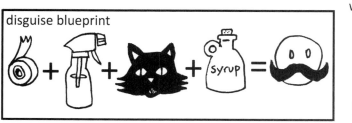

Players are generally smarter than you think when it comes to solving puzzles, but don't resort to cryptic or nonsensical solutions. An example of this is in an adventure game where the player had to disguise themselves as a non-player character to gain entry into a location. In order to create the disguise, the player had to stick tape over a hole in a fence that a cat passed through. The cat's back would rub against the tape and hair would stick to the tape which the player would use to create a mustache disguise. However, the non-player character that the player was disguising themselves as DIDN'T EVEN HAVE A MUSTACHE!! My **very important motto** for creating puzzles has since become:

NO CAT MUSTACHES

In other words, don't be so damn clever. If you have created a Rube Goldberg style[12] solution to your puzzle, then you've overthought it and it needs to be simplified. The conflict isn't "game designer vs player" but "player vs puzzle." So check your ego at the door and do what's right for the player and the game.

Of course, up to now, we've been talking about puzzles that you find in story-based games. But there are plenty of other puzzle-based games:

- Dexterity-based action puzzles like *Bejeweled* or *Puzzle Quest*
- Observation puzzles like the *Mystery Case Files* games
- Pure puzzles like *Sudoku* or crosswords
- Knowledge puzzles like *Buzz!* or *You Don't Know Jack*.

When creating trivia and knowledge puzzles, don't assume everyone knows what you do. Keep your questions short and clear. Do your research and determine what kind of questions your audience would want to answer. Make sure you have a wide range of difficulty from simple to obscure, but mostly simple. Write **lots** of questions. Knowledge games cease to be fun the minute you have answered all of the questions.

There are many different ways a player can answer a question. Which one is right for your game?

Multiple choice: give players a range of choices—at least three. Create "close answers," with answers that are similar to the real answer or ones that could be easily confused with the real answer. Remember to change things up by allowing the player to select the **wrong** answer from a group of correct ones.

Find the object/image: the player must hunt for the answer among a variety of images or objects. Don't make the hunt be pixel perfect, allow for

---

[12] Rube Goldberg was a newspaper cartoonist who drew very complex and amusing contraptions to do very simple things. The famous board game "Mouse Trap" is unofficially based on his cartoons.

plenty of space around the item so the player can eventually spot and select the answer. Play with image orientation, color, and size to keep your players hunting.

Fill in the answer: this requires keyboard or writing tablet input. Make sure your word parser is flexible enough to allow for synonyms, colloquialisms, and regional terms. DS game *Scribblenauts* has 22,802 words in their vocabulary! If your puzzle's vocabulary is smaller than that, consider letting the player learn what words are available so they don't waste time guessing ones that aren't available.

A SHORT WORD ON MINIGAMES AND MICROGAMES

A **minigame** is a simple game created to provide variety, represent activities, and add value to a product. Many minigames are based on or are variations of classic arcade and classic home console games.

A **microgame** is a minigame that takes seconds to play. Half of the challenge of microgames is learning how to play them within the short time allotted. The *Warioware* titles are compilations of microgames.

Minigames offer many advantages to game developers. They are quick to create and test, they are easy to play, and they can be used as metaphors for complex player activities. I truly believe ANY activity can be represented by a minigame. Observe:

- Lockpicking: *The Elder Scrolls IV: Oblivion* (2K, 2006)
- Hacking electronics: *Batman: Arkham Asylum* (WBI, 2009)
- Portrait painting: *Spongebob Atlantis Squarepantis* (THQ, 2008)
- Tagging walls: *The Warriors* (Rockstar, 2005)
- Cooking dinner: *Cooking Mama* (Majesco, 2006)
- Serving dinner: *Diner Dash* (Playfirst, 2003)
- Sex: *God of War* (SCEA, 2005).

Any activity.

When designing a minigame, make sure to:

- Keep the controls simple. Minigames by their nature imply easy-to-learn gameplay.
- Keep the gameplay sessions short. No longer than 5 to 10 minutes. Microgames can last only a few seconds long.
- How does progression work? It is designed or random? Ramp the difficulty gently. Minigames are meant to provide variety, not torture the player.

- Add new elements with each progression. Progression doesn't mean every level: it can be a grouping of levels. Progression can represent a major element like a new weapon or enemy or minor like a change in an enemy's movement pattern or bonus modifier. Even a different background art, sound effect, or song keeps the game from getting stale or repetitive.

- Consider limiting the minigame's controls to only a few buttons. Assign only one action per button or control stick to keep control schemes simple.

- If possible, allow for player customization. The web-based minigame *Upgrade Complete (Kongregate, 2009)* allows the player to upgrade EVERYTHING, including the player's ship, the background graphics, and even the copyright screen!

- How does your minigame end? Does it have an end? Make sure the victory condition is clear to the player. Some games can be played "forever"—or at least until the kill screen appears.

Minigames don't even need to be segregated from the core game. The platformer/puzzle game *Henry Hatsworth in the Puzzling Adventure* (EA Games, 2009) and the RPG/puzzle game *Puzzle Quest* (D3, 2007) combine two styles of gameplay; platforming and puzzle. If you do this in your own game, just make sure you allow time for the player to make a "brain shift" between the two gaming styles; give them a second to reorient themselves with a "ready" screen or pause in the action.

And finally, when you've run out of all other creative ideas of minigames and puzzles, you can always resort to "Whack-A-Mole."

I consider "Whack-A-Mole" the last stop on the designer's creativity train. And here's why:

- It relies solely on the player's reaction time, which requires no thought or decision making from the player.
- It's random, which doesn't allow the player to utilize strategy.
- It's very repetitive. There's no variety to the gameplay other than possibly the speed of the popping moles.
- It requires almost no input from the player other than a single motion, button press, or click.
- It is an "endless game"—there is no end unless the designer dictates it. Usually the player stops because they're tired of playing it.

I know you can design something more engaging than that! Let's move on to something more exciting: power-ups!!

Level 12's Universal Truths and Clever Ideas:

- Design mechanics, hazards and props that work with enemies and complement each other.

- Good game design is like music: it has a rhythm that the player can feel.

- Games should be challenging, not overly difficult.

- No rocks on the heads of the player: be fair when punishing your player.

- Be creative: don't resort to worn-out clichés like crates and whack-a-mole unless you have to.

- No cat mustaches: don't make puzzles so cryptic that the player can't use logic, knowledge, or skill to solve them.

- A puzzle is a challenge that has a right answer.

- Show them the door and then send them after the key.

- Give the player opportunities to catch their breath by providing plenty of checkpoints.

- Keep minigames and microgames simple and short.

LEVEL 13

NOW YOU'RE PLAYING WITH POWER

The **power-up** can be found in every genre of gaming, from driving and puzzle games to action-adventures and shooters. They are dropped by defeated enemies, hidden in treasure chests and breakable crates, and sometimes just lying all over the place in the middle of the road.

A well-designed power-up is concentrated action! A player only has to touch it to become energized to move at lightning speeds, blow up the world and return from the dead! The great thing about a power-up is its effects are **immediate**: who wouldn't want to immediately gain awesome power?! The only downside is that its effects are usually **temporary**, so use that power wisely. A designer should be wise when creating power-up and ask the following questions:

- What does the power-up do?
- What does it look like? How will it (or its effects) visually stand out in the world? Does it glow or strobe? Rotate or bounce?
- Can power-ups be combined or can the player only have one active at once? Can the player retrieve power-ups that are unused or discarded?
- How does it affect the player's movement? Rate of speed? Number or type of attacks? Health or status?
- How are its effects communicated to the player visually? Aurally?

- What is the player's trade-off for using the power-up? Some reduce speed or mobility or the type of moves you can do while under the influence of the power-up.
- If the power-up ability is temporary, what cues will let the player know they are about to expire? Is there a HUD element? A visual cue? A sound cue? A music cue? Does it last until you lose a life?

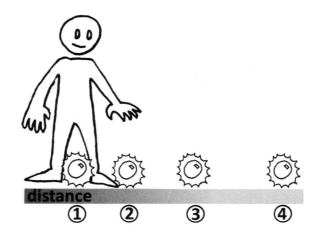

Consider how the player will be collecting the collectable or power-up.

- Do they have to walk over it to collect it?
- Do they have to reach out and actively choose to pick it up?
- Some power-ups are automatically drawn towards the player when they get a certain distance from them. If so, how close does the player have to be, how quickly does this happen and so on?
- Perhaps the power-up or collectable is activated when the player gets into its proximity?

Knowing how close the player needs to get will help you determine the effects of the power-up once it's collected.

Power-ups boil down into four categories: **defensive**, **offensive**, **movement**, and **game changers**.

Defensive power-ups help boost the player's ability to survive damage and continue progress in the game. The most common defensive power-ups include:

- **Health-up:** refills the player's health meter. Can be a partial or full refill. If they fill up different amounts, make sure they look different.
- **Ability recharge:** like a health-up but recharges an ability meter rather than the player's health.
- **Extra life:** when collected, the player gains one more life/restart that will allow them to continue the game after they lose all of their health.
- **Invulnerability:** the player cannot be hurt when hit by an enemy or their attack. An invulnerable player is usually still open to affects from hazards that use physics and geometry, (for example, falling off a cliff edge) otherwise problems can arise with collision detection.
- **Invincibility:** as with invulnerability—the player cannot be hurt when hit by an enemy or their attack—but they can also automatically destroy most enemies by colliding with them, as seen in *Metroid*'s screw attack and *Mario Kart*'s super star. Many games don't allow this kind of ability to work on bosses or only cause minor damage.
- **Protective:** temporary forcefields, physical shields, or auras that protect the player from enemy projectiles, fire, or poisonous floors. Protective power-ups may or may not have their own "health meter" to show how much use remains. Protective defenses are different from invulnerability and invincibility because they usually can be improved, modified, and extended by the player.
- **Indirect attack:** commonly found in fast-moving car combat and kart-racing games, this power-up lets the player "fire and forget" smokescreens, oil slicks, and black bombs with fuses on top, causing havoc to those unlucky enemies and players behind them.

- **Smart bomb:** A clear the game screen when things get too tough or the player needs a moment to breathe during all of the action.

we're boned.

Offensive power-ups improve or modify attacks, allowing players to defeat enemies faster, more efficiently, or more spectacularly.

- **Ammo boost:** the player's ammunition is fully restocked. Most ammo boosts pertain to a specific weapon in the player's inventory.
- **Buffs:** from hacking orcs to shooting hoops, these power-ups increase the player's skills and abilities for a short period of time. Awesome flame effects are optional.
- **Multi-weapon:** a power-up that improves your current weapon without fundamentally changing it. *Contra's* spread attack fires five projectiles in a fan-shaped configuration while heat-seeking rockets will home in on enemies.
- **Weapon upgrade/swap:** this power-up increases the strength, speed, and damage of the player's attack, or can change their weapon to an entirely new one (sometimes more powerful, sometimes as powerful but with differing capabilities that may be more suitable—and hence more useful—in a particular situation). New visuals usually accompany the change. *Ghosts 'N Goblins* lets the player change from lance to dagger to torch. Flamethrowers, rocket launchers, and shotguns are popular choices.
- **Damage modifier:** Flame! Poison! Ice! Electricity! These power-ups improve the player's base damage, usually accompanied with a dynamic visual.
- **Direction:** this power-up allows the player to change/augment the direction of their attack, most commonly found in shooters to allow the player to shoot behind as well as above and below them. The change in

direction can also be applied to the projectile, as in the case of enemy-seeking missiles.

- **Companion:** when picked up, a small object appears next to the player that can provide an additional attack or shielding function. The companion may or may not have hit points. Many last until the player is destroyed or for a specific duration of time. *Galaga* (Namco, 1981) added the novel twist that a captured ship became your companion. You lost a life, but you gained double shot ability.

told ya.

Movement power-ups allow the player to improve their existing movement, or add some new ones. Be particularly careful to account for these power-ups when designing player metrics.

- **Speed change:** nitro boosts and other power-ups allow the player to move at incredible speeds. As a trade-off, the player usually has less control of the vehicle or character because of the faster reaction time needed.
- **Access:** the player gains access to locations normally unreachable via an ability bestowed by the power-up. The access methods are as varied as flying, helicoptering, gliding, and swimming. For example, Mario's bee suit in *Super Mario Galaxy*.
- **Size change:** depending on the game, changing size can allow a whole suite of abilities, least of which is being able to get into tiny holes. In *Super Mario Bros.* the super mushroom not only increases the player's size, but it allows the player to take one extra hit, and to break bricks to access new locations. The mini mushroom in *New Super Mario Bros.* causes Mario to shrink, allowing the player to leap great distances.

Game changers alter the dynamics of the gameplay and the player's interaction with the game in a significant manner.

- **Score/treasure modifiers:** whether it's a *Crazy Taxi* fare multiplier or *Rock Band's* star power, the value of any points/treasure collected by the player is increased for a short period of time.
- **Change state:** this power-up changes the play dynamics in the game. For example, in *Pac-Man*, the player flees from the enemy ghosts. When he eats a power pellet, the ghosts become vulnerable and the player can become the aggressor.

- **Magnetic:** this power-up draws treasure items towards the player, relieving them of the risk of entering dangerous territory or having to "clean up" treasure and collectables after combat.
- **Invisibility/disguise:** the player is rendered temporarily undetectable by enemies and hazards, allowing the player to safely avoid potentially deadly combat and enter locations barred by annoyingly alert guards.
- **Comedy power-up:** a power-up that exists solely to surprise and amuse the player. *MDK*'s "Earthworm Jim" power-up drops a cow onto enemies' heads.

Most power-ups are content to sit still and wait patiently to be consumed by the player, while others have a keen sense of self-preservation. Power-ups have been known to move upon spawning out of their hiding place, like the super mushrooms in *Super Mario Bros.* Still others will run and hide when they spot the player, like the "cowardly power-up" in *MDK.* Give your player a chance to catch these **mobile power-ups**. Do not make them move faster than the player or make them resistant to the lure of a magnetic power-up.

Power-ups can be designed to work conditionally. In *Maximo: Ghosts to Glory*, we had an armor power-up that only worked when the player had collected the full set of armor. Another one required a special ability to activate. As long as the conditions for gaining these special powers are clear to the player, there's no reason why you can't add this technique to your design arsenal.

Not all power-ups are delicious and useful. Very evil game designers in their secret lair high in the Alps have created **anti-power-ups**. Like a chocolate truffle stuffed with dog poo, these sinister collectables look like regular, nice power-ups but they hold a deadly surprise. Poisonous power-ups that can sap health, slow movement, drain experience, or even turn the player into a zombie, complete with backward control schemes. While they are fun, they are only fun once or twice. I suggest using anti-power-ups judiciously and with caution.

"LOVE THY PLAYER"

↑   *Pureiya aishi nasai*   ↑

Once upon a time, a Japanese game director[1] told me this should be the motto of all game designers. I agree with him, although I have a different way of saying it:

[1] A different Japanese game director from the "fisherman" from Level 4, btw.

The game designer should be the gentle hand on the rear of the player, pushing them ever upwards[2].

There are many systems that the designer can use to enable the player during the game, and we've already talked about some of them in other chapters: checkpoints, hoists and teeters, aim assist, ramping difficulty. But there are others that are worth discussing: dynamic difficulty balancing, difficulty level adjustment, rubberbanding, game length, and autosave.

Thanks!

Dynamic difficulty balancing (or **DDB**) is a way to adjust the challenge and rewards for the player based on performance. For example, if the player dies too often fighting an enemy, then the enemy's health is reduced slightly or the enemy doesn't attack as often. If the player is low on health and opens a treasure chest, a health-up will pop out—but if the player isn't low on health when they open the chest, the player will be rewarded with treasure instead. The goal of DDB is to give the player what they need when they need it in order to propel the player along to success.

Difficulty level adjustment gives a player the option to shift the game down to a lower difficulty setting if too many parameters, such as multiple player deaths, are detected. The player can be given the option to decline or it may be that the adjustment happens automatically. Personally, I don't recommend the latter as many players find it insulting.

Rubberbanding is used primarily in racing games, but it can be used anytime the player needs to follow or catch any other character or vehicle. If

---

[2] Not as concise, but much more pronounceable.

the player gets too far behind, the opponent(s) will slow down enough to let the player catch up. A great solution because racing on an empty track sucks!

The **game's length** is actually a good tool for adjusting difficulty. Take for example a battle arena. If the player fights bad guys for about 10 minutes, with sufficient health and a modicum of skill, they should be able to survive just fine. However, make that player fight for a half-hour and player fatigue and attrition start to set in. Odds are the player won't survive the encounter. My rule of thumb for gameplay length is this **very important thing**:

IF IT FEELS TOO LONG, HARD, OR BORING, THEN IT PROBABLY IS

Trust your feelings, Luke. After you play a level a thousand times[3] you will know when your level gets boring. That said, you must be very, very careful as you can develop what I call "**designer blinders**." Designer blinders occur when you've played your game so many times that you will require a much more difficult level to feel challenged than the consumers, who will only play it a few times. It is a very common problem within game development, which I have seen happen many, many times. We'll talk about how to solve this problem later in Level 17. In the meantime, consolidate your level. Kill the boring parts. Death to boring! Don't be afraid to cut elements if it will make your game better.

Autosaving is when the game periodically records and saves game data automatically. This way, the player can concentrate on playing the game rather than micromanaging their game's save files. Autosave is helpful for when the game crashes[4] or if the player forgets to save their game at a critical part and then dies. Many games autosave whenever loading a new area (for example, *Fallout 3*).

For every positive example of player difficulty, there is at least one negative one. Here's a story illustrating what I **don't** mean about how to design player difficulty: I was reviewing an enemy encounter with a creative director. I told him that I thought the encounter wasn't bad, but could stand to be a little more challenging. He agreed and his instructions to me were, "The player has to die three times before they can progress." I thought, "I'm

---

[3] Honestly, you will play a level a thousand times (at least) between setting it up, populating it, testing the mechanics, hazards and combat, placing the collectibles and readjusting them, and then finally officially play testing it.
[4] But your game isn't going to crash, is it?

sorry, Mr. Creative Director, I know you are my boss and all, but you are an idiot." But I didn't say it because I wanted to keep my job.

What I did *do* was not design the encounter so the player had to die three times to progress. And neither should you. Player death should **never** be a yardstick for game design. "Rewarding" the player with damage or death is negative reinforcement.

In *Maximo*, one of the enemies was a treasure chest mimic: a fun enemy that, when "opened" up, snapped and attacked the player like a dog. But it had an unfortunate side effect. I saw players actually cringe before opening a chest because they expected it to be a mimic. While it was fun for the designer to watch the player get tricked, it was not fun for the player. This defeats the point of the game: to have fun. Your players will hate you for it and stop playing the game. This is bad, because the ultimate goal of any game designer should be to keep the player playing. If I ever create this kind of enemy again, I will give some clues to the player so they can spot this enemy and make preparations for it. It can be as simple as a color change or the wobbling pots with an enemy inside in *Legend of Zelda: Spirit Tracks*.

The way I see it, if the player can play through and finish the entire game, then they will be happy. They will be happy enough to tell others how much they liked your game and they will be happy enough to buy your next game. It's a win-win for all parties involved.

MORE WEALTH THAN YOU CAN IMAGINE!

I don't know, I can imagine quite a bit.
Han Solo

Game designers have many very powerful tools to keep the player playing: Mystery, delight, pride, and power we've already talked about, but now we come to the two most powerful of these tools: greed and reward.

Greed will get players to do interesting things. They will grind their way through the grindiest MMOs to get that stronger sword, that unique hat, gain that next level. They will jump onto the smallest platform festooned with the deadliest traps just to grab that one additional coin. They will fight the biggest, meanest enemies just to find out what comes next in the story. Or to score that achievement. The following **very important thing** rings true:

NEVER UNDERESTIMATE THE GREED OF THE PLAYER

But … instead of using the player's greed for evil—luring the player to their death to prove that you, the game designer, are cleverer than the player—use their greed for good instead:

- Use the promise of treasure and items to motivate players to fight enemies.
- Give the player a personal and customizable space to show off their trophies and rewards. Once they start seeing some of the "shelves" filling up, they'll want to "catch them all."

- Exploit the "me too" factor. Keeping up with the Joneses is a powerful urge for the player, especially in the multiplayer space. I was once playing *World of Warcraft* and minding my own business when I saw another player ride by on a mechanical chicken mount. All of a sudden, my player agenda went from "get to the next level" to "MUST OWN ROBOT CHICKEN!"

- Create "guidelines" when placing treasure and hidden objects. Sharp players will pick up on these guidelines and their observations will be rewarded. For example, in *Maximo: Ghosts to Glory*, buried treasure chests were placed next to trees. If there weren't trees in the level, they were hidden next to similar vertical architectural elements like pillars or gravestones.

- Like the dots in *Pac-Man World* or rings in any *Sonic the Hedgehog* game, you can string collectables through the level to guide the player where to go next.

- The designers of *Half-Life* (Valve, 1998) have an interesting method of introducing a new weapon or item to players. First, the player hears about the new item from another character. Second, the player sees the item in the possession of another character. Third, the player sees the item being used by another character and finally, the player obtains and uses the new item for themselves. By the time the new item is in the player's hands, not only have they learned what it looks like, what it is and what it does, but they want it for themselves.

Like greed, **rewards** are a powerful player motivator. A reward is what the player is ultimately working towards. After all, you can't have a game without a victory condition, and you should never have a victory without a reward.

- Expose the player to what rewards are available early in the game. This way they have a laundry list of things "to do" throughout the game and what they will get for achieving them.
- Reward the player as soon as possible, reward often, and provide some variety and surprise to the rewards.
- A win condition needs to show evidence of success. There's no such thing as enough fanfare. Be dramatic, exciting, and even a little goofy. Or a lot goofy! Set off fireworks, do exciting camera pans around the player, have the player character jump in the air excitedly, play cheering crowds and slot-machine sound effects. Use visual effects and particles, lots and lots of particles! The more, the better! You want the player to feel like they are the victors of World War III, the scorer of the winning run at a baseball game, and a lottery winner all at the same time.
- Whatever the reward is, make it matter to the player. Award the player something that gives them the edge on the next level and is the solution to a problem that plagued them on the last. The best reward is the one a player doesn't realize they need until they get it.

In video games, rewards come in many shapes and sizes: **scoring**, **achievements**, **treasure**, **loot**, **power-ups**, **souvenirs**, **bonus materials**, **praise**, **surprise**, and **progression**.

Back in the prehistoric era of video games[5] the player's only reward was a **high score**. Scoring is a useful system to showcase the player's success in a very simple way: a number and three little letters. It's a little hard to describe to someone these days why seeing your three initials displayed on an arcade game screen was so exciting, but it was a little like writing your name in wet cement: something the whole world can see to show that YOU were the master of the game—at least until the game's power was turned off for the night and the scoreboard reset[6]. Many gamers thrive on competition, even when it's against themselves, and love having the bragging rights that come with getting a high score. But is scoring in gaming still relevant?

That was the question many game developers asked themselves in the late 1990s. As the arcade scene was dying and most gaming had moved to PCs and home consoles, scoring represented the old school. Scoring was regarded as a remnant of game designs whose sole intent was to keep players dropping quarters into the slot. Scoring soon became regarded as a meaningless number compared to collecting 100% of the game's secrets and finishing the game's story. A simple numeric score just wasn't as sexy or cinematic as a full-blown ending cutscene. Scoring in gaming was almost as dead as the dodo.

Almost.

In the early 2000s, scoring started to matter again with the rising popularity of browser games like *Bejeweled* (Popcap, 2001) and *Feeding Frenzy* (Popcap, 2004). When **leaderboards** were introduced to Xbox Live (and later to the Playstation Network), scoring was off and running again, where it remains a lively part of gaming to this day.

Achievements are high scores with personality. Debuting with *Halo 2* on the Xbox 360, achievements motivate players to show off their in-game skills and brag about their accomplishments. Doing a task X number of times; completing game goals like defeating bosses, collecting one specific item (or all of them), or just finishing the game are all valid achievements.

---

[5] Back in those days, the only video games we had to play with were two rocks connected by vines to one bigger rock. Now get off my lawn, you darned kids!

[6] This is why it was always better when you got the high score at a 7-11. Those places NEVER closed!

Achievements are great fun for the developer to create—as much as they are for the player to collect. You can give your achievements clever names and fun icons. Usually published before the game's release, achievement lists act as a play "to-do" list. Achievements are a great way for designers to point out gameplay concepts to players that they otherwise may not think of attempting. Achievements can be awarded for anything the developer desires. Here are a few of my favorites:

- Easiest achievement ever: press start to play (*The Simpsons*)
- Not bulletproof: died on easy level (*50 Cent: Bulletproof*)
- Street cleaner: hide five dead bodies in bales of hay (*Assassin's Creed 2*)
- Be polite: provide an enemy with a freezecam shot of you doffing your hat (*Team Fortress 2*)
- Six degrees of Schaefer: played with or against any player who has this achievement (which means that at least one player in the chain has played the game with creator Tim Schaefer) (*Brütal Legend*)
- You've wasted your life: be idle for 5 minutes (*Saw*)
- Losing his mind: decapitate a captain with a shield (*Conan*)
- Wheeeeeee!: slide 330 feet continuously through blood (*Fairy Tale Fights*)
- Skidmark: give 50 wedgies (*Bully: Scholarship edition*)
- I feel so funky: get slimed by a charging ghost (*Ghostbusters*)
- Jawa juicer: crush five Jawas by using the grinder in the garbage processing room (*The Force Unleashed: Ultimate Sith Edition*)
- The cake: you found the cake, yummy! (*X-Men origins: Wolverine*).

Money! Money! Money! Who doesn't love getting **treasure**? The way the coins jingle merrily when they pop out of a treasure chest… The way they glitter and sparkle on the ground after spilling out of a headless enemy… The way they spin in place, luring you to jump through a flaming hoop of death and over a pit of needle-sharp pungie knives…

Yeah, collecting treasure is great and all, but what are you going to spend it on? In order to make treasure mean anything, you need an **economic system**. When designing treasure items for your game, create them in escalating values. 1, 5, 10, 50, 100… You get the idea. But don't spread your values too far apart either. The last thing you want is the virtual equivalent of pennies; treasure that no one wants to pick up.

One of the things I love about video games is that I am far richer than I am in real life. A player feels great when they are flush with cash. The benefit of having wads of dough is that the player has lots of choices when shopping—but to do that you have to make sure there are plenty of items for the player to buy. It's always fun to give the player choices between two really good things. Not only do they have the delicious agony over what to buy, but it gives them something to look forward to buying the next time they go shopping. Stock your stores with a variety of things and find ways to rotate the stock to keep the selection from getting stale. Next, determine the price your items will be. Start by classifying your treasure, loot, and other buyable items by their rarity: common, uncommon, rare, and unique. Then apply a price to each of the items. Think about what items you want available to the player from the beginning of the game. Always have some items that can be bought quickly and others that lie tantalizingly out of reach. If I only had a few more coins!

Once you've created a preliminary economy (don't worry about setting it in stone, prices will change over the course of production as you figure out what the player will want or need) then think about placing treasure in the world. If you want the player to be able to afford $300 worth of items, then make sure there is at least $300 worth of treasure in the level. You will have to answer the question, "does treasure regenerate?" If it does, then be aware that players can "mine" levels for treasure, which can completely screw up your economy. On the other hand, replaying a level without any treasure to act as a motivator isn't fun for the player. You may want the player to replay a level multiple times so they can collect enough money to buy what they need. A shortage of funds encourages replay, or exploration off the beaten path. By exposing the player to all the items they could buy at the beginning of the game (via an "ability tree" like in *Dante's Inferno*), the player can start to plan how they are going to spend their money once they earn it. Sometimes the player might have to buy cheaper and necessary gear like ammo or health-ups in order to progress. Give the player options.

Use color to clarify your treasure's value like the old standbys of copper, silver, and gold. Or use different shapes like coins, bags, and gems. Don't get too diverse or crazy, otherwise players will mistake treasure items for power-ups.

Does your treasure have encumbrance, meaning there is a limit to what the player can carry? If so, then how are they going to carry it? Many RPGs and MMOs have a limit to encumbrance, forcing players to find other storage solutions such as magical bags of holding or a bank. Whatever the solution, make sure that the player doesn't have to shuttle cash from their storage to the store. Just have it come out of the player's account to avoid all of the hassle.

Your treasure doesn't even have to be money. Treasure can be bolts as in *Ratchet and Clank*, studs as in the *Lego* games, souls as in *God of War* series—even trash, such as the bottle caps in *Fallout*. It doesn't matter what it looks like, as long as it's sparkly and makes a satisfying cha-ching! sound effect when you collect it!

Speaking of all that treasure, where is your player going to spend it? Most RPGs have friendly (and not so friendly) stores that sell all manner of adventuring goods. *Borderlands* and *Bioshock* use vending machines. Make your store specific to the game you're making. A racing game could have a garage where players can buy car upgrades and customizations. A sports game could have a sporting goods shop. It's just one more way to add character and theme to your game.

Hey, maybe that slightly creepy guy in the trenchcoat over there in the alley has the magic sword we're looking for? Let's go talk to him.

Who's there? Come in, come in. I have everything the daring hero needs to survive. Take a look around and don't be afraid to ask for help:

Offense. Need a new sword? Lusting after that more powerful gun? How about a nice magic missile spell? It was owned by a little old witch who only used it on Sundays...

Defense. Armor, shields, helmets, forcefield generators: I've got everything that can repel a blade or deflect a laser beam.

Repairs. Swung that sword a little too hard, did ya? Well it will only cost you a few coins to get it swing-worthy again...

Replenishable resources. Ammunition, health potions, batteries, gasoline; we'll get you back up and running again!

Skills. Want to learn a whirlwind sword attack? Or how to add +2 to your accuracy skill? How about a nice set that grants a lock-picking ability? All ya need is some cash...

Access. I've got keys, treasure maps and even a statue that looks like it may fit into a hole. I'll bet it opens a secret door somewhere...

Vanity. That hat looks very stylish on ya. So does that new costume; much better than your old one, if I do say so myself.

Whimsy. Oh, I absolutely think your hair would look better pink, sir. And yes Ma'am, a mustache is just the thing ya need.

Information. For just a few coins, I can tell you where the King is handing out jobs for adventurers such as yourself...

Saves. Only the cruelest of designers would charge someone to keep playing... that will be $100 gold, good sir. Thanks and come again!

Let's get out of this place; it's horribly overpriced, especially since you can find most of this stuff lying around the levels.

Loot is all the great stuff you can buy, but it's FREE! Well, if you consider navigating through the temple of eternal pain and defeating the goblin army free. The difference between loot you buy and loot you find is you should always find much better loot on your adventure. Save the best weapons, the strongest armor, and the shootiest guns for loot. Let the player earn their keep by solving puzzles, surviving hazards, and defeating bosses. And remember this **very important thing**:

THE BEST REWARDS ARE HARD WON

Souvenirs are physical (well, virtual) reminders of the player's adventures during the game. Souvenirs can be displayed back at the player's base or castle or spaceship or condo. Give the player a special place to show them off, like Lara Croft's trophy room in *Tomb Raider Anniversary* (Eidos, 2006) or a nice shelf with proper lighting. They can be animated interactive exhibits like those found in *Lego Indiana Jones: the Original Adventures* (Lucasarts, 2008) or virtual museums like the one in *Uncharted 2: Among Thieves*. No matter which style you choose, use a tight camera or viewer to let the player get a good look at 'em and a label to remind them where they found the souvenir.

Sweet boots!   **Level 70 Red!**

Not all souvenirs should be kept on a shelf. Turning souvenirs into useful game items gives those items more meaning. Defeat the Lich King in *World of Warcraft* and take his sword. *Mega Man* takes the powers of the Robot Masters as he defeats them. Instead of awarding a dragon skin rug, why not give the player a pair of dragon skin boots? That way, as long as the player wears the boots, everyone will know who slew the red dragon. Make sure to give the souvenir items special properties too. Those red dragon boots may allow a player resistance to fire attacks or let them walk over hot coals or on lava. It may even give them a special flaming kick attack. Make it special and the player will want to get to the next encounter to see what they can win.

The biggest problem with **bonus features** is they are usually created at the last minute by the production team. Design them early but they should be one of the last things you create. This way, you can judge just what constitutes a "bonus" to the player by comparing it to the rest of the game's content. Bonus materials may include:

- **Costume changes.** Costume changes help add a little variety—and humor—to your bonus features. The Starkiller from *Star Wars: The Force Unleashed* can wear costumes from the game's other levels. Kratos in *God of War* can unlock a business suit or chef's costume.

- **Alternate models.** Create a new look for your hero or villains! In *Uncharted 2: Among Thieves* players can unlock a fat version of the hero, while in *Batman: Arkham Asylum* players can turn all the enemies into skeletons.

I'm not sure why this is hilarious.

- **Alternate modes.** Ah, big head mode. You are so easy to code and yet you get so many laughs. Is it any wonder why we love you? Silly modes run the gamut from changing an enemy's exploding body parts into birthday presents to turning all the cars in a game pink. You are only limited by your imagination and how much time you have left in your production schedule.

- **Downloadable content (DLC).** Usually downloaded via console networks like Xbox Live Arcade, Playstation Network or WiiWare, downloadable content can take many forms, including many of those bonuses included on this list. DLC offers a way for games to live beyond their average play life with additional weapons, gameplay modes, achievements, character models, and new levels.

- **New levels.** The most time-consuming of all bonus materials to make, new levels (and game content) is becoming more popular as DLC. By scheduling it as additional material that is released after the game has shipped, the development team can put more time, effort, and polish into the levels—thus keeping up the quality of the material.

- **Music.** Want to listen to the game's music without playing the game? Simple. Create an audio player to allow the player to hear the music. Or you can just let them insert the game disc into a CD player.

- **Commentary.** An audio track of the team talking about the game's development. Starting with *Half-Life 2: Lost Coast*, developer Valve has made interactive in-game commentary one of their standard bonus features.

- **"Making of" video.** A documentary-style featurette (or feature) that explores the game's creation. These are very time-consuming to make; however, they can be a great way to spotlight your hard-working team.

- **Model viewers.** Players can view the 3-D models and assets in the game. Allow the player camera control to pan around, rotate, and zoom in and out on your models to show them off in the best possible light.

This feature is particularly good in games like RTSs, where the characters are normally viewed from a more distant camera angle.

- **Art viewers.** The most common of bonus features: just scan your preproduction art and Voilà! You're done! OK lazy, you can do better than that. Don't be content to just show a slideshow of your team's art. Set the images to music or commentary from the artists. They don't often get a chance to speak up. Show more than just drawings of characters too: show off environments, props, maps, and design materials that will make the player appreciate all the hard work you've put into your games. Make sure the player has control over the pace of the presentation. Don't make them wait around for the next piece of art to appear. How about a magnifier so they can zoom in closely to examine the art? (You can even hide a reward within the art for the player to find!) Or have the player collect pieces of the art to be assembled like a puzzle, which gives a reward based on the artwork when solved.

- **Promotional materials.** Promo materials are more commonly found in sequels as the assets are usually created late in the game's production process. If included with long-standing franchises, they can be particularly interesting for nostalgia purposes.

- **Trailers.** Movie trailers (especially relevant if the game is a movie tie-in), previews of other games, a sneak peak at a sequel. Just don't make watching them mandatory: allow the player the option to skip them.

- **Minigames.** While some whole games are collections of minigames[7], don't forget to include them in bigger games too. They provide the player a chance to take a break from the protracted grind of a longer adventure without ever having to "leave the disc." Give your minigame a place to live, such as an arcade. Minigames are moderately easy to make: just identify some of your game's most fun gameplay and re-contextualize it. In *God of War*, we did just that—everything in the "Challenge of the Gods" was already in the game code, it just gave the player a different set of victory conditions. Some minigames give rewards that can be used back in the main game's economy system. Sometimes they are promotional tools, as seen in the case of the iPhone game *Mass Effect Galaxy*, which gives players a reward in *Mass Effect 2* for completing it. Or you can just rip-off Galaxian like everyone else.

- **Multiplayer modes.** While describing multiplayer gameplay could take up an entire chapter[8] there are still other modes that aren't directly related to gameplay. Asset trading, chat functions, spectator modes, friends, and rival rosters that allow you to check your friend's game stats—these additional modes will give your game value. Remember to keep their interfaces intuitive and user-friendly. Follow the rules found in Level 8: not

[7] For examples, just check out most of the games on the Wii.
[8] It does, in Level 19. Coming up next!

too many clicks, keep the game screens down to a minimum, use icons over text, and so on, to keep functions and intent clear.

- **Alternate endings.** Will the player turn out good or evil? Save the world or get blown up? Get the girl or get the boy? Many RPG, adventure, action, and survival horror games offer multiple endings to their stories. Examples include *Star Wars: Knights of the Old Republic,* the *Fable* series, *Heavy Rain* and the games in the *Resident Evil* series. Multiple endings are a great way to get the player to replay the game, as long as the player knows there are multiple endings to be seen. I've found that it's no longer enough to just have a few different endings based on the decisions made at a few key moments in the game. The struggle between good and evil is much more interesting if they are evenly matched. Build systems and opportunities for the player to "course correct" towards one outcome or another. Make the outcome be the player's choice, rather than one decided by the game.

- **Cheats.** Cheats are usually reserved for use by the development team during production. Cheat modes can be enabled to give the player unlimited resources like health, ammo, lives, or just plain ol' invulnerability. I suggest that you don't enable cheats until the player has played through the game once, otherwise they are CHEATING!!!… themselves out of experiencing the game the way it was meant to be played. Some games go as far as to encourage "proper" play: cheats might not get the "good" ending of a game or they might be marked out as a cheater as in *GTA*. In *Team Fortress 2*, anyone who didn't use a cheat received a special wearable angel's halo called "the cheater's lament."

As an industry, we are really, really good about making the player feel really, really bad. We kill player characters at the drop of a hat, force them into near impossible situations, and then mock them when they fail. We'll steal from them in a heartbeat and we'll mess with their minds any chance we can get. What we're not very good at doing is offering **praise**. And as an industry, we wonder why players complain about games. But as anyone who deals with children knows, praise is the best way to get people to do what you want them to do. What we need to do is make the player feel like the best person in the world instead. The best example I've seen of giving a player praise is in *Zak and Wiki: the Quest For Barbaros' Treasure* (Capcom, 2007). Whenever the player does something correctly, the following happens:

- A "success" musical sting plays.
- The hero does a funny reaction or victory animation.
- There is a particle effect coming off the hero.
- Wiki, the player's monkey sidekick congratulates the player (in text form) on how good they just did; Wiki also has his own musical sting and particle effect.

Not only does all of the above play out whenever the player completes a puzzle, but also:

- A burst of special effects tints the screen yellow with streaking stars.
- A success musical tune plays, longer than the sting.
- A "look at me!" animation from the hero displaying the puzzle piece or item they've just won.
- The name of the item the player has just won.

Eight things to support praising the player in the forms of character animation, visual effects, music, and text for solving one puzzle! Fantastic! This game made me feel like I was the smartest player in the world and as a result, I wanted to keep playing! Just remember that you can have too much of a good thing. Praise ceases to be meaningful if you receive it for doing nothing or insignificant acts.

See how often you can stroke the player's ego during the course of the game. NPCs in *Fable* either recoil in horror or compliment the hero depending on what alignment he is, which is exactly what the player wants to hear, especially since they've spent so much time cultivating their goodness or evil.

There are other rewards than just treasure… I'm talking about **surprise** and fun. At Disneyland, Pirate's Lair is a pirate-themed playground. Guests at Pirate's Lair can interact with several items, including a bilge pump and a turn wheel.

As you turn the wheel, a rope on a pulley starts to pull a treasure chest up from underwater. In a video game, once the treasure chest is revealed, the player would get their treasure and go on their way.

However, if you keep cranking the wheel and raising the chest, a clinging skeleton is revealed who is trying to keep the chest for himself. The skeleton serves no purpose other than to get a laugh out of the viewer. There's no reason why video games can't have little moments like this. Some game developers do similar things such as Marvel Comics creator Stan Lee appearing in *Marvel Ultimate Alliance 2, Ape Escape*'s monkeys in *Metal Gear Solid 3*'s jungle level, or *Braid*'s homage to Mario's World 1-1.

Some will argue that **progression** isn't much of a reward, and that the player shouldn't be rewarded for merely finishing the game; after all, isn't the point to finish it? There are a lot of things competing for your player's free time. What can be done to keep them engaged? You only need a great story, intriguing level design, ridiculously cool boss battles, and awesome upgrades. Easy, right? But what if more than one player wants to play? Well, that's why we're moving on to Level 14!

Level 13's Universal Truths and Clever Ideas:

- Create power-ups that are compatible and complementary to the player's actions and attacks.

- Love thy player! Give them the tools to succeed like DDB and rubberbanding.

- If something in your game is too difficult or boring, then it is. Get rid of it.

- Never underestimate the greed of the player, and use it to prompt interesting scenarios and challenges.

- Plan out your economy for the entire game. Price items according to when you want the players to earn them.

- Provide enough money for the player so they have choices when shopping.

- Have a variety of cool things to buy. Make the player have to choose over (at least) two really good things, so they come back for more.

- Determine whether scoring is right for your game, then reward the player when high scores or achievements are obtained.

- Don't forget bonus materials and DLC. Remember that it takes time to make this content so don't leave it until the end of your production.

- Some rewards are just for fun.

LEVEL 14

MULTIPLAYER—THE MORE THE MERRIER

The first true multiplayer game I remember playing was *Gauntlet* (Atari, 1985) where up to four people were able to play together. Because of the arcade cabinet's configuration, what I remember most from playing *Gauntlet* (other than "elf needs food badly") is that my friends and I would push and jostle each other as we played the game. Even though *Gauntlet* is a cooperative game, we sure didn't play it that way. We were always trying to grab the health or be the first to activate the "smart bomb" potion.

The jostling continued through the years with *Teenage Mutant Ninja* Turtles (Konami, 1989) and *Captain America and the Avengers* (Data East, 1991). When *Doom* (id Software, 1993) reared its ugly demon head, the jostling became virtual via our local area network (LAN) connection. And by jostling, I mean blasting each other with plasma rifles during death matches. Multiplayer jostling has since evolved even further:

Head-to-head: two or more players compete against each other in real time on the same game system. Most sports, action, and some FPS games allow for head-to-head play.

Network/peer-to-peer: two or more play with and against each other in real time on machines connected via LAN or wide area network (WAN, aka "the Internet"). The difference between the two is proximity: WAN extends past a room, office, or campus. LAN parties (where everyone brings their computer over to someone's house to play a FPS) are still quite popular social events. Or they can be wireless as with the Nintendo DS.

Client server LAN: a computer that is big and fast enough to handle multiple users at once. Some MMO games and MMORPGs use client servers to handle the enormous traffic, and have many LANs to handle the user demand.

Once you've decided how your player is going to connect, you have to determine what they are going to play. There are broadly three different styles of play found in multiplayer games:

In **competitive** games, players have the same objective but work against each other—often fighting to the "death" to complete an objective first or achieve the highest score.

Cooperative games give players the same objective while (in theory) working together to achieve them. After playing *Gauntlet* with my stupid friends, I realized even a cooperative game can easily dissolve into a competitive one.

Conjugate gameplay has players sharing the same gameplay space but not the same goals. With the rise of **massively multiplayer online** games (**MMOs**) and **massively multiplayer online role-playing** games (**MMORPGs**), conjugate gameplay has become increasingly frequent as dozens if not hundreds of players dash around the game world at the same time, each with their own agendas and motivations.

So just what are these motivations? Well, I'm glad you asked, otherwise I wouldn't have had anything to write about for the next few pages. Look at all of these game modes found in multiplayer games; some unique to the genre. You can easily combine these modes to create conjugate gameplay scenarios:

- **Death match/free-for-all.** It's every man for himself as players battle each other for high scores or jockey for the best weapon. Usually players all start on common ground at the beginning of a death match and gain (or lose) equipment that gives them an edge over the course of the game.

- **Team death match.** This mode has teams of players killing each other for dominance. There can even be competitive goals within this mode, where players on the same team can compete for the highest score.

- **Fighting.** Two players enter, one player leaves. Starting with *Karate Champ* (Data East, 1984), fighting games quickly evolved into their own genre of game. Fighting games often feature head-to-head play, as slow data transmission can cause lag which would interrupt the crucial split-second timing required. This problem seems less of an issue as the release of classic fighting titles such as *Street Fighter* and *Mortal Kombat* on Xbox Live Arcade has shown.

- **Survival.** Usually the goal of survival game mode is to defeat all of the enemy or survive getting from point A to B. Players of the *Left 4 Dead* series watch each other's backs in combat as well as help each other heal when in danger. Survival mode most resembles that found in single-player games with cooperative modes.

- **Area/territory control.** The player has to travel to and protect/defend a certain location from AI enemies or human players. The excitement comes from the tug-of-war struggle of attacking, retreating, and retaking an objective as you attempt to "move the line" closer to the final area.

An area control map game can last hours given the right two teams.

- **Defend/king of the hill.** Much like area control, but one team of players is given a certain location, which needs to be defended for a designated period of time.

- **Capture the flag.** This game mode has one player become a target of the other players, either by possessing an object (like a flag or *Halo's* oddball skull) or being designated as "it" by the game code. The player that is "it" is sometimes handicapped while they are "it." This can be played both competitively and cooperatively with other team mates protecting the player.

- **Race/driving.** Racing modes have players competing for position or time. Often that competition can get nasty if players are given the means to mess with the other players during the race (such as *Mario Kart*'s power-ups). For combat races, use a regressive system where the player in front is the most vulnerable to attack from the other players who are coming up from behind. *Burnout Paradise* (EA, 2008) introduced the "Easy Drive" mode where multiple drivers can participate in events and socialize as they drive[1].

- **Team objective.** The players are given an objective, usually one that can only be achieved by working together. The *Army of Two* series and *Fat Princess* requires "all hands on deck" in order to win the game.

- **Man vs God.** One player is God who controls almost everything. The other is man who has limited resources. God makes life difficult for man. Man tries to survive despite overwhelming odds[2].

- **Gambling.** Games of chance where players play competitively or in conjugate to achieve the highest score (or at least beat the odds.) Avoid progressive systems where the rich get richer, and the poor get poorer.

---

[1] I wonder if this will lead to virtual cell-phone laws?
[2] Unless you are a masochist, this only sounds like fun if you are God.

- **Reflex.** How fast is your trigger finger? Quiz and puzzle games often have players see who's faster to determine victory, or at least give them an opportunity to use their…

- **Knowledge.** There's nothing like proving you're smarter than the guy sitting next to you on the sofa. This genre has remained consistently present in video games such as the *You Don't Know Jack*, *Buzz!* and the *Scene It?* series.

- **Creation.** *LittleBigPlanet*, *The Sims* and *Spore*'s multiplayer components consist of players visiting or interacting with a player's creations. It's a great way to extend the life of a game, as your players are creating the content for you! For example, *LittleBigPlanet: Game of the Year Edition* showcased 18 brand new levels that were created by the communities' top-rated player creators. A whole subgenre of "play" emerged when players of *The Sims* were given tools to make "stories" of their characters. These movies became just as popular as the game!

- **Virtual life.** Playstation's *Home*, *Second Life* (Linden Research Group, 2003) and *Animal Crossing* (Nintendo, 2001) are just a few of the virtual worlds where players can customize their world and interact with other online occupants. What started as text-only chatrooms have become the reality described in Neil Stephenson's visionary book *Snow Crash*.

HOW MANY IS THE RIGHT NUMBER?

You may be wondering how many players should multiplayer support? Take, for example, a melee-based fighting game like *Street Fighter*; With more than two players, there would be all types of problems. Players would bunch up as they fought making it hard to see individual players. Collision detection would be problematic and it would all just devolve into mob warfare rather than the contest of skills that make a good fighting game. On the other hand, an MMORPG like *World of Warcraft* would feel empty if it only allowed a few hundred players to roam around at the same time. Well, you might not be, but I am. So, how many players should there be? Let's look at the numbers:

- Fighting game (*Street Fighter*) = 2 players
- Fighting game (Power Stone) = 4 players

- Social games (*Uno*) = 4 players
- Action platformers (*LittleBigPlanet*) = 4 players
- Driving (*Burnout Paradise*) = 8 players
- FPS (*Call of Duty: Modern Warfare 2*) = 16 players
- FPS (*MAG*) = 64, 128 or 256 (depending on game mode)
- MMORPG (*World of Warcraft*) roughly 4000 to 5000 *per server*.

As you can see, there is a HUGE difference between the numbers of players. So, the answer to the question is: "whatever is right for your game."

MMORPGS, OR HELL IS OTHER PEOPLE

The MMORPG genre has evolved rapidly to have its own set of tropes and methods of play, some of which hardly qualify as "playing" at all. Becoming familiar with these tropes and including them in your own design will not only fill out your game but keep you competitive.

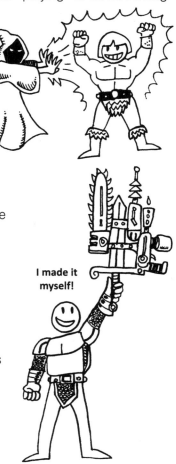

I made it myself!

- **Buffing.** Spell casting that affects not only the caster, but the entire party. This allows players to assume certain roles during gameplay. For example, if a cleric is able to prepare a healing buff (via hotkey), as players take damage he can restore them fully to allow them to continue fighting.
- **Character customization.** A huge appeal of any MMO is being able to assume the role of another character and to get lost in that fantasy life. The level of player character customization can range from preset character templates to making characters fully customizable down to sex, eye color, and nose length. Within the game, further encourage customization and let the player buy or win clothing, weapons, armor, gear, and mounts that fit the personality and class of the character they are playing.
- **Chatting.** A text or voice chat system in your game is expected these days. Players will use MMOs as a social gathering place as much as a place to play your game.

- **Crafting.** Crafting is combining harvested, found, or bought items to create new gear and weapons. Players first need to find "recipes" and "components" for creating items in order to craft objects. Just like creating characters, it's better to let the player craft items so they become recognizable as "their creations." As crafting can create powerful items and weapons, the time it takes to make these creations is usually time consuming. Sometimes players can craft in workshop locations to reduce crafting time. You can use skill-based minigames to successfully initiate the crafting process. Some games allow for "trial and error" style crafting, with the player running the risk of destroyed components if they fail in their attempt. Just don't allow a player to destroy a hard to get an expensive crafting item. It's not fair to punish the player twice!

- **Economy.** Many MMO games thrive on an economy system. Players win treasures that allow them to customize characters, buy better weapons and gear, craft items, and buy housing and mounts, even their own castles! (Or space stations, secret HQs, and so on.) Be sure to balance the effort the player puts into earning the money and the items they can buy with it. Allow for players to carry treasure as well as store it away in personal safes or public banks. Many MMOs have developed an economy that spills over into the real world, where players buy in-game money for real world cash. Many game creators frown on this practice, preferring to control the world's economy themselves.

Howabout you *don't* kill eight of us and we'll buy you those boots instead?

- **Grinding.** As the players level up their characters, the rate of their progression slows down. Many quests require quest items to complete, and obtaining those items can be time consuming as well. For example, in *Mafia Wars* (Zynga, 2009), to complete the "Extort a Corrupt Judge" job, you must own the relevant blackmail photo items. To earn blackmail photos you must complete the "Take Compromising Photo" job. But before that, you must have a disposable camera, which can either be gifted to the player by other players or dropped during the "Rob an Electronics Store" job—but there is no guarantee that you'll get the item when you pull the job! As you can see, placing several steps between the player and completion of the goal can get very time consuming...

and it can also get very frustrating for the player who feels like their progress has been artificially slowed. If anything gets a player to quit playing a MMO, it's the "grind." While it's not really possible to remove grinding completely from long-term MMO gaming, whatever can be done to reduce this phenomenon, or at least make it entertaining, will be appreciated by your players.

- **Instanced dungeons.** In order to make MMO gaming a unique experience for your players, dungeons are instanced. Content such as enemies and loot or even the level map are randomly generated to provide a different experience each time it is played. These dungeons exist "outside" of the game world, allowing for several groups of players to be in the same albeit alternate versions of the dungeon at the same time. That way, players don't have to wait for the dungeon to "restock" between player interactions.

- **Item collection.** Item collection is a huge motivating factor for players in MMORPGs. Create items that not only improve combat but other in-game abilities—especially tedious ones like crafting, mining, or harvesting resources. Most items fall along a rarity scheme: common, uncommon, rare, and unique. Create special items that can only be gained by defeating specific creatures (getting these items is known as "drops"), seasonal items that are only available at certain times of the year, or by attending specific world events.

- **Open world structure.** Most MMOs feature sandbox worlds where the player can (presumably) go anywhere and do anything. However, that is merely an illusion you will need to maintain for the player. In reality, you will need to build the world in the way you want the player to play the game. **Gating mechanisms**, such as level or gear requirements will prevent players from travelling to places they aren't ready for. Some games allow players to wander into higher-level sections, but the ass-kicking they receive at the hands of the enemies will usually force them to retreat until they've reached the necessary level to tackle the area's foes.

**Not cool, dude.
Not cool.**

- **Griefing.** Griefing is when a player will harass another player by constantly killing them. Design systems and create a rule structure for your world to combat this bad behavior. Make sure your policies are clear to the players, and a warning/zero tolerance system helps keep the peace.

- **Guilds.** Players are social animals and, as a result, they form groups. Players will form parties of characters, called guilds, in order to explore, socialize, and run raids. As a designer, you will want to create in-game meeting places for guilds to socialize. While it requires a lot of work, you may want to also design tools to promote guilds within your game world. Useful guild tools include communication tools, stat tracking, calendars for running raids, and guild asset customization.

- **Player housing.** Everyone likes to play house. Give your player a personal space to show off their achievements, display their souvenirs, or just "park" their player safely between game sessions. Having a home base will make the player feel much more connected and "at home" in the game world, which will make it become a place they want to return to again and again.

- **Player vs player.** Players love to see how strong their characters are by killing other player characters. However, not everyone wants to run the risk of being randomly killed while they play. As a precaution, many

MMOs have dedicated PvP servers. Another alternative is that your world has PvP combat restricted to certain locations.

- **Raids.** Raids are when players team up to defeat difficult game scenarios, such as storming a castle or battling a particularly fearsome enemy. Players that assemble and lead a raid need to be one part strategist, one part manager, and one part social director. As a designer, you want to create scenarios that can be overcome by a variety of party configurations, and even allow for the player's creative thinking or just plain dumb luck. Creating and cultivating the legends of these raid targets will let the players know that they have to marshal their forces to defeat them. Design systems that make it easy for players to share the loot after the raid is over based on each player's performance.

- **Spawn camping.** A practice by players who wait for an enemy or player to appear at a spawn point to kill them. It's a practice frowned upon by most MMO creators and you will have to develop safeguards into your game to discourage or disable this kind of behavior.
- **Trading/auctions.** Because players often end up with lots of identical loot, or with items that their character class can't use, trading and auctions are good solutions to help players clear out inventory. Make

sure it's simple for your players to trade items without ripping each other off. Create locations in your game world to promote trading. Some games have auction houses, where regular auctions are held and players can bid on items using in-game treasure.

As you can see there are lots of ways to design play and activities for multiple players. Just remember this **very important thing**:

**PLAYERS WILL ALWAYS DO THE LAST THING YOU EXPECT…
AND SOMETIMES YOU SHOULD LET THEM DO IT**

Multiplayer offers some great opportunities for players to "find the fun" in your design. Give your players a chance to personalize the way they play, just don't let them exploit it in ways that ruin the fun for other players.

Design your game systems thoroughly, and you will be able to anticipate problems before you start production.

Level 14's Universal Truths and Clever Ideas:

- Offer your players a variety of game modes and objectives.

- The right number of players is whatever is right for your gameplay.

- Allow players to customize their characters, their objects, their world.

- New play patterns will emerge when players are given the tools to create.

- Determine what level you want players to negatively interact with other players (like PvP).

- Players will always do the last thing you expect, but sometimes that's OK.

LEVEL 15
SOME NOTES ON MUSIC[1]

When the imagineers were creating the *Star Wars Star Tours* attraction at Disneyland, they initially intended the experience to be "realistic"; the audience would hear only the sound of the Starspeeder 3000 and the pilot's dialogue. However, when they tested the attraction, something didn't feel right. Without John Williams' music, the attraction just didn't seem like "Star Wars" and so the classic theme was added in.

Music brings a lot to any entertainment experience, be it a theme park attraction, movie, or a video game. But it also requires a lot of work and coordination between many members of a team, which contributes to why music and sound is usually left until late in production. This is a mistake. Sound and music can bring so much to a game that to leave it to the last minute is missing out on great design opportunities.

[1] Get it? Notes?

Music and sound in gaming has come a long way in a short time. Back in the 1970s and 1980s, arcade and console programmers had only electronic beeps and boops to play with. Even with the limitations, game creators were able to create some simple but memorable musical themes (or even just jingles) for games like *Pac-Man*, *Donkey Kong*, and *The Legend of Zelda*. Sound advances happened with almost every system; voice synthesizing and MIDI format audio meant that music became more lush. However, game creators were limited because sound and music files took up a good amount of memory on cartridges.

The big jump in game music came with CD media games. Starting with Red Book audio (Red Book being the set of standards for CD audio), music and audio in games was not only able to sound just like any other recorded music, but it was possible to store more of it on the CD. As games moved onto DVD media, the biggest problem with sound and music, storage space, was no longer an insurmountable issue. Nowadays streaming sound (compressed into MP3s, Ogg Vorbis, or console-specific formats and decompressed as needed by the sound chip) is used on modern PC and console games. Emphasis shifted from the programmatic issues with music and sound to what to do with it creatively.

The first question you need to ask yourself when thinking about music design is, "what kind of music do I want?" There are really two answers to this question: licensed or original.

How the heck do you draw a
picture of licensed game music?

Licensed music is previously recorded music that can be "licensed" for use in a game for a fee. While music publishers own the rights to the recorded music, there are also companies that work on behalf of the publishers to negotiate licensing deals including ASCAP (the American Society of Composers, Artists and Publishers) and Third Element. Obtaining the rights to music licenses and negotiating deals is usually handled by the game's publisher.

Because video games currently don't generate royalties once published, game publishers will negotiate **one-time buy-out fees** for music licenses lasting over a period of 7 years to "life of product." Licensing fees can range from $2,500 to over $30,000 a song. The more popular and prestigious a song is, the higher the licensing fee. I don't want to think how much the licensing fees were for *The Beatles: Rock Band* (EA, 2009).

If the song you want for your game is too expensive for your budget, don't fret—there are still plenty of options. You can license a less-expensive cover version of a song—this was done in the first *Guitar Hero* (Activision, 2005). Or, you can find a similar sounding but less expensive song at a music library. In fact, libraries are great if your game calls for a wide variety of musical styles or requires incidental music, like that heard on a radio or in the background of a bar scene.

Your other option is to use **original music**. Original music is a composition that is created specifically for your game. Unless you can compose, perform, and record your own music, then I suggest hiring a music director to work with your team[2]. Not only will they create the music, but they can also handle the resources required for performing, recording, and preparing the music for your game. Even though that's a lot of work, there is still plenty of prep work for a game designer to do before you even get to that stage.

I find it helps to be able to talk to a music director in their own language, even if you can't write music, play an instrument, or carry a tune. You just have to know what you like and have an opinion about it! Provide examples of what you want for your composer: try to cut out as much of the guesswork as possible. For *Maximo: Ghosts to Glory*, I gave the composer a "mix tape" of music from movie soundtracks and songs I thought would be appropriate for the game's levels. While they say that "a little knowledge is dangerous", I have found it useful to develop a musical vocabulary so you are speaking the composer's language. It will make it that much easier to request changes when you know what to listen for and what it's called.

---

[2] That is, if you don't already have a music director working on your team.

Here are a few **musical terms** that I have found useful to know:

- **Accent:** to place emphasis on a beat to make it louder or longer. As in, "that beat could use a little more accent."
- **Beat:** the "pulse" of the music. Music is measured in beats. Music can have fast beats or slow beats.
- **Chord:** three or more tones that create a harmony.
- **Instrument:** an object that produces music. Synthesized music replicates the sounds instruments make. The instrument used can greatly change the theme and mood of a piece.
- **Mood:** the "feel" or theme of a musical piece. The mood of a musical piece can be based on emotion (fear, excitement), action (sneaky, combat) or even location (tropical, Russian). Mood is created by instruments and changes in tempo and beat.
- **Octave:** this is the interval between one musical pitch and another with half or double its frequency; one octave up has twice the pitch. One octave down has half the pitch. Usually, I find that you will be telling the composer to bring something "up an octave" or "down an octave" to make it sound higher or lower pitched.
- **Pitch:** the highness or lowness of a tone. A tone's pitch can be adjusted either higher (to sound like the Chipmunks) or lower (to sound demonic). A tone's frequency is adjusted to add variety into game sounds without creating new sounds, for example a sword clanging on metal can have its frequency changed so the player doesn't have to hear the same sound over and over.
- **Rhythm:** the controlled movement of music in time. Ravel's *Bolero* builds in rhythm to a frantic conclusion.
- **Tempo:** the rate of speed of the music, which can range from very very slow to very very very fast. There's even a specific tempo for walking speed called *andante*!
- **Theme:** the "heart" of the musical composition. Usually a composer will come up with the theme first and then "flesh it out" to fit the length required. For example, John Williams' *Raiders of the Lost Ark March* was created when Steven Spielberg couldn't decide between which of two themes he liked better... so he had Williams combine them together!
- **Tone:** the sound or characteristic of a particular voice or instrument.
- **Upbeat:** refers to the last beat of a measure, but can be used to refer to making the music sound happier, friendlier, or faster.
- **Volume:** referring to the softness or loudness of the music.

Now that you can communicate with your music director, you need to consider the genre of your game. What style of music do you want for your game? A traditional route would be to use the style of music generally associated with that genre. Say you are making a sci-fi game. Do you want orchestral music like John Williams' score from *Star Wars*, or something like Vangelis' synthesized music from *Blade Runner*, or go old school with 1950s theremin music in the style of the original *The Day the Earth Stood Still*? Feel free to go in another creative direction: how would a sci-fi game feel with a hip-hop soundtrack? Or a trance soundtrack? Or polka?

Creating a **temporary soundtrack** of your game will cut down on the guesswork for your composer and give them clear examples of what you want. Finding music for temporary tracks is amazingly easy in this age of digital miracles and wonders. By using the Internet, finding music is incredibly simple compared to the past, when we had to scour our CD collections or go into "the field" with microphone and recorders to get samples from the real world. But with the advent of iTunes, YouTube, Pandora, and other music-finding websites, assembling tracks is a breeze— put in a couple of keywords and you'll get hundreds, if not thousands, of results. You can even have the programmers insert this music into your game as is, but there is a danger that your team will really start to like (or hate) the temp tracks and complain if they are changed! Also, **make absolutely sure** you don't leave any music in your game that you don't have a license for—you may have to pay huge amounts to use the sample, or scrap all the work!

Next, prepare a list of your musical needs. To determine this, figure out how many levels/environments/chapters/race tracks/unique encounters your game has. Each one of these levels will require **background music**, literally music that plays in the background as a kind of audio backdrop for gameplay.

Traditionally, background music is themed towards the level. Spooky music on the haunted house level, medieval music for the castle level, jungle drums for the jungle level—you get the idea.

Background music tracks usually run for a few minutes and loop over again to save space in memory and composition time. Work with your music director to make sure the transition between the beginning and the end of the song sounds correct and isn't marred by silence or an awkward change in tempo.

The next question to ask is do you want—or more realistically, can you afford—to have background music on every level? You may have to re-use tracks throughout the game. For example, in *Maximo vs. Army of Zin*, we had two songs created for each world and alternated between them so the player wouldn't have to hear the same song twice in a row.

Instead of having a straightforward song-per-level system, you may want to work with your sound programmer and music director to create a **dynamic score** instead. In this method of scoring a game, music is broken up into themes that play when a certain situation arises. For example, dynamic music can kick in during combat to make a fight feel more exciting and fast paced. The main theme music will come back in once the fight is won.

Hey! Sweet theme music!

Dynamic scoring is similar to the music convention **leitmotif**, in which a specific character or scenario has a specific musical theme associated with them. One of the most commonly known leitmotifs is from the *Star Wars* films. Darth Vader, Luke Skywalker, Yoda, and the Princess Leia/Han Solo romance all have unique themes that play whenever the characters are on screen. The most commonly encountered dynamic score themes include:

- **Mystery.** The player has entered a new and mysterious locale. A little bit of mysterious music can help set the mood.

- **Warning.** Sinister or menacing music that plays whenever the player is entering a hazardous area or about to encounter enemies. This type of theme can be found in many horror games.
- **Combat.** Exciting music that plays whenever the player is engaged in combat.
- **Chase/fast movement.** Chased by dinosaurs? Pursuing villains? Giant boulder hot on your heels? A fast-paced chase theme will make the action feel even more exciting.
- **Victory.** Be sure to sonically reward your players, even if it's a "sting" (a very short piece of music) to let the player know when a fight is over and they are victorious or to celebrate a successfully accomplished event in the game. *The Legend of Zelda* games have some great examples of rewarding players with music.
- **Walking.** While most games play "walking" music, I believe that if you play slow music, then the player is going to move slowly. But if you make the music's beat faster than the player can walk, it will motivate the player to move faster. In other words, remember this **very important thing**:

ALWAYS MAKE THE MUSIC MORE EXCITING THAN THE ACTION ON SCREEN

Don't forget to budget in music for your title screen, pause/options/save screen, game over screen or any bonus or minigames your games may have. Your opening theme is very important: it's the first piece of music the player hears and will set the stage for the rest of the game. I suggest using your best piece of music for the start screen to really get the player excited about playing your game.

Environmental effects are the music of the world around us. Locations have their own special background sounds; a graveyard at night sounds very different to a city during lunch hour. Sometimes music can just be too overbearing or not "right" for certain environments or games. Combining environmental effects with a dynamic score to punctuate action can be very effective. In *Maximo: Ghosts to Glory*, the hub levels were designed to have environmental effects to help the player get into the mood of the locations while the gameplay levels had more traditional background music.

When is a sound not a sound? When it's **silence**. Silence has a powerful effect on the listener. Often sound is used judiciously to indicate that something special is happening to the player or the world. It can be used to indicate great speed (when the music drops off as the player engages the boost in *Burnout*), intense action moments (as in "reflex time" in *F.E.A.R.*), for suspense, or even a character's failed attempt at humor[3].

SOUNDS LIKE A GAME TO ME

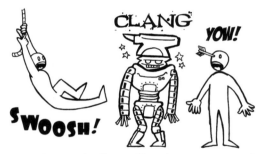

Next, assemble a list of sound effects. Develop your sound effect lists as you develop the move sets of your characters and enemies. Start with cataloging the basic sound effects for your main character:

* **Movement.** Start with the sounds for walking and running on specific surfaces like stone, gravel, metal, and splashing through water to make your character feel grounded in the world. Jumping, landing, rolling, and sliding all need sounds too to let the player know they've pulled off the moves.
* **Attacks.** Making swings and kicks "swoosh" will make them sound more dynamic. Make unique attacks sound distinct, like Pac-Man's "eating a ghost" or Mario's jump/stomp.
* **Impacts.** A nice meaty "whack" will make a punch or kick feel more powerful. Weapons, spells, and explosions all need dynamic and loud sounds to make the player know they've hit something or someone. Don't forget object reaction effects like breaking wood, shattering glass, and clanging metal.

[3]Usually accompanied with the sound of crickets—so I guess it isn't silent after all...

- **Weapons.** Guns bang, swords clang, and laser blasters "pew pew!" The bigger the weapon, the bigger the sound effect. Your weapons can also sound as unique as they look: for example, *Star Wars'* iconic hum of a lightsaber.

- **Hit reactions.** "Oomph!s", "Ow!s", and "Aarrgh!s" may sound funny while you are recording them, but they are some of the most important sounds in the game. Whenever the player gets hit, they need to know it!

- **Vocal cues.** Need to communicate to the player? Use your character. Having your hero say "What's this?" when they spot treasure or "That's better!" after being healed will not only let the player know what's been accomplished or is possible but it's a chance to add some character to your character. Don't forget effort cues, such as grunts of exertion when pushing moveable blocks and pulling stubborn levers.

- **Death.** Nothing says "you're dead", better than a good blood-curdling scream. Make sure you account for all the horrible ways to go, from a groan when getting slain to the gurgle of death by drowning to a long scream when plummeting off a cliff.

- **Success.** Use both "musical" and vocal sound effects to indicate success to your player. Play a "sting" to let players know they're a winner and don't forget to have your character celebrate vocally with a "woo-hoo!" or "yeah!"

For temporary sound effects, I suggest buying CD libraries from sound-effect providers like *Sound Ideas* or *Hollywood Edge*. Their libraries have sounds for things you can't even believe anyone would ever need: cougars sneezing or the hum of a nuclear reactor. They even have sound effects from some of the most popular Hollywood movies and TV shows. Even if you don't have a dedicated sound effects designer on staff, they are useful tools to have around the studio. Be prepared to spend many hours trying to find "the right" sound effect.

You can also find many sound effects online for free (though of course always check for copyright and so on—better to be sure than on the end of a zillion dollar lawsuit later). However, even with all of these great resources online, sometimes you just can't find the effect you need. This is why I turn to sound editing tools like *Sound Forge* or *Vegas*. With these programs I can quickly and easily mix together two or more sounds to get an idea across to my sound effects designer.

Decide whether your sound effects are realistic or cartoony. This will generally be set by the theme of your game, but sometimes there are exceptions. Realistic sounds make the world feel grounded in reality but sometimes the sounds can be too subdued. Cartoony sound effects are exaggerated and great for "video game-y" things like extra lives and treasure collection, but sometimes they are a little too "on the nose" and risk taking the player out of the game's world. Make sure your sound designer is using sound to its greatest potential. Make sounds go "up" in pitch and tempo to make something sound positive, like collecting an extra life or completing a task. Make sound effects go "down" to reinforce negative and failure situations.

Regardless of which style you choose, sometimes your sound designer will have to "sweeten" a sound effect because the real world version just doesn't sound right. For example, I have found that breaking bones never sound right; they sound more like dry twigs cracking. Instead, we "sweetened" the effect with the sound of a bowling ball cracking into pins.

When you are creating attack and reaction sound effects for your characters, work with your animators to determine **timing**. You want to make sure your sound effect doesn't last longer or end before the animation does. Once you have determined the animation's timing, create the sound effect to fit. Make sure your sound programmer knows what frame of animation the sound effect is supposed to play on.

Sounds can be used to give the player a warning or clue to something else in the game. The whistle of a falling bombshell can give the player enough of a chance to dive for cover. A crackle of electricity or ominous thrum of magical power will give the player pause when approaching a protected doorway. A player can search for an item like a lost pocket watch or misplaced cell phone by following the sound of its ticking or ringing.

Be careful not to have too many sounds playing at once. To prevent sound effects from creating cacophony, you will have to prioritize them. Your sound programmer can help you designate sounds into three categories: **local, distant**, and **priority**.

Priority   Local   Distant

Local sound effects play when the player is close to the source of the sound effect. This may be a babbling brook, a ticking clock, a ringing phone, the hum of machinery, or the growls of an enemy. As the player gets further from the source, these sound effects fade away.

Distant sound effects are sounds that the player can hear even if they are far from the sound's source. These include explosions, a wolf's howl, approaching vehicle engines, or the ominous thrum of a tower o' doom.

Priority sound effects are sounds that will always play regardless of where the player is. These are sounds that provide the player gameplay feedback, including: loss of health, collection of treasures/goodies, score or combo increase, power-up or countdown timer, successful enemy hit, death, world interaction such as landing, collision or weapon impacts, and footsteps/swim strokes/wing flaps.

Just as when naming level files, give your music and sound cues descriptive but short names so the viewer doesn't have to guess what they are. For example, music for level 2 of your game may be called Lv2Song.wav, and the sound file for a variation on a robot enemy's blaster shot may be roblast2.wav.

Sound is not only effective for communicating what is going on in the game, but it can be used for gameplay. Whole genres of games are centered on music, from *Dance Dance Revolution* (Konami, 1998) to *Band Hero* (Activision, 2009). When creating sound-based and music-based gameplay, don't rely completely on the sound. Create visuals to echo the music and sound. You can never provide too many clues for the player and you get the benefit of creating gameplay that can be played by impaired players.

Short-term memory games like *Simon* (Milton Bradley, 1978) or *PaRappa the Rapper* (SCE, 1996) require the player to memorize and repeat a short piece of music. It helps to have a visual component to the gameplay, not only to help players remember which notes to play, but also to accommodate deaf (and tone deaf) players.

Rhythm games like *Taiko: Drum Master* (Namco, 2004), *Rhythm Heaven* (Nintendo, 2008), and the *Guitar Hero* series require the player to keep the beat in time to the music. Many of these games require or come with specific peripherals resembling instruments from guitars to maracas. When designing rhythm games, make sure you account for player fatigue as many of these games require constant hand and wrist movement. Provide mandatory breaks between songs or levels for players to prevent injuries.

Pitch games have players sing in order to match a song's pitch. These games require a microphone to play as seen in the *SingStar* or *Karaoke Revolution* series of games.

Music creation games blur the lines between music creation tool and game. *Electroplankton* (Nintendo, 2005) and *Fluid* (SCEI, 1998) feature charming player characters and dynamic on-screen activity but their end goals are not to win, but to create and enjoy.

Other music games defy classification: *Vib-Ribbon* (SCE, 1999) creates platform-esque gameplay based on whatever CD the player inserts, creating different play experiences with every game. *Rez* (Sega, 2001) is a classic rail shooter with the added layer of the player creating complex electronic music with each enemy they destroy. *Battle of the Bands* (THQ, 2008) is a rhythm game where players play a musical tug-of-war (from disco to country for example) as they launch attacks at each other.

As you can see, there are plenty of ways to use music and sound in gameplay. Don't neglect them; they're one more tool for a designer to use.

Level 15's Universal Truths and Clever Ideas:

- Determine sound needs early in production: don't wait until the last minute.

- Learn how to "speak musician" to communicate your desires to the composer.

- Communicate important game actions to the player using sound effects and vocal cues.

- Don't use music and sound effects you don't have the rights to use.

- Use music to move the game's action.

- Use leitmotifs to help tell your story.

- Determine sound and music's proximity and timing to make it feel more realistic and interactive.

- Silence can be as powerful as music.

- Use music and sound effects as gameplay (but make sure you have accompanying visuals for sound-impaired players).

LEVEL 16

CUTSCENES, OR NO ONE'S GONNA WATCH 'EM ANYWAY

A **cutscene** is an animated or live-action sequence used to advance the story, create spectacle, and provide atmosphere, dialogue, character development, and reveal clues that would otherwise be missed by the player during gameplay. The player often has no control over the game while a cutscene plays.

Why can't it just GET TO THE GAME?!!

I find cutscenes to be a double-edged sword. On one hand, they usually look fantastic, allowing your game world and characters to be shown in a way that may not be reproducible in the game engine. However cutscenes carry a stigma. There is a history of many cutscenes being too long, not necessary to the story or a downright chore to watch. Many players will skip through cutscenes (if the game gives them the option to do this!) in order to "get to the game." To avoid this, you should first ask yourself this **very important thing**:

CAN IT BE DONE IN THE GAME?

We'll answer that in a minute. Just as there are many ways to make movies, there are many ways to make cutscenes: full motion video, animated, flash animated, prerendered, puppet shows, and scripted events.

Full motion video (or FMV) cutscenes were popular when video games were first being published on CD media. Titles like *Wing Commander III: Heart of the Tiger* (Origin, 1994), *Command and Conquer* (EA, 1995), and *The Horde* (Crystal Dynamics, 1994) featured live-action cutscenes featuring Hollywood actors and production values. FMVs are usually produced by an outside production company, as they require all the resources of a motion picture production.

FMVs became so popular during the mid-1990s that several systems dedicated to playing **interactive movies** were produced. Game systems like the 3DO Interactive player, Philips CD-I, and Sega Mega CD (as well as PCs) specialized in games with extensive or playable FMV sequences such as *Night Trap* (Sega, 1992), *Sewer Shark* (Sony Imagesoft, 1992), *Phantasmagoria* (Sierra Online, 1995), and *Psychic Detective* (EA, 1995). Even though DVD media can easily handle the file size of the videos, FMVs have become less popular with game developers these days. They're usually deemed too expensive to produce for something the game's audience may not even watch.

Animated cutscenes or **full motion animations** offer a stylistic alternative to FMVs. A cell animated or stop motion animated cutscene is converted into a video format playable by the game's engine, which is then shown during the game's title and story sequences. Players have no control over the game during these sequences. Due to the involved production, generally long shooting time and cost, animated cutscenes are scarce in video games. However, there have been many gorgeous examples of animated cutscenes such as the *Neverhood* titles (Dreamworks Interactive, 1996), *The Curse of Monkey Island* (Lucasarts, 1997), and the *Professor Layton* series (Nintendo, 2007).

Flash animated sequences are animated sequences created in Adobe Flash, which, due to the use of still images and simple movement, lends the animation a certain distinctive visual style. While Flash is often used for a game's animatics, some games used Flash animations for their cutscenes such as in the *Sly Cooper* series (SCE, 2002), and the first *God of War*.

Prerendered cutscenes are created using high-resolution versions of the game's character models and environments, with cinematic cameras to create dynamic and dramatic choreography, imagery, and storytelling. Players have no control over the game during these sequences. With enough money, time, and manpower, these prerendered cutscenes can look spectacular—check out any Blizzard title, Final Fantasy series game, or Namco[1] fighting game to see what I mean.

Puppet shows use in-game assets such as characters and environments to create cutscenes. These are called puppet shows because the characters in early versions of these cutscenes moved unnaturally, giving them the impression of marionettes. Visually, they are only distinguished from gameplay by the use of a cinematic camera. Puppet shows can be non-interactive or allow the player limited character and camera movement (such as looking around with the main character's head) as seen in *Assassin's Creed* (Ubisoft, 2007), and the *Call of Duty: Modern Warfare* series.

Scripted events are similar to puppet shows where in-game assets are used to create animated sequences, but here the player is allowed limited to full interaction with the game during the sequence. Since their inclusion in games such as *Half-Life* (Valve, 1998), *The Operative: No One Lives Forever* (Fox Interactive, 2000), and the *Call of Duty* series, scripted events have become the preferred method to convey story without upsetting the pace of gameplay. They are quite common in FPS and action games, but if not properly choreographed players run the risk of missing/not seeing the event. They can also get repetitive if the player has to experience them repeatedly due to dying before the event's objectives can be completed[2]. Here are a few ways to make sure your player is watching your scripted event:

- Have your events activate only when the player character is actually looking at/facing the scripted event.
- Build your level geometry to "frame the scene" so the player gets a clear view of the action.
- Move the camera around the environment to give the player an idea of its layout and space.
- If you have a mobile camera, be sure to start your event from the player's POV or position. This is particularly important for cutscenes that

[1] During the production of Tekken 3, I remember the game's Japanese producer proudly telling me that the game's spectacular cinematics were the work of just two animators. He then told me that both of them ended up in the hospital due to exhaustion.

[2] This often leads to the "Groundhog Day" phenomenon, where the player feels like they are caught in a time loop having to live out the same sequence of events over and over again.

use the in-game camera to show events like geometry changing position or when giving hints about puzzle elements or revealing enemies. You want to use the camera to always show a clear cause and effect, such as "pull this lever and that door opens."

The good news is, you can now determine which type of storytelling device is best for your cutscene. The bad news is, you now have to write it.

HOW TO WRITE A SCREENPLAY IN EIGHT EASY STEPS

There are so many books on screenwriting, I'm not going to even attempt to go into the level of detail that they do. If you are interested in reading an in-depth analysis on screenwriting, then I suggest the following books[3]:

- *Screenplay: the Foundations of Screenwriting* by Syd Field (Dell, 1984)
- *Story; Substance, Structure, Style and the Principles of Screenwriting* by Robert McKee (It Books, 1997)
- *Screenwriting 434 (a Practical Guide to Step-Outlining & Writing Your Screenplay)* by Lew Hunter (Perigee Trade, 2004).

Since you are reading this book and not theirs, here is a quick and dirty guide to teach you how to write your screenplay like a professional, so it can be used by storyboard artists, cutscene animators, or voice actors.

Step 1. Outline your story. If you don't know the beginning, middle, and end of your story, you won't know what the heck you are writing. But you've already learned this back in Level 3, right?

Step 2. Break your story down scene by scene to determine which characters are in each scene and what locations they take place in. This is going to be important for staging as well as asset creation purposes. You may not be able to have 10,000 Orcish warriors charging over a hill in a puppet show cutscene. You may want to play around with the order of your cutscenes. Maybe you want to start with a flashback, because there is more action in a later scene than in your first scene. For example, in *SpongeBob Squarepants: Atlantis Squarepantis* (THQ, 2007), we started the game at the end of the story because it was the scene with the most action and we wanted the game to start with a high action scene. I find it better to start with a bang to grab the viewer's attention.

---

[3] Do me a favor and read them AFTER you've finished this one, OK?

Step 3. Determine which scenes of your story are going to be cutscenes vs being told through gameplay. I prefer to tell as much of the story through gameplay as this is what the player will be doing the most—playing the game. You want to save cutscenes for big moments—kissing and blowing things up—things that the game engine cannot support.

Don't make the player watch something they should doing. It's always better to have the player do than watch… Wait a second, that's a **very important thing**. Let me try that again.

IT'S ALWAYS BETTER TO HAVE THE PLAYER *DO* THAN *WATCH*

Step 4. Write your scenes and dialogue. Determine what needs to happen and what needs to be said. Try to communicate it with action as much (if not more) than with words. Write to entertain. It doesn't hurt to be funny either. What you do need to be is brief. As Shakespeare once said, "brevity is the soul of wit." Or in other words, **keep it short**. Don't bore with a lot of yapping and psycho/technobabble[4]. Try to get your point across in as few words as possible. I used to treat writing dialogue like a game of "Name that Tune." "George, I can write that dialogue in 12 lines." "Oh yeah, well, I can write that in eight lines or less." "Write. That. Dialogue!"

Step 5. Write your script in the official screenplay format. If you are going to be a writing professional (hey, you're writing a video game, so guess what? You are a writing professional) then you'd better learn to do it the way the pros do. Every other entertainment professional uses this format, so there's no reason to reinvent the wheel. Here's a simple style guide:

```
SCENE #. INT./EXT. (choose one) — LOCATION — TIME OF DAY
CAMERA ANGLE
Describe the setting, introduce CHARACTERS in ALL CAPS,
highlight any ACTION in ALL CAPS too.
CHARACTER'S NAME
(actor's direction goes in parenthesis)
Dialogue is written here. Keep it brief.
```

That's pretty much the basics of screenwriting format! There are plenty of screenwriting formatting programs like *Final Draft* or *Movie Magic* available if you want to save time pressing the "tab" key on your keyboard.

Step 6. Read your dialogue. Out loud. Dialogue often sounds great "in your head" when you've written it down, but sounds strange or clunky when it's read out[5]. Expect to rewrite (and rewrite and rewrite) your dialogue.

---

[4] Yes, Metal Gear Solid series, I'm still looking at you.
[5] I am reminded of Harrison Ford's quote to George Lucas about Star Wars' dialogue:
"George, you can type this sh*t, but you sure as hell can't say it."

Step 7. Let it simmer for a day or two. Often you will get new ideas, think of better ways to write scenes or dialogue. Have someone else read it and give you their feedback. Try not to hover too much over them as they do it.

Step 8. Prepare your script for voice actors using a spreadsheet program like Microsoft Excel. Break out the character's dialogue line by line as this is the way voice actors read and record their dialogue. Having the actor's lines isolated will make it easier for them and you to get through what they need to read without having to page through a lengthy script. Make sure to retain scene numbers on your spreadsheet. Remember to give each line of dialogue a file name so the sound engineer has something to name each sound file when they cut up the session tracks. This will be the same file your programmer uses to put the track into the game.

Cold Steele VO Script: Jake Steele dialogue (Actor TBD)

File Name	Dialogue	Notes
Opening_01_01	Those terrorist bastards have hidden from us for too long, Montoya.	Opening cinematic
Opening_01_02	Well, they're about to get a taste of COLD STEEL.	Place emphasis on "cold steel"
Opening_01_03	Saddle up amigo, we're going hunting.	
Opening_01_04	Heh. You can say that again.	
Opening_01_05	Montoya! Noooooo!	Montoya is killed by terrorist
Cutscene_01_01	Just because you've got me trussed up like a Thanksgiving turkey, doesn't mean you've won, Von Slaughter.	
Cutscene_01_02	I wouldn't give you the map even if I did have it… Ungh!	Jake is slapped by Von Slaughter at end of line
Cutscene_01_03	Go ahead, sucker. Do your worst.	Hurt, but not defeated
Jake_Climb_01	Unnnh!	Climbs mountain
Jake_Climb_02	Umphf! Umphf!	Alternate climbing take
Jake_Collect_01	Come to papa.	Collects pick-up or cash
Jake_Collect_02	This will come in useful.	Collects pick-up or cash
Jake_Collect_03	Heh heh.	Collects pick-up or cash
Jake_Health_01	Oh yeah, that's the stuff.	Drinks health tonic
Jake_Health_02	That was a good one.	Drinks health tonic
Jake_Yell_01	Yaaaaah!!	Jake's charge move
Jake_Yell_02	Here I come, suckers!	Alt charge move
Jake_Victory_01	Take that, sucker!	
Jake_Victory_02	Ha ha! That's how we did it in the old days!	

File Name	Dialogue	Notes
Jake_Hit_01	Ow!	
Jake_Hit_02	Oomph!	
Jake_Hit_03	Aarrgh!	
Jake_Death_01	Yaaaaaaaah!	Jake falls off cliff
Jake_Death_02	Ung! Ooooh!	Jake is shot and drops to his knees
Jake_Death_03	Not again! Uhhhhh!	Alternate death take
Jake_Death_04	YAAAAAAAAAAAAAAAAAAA!	Burned to death

As you may have noticed from above, VO (that stands for **voice over**, btw. And **btw** stands for by the way, btw) scripts have a lot of "YAAAAAAAAAAAAAAA!" and "Oomph!" and "Unngh!" in them. Voice actors read these lines very literally so write it the way you want it to sound. There's a big difference to a voice actor between "Arg!" and "Aaaargh!". One's a pirate and the other is a death rattle.

If you're not sure how to spell a grunt, hit reaction, or death cry, I suggest reading comic books. They're filled with all sorts of onomatopoeic[6] words like POW! CRASH! And AIIEEE!

ARG! vs. ARGHH!!

[6] That's a fancy way of saying "It's spelled like it sounds."

Now that you've written your script and broken it out, I find it helpful to record a **temp track**. This is a track of moderately talented amateur actors and team members—such as you—reading the lines for the purposes of determining audio file size and length. All you need to record a temp track is your script, a willing actor, a decent microphone, computer software that can record audio, and a quiet, non-echoing place to record. Try to do your best to read the line the way you will eventually want it performed by a professional voice actor. However, it's a bad idea to animate a character's lip synch to a temp track: the actor's performance is going to end up very different than that of the temp actor. You should only use temp track audio for timing and blocking purpose.

Speaking of **voice actors**, while *you* could play the part of Jake Steele, international terrorist killer, you really should hire a professional actor for the final game. I've had the privilege of working with dozens of VO actors over the years and, believe me, there is a HUGE difference in the performance you get from an actor versus an amateur. You want the best for your game, right? So hire an actor. (Or two. Or three. Or a dozen.) But before you can hire an actor, you're going to need to hire a **voice director**.

Voice directors are extremely helpful people (and usually very nice too). They will help you cast your game's characters based on the description of the character you give them. Make sure you're accurate with what you send them and don't be vague. If necessary, give the voice director the name of an existing actor you are imagining would be perfect for the role. Who knows, you may even be able to get them for the part[7]! They will book the studio time and help you get the best rate. A voice director will help you schedule your time to get the most recording time with your actors. They will direct the actors during the voiceover sessions and work with the sound technicians to get the best quality results.

As you get ready for the voiceover session, send the script to the voice director. It doesn't have to be the final draft, but make sure you let the voice director know that you will be bringing changes to the script with you. On the day of the voice session, be sure to bring the following with you:

- Extra physical copies of the script.
- A highlighter, for calling out lines to the actor in the script during the session.
- A ballpoint pen or pencil, to make notes and to keep track of changes to the script. (Trust me, there will be changes.)

[7] This happened to game developer Tim Schaeffer, who thought he could never get Jack Black to play the lead in Brütal Legend.

- Images of the characters the actors are playing. Bring whatever you can to give the actor an idea of what the character looks like. In many cases, VO actors will play several parts in your game so even if it's "drooling alien no. 2" bring an image to help them bring that character to life (and send it ahead of time to the voice director as well to aid in casting).
- A book or handheld game. "Hurry up and wait" is the motto of the entertainment industry. There is always plenty of "down time" as actors and sound technicians prepare for the session. Keep out of their way, but don't wander off too far.
- Beverages and snacks—voice sessions can last all day if not all week. And even though all you're doing is sitting and listening to actors all day, it can be exhausting! Be prepared!

If you aren't the game writer/designer, make sure your writer/designer is on hand when it's time for the voiceover recording session too. Very often, there will need to be script rewrites and the actors and voice director don't always know the context of the line. You may need something very specific for your game: don't leave it up to someone else. Not that there's any problem with improvisation—giving an actor free reign to create great additions and alternate takes on your script will not only give you plenty of material to work with, but the actors enjoy doing it too—and if they enjoy working with you, they will want to work with you again in the future.

And finally, **have fun**! Remember, you are getting paid to sit in a room listening to actors say lines that you have written! It doesn't get much better than that!

Check. Check 1. Sibilance! Sibilance!

Is this thing on?

Level 16's Universal Truths and Clever Ideas:

- Your cutscenes should fit the style, budget, and schedule of your game.

- Learn and write your script in the standard screenwriting format.

- Start your game off with a bang to draw audiences in.

- It's better to have the player do than watch: tell your story using gameplay.

- Allow the player to skip cutscenes, and don't make them watch them over and over again.

- Keep your cutscenes short to save player's time and your money.

- Use cutscenes for kissing and explosions: save your cutscenes for big spectacular moments and intimate ones. Do everything else in gameplay.

- Professional actors make a big difference. Use them whenever possible.

- Break out your actor's material when preparing for voice acting sessions.

LEVEL 17

AND NOW THE HARD PART

If you followed the instructions in this book, you are now the proud creator of a great game idea and a 200-plus page game design document. You have everything you need to make an actual video game, right? Wrong! Your work is just beginning. Before you actually **make** the game, you will have to find a publisher to **publish** your game. And to find a publisher, you will need a **pitch**.

A pitch is a streamlined, easily digestible version of your game design document. It contains everything that's great and original about your game without all the "twiddley bits[1]."

Since most pitches are presented to groups in boardrooms, I highly recommend using Microsoft *PowerPoint* or some other presentation software to create your pitch document. To help, I have included an outline of what you should include in a pitch presentation in Bonus Level 9. The basics of this document are these:

- Title screen with logo
- Company profile
- High concept
- A few pages of details
- Proof of why your game will be awesome/make everyone lots of money.

When creating a pitch presentation, remember the basics of making presentation slides: choose a font that you can read, don't put too much information on one page, and everyone loves pictures.

---

[1] "Twiddley bits" is game industry lingo for all the details you've worked really hard on but other people don't really need to hear about when you are telling them about your game. They're important to making the game, but not to selling it to a publisher.

NO ONE CARES ABOUT YOUR STUPID LITTLE WORLD

Putting together a good pitch presentation is like putting together an artist's portfolio: you want to show off your best work, but not include too many pieces and overwhelm your audience.

This was a story pitch I once sat through. The minute the writer started telling us the intricate machinations of his fantasy world, I tuned him out. It was just too much information to process at once. While worlds are fun to create and inventing a world's details is important to making a world feel real, realize that nobody else cares about your world and those details at this stage. I didn't care who the Nebulons were or what the significance of a Galactic Imperium was. I just wanted to know how the game played. Don't overburden your reader with story details. Keep it simple and more importantly, keep those details to yourself… for now.

Here are a few more rules of thumb when pitching:

- **Pitch to the right people.** Just like when you created your game outline, you need to consider to whom you are selling your idea. Too many times, coming out of a pitch presentation, I've heard "That was a great pitch, but we'd never publish that type of game." This is sad, because if the developer had taken a little time to do some research about the publisher, that situation would have never happened. You don't want to waste your time (not to mention the publisher's). Some publishers only publish certain genres of games. Don't pitch a family game to a publisher who specializes in hardcore action games. That said, many publishers do publish a wide range of titles and their company objectives may change. Timing is everything. You may make a pitch right when the publisher decides they want to make a RTS about cybernetic death mecha piloted by farm animals. Then again, maybe not.

- **Pitch in a controlled environment.** You can never be sure where a pitch presentation is going to take place, but you want to pitch your game in a location where the audience's attention is on you and your presentation. Pitching on the show floor of E3 = not good. Pitching in a private meeting room at E3 = much better.

- **Be prepared.** Just like any other type of performance, you need to practice. Practice giving your pitch in front of your peers. Invite them to give you feedback on content as well as your performance. Don't be afraid to access your inner actor. You will be telling the story and the narrative of your game to the publisher, so you want to get them as excited about your game as you are excited to make it. If there is someone on your team better suited to speak in front of a group then have them give the presentation instead—with your supervision of course. You will still want to be present at the pitch to help them answer questions and fill in details. You want your game to shine in the best possible light and you only have one chance to impress. Make sure your computer is compatible with any type of set up, and always bring backup data on a thumb drive or disc. I have seen presentations stop cold because the sound isn't working correctly. Bring plenty of copies of documents. This is a little harder to predict because the number of attendees can be unpredictable. Here's another situation to consider: would you still be able to make your pitch if the power went out? So, as the Boy Scouts say, be prepared.

- **Know your project inside and out (and then some).** Even though your game hasn't even been made yet, you should know everything you can about it. Publishers will ask questions to try and poke holes in your design. It's not that they're malicious; they're just looking for topics that may cause trouble once the game starts production. Be able to talk about your game in-depth but remember not to go on and on; you don't want to drown your audience in details unless they ask for them. If you don't know an answer to a question, it helps to say, I'd like to hear your thoughts on that."

- **Keep the focus.** Production teams sometimes bring in several pitch ideas in an attempt to find out what the publisher is interested in. I'm not sure I agree with that strategy. More pitches means that (a) the meeting will go on longer, (b) less time will be spent on each game presentation, and (c) you may not get consensus on which idea is the best. There will always be one idea that stands out from the others, so why muddy the waters? I say let the attendees concentrate on that one idea. You may have to revisit the publisher to pitch another game idea. If you do present several ideas at a pitch meeting, then make sure that all of the presentations are at the same level of quality.

- **Pitch to represent.** Even if you don't have a great game pitch or truly original idea, but you have a great piece of technology or a prototype gameplay mechanic then it may not hurt to present it to a publisher. Sometimes a publisher has a license but hasn't picked a studio to develop it into a game. Sometimes, timing and good luck play just as much a part of the pitch process as having a great game idea and strong presentation. In my 5 plus years working at a publisher and hearing scores of video game pitches, I have developed the "**pitch equation**":

GAME DEMO > GAME DESIGN DOCUMENT > PRESENTATION > PITCH

Game demos are a lot of work. If not planned for properly, they take time away from the production of the main game. They can really disrupt the flow of your production and can lead to crunch time: long hours trying to get content into your game. However, demos show you are serious about making your game and allow potential publishers a chance to get their hands on code, which sometimes is the best way to sell the game.

VIDEO GAMES IS A HAAAARD BUSINESS

Making video games may sound like fun and games, but it is a lot of hard work. It takes lots of effort and hours to design and create a game. And even after all of that hard work, a game that may seem like a "sure hit" may get poor reviews or mediocre sales. There are plenty of examples of well made and fun games that received great reviews and still did badly sales-wise. Sometimes the publisher may not be able to finance the promotion of the game to the level you feel it deserves. Sales projections may be set at levels that the game just can't reach. It's not all the publisher's fault though. Sometimes team members may not put their best work into the game; family and health issues may distract them from their jobs. God forbid your lead designer or a key team member gets sick or dies during production. Remember this **very important thing**:

VIDEO GAMES ARE MADE BY PEOPLE

These things happen, so you want to give your game a fighting chance to be the best possible. Most games that go badly are the result of bad planning. Here's a list for troubleshooting your game during production:

- Plan ahead. Prepare for team illnesses and vacation. Prepare for hardware failure, brown-outs, or other technical issues.
- Be smart when creating your design. Don't overpromise content and bite off more than the team can chew.
- Try to lock down design and content as soon as possible; constantly changing content in the pursuit of perfection will eventually wear down your team and may even kill your game.
- Players will always find ways to break your game, so make sure to play the game like they would. Don't just play the game the way it's "meant to be played." Do unusual things and bang on the game until it breaks. Then fix it and keep working.
- If you are creating an international version of your games, make sure you account for sensitive cultural difference. For example, Titan Studios, the

creators of *Fat Princess* (SCE, 2009) had to redesign their cartoony four-fingered game characters to have five fingers[2] for the game's release in Japan.

- Find ways to remove **design blinders**, the phenomena that happens when you are too close to your game. It results in game creators thinking their game is too easy or half-baked elements "good enough." Recruit other people to play your game and give feedback. Use focus group testing when applicable and iterate on your game design in all stages of production. This is something that publishers are really good at… providing what I call the "10,000 foot view"—an objective look at your game. They'll help you identify weak spots and strengthen the good parts.

- If something doesn't work, then throw it out. Don't be precious with your ideas. They're a dime a dozen. When you do throw something out, have a backup plan in mind. Don't make throwing away work a habit. It's better to plan things out to anticipate problems than to waste work. It's better to be getting rid of good ideas; that means you have too many good ideas! You can always use them on the sequel[3].

Cutting content happens in every game. But the more you cut during preproduction, the less you will have to cut during production. Make sure you are cutting content for the right reasons. Don't cut or change content that connect and have an impact on multiple game systems or you will be asking for trouble.

[2] There are at least three explanations to why the four-fingered visual is considered taboo in Japan. Yubitsume is the practice done by members of the Yakuza; the cutting off at the knuckle of the pinkie finger as atonement. The resulting mutilated hand has the appearance of having four fingers. The number four, pronounced Shi, also means death. It's an unlucky number; much like 13 is in western cultures. The Burakumin are a social class that is still met with discrimination. The four-fingered sign was used to designate Burakumin (because they often worked with four-legged animals) and became a derogatory gesture. Modern Buraku activist groups have sued over the use of the four-fingered sign in Japanese media.
[3] S.I.F.S.—"save it for the sequel"—was a popular saying at many of the studios I worked at.

I don't want to go too much into game production (that could fill an entirely different book) but you should consider how to go about building your game. Some teams create a **vertical slice** that acts as a demo to be shown to publishers and a template for the rest of the game. A vertical slice is a level or sequence of your game that has been designed, built, and polished to the highest level of playability possible. A vertical slice has the highest quality of controls, camera, visuals, gameplay, code, effects, and audio that the final version of the game will have. Usually the target is 80% of final game quality. While experienced teams can create vertical slices in a matter of months, it is a very time-consuming process that can lead to **crunch time**—long working hours that can be very stressful to the team as they rush to create, insert and test content into the game.

May I have another vertical slice, please?

A **horizontal layer** is another alternative to game production. The team bring all elements of the game, from beginning to end, "up" at the same time in **gray box** form. When creating gray box levels, geometry is roughly built and character animation assets are mostly placeholders. Details such as texturing, effects, and sound are generally absent at this point. Once all game assets have been play tested and approved, then the team oves on to the next step of "prettying up" and polishing the game even further.

It may not look like much now, but you've got to imagine it with stone walls, the skull torches, the spike-filled pit and the goblin henchmen...

The hardest thing about presenting gray box gameplay to other team members (and publishers and marketing partners, and so on) is that it requires them to **use their imagination**. Don't laugh, even in a creative industry such as making games, that ability is rarer than you'd think. The trick is to not let these people get the wrong idea about your game. Make sure there is concept art on hand to help communicate these visuals before they are in the game. What's great about this type of iteration is it gives the team a chance to play around with the game and discover what's great about it. If bouncing off of enemies' heads turns out to be more fun than fighting them, then it's not too late to adjust the design to compensate for the gameplay.

There is a design concept called **emergent gameplay**; gameplay that will "just happen" if the player is given a set of gameplay tools and a chance to play with them. However, the problem arises when designers use the concept of emergent gameplay as an excuse to underdesign gameplay, hoping that the player will "find the fun."

I say "emergent, eschmergent!" There's no such thing as accidental design. Knowing how all of the gameplay elements work with each other is part of the design process. If you take the time to plan and think about how the elements relate to each other, the outcomes of those relationships can be predicted. Granted, unusual relationships can emerge from bugs and other inconsistencies, but you should never plan your game design around those! If something unexpected does happen and it doesn't break your game, remember: "it's not a bug, it's a feature!"

Planning ahead. That's the secret to successful game production.

WHAT TO DO FOR AN ENCORE?

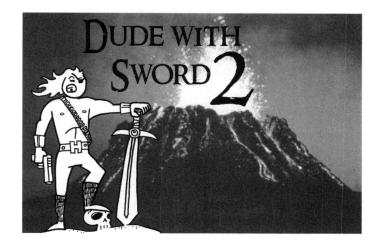

If your game reviews well or sells well, or if your publisher can afford to pay you a second time around, then you may get to make a sequel. Publishers like sequels. Now that I have worked for both a developer and a publisher, I think I have a good perspective on sequels. Just like in Hollywood, they are **safe(r) bets**: proven intellectual property (IP) that doesn't need to be explained to the audience: "if you loved the first one, you'll love the second!"

It's easy to understand why that is appealing to a publisher, but it's not without its problems. Sequels often sadly seem to represent a missed opportunity. Some teams just "phone in" or rush to make their sequel, creating retreads of the last game. Sequels should be treated as an opportunity to get it right. The first time you make a game, you are limited by several factors: you have to build a team, build an engine, figure out just what the heck this character and the gameplay is going to be. Get the whole thing to work and actually be fun. Then you hope that the audience is going to like and buy it. Once you've finished that, you've licked the hard part—especially if you've sold well enough to warrant a sequel. You should start your preproduction with the driving desire to make the game perfect[4].

---

[4] OK, odds are you will never obtain perfection, but it's not a bad goal to shoot for. Then again, it didn't help Duke Nukem Forever, did it?

For example, after finishing the first *Maximo* game, I went to my producer with a list of 40 things I thought were broken and needed to be fixed in the sequel (to my delight, I was able to get 39 of those requests fulfilled!). While the first game sold better, I still think the second game is a better game. We wouldn't have had the opportunity to make that better game if we didn't have a chance to make a sequel.

Besides, if there were no sequels, there would be no *Grand Theft Auto 3*, *Call of Duty: Modern Warfare*, *Burnout Paradise*, *Curse of Monkey Island*, *Resident Evil 2* or *Resident Evil 4*, *Lego Star Wars original trilogy…* you get the idea. Here is some advice on making a video game sequel:

- Use the "spine" of the original game as a basis of your gameplay design for the sequel. Take everything that was good in the first game and improve on it. Take everything that was bad and throw it away. It seems like common sense, but it's not all that common—things like lousy camera, controls, and gameplay mechanics are "justified" by teams because they were in the first game. Just because they were in the first game, doesn't mean they were that good. Don't be afraid to cut out the bad bits. If it's better than the original, no one will complain. My friend, project manager George Collins recommends that every sequel should be "30/70": 30 percent new material and ideas and 70 percent based on the original game. It's not a bad formula to follow.

- Don't let the player down. They expect certain things in the sequel and you shouldn't disappoint. For example, if your audience loved the wall-running mechanic in your first game, then by all means, keep wall running in the sequel.

- Name it something other than "*GameName 2*." Names are really important to a game. Personally, I think both the *Batman* (*Batman Returns*, *Batman Begins*, and so on) and the *Indiana Jones and the…* movie franchises did it right. Their titles are mysterious and keep furthering the fiction rather than reducing it to a numbered outing.

- Always introduce something new… This may seem to be pandering to marketing, but make sure there are **five** new things in your game for the back of the box, preferably new gameplay concepts to bring something fresh. Also, try to introduce at least one new hero and villain to the franchise. Remind the player that this is a new experience, not just a rehash.

- … But don't make it too new. In *Maximo vs. Army of Zin*, we didn't realize that the players wanted to fight more supernatural enemies; we had them battling clockwork creatures instead. The fans were unhappy because we deviated away from what they liked in the first title.

- The further down the road you are, the more opportunity you have for change. Why not try doing something wildly different? This, of course, requires buy-in from your publisher and marketing department so it can be tricky to pull off. I've worked on franchises that were in their 5th, 8th or even 16th incarnation and sometimes a completely new direction is what it needed to shake things up. Give it a try, it worked for both the *Grand Theft Auto* and *Wolfenstein* franchises[5]!

Level 17's Universal Truths and Clever Ideas:

- Demo > GDD > pitch presentation > pitch outline.

- Cater your pitch to the right audience.

- Be prepared for any technical problem.

- Know your game completely to answer any question your audience might have.

- Practice your pitch in front of an audience.

- Video games are made by people: schedule in "people issues", both good and bad.

- Remove designer blinders by looking at your game holistically and through focus testing.

- Build games using either horizontal layer or vertical slice style production—pick one and go!

- If something doesn't work in your game, throw it out, but try to plan ahead to avoid this.

- Avoid crunch time with responsible design goals and detailed production planning.

---

[5] Just be aware that it may not work too. Nothing is ever guaranteed in video games.

- Don't rely on emergent gameplay to make your game fun. All good design is preplanned.

- Use the 30/70% rule when creating sequels: repeat all the stuff that was great in the first game, throw out everything that didn't work.

- Don't let legacy keep your sequel down. Take a hard look at what can be improved from the first game.

- Don't let the player down.

CONTINUE?

TIME TO LEVEL UP!

So, let's see… We've thought up some game designs, we've written some game design documents, we've eaten some chili, and we've pitched our game.

Congratulations! You've leveled up!

And just like in games, you're just getting started. Now it's time for you to learn firsthand that making video games is the best job in the world. Do me a favor, as you zoom ahead and make your own games, keep this book in your back pocket; hopefully it will come in helpful the next time you get stuck.

Finally, always remember these three things:

- Take a break every once in a while. You're only human and you're only making games. You're not a heart surgeon. No one is going to die if you leave something until tomorrow.
- Always be fair and generous. This is a very small industry and word gets around very fast when you aren't.
- Always keep playing games—even the bad ones.
- Not many people make games for a living, so enjoy every minute of it: after all, you could be flipping burgers instead.

OK, so I lied, there were four things.

BONUS LEVEL 1
THE ONE-SHEET SAMPLE

The following are examples of one-sheet templates used for creating a concept overview. The one-sheet template is a very important document; not just for the team and managers to "be on the same page" with the project priorities and objectives, but as a tool to pass on to management, marketing, sales, licensors, and get them excited about your game.

Ultimately, the style in which you create the one-sheet doesn't matter as much as the information in it. The first example is a text-only version, while the second adds images. No matter what the format, keep them short and informative.

Reiterate the points on the one-sheet every time you talk about the game. You'll know when it eventually sinks in to your team mates when you talk to them about a design feature and they reply with "But that's not what it says on the one-sheet" and they're right. Consider it a victory. (We designers need to take them where we can!)

Farm Wars (game title) concept overview

XBOX LIVE/WII WARE/PS3 Download (Game platform)
Target Age: **15-21 (target audience)**
Rating: **E10**

Game Summary: Old MacDonald has a farm... and those animals are fed up! Tired of being exploited, the animals build cybernetic death armor and attack! Farmer MacDonald must fight frenzied waves of killer cows, sinister sheep and crazed chickens to protect his produce. Sell your crops to upgrade the farm and buy weapons! Farm as well as you fight, otherwise you'll "buy the farm!" **(Include the beginning, middle and end of the game story, give an indication of the game play style, the player's objectives and elements. Keep it short and sweet.)**

Game Outline: Players create and maintain a basic farm, plants and cares for crops during the *Farming Round.* Enemies attack during the *Battle Round.* Harvest and sell remaining produce during the *Selling Round.* Use profits to buy new seed, rebuild your farm and upgrade your weapon in the *Buying Round.* After a *Season* (4 sets of 4 rounds), the player fights a boss to progress to the next Season. Later seasons will feature weather that will affect farming, selling and battle rounds. **(Don't go into great detail, but it needs to be more in-depth than a summary.)**

USP (Unique Selling Points)

- RTS action meets farming simulation!
- Build and breed unique farm, weapons and crops. Hundreds of combinations!
- Over 50 weapons from a simple hoe to the DeathBringer3000!!
- Fight hordes of enemies and bosses!
- Multiple game endings based on player's performance.
- Multiplayer "Barnyard Brawl" battle mode.

(Use USPs to highlight cool and unique features – game play style, game modes, single or multiplayer, technology innovations, cool features. There shouldn't be more than 5-7 of these)

Similar competitive products:
Tower Defense, Harvest Moon series, *Lock's Quest*

Choose competitive products that are successful, recent or very well known - preferably all three.

MAXIMO VS The ARMY of ZIN

A Compelling Story, A mystery that unfolds thru cinematic and puppet story sequences

Excitement! Fun! Heroic!

A Single Player Combat / Action Game!

The Sequel to Maximo: Ghosts to Glory

The Second Saga Begins....

Eight months have passed since Ghosts to Glory and Maximo and Grim have searched in vain for Sophia.... Their search is suddenly interrupted when they encounter a maiden menaced by a strange "clockwork" monster ...

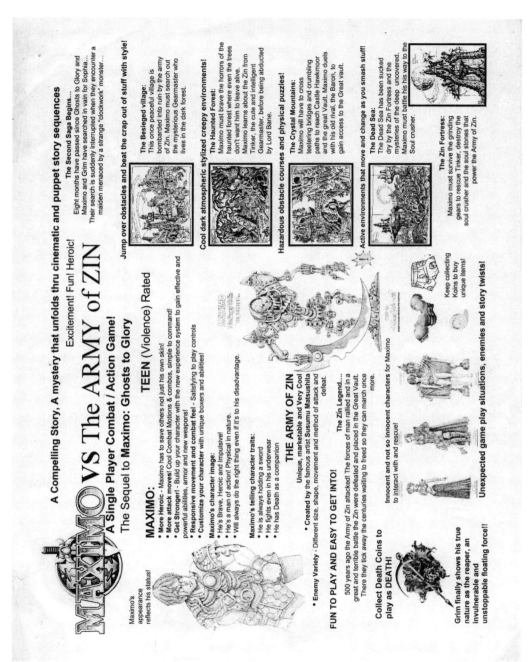

Maximo's appearance reflects his status!

MAXIMO: TEEN (Violence) Rated

- **More Heroic** - Maximo has to save others not just his own skin!
- **More attack moves!** Cool Combat Motions & combos, simple to command!
- **Get Stronger!** - Build up your character with the new experience system to gain effective and powerful abilities, armor and new weapons!
- Responsive movement and combat feel - Satisfying to play controls
- Customize your character with unique boxers and abilities!

Maximo's character image:
- He's Brave, Heroic and Impulsive!
- He's a man of action! Physical in nature.
- Will always do the right thing even if it's to his disadvantage.

Maximo's telling character traits:
- He is always holding a sword
- He fights even in his underwear
- He has Death as a companion

THE ARMY OF ZIN

Unique, marketable and Very Cool

- **Created by the famous artist Susumu Matsushita**
- **Enemy Variety** - Different size, shape, movement and method of attack and defeat.

The Zin Legend....

500 years ago the Army of Zin attacked! The forces of man rallied and in a great and terrible battle the Zin were defeated and placed in the Great Vault. There they tick away the centuries waiting to freed so they can march once more.

FUN TO PLAY AND EASY TO GET INTO!

Innocent and not so innocent characters for Maximo to interact with and rescue!

Collect Death Coins to play as DEATH!

Grim finally shows his true nature as the reaper, an invulnerable and unstoppable floating force!!

Keep collecting Koins to buy unique items!

Unexpected game play situations, enemies and story twists!

Jump over obstacles and beat the crap out of stuff with style!

The Besieged village:
This once peaceful village is bombarded into ruin by the army of Zin. Maximo must search out the mysterious Gearmaster who lives in the dark forest.

Cool dark atmospheric stylized creepy environments!

The Haunted Forest:
Maximo must brave the horrors of the haunted forest where even the trees don't want him to leave alive. Maximo learns about the Zin from Tinker, the cute and intelligent Gearmaster, before being abducted by Lord Bane.

Hazardous obstacle courses and physical puzzles!

The Crystal Mountains:
Maximo will have to cross teetering bridges and crumbling paths to reach Castle Hawkmoor and the great Vault. Maximo duels with his old rival, the Baron, to gain access to the Great vault.

Active environments that move and change as you smash stuff!

The Dead Sea:
The Dead Sea has been sucked dry by the Zin Fortress and the mysteries of the deep uncovered. Maximo must battle his his way to the Soul crusher.

The Zin Fortress:
Maximo must survive the grinding gears to rescue Tinker, destroy the soul crusher and the soul stones that power the Army of Zin.

BONUS LEVEL 2
THE TEN-PAGE DESIGN
DOCUMENT SAMPLE

Unlike the one-pager, which should be kept to one page, the ten-pager is more a set of guidelines than a strict policy[1]. It's more of a "ten-pointer" than a ten-pager, but feel free to dedicate a page to a topic.

What's important is that all the broad strokes of information are included and the document is accessible and exciting to read. The foundation of this document will turn into your pitch and GDD.

Page 1: Title Page

Include a graphic if possible, a title (preferably a logo) and your contact information, target platform, target audience, target rating, and expected shipping date.

Page 2: Story and Gameplay

Page 2 should include a few short paragraphs about the story (beginning, middle, and ending … or at least a cliffhanger) mentioning the setting, the characters, and the conflict. Gameplay description should give a brief idea of the flow of the game—break it into stages or bullet points if its easier to convey info that way.

---

[1] Kind of like the pirate's code.

Page 3: Game Flow

How does the player grow as the challenges increase? How does this tie into the story? Briefly describe how these systems will work (experience points, money, score, collectibles) and what the player gains as they grow (new abilities, weapons, additional moves, unlockables).

Page 4: Character(s) and Controls

Who does the player control? What is his/her/its story? What can they do that is unique/special to this game? Can the player do several types of activities? (Driving, shooting, and so on.) Does the player ever change characters? What is the difference in play?

Show control mapping highlighting some of the special/unique moves to this product. Include image of SKU's controller for reference.

Page 5: Main Gameplay Concepts and Platform Specific Features

What kind of play does the player engage in? What genres are they? (Driving, shooting, platform, and so on.) How is the sequence of play broken up? (Levels? Rounds? Story chapters?) If there are multiple minigames, list them out by name and give short descriptions. If there are specific cool gameplay scenarios, list them. USPs from the concept overview should be included and briefly detailed here. Diagrams are good to illustrate game concepts.

What game features are unique and capitalize on the platform's hardware? (Hard drive, touch screen, multiple screen, memory card, and so on.) Provide examples.

Page 6: Game World

Where does the gameplay take place? List the environments the player will visit with short descriptions. How do they tie into the story? What mood is being evoked in each world? How are they connected? (Linear or hub-style navigation?) Include a simple flow diagram of how the player would navigate the world.

Page 7: Interface

How does the player navigate the shell of the game? What mood is evoked with the interface screens? What music is used? Include a simple flow diagram of how the player will navigate the interface.

Page 8: Mechanics and Power-ups

Gameplay mechanics. What unique mechanics are in the game? How do they relate to the player's actions? How will they be used in the environment?

Power-ups. If applicable, what kind of power-ups/collectibles can the player collect? What are the benefits of collecting them? Can they be used to buy items, abilities, and so on?

Page 9: Enemies and Bosses

Enemies. If applicable, what kind of enemies does the player face? What kind of cool attacks do they have? Describe the enemy AI. What makes them unique?

Bosses. If applicable, what kind of boss characters does the player face? What environments do they appear in? How does the player defeat them? What does the player get for defeating them?

Page 10: Cutscenes, Bonus Material, and Comps

How are the cutscenes going to be presented? When do they appear; in between levels? At the beginning and end of the game? What format have they been created in? (CG? Flash? Puppet show?)

What material will the player be able to unlock? What incentive is there for the player to play again?

What other games will be your competition upon market release?

FARM WARS

Design by Scott Rogers
For XBOX Live Arcade, PSN and WiiWare
Rating: E10+
Ship Date: TBD

FARM WARS

Name and Contact Info   Date

Game story:

Farmer MacDonald has a farm… and that farm is under attack! Tired of being exploited for their milk and eggs, the farm animals join forces to mail-order giant mechanical Deth-tech suits and invade! Farmer MacDonald must battle off waves of killer cows, sinister sheep and crazed chickens who threaten to stomp his crops under grinding mechanical feet! As the war escalates and spreads across the county, each side adds new technology and allies to the fight. Who will win the **Farm Wars**? Can Farmer MacDonald defend the homestead or will he "buy the farm"?

Game play:

In **Farm Wars**, the player is Farmer MacDonald defending his farm from death-dealing cows, sheep and chickens. The game play is separated into five distinct phases each with a limited time of play. Players plant and raise crops on their farm for sale to purchase defense and weapon upgrades. Players defend their customized farm from waves of enemies, sell the surviving crops at their roadside produce stand, buy and plant some new ones and upgrade the farm's defenses in preparation for the next wave… or save up to build or buy Deth-tech of their very own! Each game play round lasts fifteen to thirty minutes - with six environment maps, six weather conditions and six boss rounds to offer over ten hours of game play.

Elevator pitch:

Farmville meets Tower Defense meets MechWarrior

FARM WARS

Name and Contact Info   Date

Player Character:

Farmer MacDonald: A starting **Farm Wars** player can customize their character's face, hair and clothes and sex. As the player upgrades their character over the course of the game, they can purchase new headgear, clothing and armor as well as upgrade tools, weapons, defenses and mecha.

Over the course of the game, the player can elect to spend cash to research down tech trees. Technology advances visually as well as functionally from traditional rural farm equipment to steam-punk themed gear to chrome and steel technological equipment.

Each advancement in technology offers its' own advantages and disadvantages. A high-tech piece of armor will offer more protection, but makes the player move more slowly than its' low-tech analog equivalent.

Player controls (XBOX 360):

FARM WARS

Name and Contact Info   Date

Game World:

The world of **Farm Wars** is inspired by the charming farming world of Harvest Moon, the stoic animals of "The Far Side" and the steam-punk meets mecha Deth-tech by way of Brian Despain and MechWarrior.

Farms are created to be extremely customizable but of manageable sizes to allow players to travel from one end to the other within the game play session. Players can customize crops, buildings, defenses.

Randomly generated world elements on six different farm maps and six weather conditions (Summer, Winter, Spring, Fall, Tornado and Rain) create a depth not seen on any other action strategy game.

Game Experience:

A "Round" of game play is broken up into five "Phases." **Buying, Planting, Defending, Boss** and **Selling**.

Buying - Using their ACME mail order catalog, the player can purchase seed and farming equipment for use in the Planting phase. New vegetables, farming equipment, fertilizer, irrigation, defense systems (fences from wooden to laser beam) and even weapons and "special" items can be bought as the game progresses. You can even eventually build and upgrade your own robotic-death suit! (which can double as a tractor/combine)

Planting - A farmer must tend to his crops and the player is no different. During this phase the player moves about a 3D isometric dynamic farm. The land must be tilled, the vegetables must be watered and the guidance missile defense systems must be erected. Crop selection, tending and placement is very important to victory. Crops are also affected by seasons.

Defending - Initially armed with a hoe, you must defend your crops from the attacks of vengeful farm animals and their mechanized death-suits. They will try to ruin your crops and destroy your land in an attempt to drive you out of business. Or they might just try to kill you outright. The right defenses and a little skill will keep you from "buying the farm."

Boss - Every four "rounds" the player squares off against one of the main animals (Pig, Cow, Chicken, etc…) in a fight to the finish. If MacDonald

FARM WARS

loses, he's mulch, but if he wins… well, let's just say there will be fresh bacon or beef for the selling phase…

Selling - In addition to farming, the player runs a little stand at the side of the road where he sells fresh vegetables. Customers give advice from the best way to manage resources and defeat enemies to what the upcoming season will be like or what crop will be "hot" next season…

How to win - Survive and defeat all of the animal bosses.
How to lose - Go broke, have your farm devastated or even get killed in combat. Who said being a farmer is easy?!

Game Mechanics:
Play in **Farm Wars** in an isometric view of 3D characters, elements and terrain. The camera can be zoomed and rotated 360 degrees to allow for either a close or far view of the farm battlefield. The player runs over the map in real time, farming, building and fighting advancing enemies. A HUD mini-map helps the player navigate, locate enemies and check the status of defenses during the battle.

Farm Wars players perform simple actions - build defense, use tools, plant crops and wield weapons. Over the course of the game, controls remain contextual - advanced technology and weapon upgrades utilize the same basic control scheme. After the battle, any surviving crops are harvested automatically and added to the player's inventory to be sold during the selling phase. The selling phase takes place on a simple static screen that also utilizes in-game assets.

Farm Wars players can research, buy and build defenses and tools over the course of the game. Every item will have several levels of improvement each with a distinct visual and effect. Unlike most games, the technology doesn't supplant the previous one, it just adds to the player's arsenal - the only limiting factor is the player's choice and finances on any given round.

A sample defensive technology progression would look like:

Fence < Barbed Wire < Electric Fence < Force Field < Laser System

FARM WARS

Enemies:

Each Boss animal not only has its own devastating attacks and Deth-Tech mecha, but is usually accompanied by minions that escalate in power as each game season progresses. Below is a small sample of animal enemy's attacks and minions

Chicken:

- Kamikaze Egg-men minions egg-splode on impact
- Chicken's scratch attack rip up crops

Sheep:

- Woolie minions fry farmers with static electricity discharge
- Sheep's Battering ram attack smashes down structures

Duck:

- Duck Hunter minion can emerge from bodies of water to blast at player
- Duck's Rotten egg attack explodes into a cloud of poison gas

Rooster:

- Cock Fighter minion's powerful peck can shatter the toughest armor
- Rooster's Cock-A-Doodle-Destroy! sonic attack stuns players and overloads sensitive electronics

Pig:

- Battle Boar minions charge players to gore them with tusks
- Pig's Muckmaker 3000 turns fertile land into useless mud fields

Cow:

- Heifer Hellion minion sprays sour milk that wilts crops
- Cow's cud cannon launches a powerful and gooey projectile

FARM WARS

Name and Contact Info   Date

Cutscenes:
Narrative cutscenes will use in-game assets to create short puppet-show sequences.

Bonus Materials:
We plan on supporting **Farm Wars** with at least six months of downloadable content that expands on the existing game:

- Additional farm maps
- New crop selections
- Crop trading with other players
- New Deth-Tech and defense upgrades
- Farmer's dog companion character
- Holiday themed player costumes
- Cooperative and competitive Multiplayer modes

FARM WARS   Name and Contact Info   Date

BONUS LEVEL 3
GAME DESIGN DOCUMENT
TEMPLATE

The following pages are a template for creating a game design document or GDD. The GDD is skewed towards an action, adventure, platform, RPG, and shooter-style game. However, most of the elements listed in the template can be adapted for any style of game.

Don't feel like you have to fill in every detail of information while creating the GDD, but it is better to have areas of the design roughed out than to not have them at all. I tell the developers I work with that a "TBD" is better than nothing at all.

Remember that a GDD is a living thing: everything in it is liquid and might change due to anything from technology limitations to production time realities.

In the end, use the information in this template in the way that's best for YOU and your team. If you need to draw more pictures, then do so. If you need to break the data up into "one-pagers" then do that. (See Bonus Level 1.)

COVER

(Insert evocative cover image here)

YOUR GAME'S TITLE

Document version number (keep this current!)

Written by (your team name here)

Point of contact (producer or lead designer w/phone number)

Date of publishing

Version number

Footer should always have:

Copyright Company Date   Page number   Current date

GDD Outline (for action, adventure, platform, RPG, or shooter-video game)

Table of contents—remember to keep this current

Revision history—update this with publishing dates and track which author updated the material

Game goals—this includes:

Game's "high concept"

The "back of the box" listing of any new/novel mechanics or gameplay features

Include all Internet and wireless features

Story overview—remember to keep this short and frame it in the context of the gameplay. This includes:

Set up—how does the player start the game?

Locations and how they relate to the narrative—how does the player get from one location to the next?

Finale—what is the ending? What is the player expected to be/have done by the end of the game?

Game controls

Overview—list specific moves the player will be doing, but don't go into detail on the actual moves … yet

Control scheme

Show an image of a controller (controllers if game is on multiple platforms) with corresponding button mapping

Technological requirements—keep this brief as many of these features will be included in the game's technical design document (TDD).

What tools is this game going to use?

- How are camera, physics, bosses, and so on going to be done? Implemented by programmer? By designer? Hard coded? Scripted?

What design tools is this game going to use?

- Level creation tools
- Scripting system

Proposed tools for cheats—include controls for cheats

- Level cheat
- Invulnerability cheat
- Camera cheat
- Other cheats (full health, full armor, full money, and so on)

Front end of the game

Indicate what credit screens will be shown when game is first turned on including:

- Publisher
- Studio logo
- Licensors
- Third party software manufacturers
- Legal screen

Cutscene description (if applicable)—no need to reproduce the entire script here, just give the reader an idea of what it is about.

Attract mode description (if applicable)—give a description of what in-game material will be shown if the game is left idle on the start screen.

Title/start screen—what is the first impression of the actual game? Include:

An image of the title/start screen

Detail of what is presented to the player

- Title name and how it appears on screen
- Any associated animation/graphics

A list of what selection options are available to the player

How the player interfaces with the options (cursor, d-pad, and so on)

Save/load file—describe how a game file is saved and loaded

How to name/designate a save file—keyboard or other file-naming convention

List details of saved file shown to player

- Name
- Date
- Level location or chapter name/number
- Time played elapsed
- An image of what a saved game file looks like (if applicable)

Detail any cross-save features

Player options—include image, sound and music, and player interface details. Detail out connecting links to options.

- Video settings
- Audio settings
- Music settings
- Subtitle settings
- Contrast tool
- Alternate control settings (reverse joystick, feedback on/off, and so on)

Other screens—these could be unlockable content accessed from the title screen. Make sure to include image, sound and music, and player interface details. Possible screens include:

Credits

- Team photo
- Studio images

Bonus material—include image of screens, how will player interact with interface, activate this material? (unlockable, buyable, Easter eggs, and so on)

- Alternate costumes or weapons
- Cheats
- Functional cheats (invulnerability, full health, and so on)
- Licensor required cheats (for marketing purpose)
- Other cheats (big-head mode, color swap, and so on)
- Art/sound/animation galleries
- Video player to replay cutscenes, movies, and so on
- Trailers for other games/products

Special features

- Commentary
- Team interviews
- Deleted material
- Documentary
- Gag reels

Game flowchart—show how all the screens from "title/start screen" to "game over" connect to each other.

Loading screen—what does player see when the game is loading? Include:

An image of the pause screen (and indicate if there are multiple images used)

Overview of data presented to player on pause screen (hints, trivia questions, minigame)

Game camera(s)—call out any specific camera types

Image of camera's point of view any of the following applicable cameras:

- First person
- Third person
- Three-quarters view
- 2.5-D view
- Forced scroll
- Spline
- Locked camera

Description of logic system for camera
- Game-specific situations requiring unique cameras
- Camera troubleshooting guide—examples of what camera will do when encountering problems

Logic for cheat/screenshot camera
- How developer/publisher can access and operate this camera

HUD system—information presented on screen to the player. Include images of all of the following:

Health/status

Lives/continues

Money/score/rank

Power/fuel

Ammunition

Abilities/skills

Timer

Map or navigation system

Options: links to outside screens

Plings/context sensitive information

Targeting system/reticule/cursor

Speedometer

If a game is HUD-less, describe how the above information is going to be conveyed to the player.

Player character(s)

Character name

Inspirational image or concept drawing of your character

Short description explaining player's motivation and relationships to other major/player characters

Player metrics

Size relationships of player character to other elements/characters in the world

Movement (walk, run, sneak, duck, roll, crawl)
- Show metrics

Navigation (jump, swim, fly)
- Show metrics
- Conditions for navigation moves

Hoist/hang
- Show metrics

Context-sensitive moves (push/pull, operate switch, swing, and so on)

- Show examples and metrics
- Conditions for context-sensitive moves

Reactions/damage/death

- Show examples and metrics

Idles

Player skills

Description of basic skills

List of skill upgrades

- Description of skills
- Skill modifiers
- Player metrics (if applicable)

Player inventory tools (equipment, spells, buffs, and so on)

List of tools

- Image of tools
- What does each tool do?
- Controls for using tool

Inventory screen

- Image of inventory screen
- How does player access inventory?
- How does player select tool from inventory?

Combat: melee combat

- Combat moves—include metrics and controls
- Combat reactions—include metrics and controls
  —Block
  —Dodge
  —Parry
  —Grab
- Types of effects (damage, knockback, stun, poison, and so on)
- Combat progression—how player improves moves
- Descriptions of combo moves
  —Controls for combo moves
  —Combo progression
- Combat gauge
  —Combat gauge descriptors/combat value modifiers based on descriptors
- Descriptions of combo moves
  —Controls for combo moves
  —Combo progression

Weapon combat

Weapon progression

- Technology tree
- Weapon inspiration/concept images
- Weapon damage and effects
  —Targeting system details
  —Lock-on system details
- Ammo required
- Range
- Special attributes (breakable, degrades)
- Controls
  —How does player use weapons?
  —How does player swap weapons?

Power-ups/state modifiers

List of power-ups/state modifiers

- Description including image
- Effect
- Duration
- Effect on controls (if valid)

Health

Health (general)

- HUD display
- How to replenish health
- Power-ups and health items
- Warning for player when health is low

Alternate states (stunned, poisoned, turned into a baby)

- Controls
- Show examples and metrics

Lives (if applicable)

- How are lives earned?
- How are lives lost?
- What happens when you run out of lives?

Death

- Instant death conditions—(combat, fire, drowning, and so on)
- Game over conditions:
  —Penalty for dying
  —Game over screen (show image of game over screen)

Checkpoints
- Continue system

Scoring (if applicable)

Point values

Bonuses
- What gives a bonus?

Leaderboard setup
- Image
- Elements that contribute to scoring

Achievements
- List
- Icon image

Rewards and economy

Monetary system
- Shopping interface
  —Description
  —Player navigation
- What does it buy?
- Cost

Vehicles

How does player enter/exit vehicle?

How does vehicle interact with world, enemies, objects, and so on

Vehicle description
- Image of vehicle

Vehicle controls

Vehicle metrics (size, speed, and so on)

Attributes (armor, weapons, and so on)
- Attribute stats
- Special effects

Major characters in story—anyone mentioned in the above story outline, preferably ones that have impact on the story or gameplay.

These include allies/helpers, love interests, rivals/villains

Include visuals
- What is their relationship to the player character?
- Where do they appear?

Game progression outline

Overview of all game levels—insert game beat chart here. Remember to:

- Include story beats to show how gameplay and story intertwine
- Indicate if story beat is a cutscene or in game

Indicate progression/reward elements for the player

- Show where new skills, abilities, weapons, and collectibles are earned in relation to the story

Gameplay classifications

Descriptions of gameplay types (stealth, battle arena, driving, flying, and so on)

World overview/level select/navigation screen

Image(s) of world overview screen (if applicable)

List of game levels available on World Overview

Description of how information is presented to player

Details on how player will navigate this screen (cursor, character, and so on)

Animation (character and/or elements) required for this screen

Sound and music required for level select screen

Universal game mechanics—list mechanics that will be found throughout the game. Always include images of each mechanic.

Platform mechanics

- Description
- Metrics in relationship to player

Portal mechanics

- Doors
    —Handle/switch operated
    —Key operated
    —Breakable
    —Hatch (context-sensitive move)
- Teleportals
    —Description and image
    —Effects
    —Navigational aids

Checkpoints

Breakable objects (crates, furniture, grass clumps, and so on)

- How is item broken
- What items are yielded/percentage of yield
- Other effects (explosion, timer, switch, and so on)

Non-breakable objects (treasure chests, and so on)

- Description and image

- What items are yielded/percentage of yield
- Other effects (explosion, timer, switch, and so on)

Puzzle objects (pushable blocks, keys, and so on)

- Description and image
- How does player interact

Switches

- Description and image
- How does player interact

Climbable/swingable objects

- Description and image
- How does player interact

Game levels—list out each of the level mentioned in the world overview

Name/title of levels

- Short description of level
- Player's objective (training, get from A to B, find key, and so on)
- Reward of level (level up, magic sword, progression, and so on)
- Major gameplay found in this level (stealth, platform, vehicle, and so on)
  —Sub-game found in level, with description of gameplay and control scheme
- Enemies found on this level
- Visual style guides for level
  —Include inspirational and concept artwork
  —Time of day
  —Color guide
- Music for level
  —Provide examples/sound files

Hub level

- Description/image of hub
- List of locations found in hub
- Requirements for travel/unlock
- State changes
- Save/load options (if applicable)

Training level

- Goals of training level
  —List of training level activities

Level specific mechanics

- Hazards (spikes, flame jet, laser fields, and so on)

—Description and image

—Timing information

—Damage/effect

—How does it affect player? (Movement, health, and so on)

—How does player avoid/thwart?

—Special effects or elements needed

Level specific contextual mechanics

- Description and image
- Timing information
- Effect
- How does it affect player? (Movement, health, and so on)
- How does player interact?
- Special effects or elements needed

General enemy rules

Behavior types (patroller, hunter, flyer, and so on)

AI rules and detection metrics

Spawn parameters

Defeat parameters

Reward yield rules

Level-specific enemies

Enemy image

Enemy description—include enemy type

Levels enemy is encountered

Movement pattern—show metrics

Attacks

- Damage value
- Damage effects (knockback, stun, and so on)

Reactions/damage/death

Idles

Special effects

Reward yield

Bosses

Description and image of boss

- Include scale

Call out weak points/attack spots

Interaction with player (will hurt player if collides, only hurt player when in specific state, and so on)

Movement patterns

- Show metrics in relationship to player

Attack patterns
- Warnings
- Specific attack
  —Damage done
  —Special effects
- Reactions/damage/death
- Idles

Description of player's experience
- Description of intro/cutscene
- Include number of rounds
- Progression/ramping of action

Description and image of environment
- Hazards and mechanics used
- Power-ups and collectibles found
- Other enemies used in boss fight

How is the boss defeated?

Reward yield

Non-player characters

NPC type overview (information, mission deliverer, escort/defend, and so on)

Character list
- Name, sex, age
- Background material
- NPC type
- Level where encountered

Interacting with NPCs
- Dialogue
- Collision

NPC rewards

Collectibles/object sets

List of items
- Images
- Level(s) found on
- What object or set unlocks (if applicable)

Minigames

Types of minigames

How are minigames accessed

Player controls

Elements needed/repurposed

Levels encountered

Cutscenes

List of cutscenes

Short outline of each cutscene

Level where cutscene is presented

Music and SFX

List of music

- Level where music is needed—don't forget title, pause, options, end credits
- Tone/feeling of music

Licensor points and concerns

Appendixes

Player character animation lists

Enemy character animations lists

Sound effects list

Music list

- Level location

Cutscene scripts

- Cutscene storyboards

VO scripts

- Player
- Enemies
- Bosses
- NPC barks

In-game text

- Warning screens
- Tutorial text
- Character dialogue/subtitles

BONUS LEVEL 4
THE MEDIUM-SIZED LIST OF STORY THEMES

- Adventure: period piece
- Adventure: pulp/"two-fisted" action
- Adventure: survival/disaster
- Adventure: swashbuckler/pirate
- Blaxplotation/grindhouse
- Caper/heist/thief
- Cartoon/anthropomorphic
- Comedy: romantic
- Comedy: screwball/slapstick
- Crime drama/police
- Documentary/showbiz
- Educational
- Erotic
- Espionage
- Family drama
- Fantasy: fairytale
- Fantasy: mythology (Greek, Japanese, Chinese, Norse, and so on)
- Fantasy: swords and sorcery
- Fantasy: whimsical
- Film noir/hard-boiled detective
- Game show
- Horror: B-movie/giant monster
- Horror: gothic (vampire, werewolf, Frankenstein)
- Horror: sci-fi
- Horror: torture porn/slasher

- Horror: zombie/end of the world
- Martial arts/ninja
- Medical drama
- Mobster/gangster
- Musical
- Music/rock 'n' roll
- Mystery
- Nurture/tamagotchi
- Political
- School/teen drama
- Sci-fi: cyberpunk
- Sci-fi: Japanese/Sentai/giant robot
- Sci-fi: realistic
- Sci-fi: retro (1930s)
- Sci-fi: space opera
- Sci-fi: steampunk
- Sci-fi: undersea
- Sports: Olympic
- Sports: racing
- Sports: team (American football, soccer, hockey, baseball, basketball, and so on)
- Superhero
- War (World War I, World War II, American Revolution, Crusades, Napoleonic, American Civil War, Iraq conflict, Vietnam[1])
- Western/spaghetti western

[1] I apologize in advance to all of my international readers for my American bias towards warfare and history.

BONUS LEVEL 5
THE BIG LIST OF
ENVIRONMENTS[1]

- Abandoned city
- Air/clouds
- Airplane
- Airport/airship port
- Alien planet
- Alien ship
- Amphitheatre
- Ancient ruins
- Aquarium
- Arcade
- Atlantis
- Bank
- Bar/cantina
- Barren rock (planetoid or moon)
- Battlefield/war zone/no man's land
- Bayou
- Beach
- Biomechanical area (à la *Alien*)
- Boardwalk
- Campsite
- Candy land
- Carnival

- Casino/Las Vegas/Atlantic City
- Castle
- Cave
- Chemical plant
- Chinatown
- Chinese temple
- Church
- Circus
- City street
- Cliff city
- Clock tower
- Concert hall
- Construction site
- Crack house
- Cruise ship
- Cyberspace/computer world (à la *Tron*)
- Desert
- Desert island
- Disco
- Dungeon/catacombs
- Egypt/Egyptian tomb
- Factory

- Fairytale land
- Famous monument
- Farm/ranch
- Fast food restaurant
- Fire level/world
- Forest
- Fort
- Fort Knox/treasury
- Freeway
- Funeral home
- Futuristic city
- Garden
- Giant-sized world (can be applied to any theme)
- Glacier/ice flow
- Graveyard
- Haunted house
- Heaven/Olympus
- Hospital
- Hotel/inn
- House
- Ice
- Indian reservation/village/burial ground
- Inside a creature/on top of a giant creature
- Japanese dojo/temple
- Jungle
- Junkyard
- Kitchen
- Laboratory
- Library
- "Little" world (where the player has been shrunken down)
- Mall/marketplace
- Mansion
- Marina/seaport
- Mayan jungle/temple

- Maze/hedge/labyrinth
- Medieval village
- Metropolis/megalopolis/arcology
- Military base/Area 51
- Mines
- Missile silo
- Monastery
- Mountain
- Movie set/TV studio
- Movie theatre
- Moving train
- Museum
- New York City
- North pole
- Nuclear reactor
- Ocean park (à la "Sea World")
- Ocean surface
- Office building
- Oil refinery
- Opera house
- Oriental temple/dojo
- Palace
- Park
- Pirate ship/town
- Playground
- Police station
- Prehistoric village/caves
- Prison
- Racetrack
- Restaurant
- River
- Rooftops
- Russian city/military base
- Rustic village
- Savannah/veldt
- School/elementary/college
- Secret lair
- Sewer

- Ship/boat deck/interior
- Sky/clouds
- Skyscraper
- Sock puppet world
- Space station/spaceport
- Sporting arena
- Strip club
- Submarine interior
- Suburbs
- Subway
- Superhero HQ/supervillain lair
- Surface of the sun
- Swamp
- Temple
- Theatre stage
- Theme park
- Topiary maze/garden
- Toy land
- Toy store
- Train station
- Treehouse/village
- Undersea base/city/grotto
- Underwater
- Underworld/Hell
- Urban city
- Utopia
- Volcano
- Warehouse
- Wild West town
- Zeppelin interior
- Zoo/wild animal preserve

BONUS LEVEL 6
MECHANICS AND HAZARDS

- Moving platforms: horizontal, vertical, diagonal
- Sinking/shrinking/collapsing platforms
- Ladders
- Swingable vine/trapeze
- Zip line
- Conveyer belt
- Slippery ice
- Spring/trampoline/jump pad/air gust
- Accelerator
- Pendulum/swinging object timing puzzle
- Rotating platform
- Spinning hazard
- Hazard that smashes down or up
- Blasting flame/wind/cannon timing puzzle
- Exploding object
- Breakable object
- Climbable wall surface
- Deadly surface/sticky floor/poison gas that slows player movement

- Object that grabs the player, requiring another move to break free
- Teleportal
- Opening/closing door/drawbridge
- Locked door requiring a key or some other method to open
- Treasure chest
- Health/ammo dispenser
- Spotlight that player must avoid (stealth)
- Push block
- Floor switch/pressure plate
- Lever
- Crank/pump
- Balance beam
- Carryable/throwable object
- Shootable target
- Catapult that launches player or object
- Two-stage openable or breakable object
- Lighting fixture to control light/darkness effect

BONUS LEVEL 7
ENEMY DESIGN TEMPLATE

Enemy name: _____

Enemy image: (insert concept or inspirational image here)

Description: (write a short description of the enemy; what is the enemy's personality and motivation?)

Animation list:

- Stand
- Idle
- Taunts
- Attacks (melee)
- Attacks (projectile)
- Hit reactions
- Death animations
- Victory animations

Movement patterns: (add as many as necessary)

- **Move 1:** (image and description of enemy's movement)
- **Move 2:** (image and description of enemy's movement)

Attack descriptions: (add as many as necessary)

- **Attack 1:** (melee, projectile, special)
- **Attack 2:** (melee, projectile, special)

Enemy is defeated by: (how will the player defeat the enemy?)

Damage description: (how is damage communicated to the player? Do they require any special visual effects?)

Particle effects: (what visual effects are required for attacks, movement or damage states?)

Projectiles: (if used, list what projectiles will be needed for attacks)

HUD elements: (are there any additional HUD elements required for the enemy fight, such as icons for QTEs?)

Sound effects list: (match the sound effects list with the animation list)

Voice effects list: (match the voice effects list with the animation list)

Special requirements for player character: (does the player need any special animations, effects, and so on to go with the enemy's attack? List them here)

Player reward: (what does the player get, if anything, for defeating the enemy?)

BONUS LEVEL 8
BOSS DESIGN TEMPLATE

Boss name: _____

Boss image: (insert concept or inspirational image here)

Description: (write a short description of the boss: what is the boss' personality and motivation?)

Animation list:

- Stand
- Idle
- Taunts
- Attacks (melee)
- Attacks (projectile)
- Hit reactions
- Death animations
- Victory animations

Movement patterns: (add as many as necessary)

- **Move 1:** (image and description of boss' movement)
- **Move 2:** (image and description of boss' movement)

Attack descriptions: (add as many as necessary)

- **Attack 1:** (melee, projectile, special)
- **Attack 2:** (melee, projectile, special)

Boss is defeated by: (how will the player defeat the boss? Does the boss have any weak spots or vulnerable states?)

Damage description: (what does the boss' health bar look like? How is damage communicated to the player? Do they require any special visual effects?)

Particle effects: (what visual effects are required for attacks, movement or damage states)

Projectiles: (if used, list what projectiles will be needed for attacks)

HUD elements: (are there any additional HUD elements required for the boss fight, such as icons for QTEs)

Sound effects list: (match the sound effects list with the animation list)

Voice effects list: (match the voice effects list with the animation list)

Special requirements for player character: (does the player need any special animations, effects, and so on to go with the boss attack? List them here)

Player reward: (what does the player get for defeating the boss?)

Boss Fight Arena

Arena image: (insert image of environment; could be a concept drawing or map)

Arena description: (write a short description of the environment and what the action is that takes place there)

Level elements: (are there any mechanics, hazards, or props that will be needed for the boss fight?)

Boss fight music tracks: (list music tracks here, including notes on any contextual music)

BONUS LEVEL 9
HIGH CONCEPT PITCH
PRESENTATION

Slide 1: Cover Page

Start with a compelling image and logo that sums up your game.

Put date of presentation on the PowerPoint so the people you present to will remember when the meeting took place.

For author credits use the studio's name; remember no one makes a game by themselves.

Include contact information: email address and/or phone number.

FARM WARS

Game pitch by Scott Rogers
DATE
Contact Information

Slide 2: Company Profile

Briefly outline who you are, what you've done, and how long you've been doing it for. This is a great place to showcase the covers of any games your studio's created.

Obviously you can skip creating this slide if you are presenting to your own peers.

TARGET SPECS

Genre: Action/Strategy

Target rating: E 10 (ages 8 – 15)

Target systems: XBOX Live Arcade and PSN

Average game length: 10 + hours

Slide 3: Target Specs

This slide covers the very basics of the game. What kind of game is it? What is it rated? Who is the audience? How long will it take to play?

STORY

Farmer MacDonald has a farm... and that farm is under attack!

Tired of being exploited for their milk and eggs, the farm animals join forces to mail-order giant mechanical Deth-tech suits and invade!

Farmer MacDonald must battle off waves of killer cows, sinister sheep and deadly ducks who threaten to stomp his crops under grinding mechanical feet!

As the war escalates and spreads across the county, each side adds new technology and allies to the fight. Who will win the **Farm Wars**?

Can Farmer MacDonald defend the homestead or will he "buy the farm?"

Slide 4: Game Story

Who is the player? What is the game's story? What's the conflict? Don't forget a beginning, middle, and end, or at least a cliffhanger that gets the reader/audience interested in knowing the ending.

GAME GOALS

- Can you farm as well as you fight? **Farm Wars** is a unique combination of two popular game genres

- **Farm Wars** features fast paced-action and massive boss battles

- From farm and crops, to your farmer and weapons, **Farm Wars** players can customize everything

- **Farm Wars'** gigantic tech tree lets player research and create hundreds of weapons, defenses and sellable crops

- Multiplayer mode allows **Farm Wars** players to band together to defend, raid and trade with each other

Slide 5: Game Goals

What are the most kick-ass features of your game? Why should the audience/reader care about your game? Aim for five "back of the box" goals.

GAME PLAY

In **Farm Wars**, the player is Farmer MacDonald defending his farm from death-dealing cows, chickens and other disgruntled farm animals. The game play is separated into five distinct game play: phases each with a limited time of play.

Players plant and raise crops on their farm for sale to purchase defense and weapon upgrades. Players defend their customized farm from waves of enemies, sell the surviving crops at their roadside produce stand, buy and plant some new ones and upgrade the farm's defenses in preparation for the next wave... or save up to build or buy Deth-tech of their very own!

Each game play round lasts fifteen to thirty minutes - with six environment maps, six weather conditions and six boss rounds to offer over ten hours of game play.

Slide 6: Gameplay Summary

This slide should briefly cover the major points of gameplay. What are the basics of play for the game? What is the camera view? How will the play expand/increase in challenge during the course of the game? What environments will the game happen in? What are the "hooks" that make this game unique?

GAME PLAY (CONT')

Farm Wars is played in an isometric view with 3D characters, elements and terrain. The camera can be zoomed and rotated 360 degrees to allow for either a close or far view of the farm battlefield. The player runs over the map in real time, farming, building and fighting advancing enemies. A HUD mini-map helps the player navigate, locate enemies and check the status of defenses during the battle.

Farm Wars players perform simple actions - build defense, use tools, plant crops and wield weapons. Over the course of the game, controls remain contextual - advanced technology and weapon upgrades utilize the same basic control scheme. After the battle, any surviving crops are harvested automatically and added to the player's inventory to be sold during the selling phase. The selling phase takes place on a simple static screen that also utilizes in-game assets.

GAME PLAY (CONT')

• **Buying** - Players can purchase seed, farming equipment, and offensive/defense systems (be bought as the game progresses). You can even eventually build and upgrade your own robotic-death suit! (which can double as a tractor/combine)

• **Planting** - During this phase the player moves about a 3D isometric dynamic farm. The land must be tilled, the vegetables must be watered and the guidance missile defense systems must be erected. Crop selection, tending and placement is very important to victory. Crops are also affected by seasons.

• **Defending** - Initially armed with a hoe, you must defend your crops from the attacks of vengeful farm animals who ruin your crops and destroy your land.
•The right defenses and a little skill will keep you from "buying the farm."

• **Boss** - Every four "rounds" the player squares off against one of the main animals (Pig, Cow, Chicken, etc...) in a fight to the finish. If MacDonald loses, he's mulch, but if he wins... well, let's just say there will be fresh bacon or beef for the selling phase...

• **Selling** – The player runs a roadside produce stand. Sell vegetables for cash to purchase farm upgrades. Get tips from customers on what crops to plant and what weapons to buy.

Farm Wars Technology Trees

Farm Wars players can research, buy and build defenses and tools over the course of the game. Every item will have several levels of improvement each with a distinct visual and effect. Unlike most games, the technology doesn't supplant the previous one, it just adds to the player's arsenal - the only limiting factor is the player's choice and finances on any given round.

Tech trees include:

Armor	Offensive weapons	Deth-Tech
Farming tools	Crops (seeds)	Defense systems

A sample defensive technology progression would look like:

Fence < Barbed Wire < Electric Fence < Force Field < Laser System

Slide 7: Gameplay details

Go into some of the more interesting details of the gameplay. The goal is to give the audience/reader an idea of what it is going to be like as they play the game. If any gameplay elements are important enough to the game, go ahead and dedicate a specific slide to them so the audience/reader is clear on how they impact gameplay and what they add to the game experience.

Download Strategy

We plan on supporting **Farm Wars** with at least six months of downloadable content that expands on the existing game:

- Additional farm maps
- New crop selections
- Crop trading with other players
- New Deth-Tech and defense upgrades
- Farmer's dog companion character
- Holiday themed player costumes
- Cooperative and competitive Multiplayer modes

Slide 8: Download strategy

Most games these days require download support to extend the life of the game beyond release. Outline these plans on this slide.

PRODUCTION INFO

Info about your team goes here:

• Number of programmers, artists, designers in your studio

• A timeline outlining your production schedule, milestones, etc.

• Estimated cost of production

Slide 9: Production Specs

Share the production plans here. How big is the team dedicated to making it? How long will it take to create the game? How much is it going to cost to make the game?

ACHIEVEMENT UNLOCKED: EXACTLY LIKE MAKING CHILI

(Feeds 6 to 8)

1/4 cup extra virgin olive oil
2 cloves fresh garlic
3 pounds beef brisket (trimmed of all fat)
2 large cans crushed tomatoes
2 small cans of beef broth
2 ancho chilis
1/2 tablespoon chili powder
1 tablespoon cayenne pepper
1/2 tablespoon of crushed red chili (seeds)
1 tablespoon Lowry's garlic salt
2 large green peppers
1 large red pepper
1 large yellow onion
1/4 cup scallions (for serving)
1/2 cup of sour cream (for serving)
1/2 cup shredded Monterey Jack cheese (for serving)

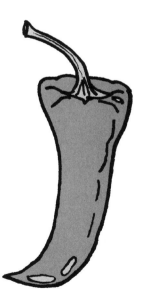

1. Slice garlic cloves. In a large pot or Dutch oven, heat oil over medium heat. Brown the garlic cloves in oil. Add beef brisket in the garlic/olive oil. Cook for about 7 to 10 minutes until browned.
2. Meanwhile, put ancho chili and beef broth in a blender or food processor. Process until the chilis are pureed. Set mixture aside.

3. When meat is browned, carefully remove it from pot to a plate. Pour off oil. Add in pureed chili mixture and crushed tomatoes (including liquid).

4. Add garlic salt, chili powder, cayenne pepper, and crushed red chili to tomato/chili mixture.

5. Bring the liquid to a boil, reduce the heat and simmer, covered for about 2 to 2.5 hours until the meat is completely cooked and tender.

6. Slice peppers (removing stem and seeds) and onion into largish pieces.

7. Remove meat from pot and shred meat with a pair of forks. Return shredded meat to pot along with peppers and onions. Adjust seasoning to taste.

8. Raise heat until majority of liquid is boiled away.

9. Spoon chili into serving bowls and top with cheese, sour cream, and scallions. Serve and enjoy!

INDEX